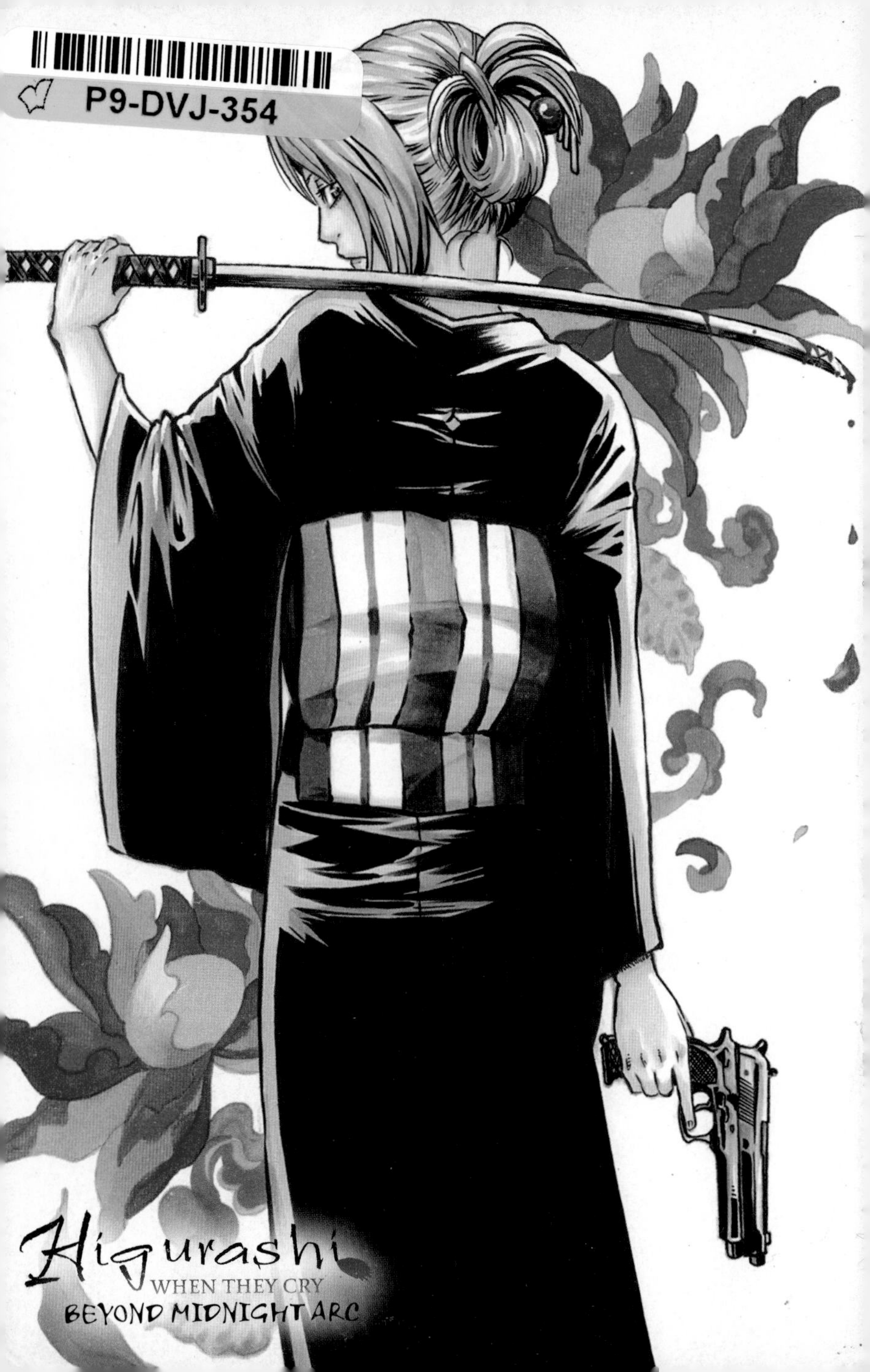
Higurashi
WHEN THEY CRY
BEYOND MIDNIGHT ARC

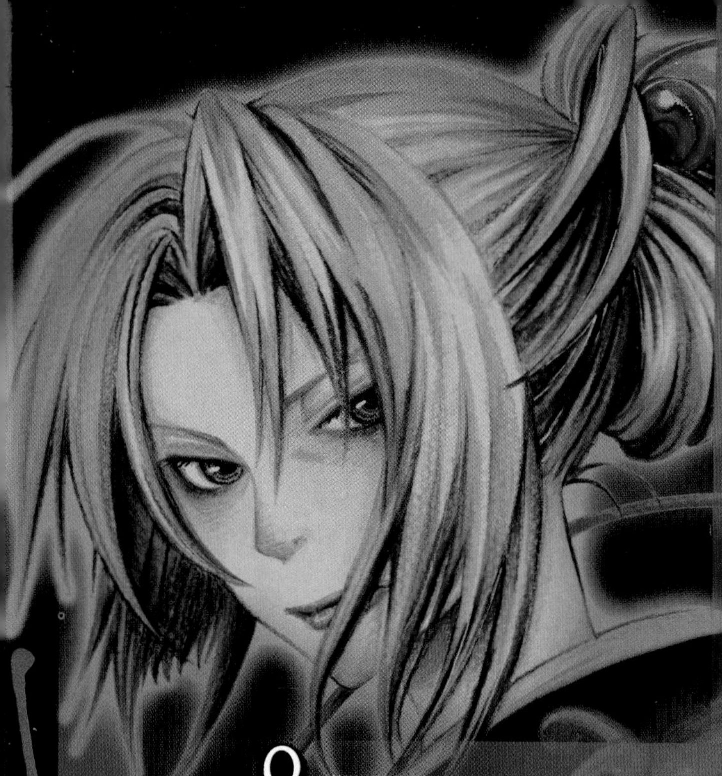

1

CONTENTS

Higurashi WHEN THEY CRY

BEYOND MIDNIGHT ARC

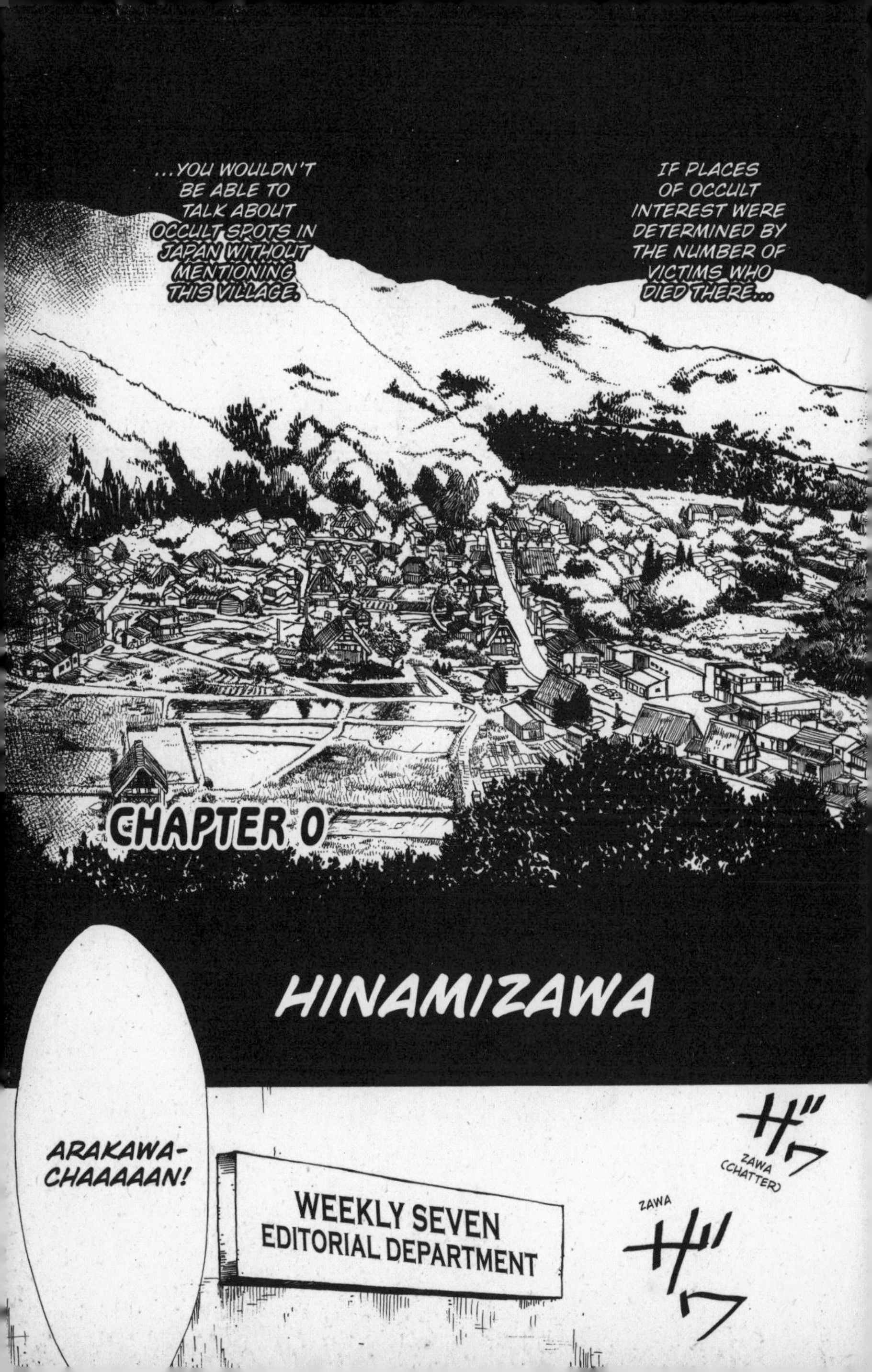
IF PLACES OF OCCULT INTEREST WERE DETERMINED BY THE NUMBER OF VICTIMS WHO DIED THERE...
...YOU WOULDN'T BE ABLE TO TALK ABOUT OCCULT SPOTS IN JAPAN WITHOUT MENTIONING THIS VILLAGE.
CHAPTER 0
HINAMIZAWA
ザワ
ZAWA (CHATTER)
ZAWA
ザワ
WEEKLY SEVEN EDITORIAL DEPARTMENT
ARAKAWA-CHAAAAAN!

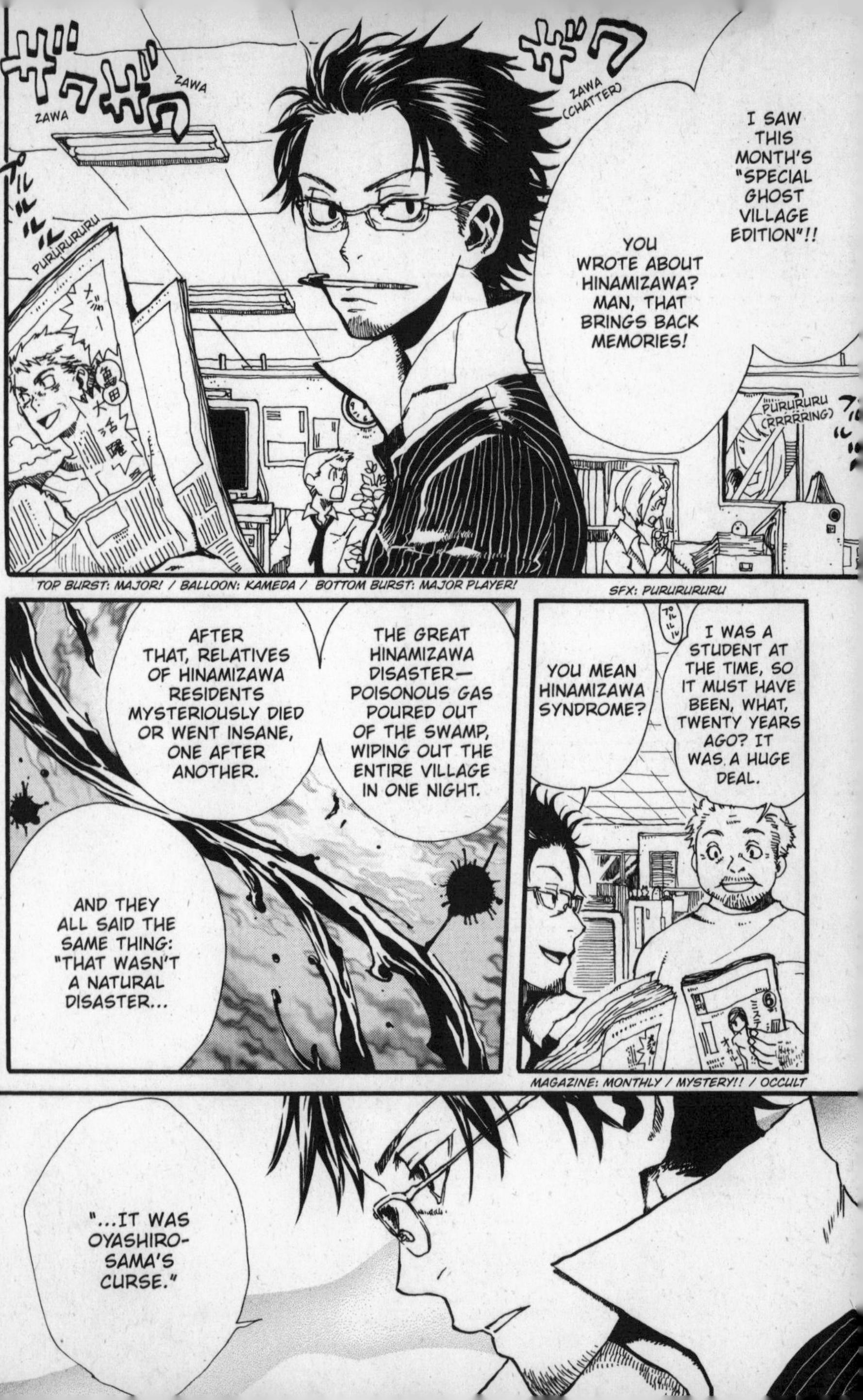
ZAWA (CHATTER)
ZAWA
ZAWA
PURURURU
I SAW THIS MONTH'S "SPECIAL GHOST VILLAGE EDITION"!!
YOU WROTE ABOUT HINAMIZAWA? MAN, THAT BRINGS BACK MEMORIES!
PURURURU (RRRRRING)
TOP BURST: MAJOR! / BALLOON: KAMEDA / BOTTOM BURST: MAJOR PLAYER!
SFX: PURURURURU
I WAS A STUDENT AT THE TIME, SO IT MUST HAVE BEEN, WHAT, TWENTY YEARS AGO? IT WAS A HUGE DEAL.
YOU MEAN HINAMIZAWA SYNDROME?
THE GREAT HINAMIZAWA DISASTER—POISONOUS GAS POURED OUT OF THE SWAMP, WIPING OUT THE ENTIRE VILLAGE IN ONE NIGHT.
AFTER THAT, RELATIVES OF HINAMIZAWA RESIDENTS MYSTERIOUSLY DIED OR WENT INSANE, ONE AFTER ANOTHER.
AND THEY ALL SAID THE SAME THING: "THAT WASN'T A NATURAL DISASTER...
MAGAZINE: MONTHLY / MYSTERY!! / OCCULT
"...IT WAS OYASHIRO-SAMA'S CURSE."

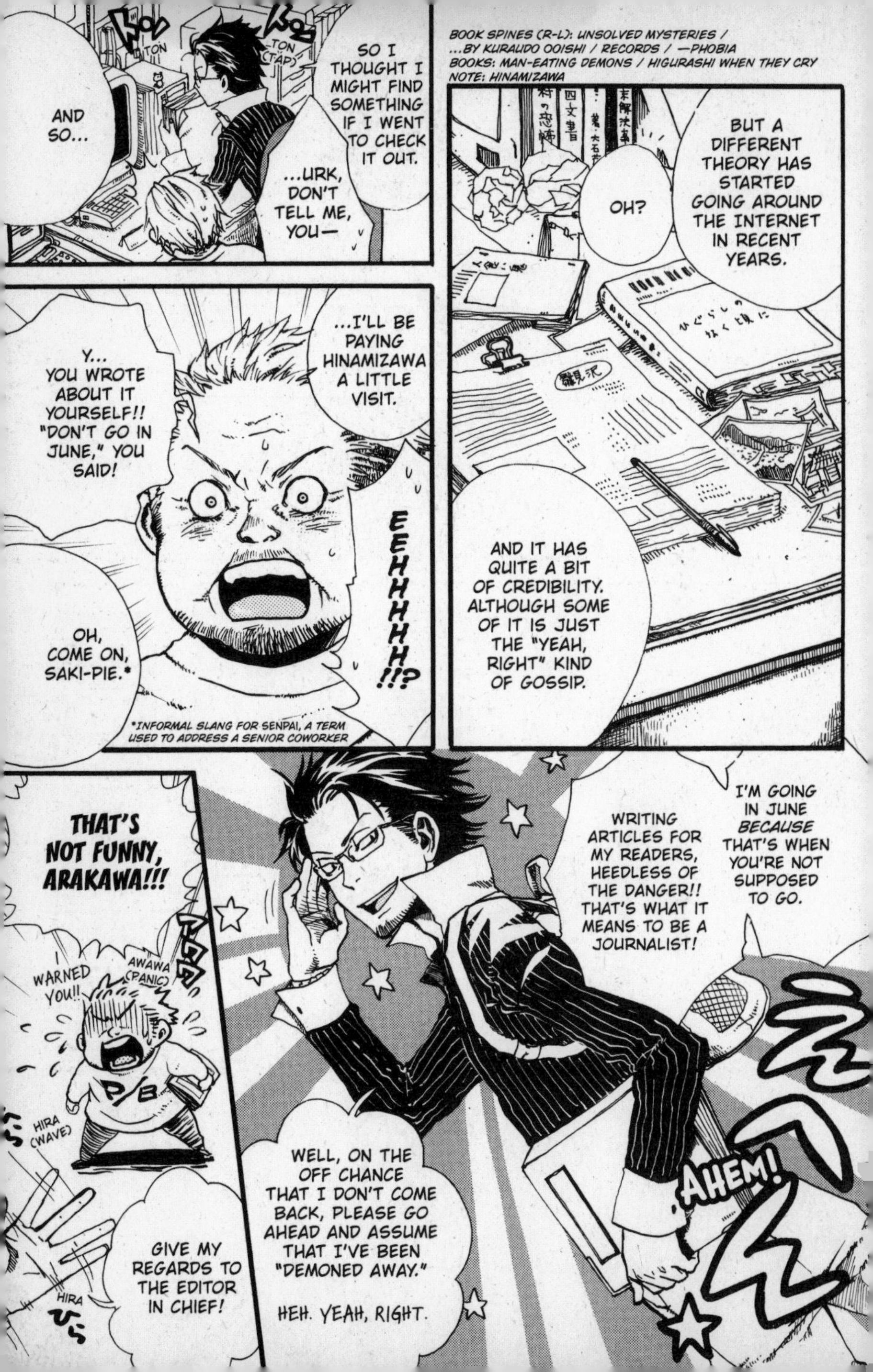
BOOK SPINES (R-L): UNSOLVED MYSTERIES / ...BY KURAUDO OOISHI / RECORDS / —PHOBIA
BOOKS: MAN-EATING DEMONS / HIGURASHI WHEN THEY CRY
NOTE: HINAMIZAWA
BUT A DIFFERENT THEORY HAS STARTED GOING AROUND THE INTERNET IN RECENT YEARS.
OH?
AND IT HAS QUITE A BIT OF CREDIBILITY. ALTHOUGH SOME OF IT IS JUST THE "YEAH, RIGHT" KIND OF GOSSIP.
TON TON (TAP)
AND SO...
SO I THOUGHT I MIGHT FIND SOMETHING IF I WENT TO CHECK IT OUT.
...URK, DON'T TELL ME, YOU—
...I'LL BE PAYING HINAMIZAWA A LITTLE VISIT.
Y... YOU WROTE ABOUT IT YOURSELF!! "DON'T GO IN JUNE," YOU SAID!
EEHHHHHH!!?
OH, COME ON, SAKI-PIE.*
*INFORMAL SLANG FOR SENPAI, A TERM USED TO ADDRESS A SENIOR COWORKER
I'M GOING IN JUNE *BECAUSE* THAT'S WHEN YOU'RE NOT SUPPOSED TO GO.
WRITING ARTICLES FOR MY READERS, HEEDLESS OF THE DANGER!! THAT'S WHAT IT MEANS TO BE A JOURNALIST!
AHEM!
WELL, ON THE OFF CHANCE THAT I DON'T COME BACK, PLEASE GO AHEAD AND ASSUME THAT I'VE BEEN "DEMONED AWAY."
HEH. YEAH, RIGHT.
THAT'S NOT FUNNY, ARAKAWA!!!
AWAWA (PANIC)
I WARNED YOU!!
HIRA (WAVE)
GIVE MY REGARDS TO THE EDITOR IN CHIEF!
HIRA

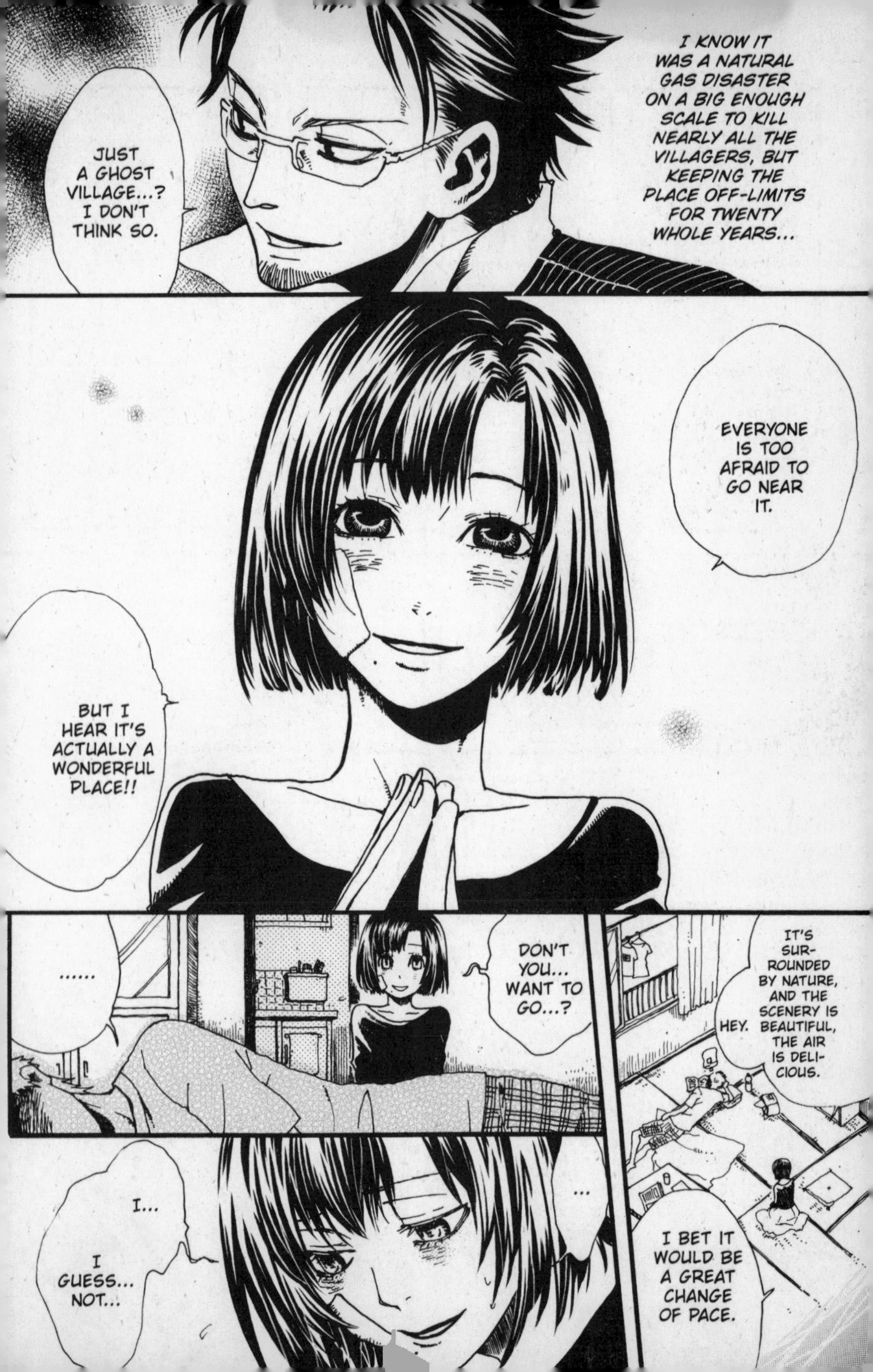
I KNOW IT WAS A NATURAL GAS DISASTER ON A BIG ENOUGH SCALE TO KILL NEARLY ALL THE VILLAGERS, BUT KEEPING THE PLACE OFF-LIMITS FOR TWENTY WHOLE YEARS...
JUST A GHOST VILLAGE...? I DON'T THINK SO.
EVERYONE IS TOO AFRAID TO GO NEAR IT.
BUT I HEAR IT'S ACTUALLY A WONDERFUL PLACE!!
IT'S SUR-ROUNDED BY NATURE, AND THE SCENERY IS BEAUTIFUL, THE AIR IS DELI-CIOUS.
HEY.
I BET IT WOULD BE A GREAT CHANGE OF PACE.
DON'T YOU... WANT TO GO...?
......
...
I...
I GUESS... NOT...

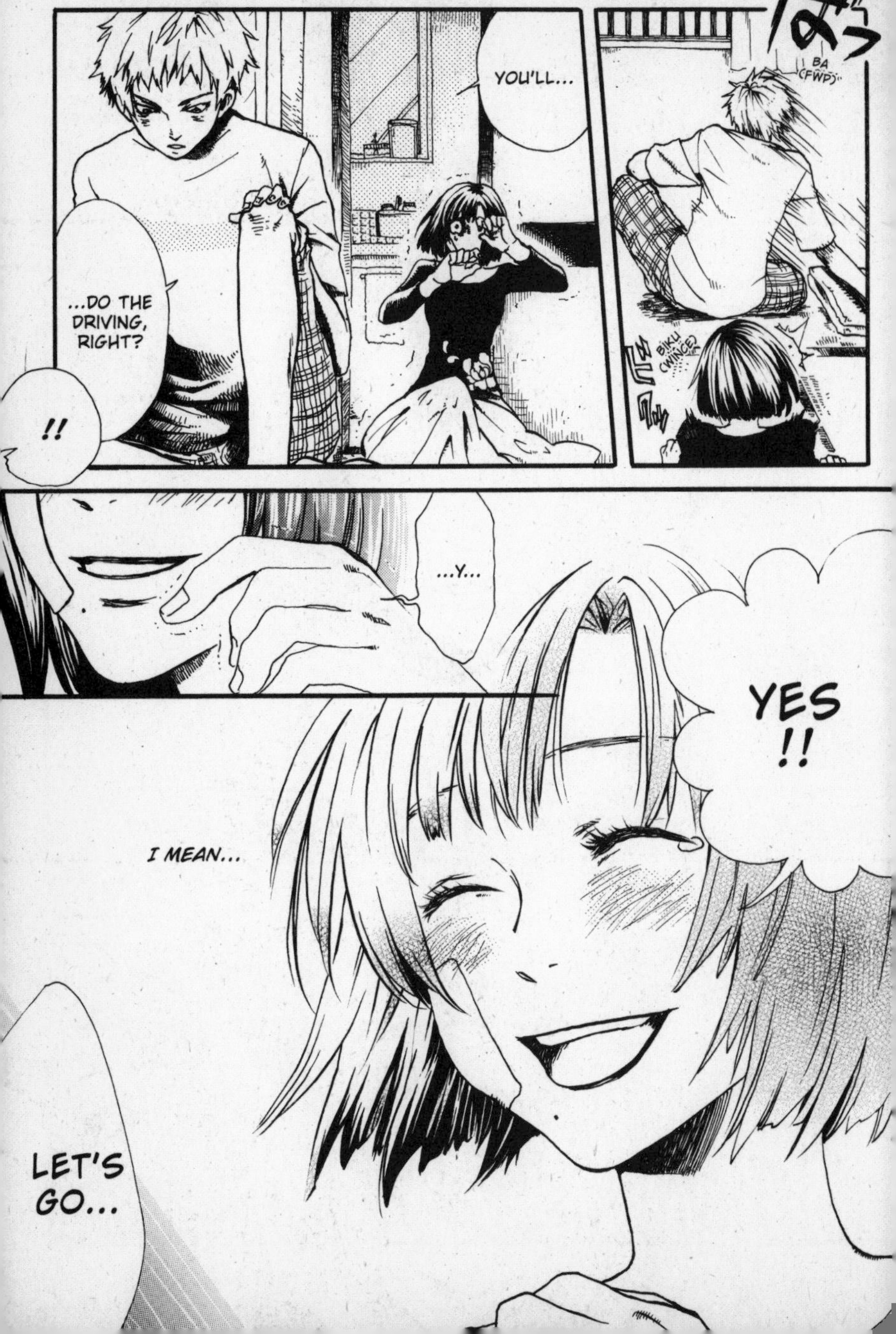
ばっ
BA (FWP)
BIKU (WINCE)
YOU'LL...
...DO THE DRIVING, RIGHT?
!!
...Y...
YES !!
I MEAN...
LET'S GO...

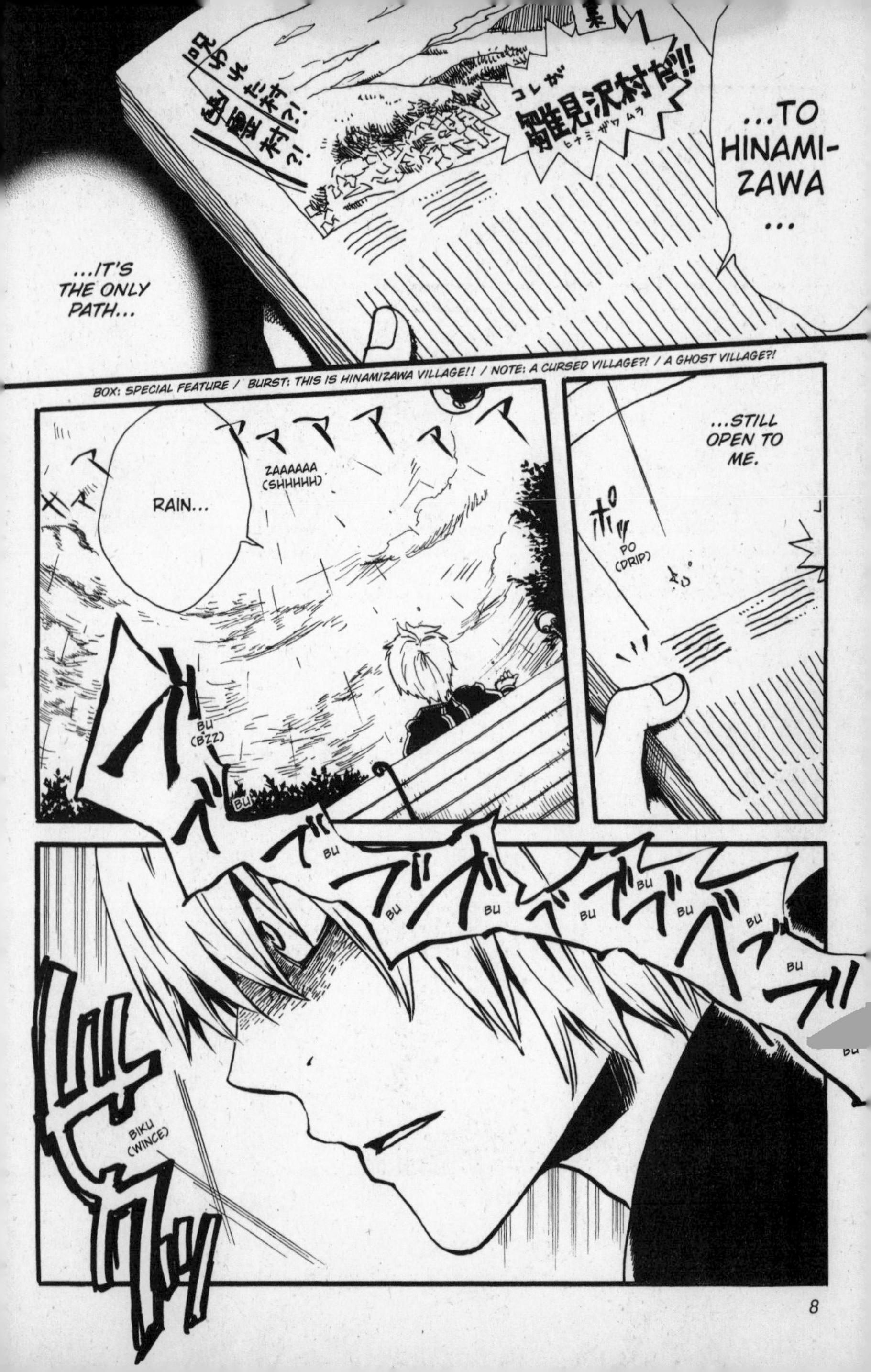

コレが雛見沢村だ!!
ヒナミザワムラ
呪われた村?! 幽霊村?!
...TO HINAMI-ZAWA...
...IT'S THE ONLY PATH...
BOX: SPECIAL FEATURE / BURST: THIS IS HINAMIZAWA VILLAGE!! / NOTE: A CURSED VILLAGE?! / A GHOST VILLAGE?!
...STILL OPEN TO ME.
PO (DRIP)
ZAAAAAA (SHHHHH)
RAIN...
BU (BZZ)
BU
BU
BU
BU
BU
BU
BU
BU
BU
BIKU (WINCE)

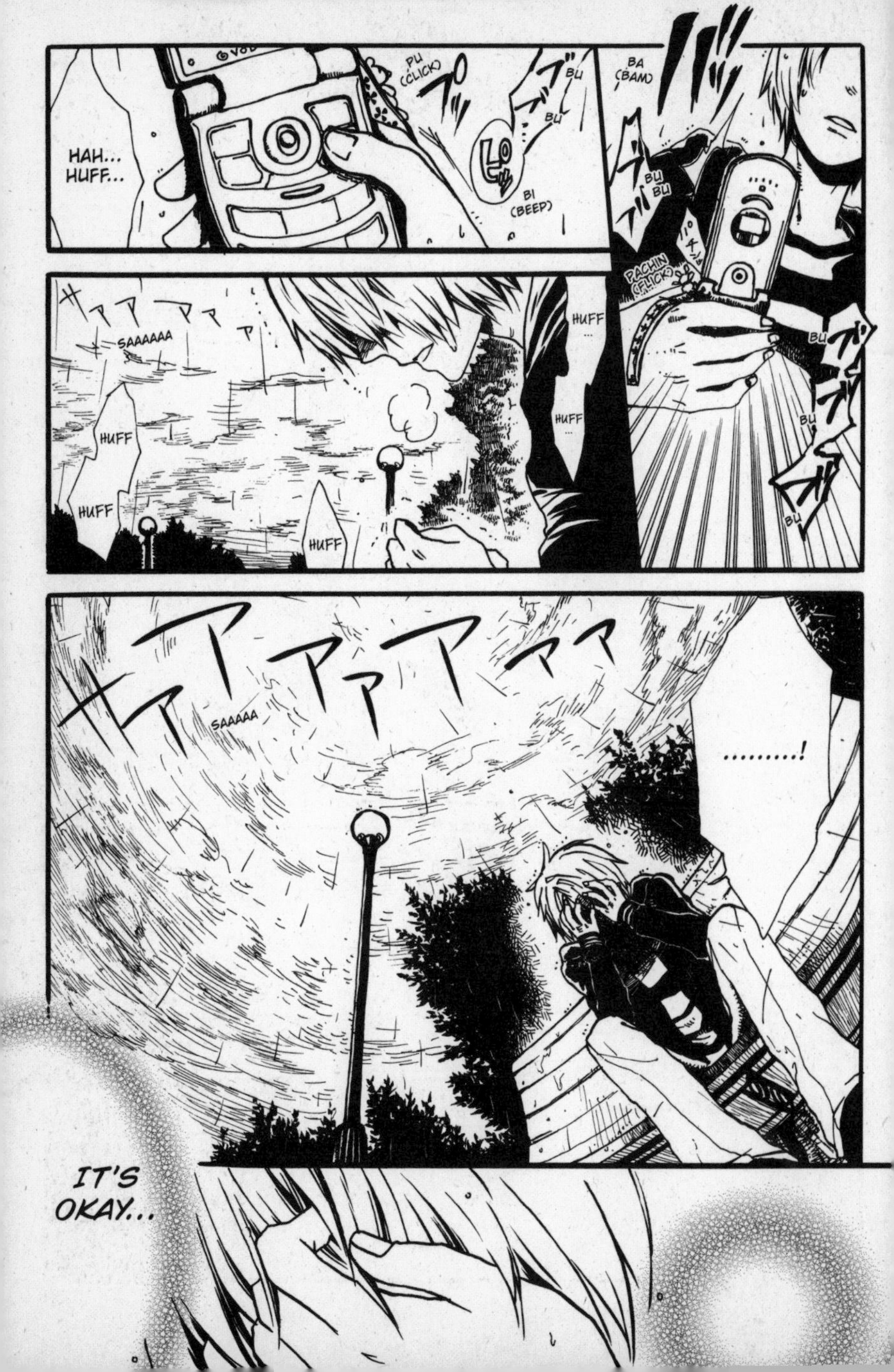

BA (BAM)
BU BU
PACHIN (FLICK)
BU
BU
BU
HAH... HUFF...
PU (CLICK)
BU
BU
BI (BEEP)
HUFF...
HUFF...
SAAAAAA
HUFF
HUFF
HUFF
SAAAAA
..........!
IT'S OKAY...

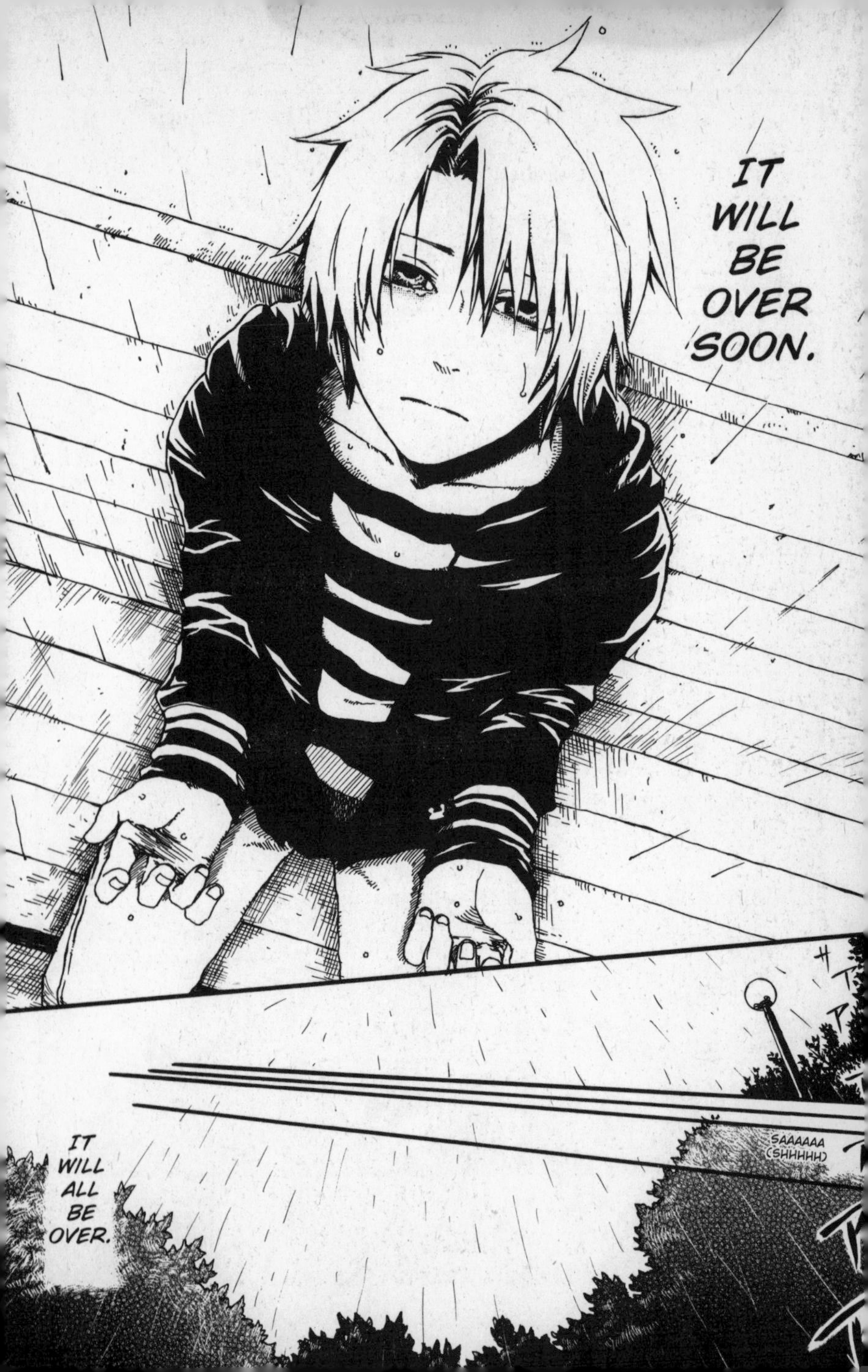
IT WILL BE OVER SOON.
SAAAAAA (SHHHHH)
IT WILL ALL BE OVER.

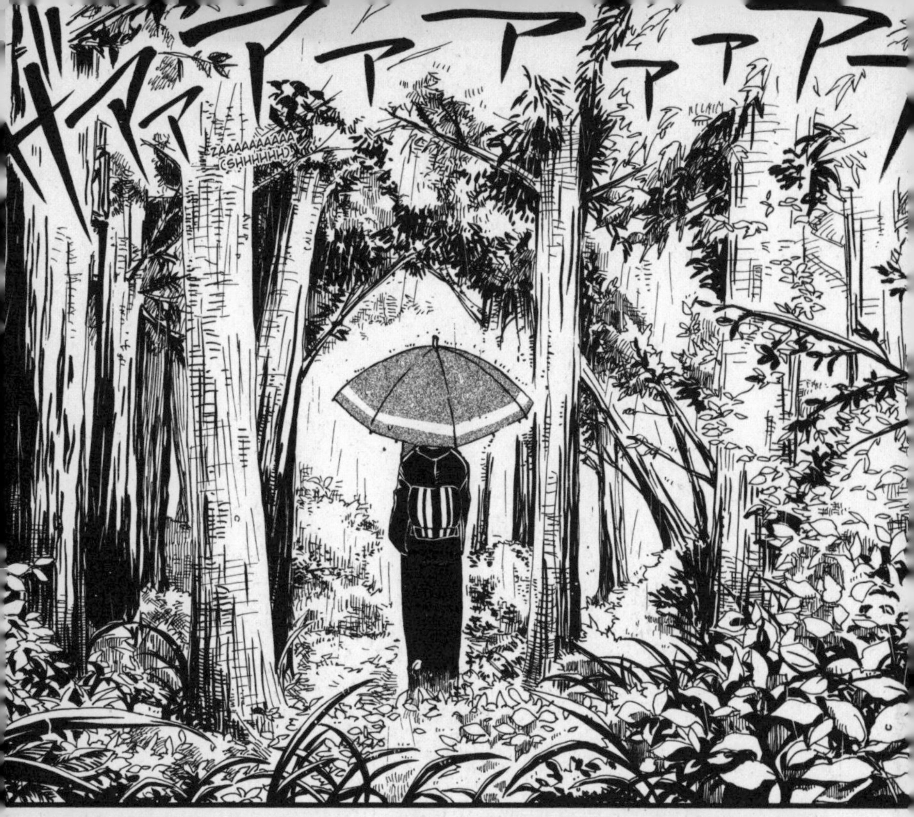
ZAAAAAAAAAA
(SHHHHHHH)
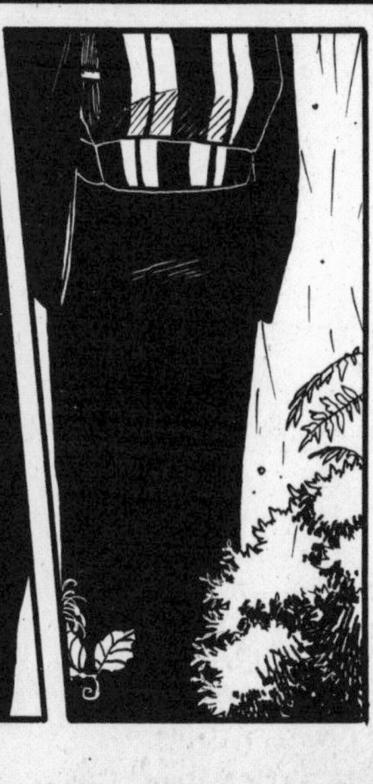
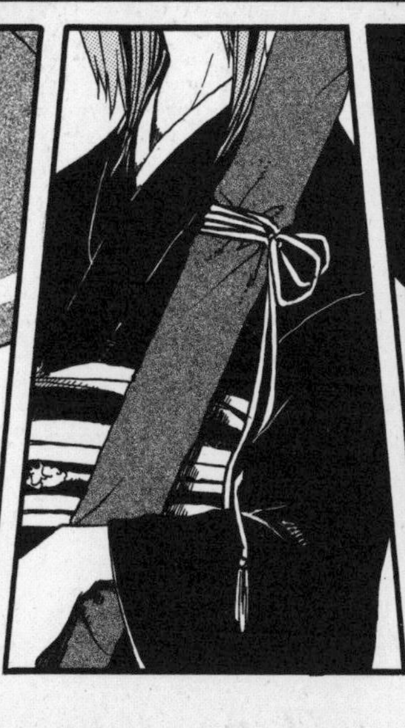
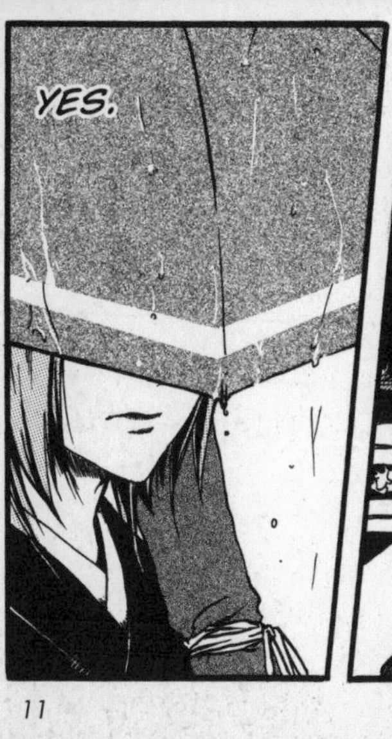
YES.

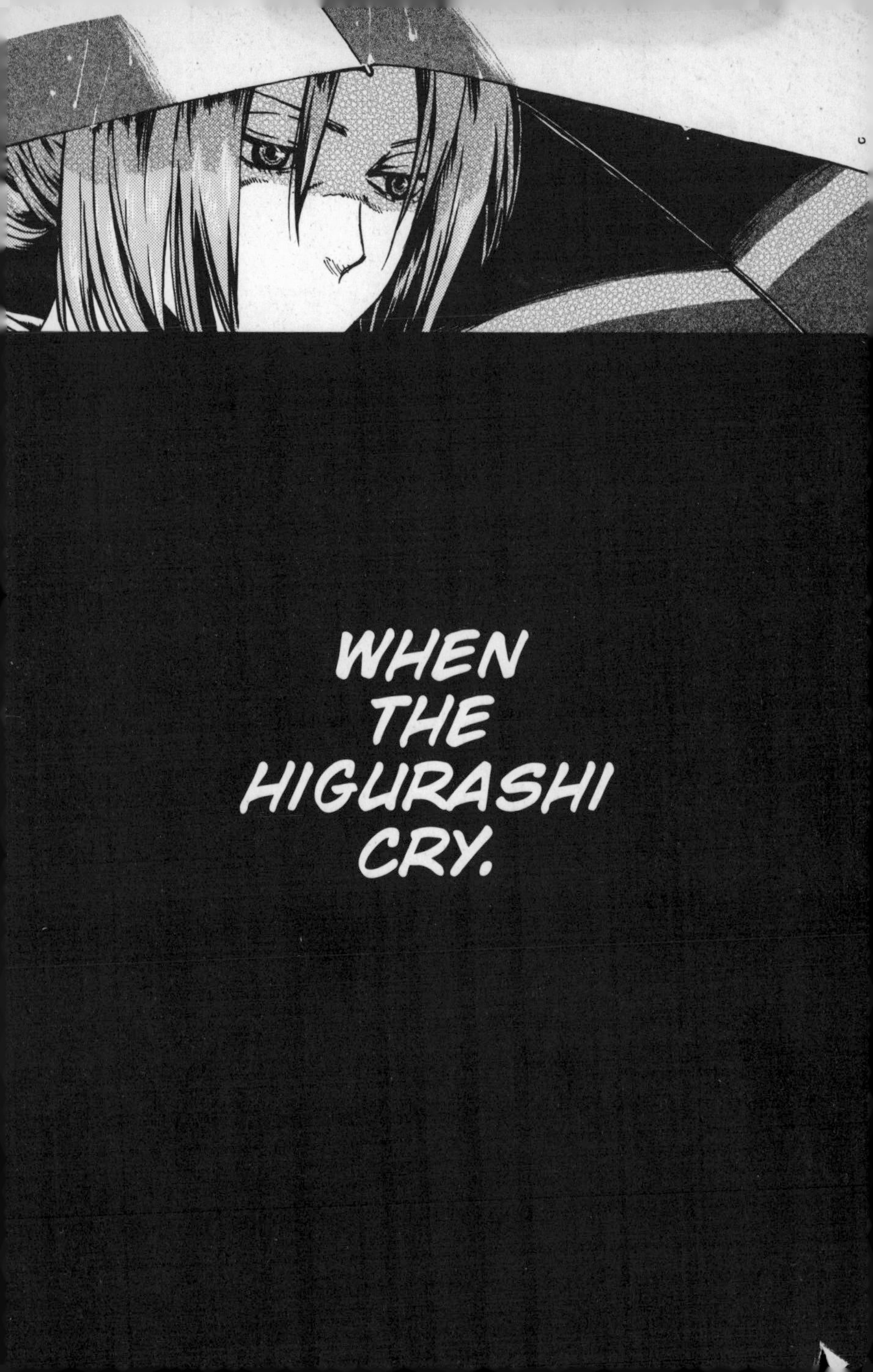
WHEN THE HIGURASHI CRY.

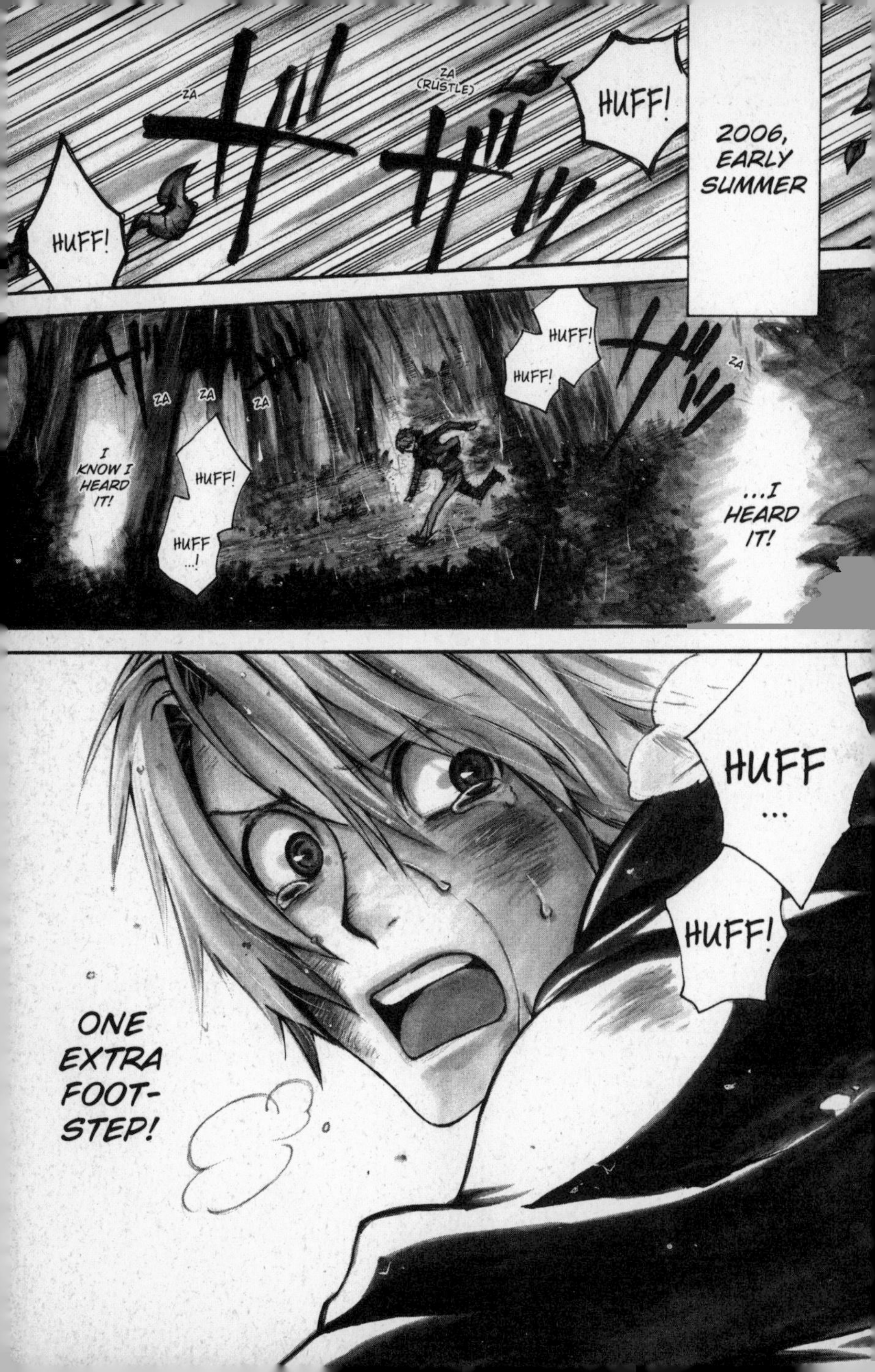
2006, EARLY SUMMER
HUFF!
ZA (RUSTLE)
ZA
HUFF!
...I HEARD IT!
ZA
HUFF!
HUFF!
HUFF!
HUFF ...!
ZA
ZA
ZA
I KNOW I HEARD IT!
HUFF ...
HUFF!
ONE EXTRA FOOT-STEP!

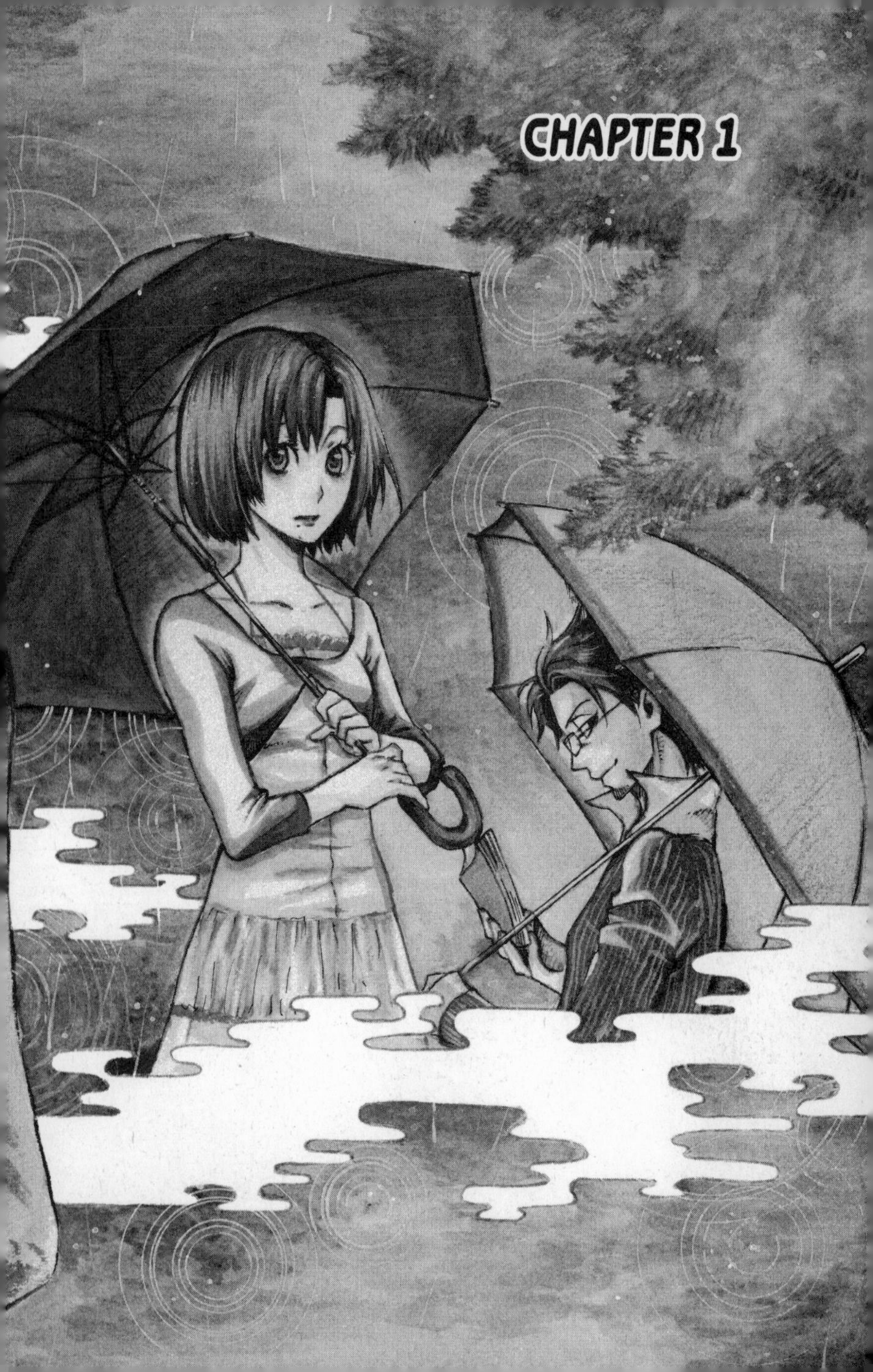
CHAPTER 1

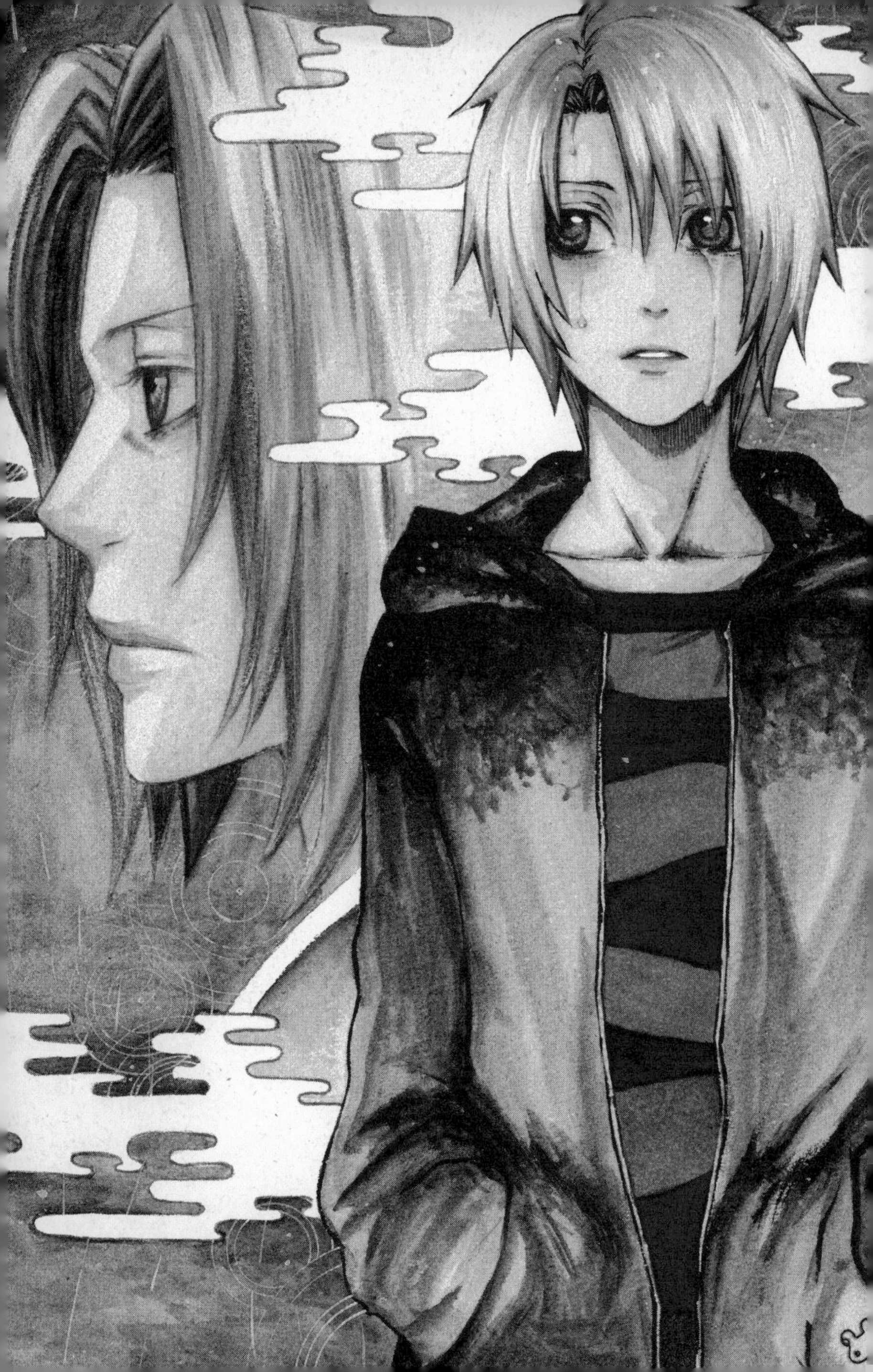

BEYOND MIDNIGHT ARC

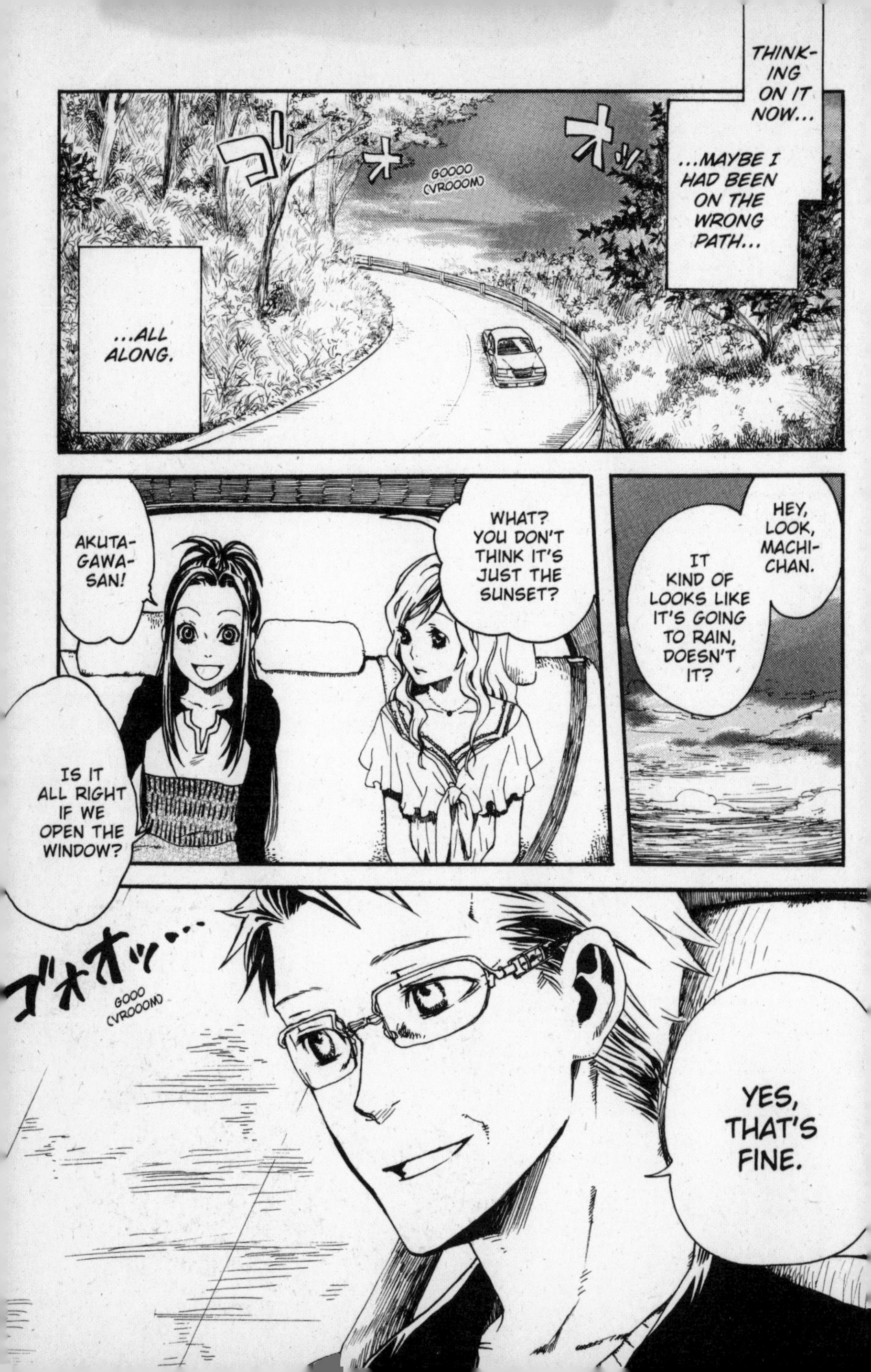
THINKING ON IT NOW...
...MAYBE I HAD BEEN ON THE WRONG PATH...
GOOOO (VROOOM)
...ALL ALONG.
HEY, LOOK, MACHI-CHAN.
IT KIND OF LOOKS LIKE IT'S GOING TO RAIN, DOESN'T IT?
WHAT? YOU DON'T THINK IT'S JUST THE SUNSET?
AKUTAGAWA-SAN!
IS IT ALL RIGHT IF WE OPEN THE WINDOW?
YES, THAT'S FINE.
GOOO (VROOOM)

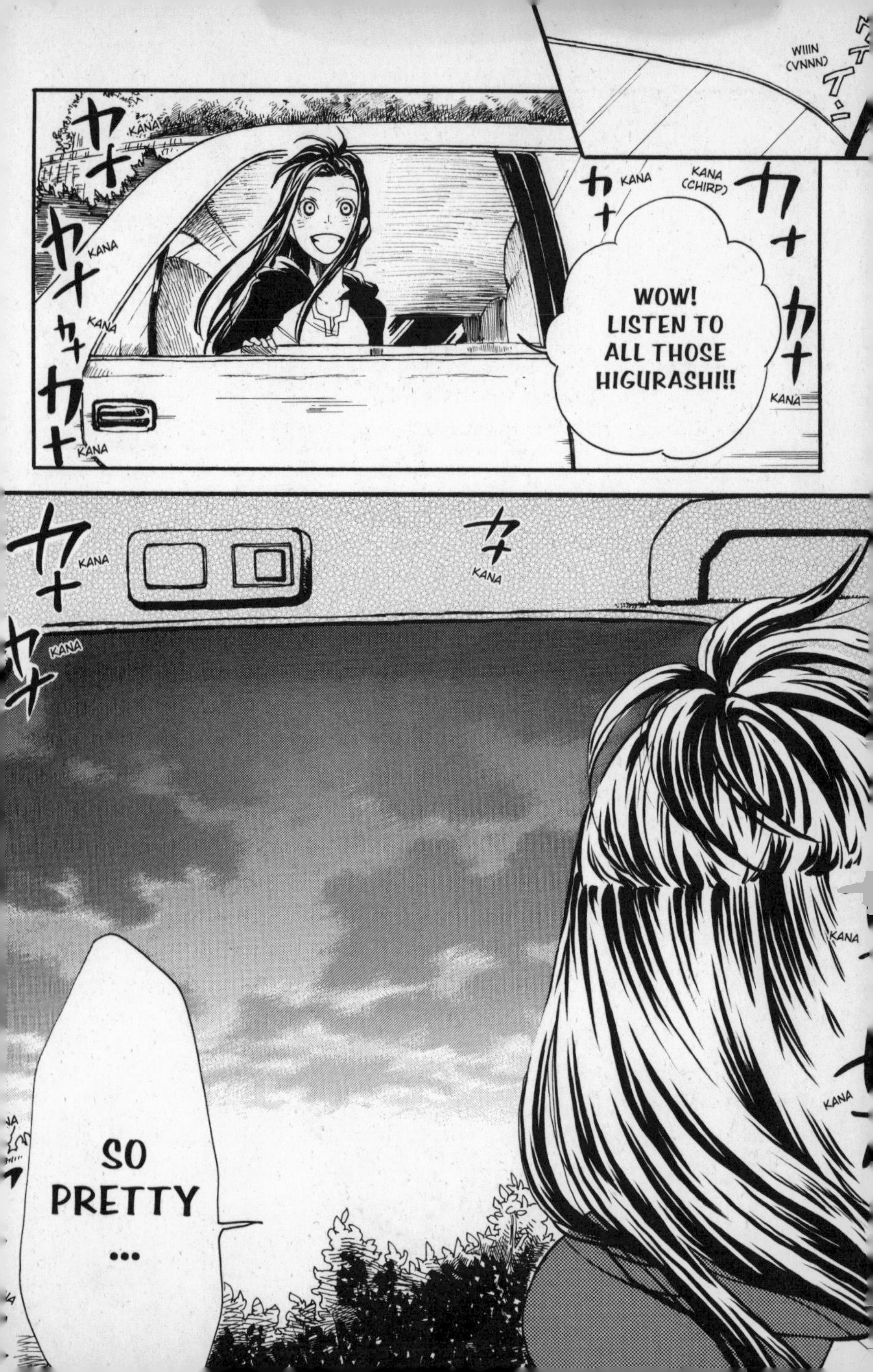
WIIIN (VNNN)
KANA (CHIRP)
KANA
WOW! LISTEN TO ALL THOSE HIGURASHI!!
KANA
KANA
KANA
KANA
KANA
KANA
KANA
KANA
KANA
KANA
KANA
SO PRETTY ...

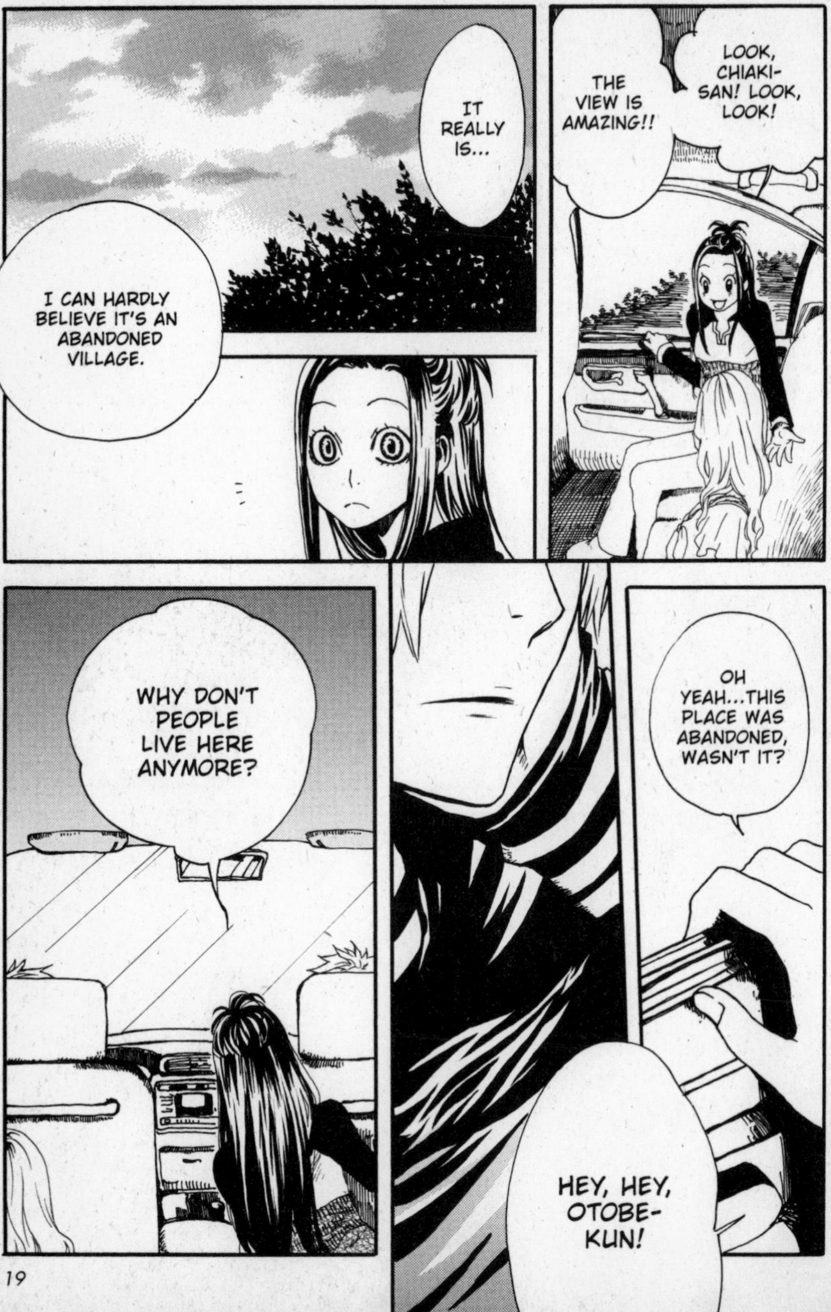
LOOK, CHIAKI-SAN! LOOK, LOOK!
THE VIEW IS AMAZING!!
IT REALLY IS...
I CAN HARDLY BELIEVE IT'S AN ABANDONED VILLAGE.
OH YEAH...THIS PLACE WAS ABANDONED, WASN'T IT?
HEY, HEY, OTOBE-KUN!
WHY DON'T PEOPLE LIVE HERE ANYMORE?

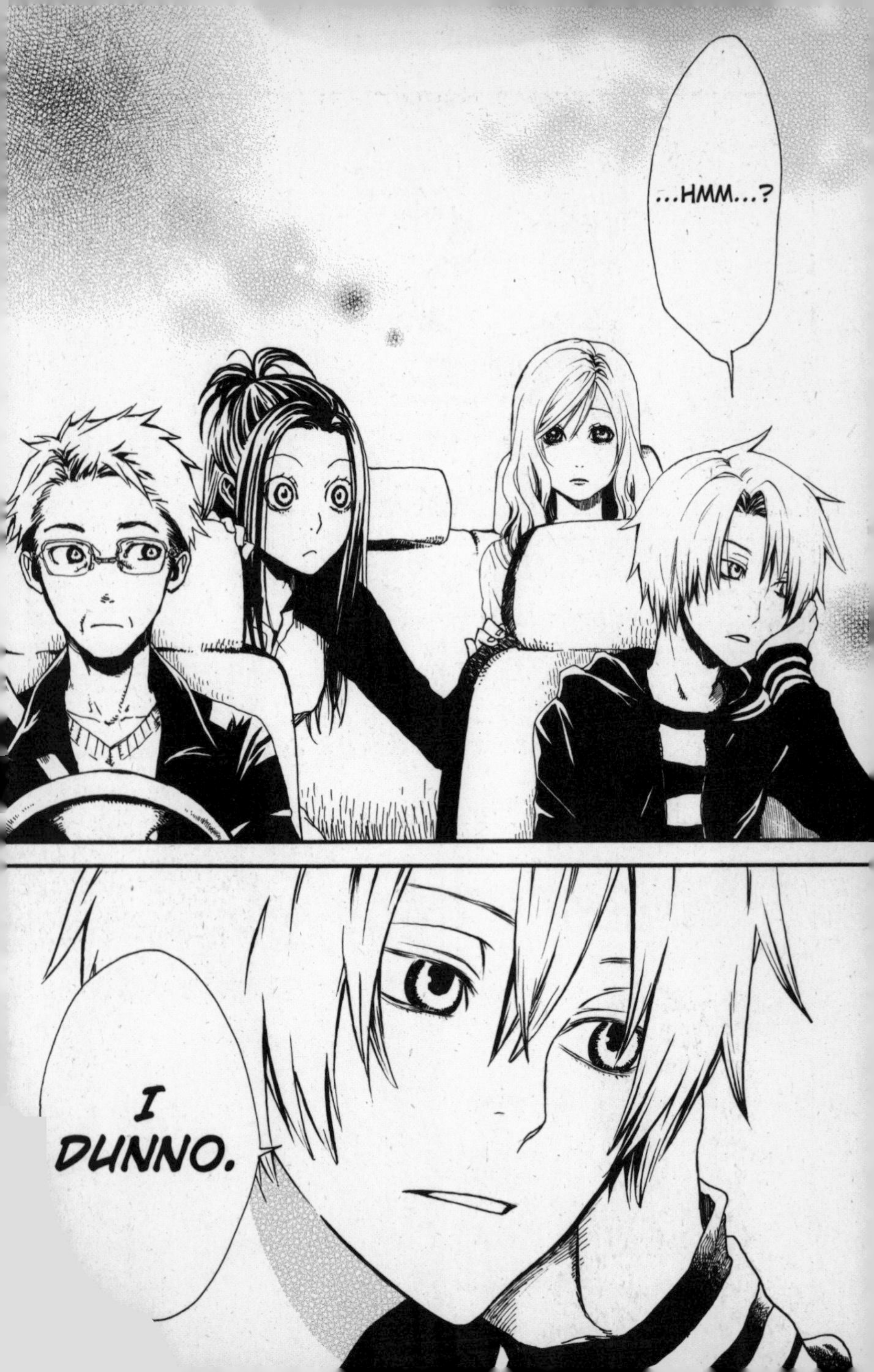
...HMM...?
I DUNNO.

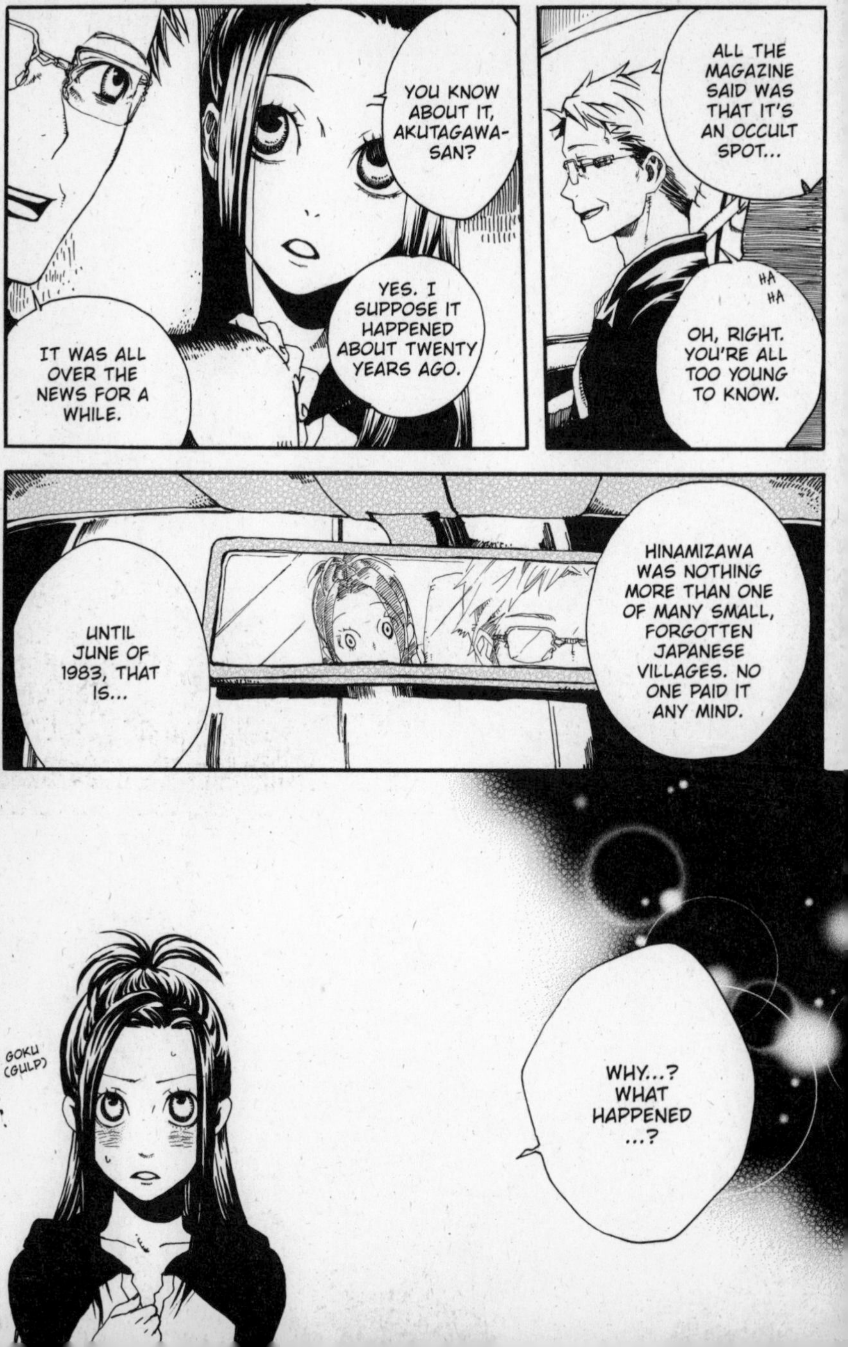
ALL THE MAGAZINE SAID WAS THAT IT'S AN OCCULT SPOT...
HA HA
OH, RIGHT. YOU'RE ALL TOO YOUNG TO KNOW.
YOU KNOW ABOUT IT, AKUTAGAWA-SAN?
YES. I SUPPOSE IT HAPPENED ABOUT TWENTY YEARS AGO.
IT WAS ALL OVER THE NEWS FOR A WHILE.
HINAMIZAWA WAS NOTHING MORE THAN ONE OF MANY SMALL, FORGOTTEN JAPANESE VILLAGES. NO ONE PAID IT ANY MIND.
UNTIL JUNE OF 1983, THAT IS...
WHY...? WHAT HAPPENED ...?
GOKU (GULP)

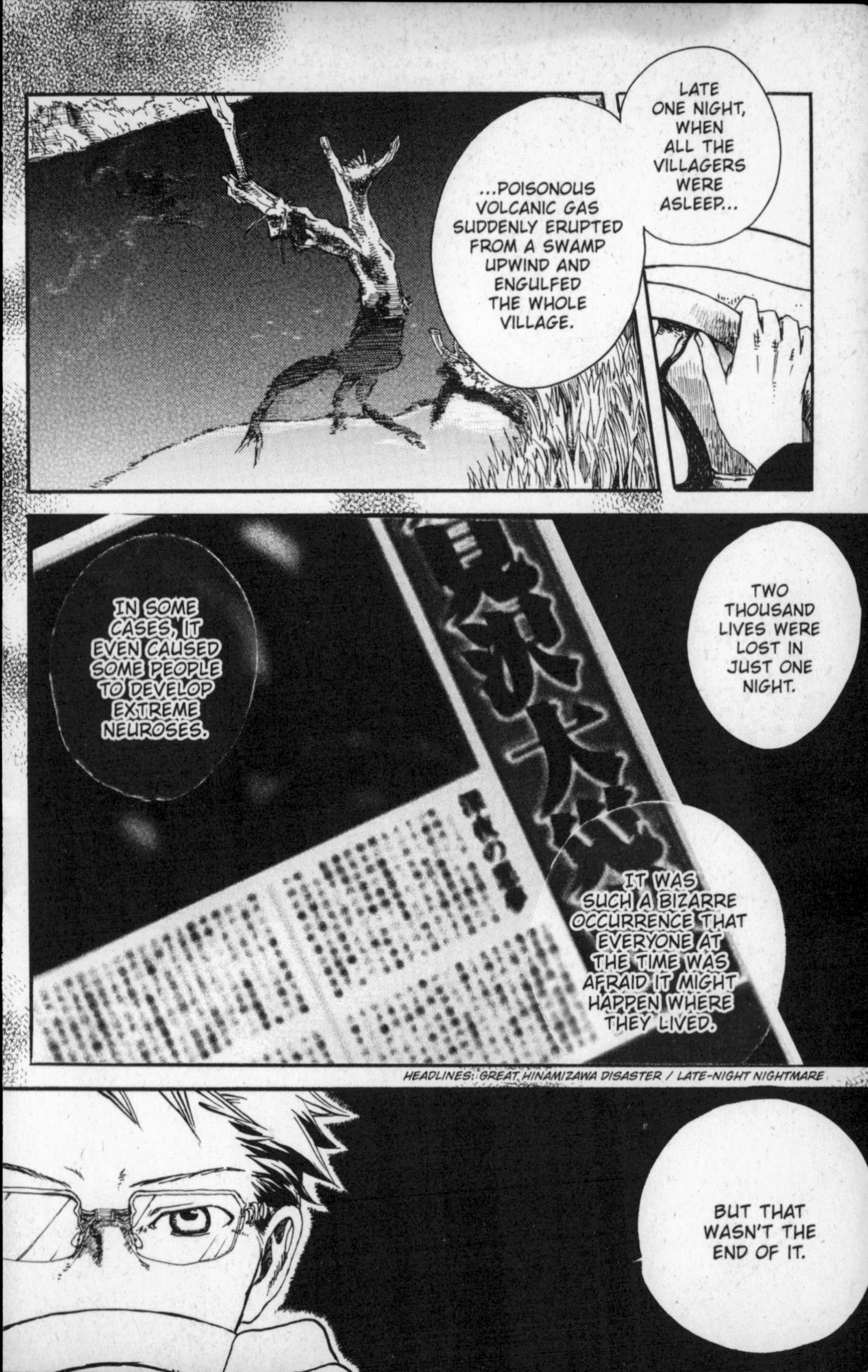
LATE ONE NIGHT, WHEN ALL THE VILLAGERS WERE ASLEEP...
...POISONOUS VOLCANIC GAS SUDDENLY ERUPTED FROM A SWAMP UPWIND AND ENGULFED THE WHOLE VILLAGE.
TWO THOUSAND LIVES WERE LOST IN JUST ONE NIGHT.
IN SOME CASES, IT EVEN CAUSED SOME PEOPLE TO DEVELOP EXTREME NEUROSES.
IT WAS SUCH A BIZARRE OCCURRENCE THAT EVERYONE AT THE TIME WAS AFRAID IT MIGHT HAPPEN WHERE THEY LIVED.
HEADLINES: GREAT HINAMIZAWA DISASTER / LATE-NIGHT NIGHTMARE
BUT THAT WASN'T THE END OF IT.

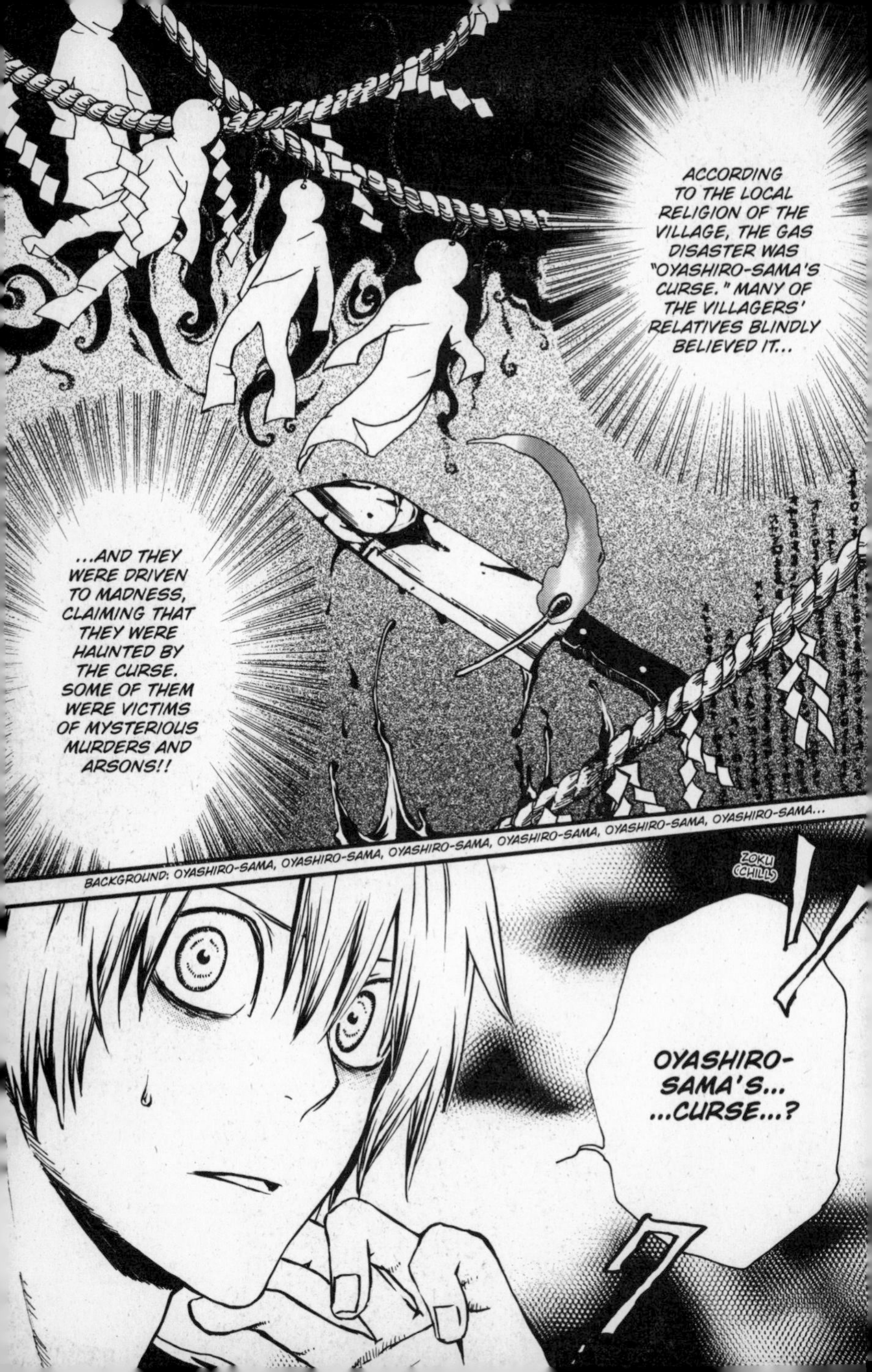
ACCORDING TO THE LOCAL RELIGION OF THE VILLAGE, THE GAS DISASTER WAS "OYASHIRO-SAMA'S CURSE." MANY OF THE VILLAGERS' RELATIVES BLINDLY BELIEVED IT...
...AND THEY WERE DRIVEN TO MADNESS, CLAIMING THAT THEY WERE HAUNTED BY THE CURSE. SOME OF THEM WERE VICTIMS OF MYSTERIOUS MURDERS AND ARSONS!!
BACKGROUND: OYASHIRO-SAMA, OYASHIRO-SAMA, OYASHIRO-SAMA, OYASHIRO-SAMA, OYASHIRO-SAMA, OYASHIRO-SAMA, OYASHIRO-SAMA...
ZOKU (CHILLS)
OYASHIRO-SAMA'S... ...CURSE...?

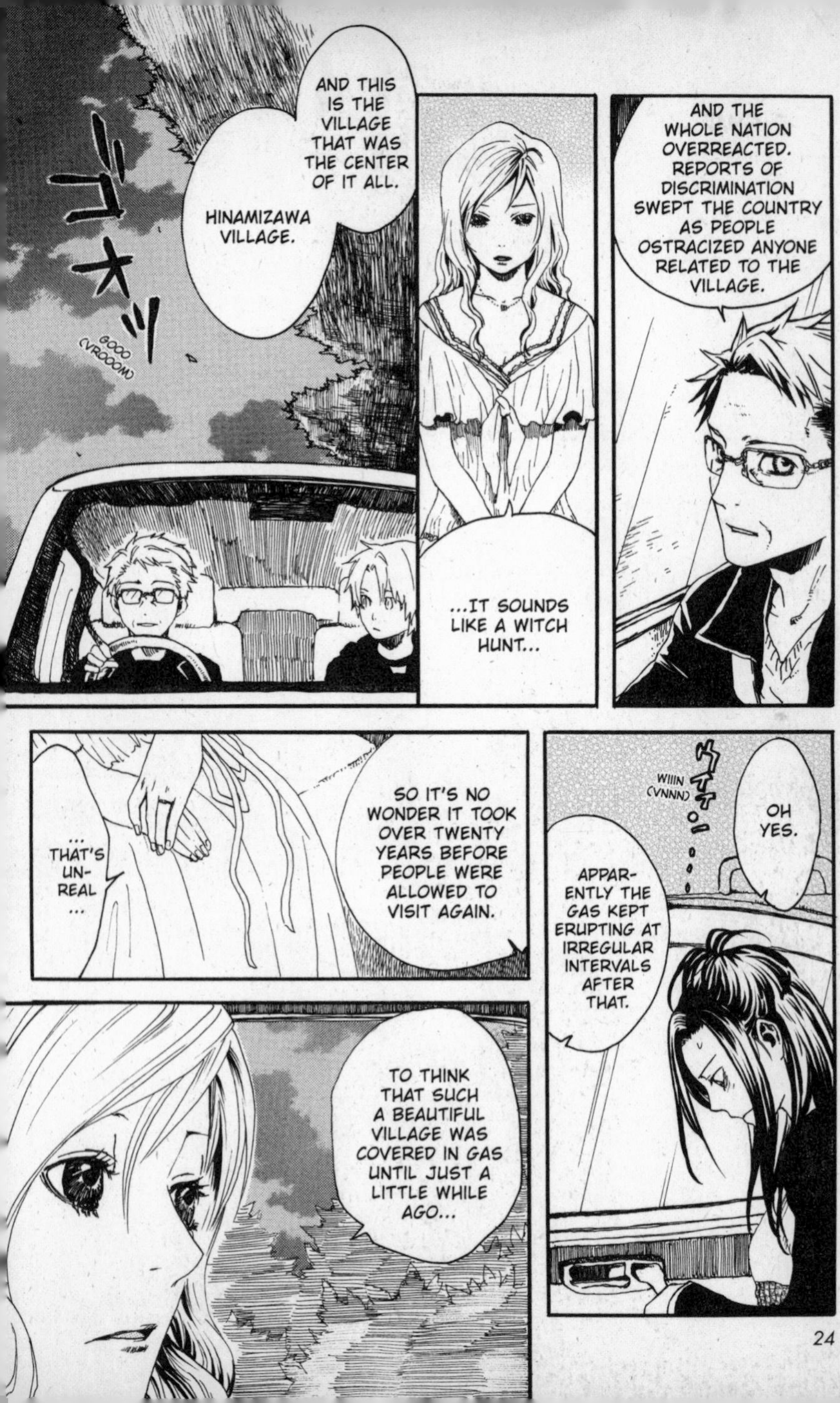

AND THE WHOLE NATION OVERREACTED. REPORTS OF DISCRIMINATION SWEPT THE COUNTRY AS PEOPLE OSTRACIZED ANYONE RELATED TO THE VILLAGE.
...IT SOUNDS LIKE A WITCH HUNT...
AND THIS IS THE VILLAGE THAT WAS THE CENTER OF IT ALL.
HINAMIZAWA VILLAGE.
GOOO (VROOOM)
WIIIN (VNNN)
OH YES.
APPARENTLY THE GAS KEPT ERUPTING AT IRREGULAR INTERVALS AFTER THAT.
SO IT'S NO WONDER IT TOOK OVER TWENTY YEARS BEFORE PEOPLE WERE ALLOWED TO VISIT AGAIN.
...THAT'S UNREAL...
TO THINK THAT SUCH A BEAUTIFUL VILLAGE WAS COVERED IN GAS UNTIL JUST A LITTLE WHILE AGO...

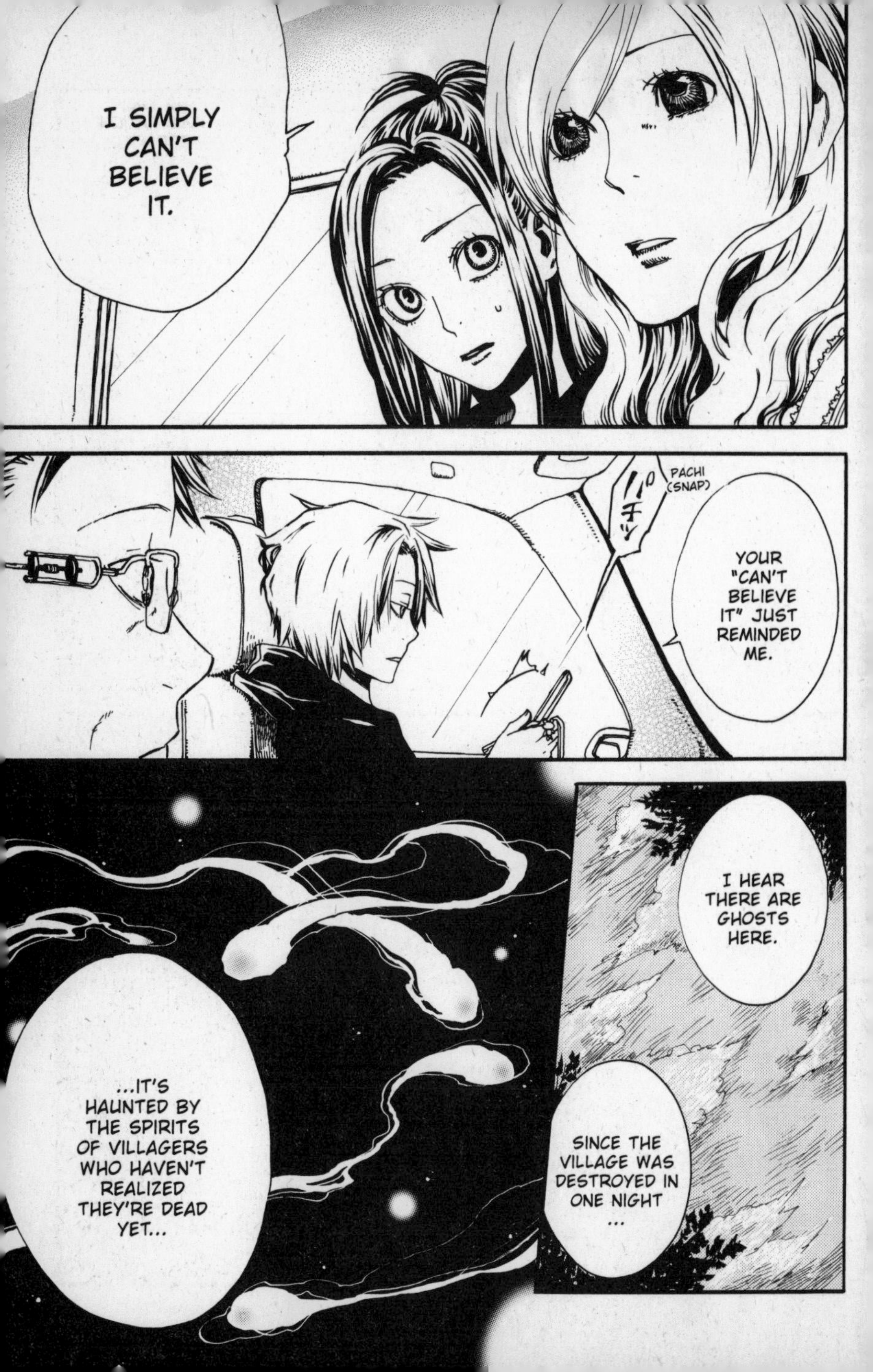
I SIMPLY CAN'T BELIEVE IT.
パチッ
PACHI (SNAP)
YOUR "CAN'T BELIEVE IT" JUST REMINDED ME.
I HEAR THERE ARE GHOSTS HERE.
SINCE THE VILLAGE WAS DESTROYED IN ONE NIGHT ...
...IT'S HAUNTED BY THE SPIRITS OF VILLAGERS WHO HAVEN'T REALIZED THEY'RE DEAD YET...

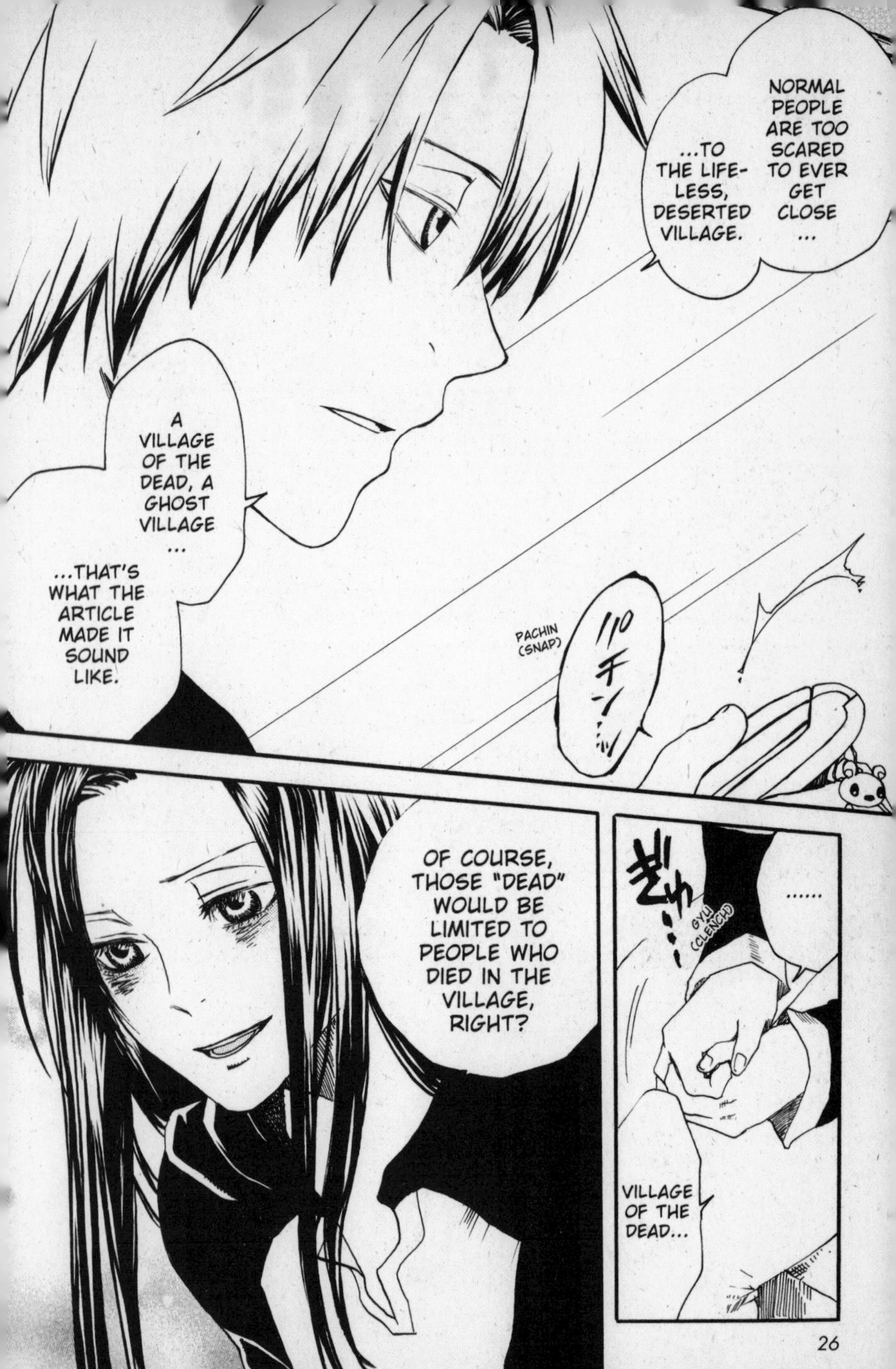
NORMAL PEOPLE ARE TOO SCARED TO EVER GET CLOSE ...
...TO THE LIFE-LESS, DESERTED VILLAGE.
A VILLAGE OF THE DEAD, A GHOST VILLAGE ...
パチン
PACHIN (SNAP)
...THAT'S WHAT THE ARTICLE MADE IT SOUND LIKE.
ぎゅ
GYU (CLENCH)
......
VILLAGE OF THE DEAD...
OF COURSE, THOSE "DEAD" WOULD BE LIMITED TO PEOPLE WHO DIED IN THE VILLAGE, RIGHT?

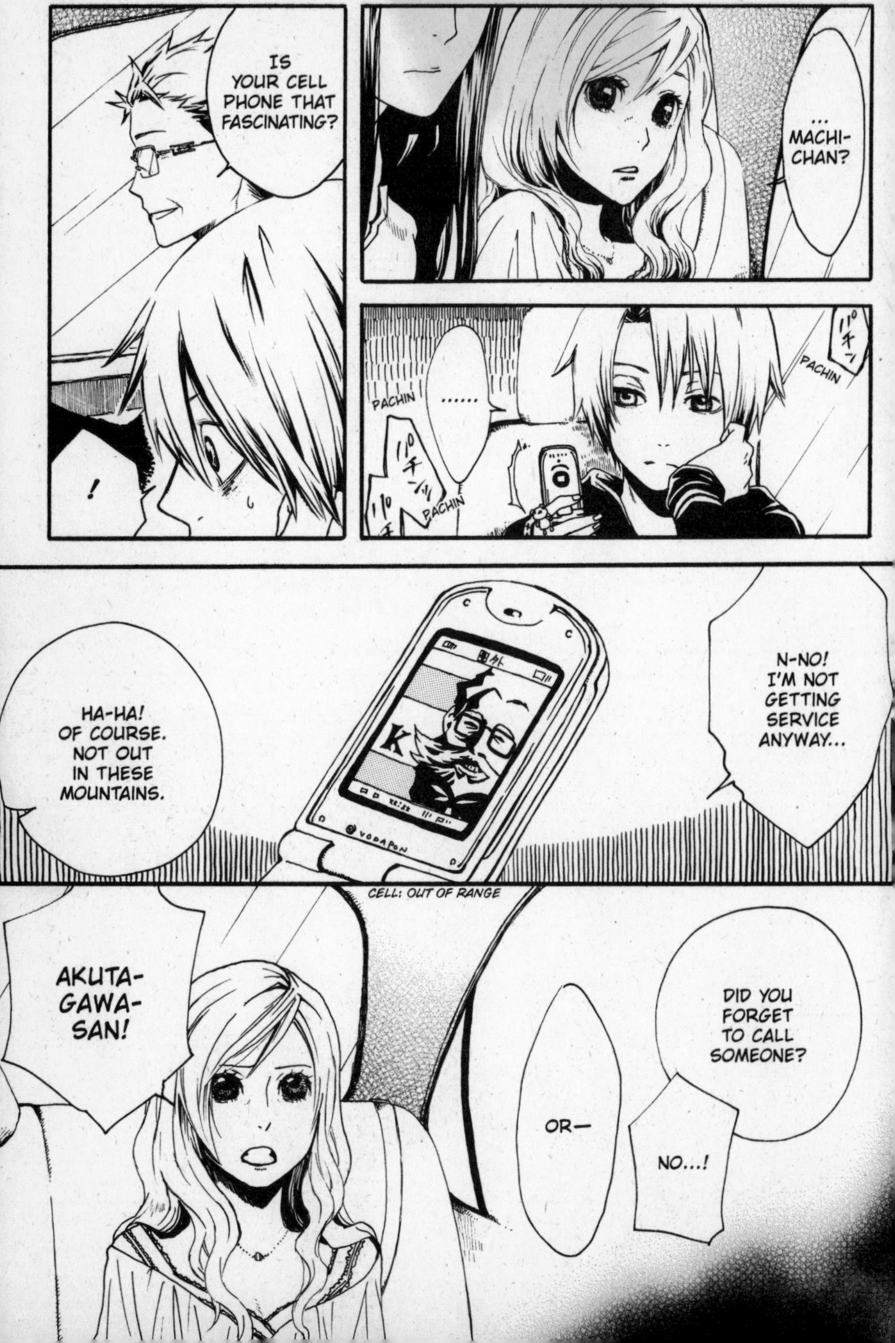

... MACHI-CHAN?
パチン
PACHIN
......
PACHIN
PACHIN
IS YOUR CELL PHONE THAT FASCINATING?
!
N-NO! I'M NOT GETTING SERVICE ANYWAY...
圏外
VODAPON
CELL: OUT OF RANGE
HA-HA! OF COURSE. NOT OUT IN THESE MOUNTAINS.
DID YOU FORGET TO CALL SOMEONE?
NO...!
OR—
AKUTA-GAWA-SAN!

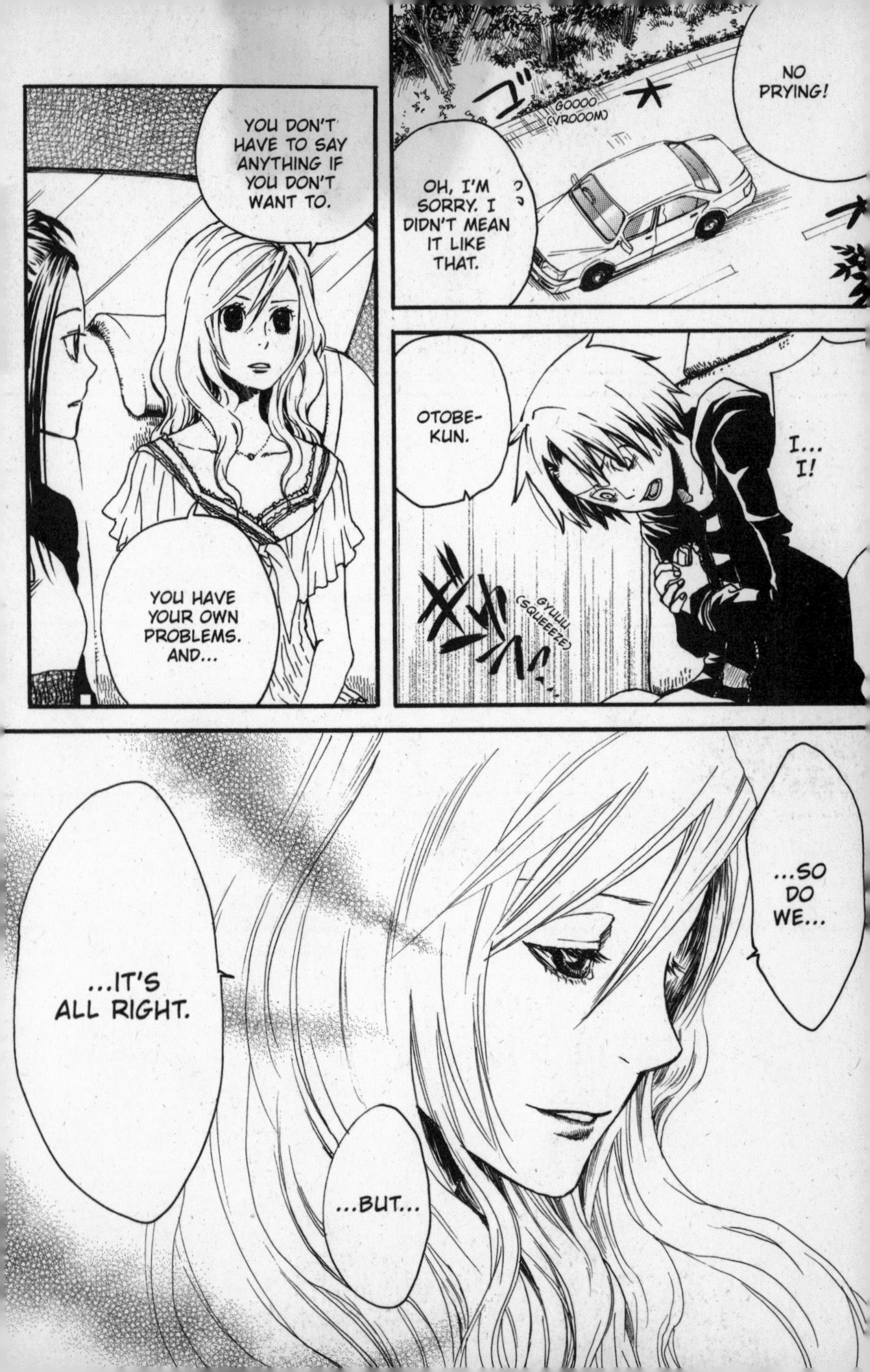
NO PRYING!
GOOOO (VROOOM)
OH, I'M SORRY. I DIDN'T MEAN IT LIKE THAT.
I... I!
OTOBE-KUN.
GYUUU (SQUEEEZE)
YOU DON'T HAVE TO SAY ANYTHING IF YOU DON'T WANT TO.
YOU HAVE YOUR OWN PROBLEMS. AND...
...SO DO WE...
...BUT...
...IT'S ALL RIGHT.

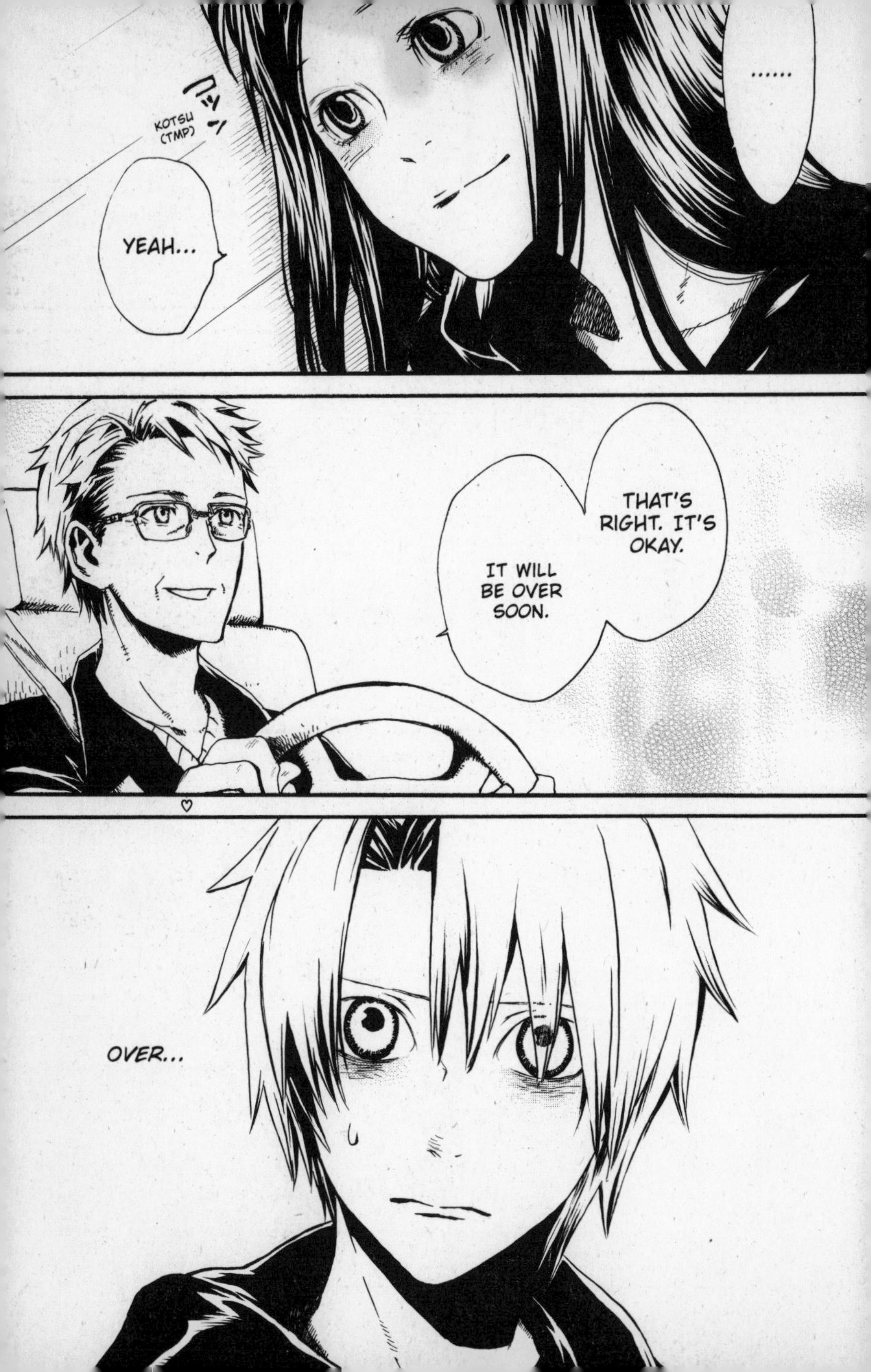
......
KOTSU (TMP)
YEAH...
THAT'S RIGHT. IT'S OKAY.
IT WILL BE OVER SOON.
OVER...

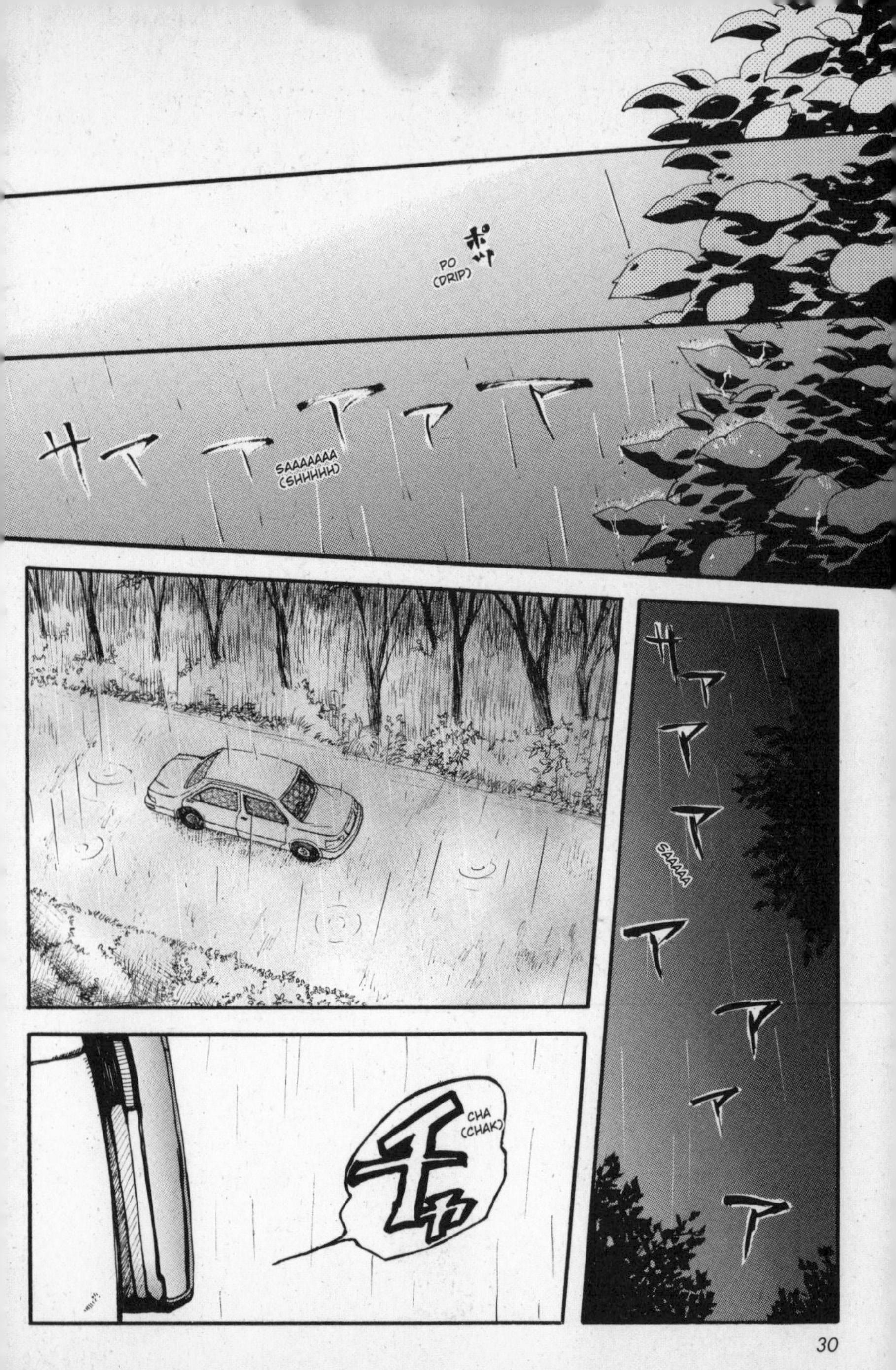
PO
(DRIP)
SAAAAAAA
(SHHHHH)
SAAAAA
CHA
(CHAK)

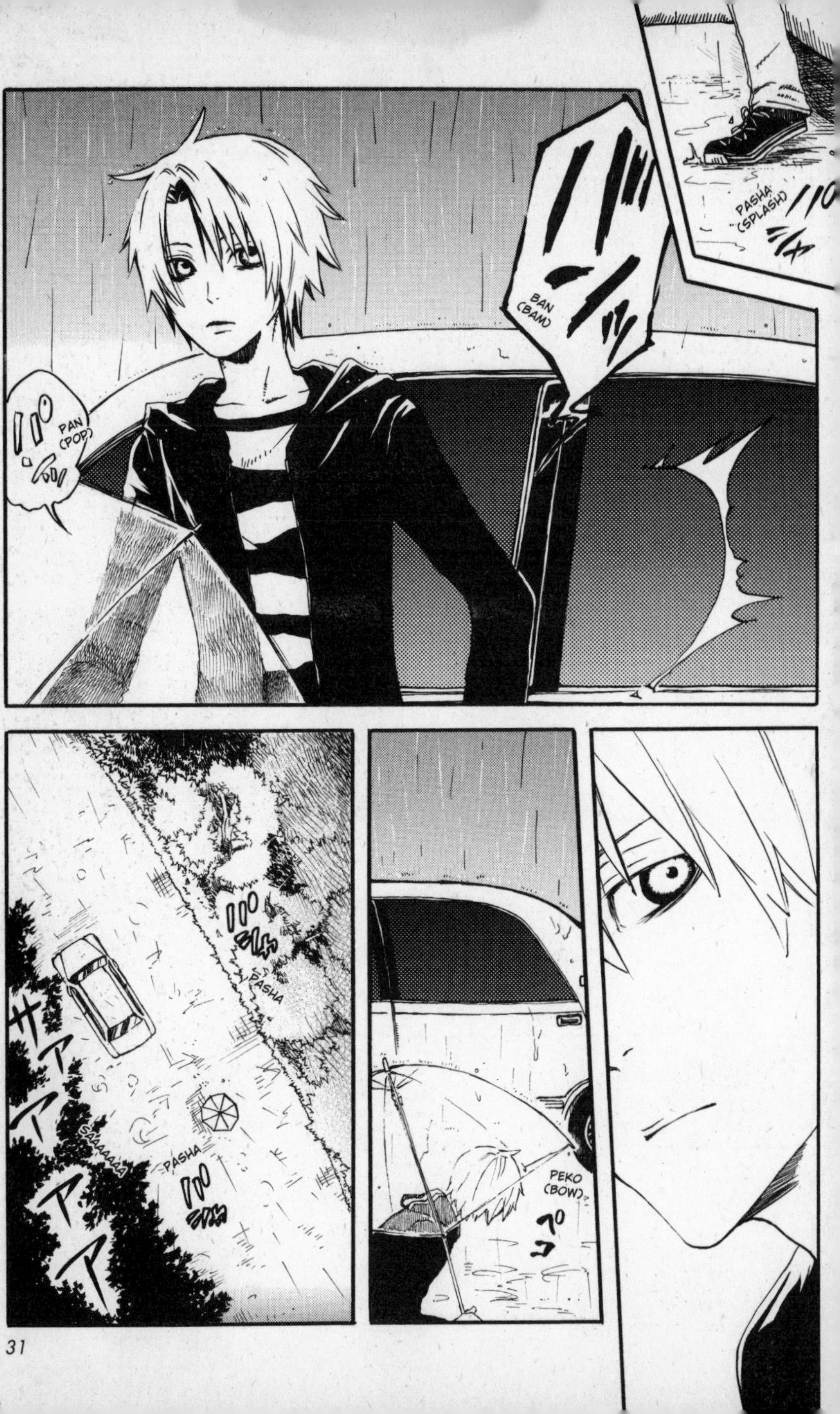
PASHA (SPLASH)
BAN (BAM)
PAN (POP)
PEKO (BOW)
PASHA
SAAAAAAA
PASHA

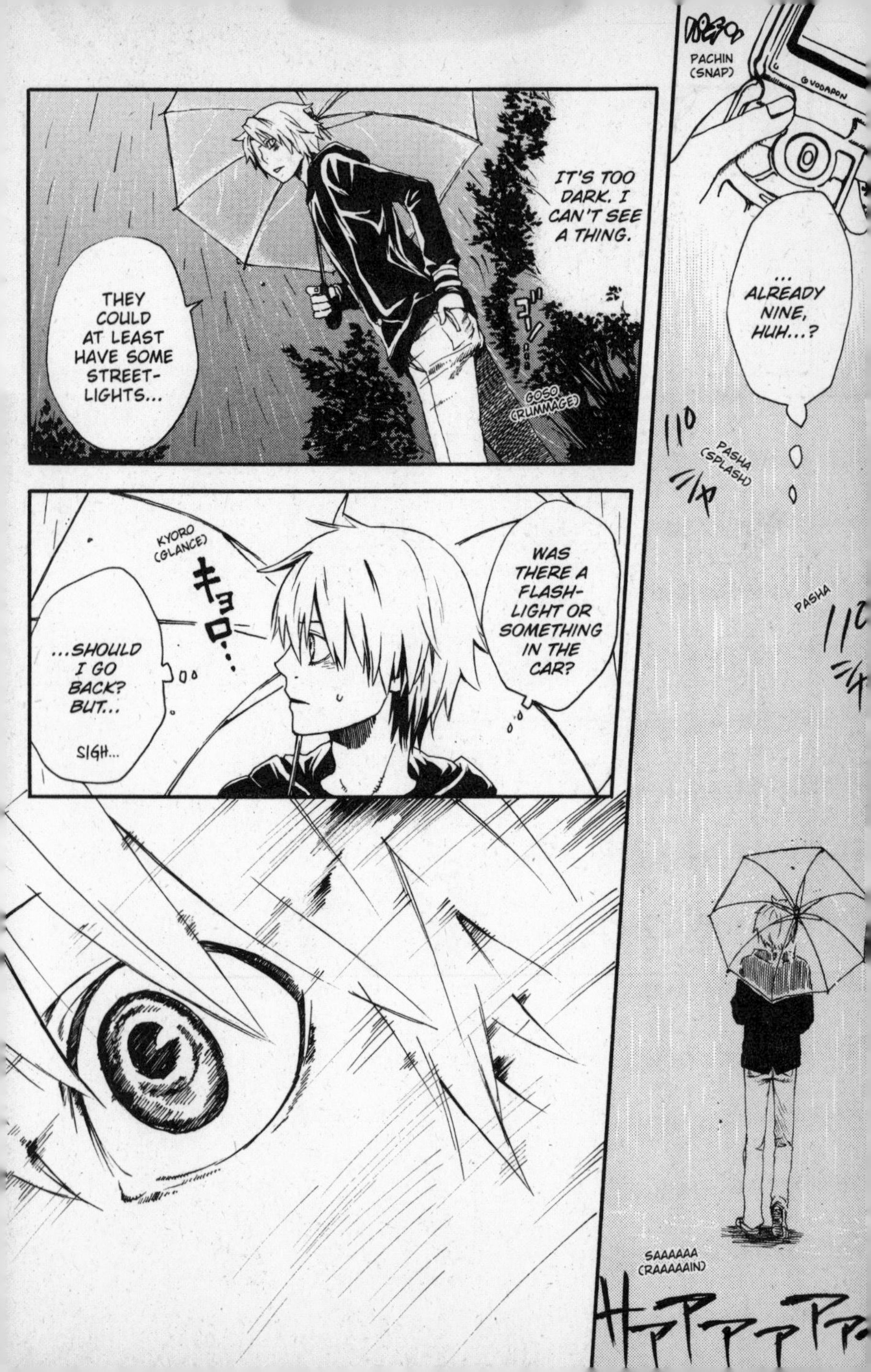
PACHIN (SNAP)
...ALREADY NINE, HUH...?
PASHA (SPLASH)
PASHA
SAAAAAA (RAAAAAIN)
IT'S TOO DARK. I CAN'T SEE A THING.
GOSO (RUMMAGE)
THEY COULD AT LEAST HAVE SOME STREET-LIGHTS...
WAS THERE A FLASH-LIGHT OR SOMETHING IN THE CAR?
KYORO (GLANCE)
...SHOULD I GO BACK? BUT...
SIGH...

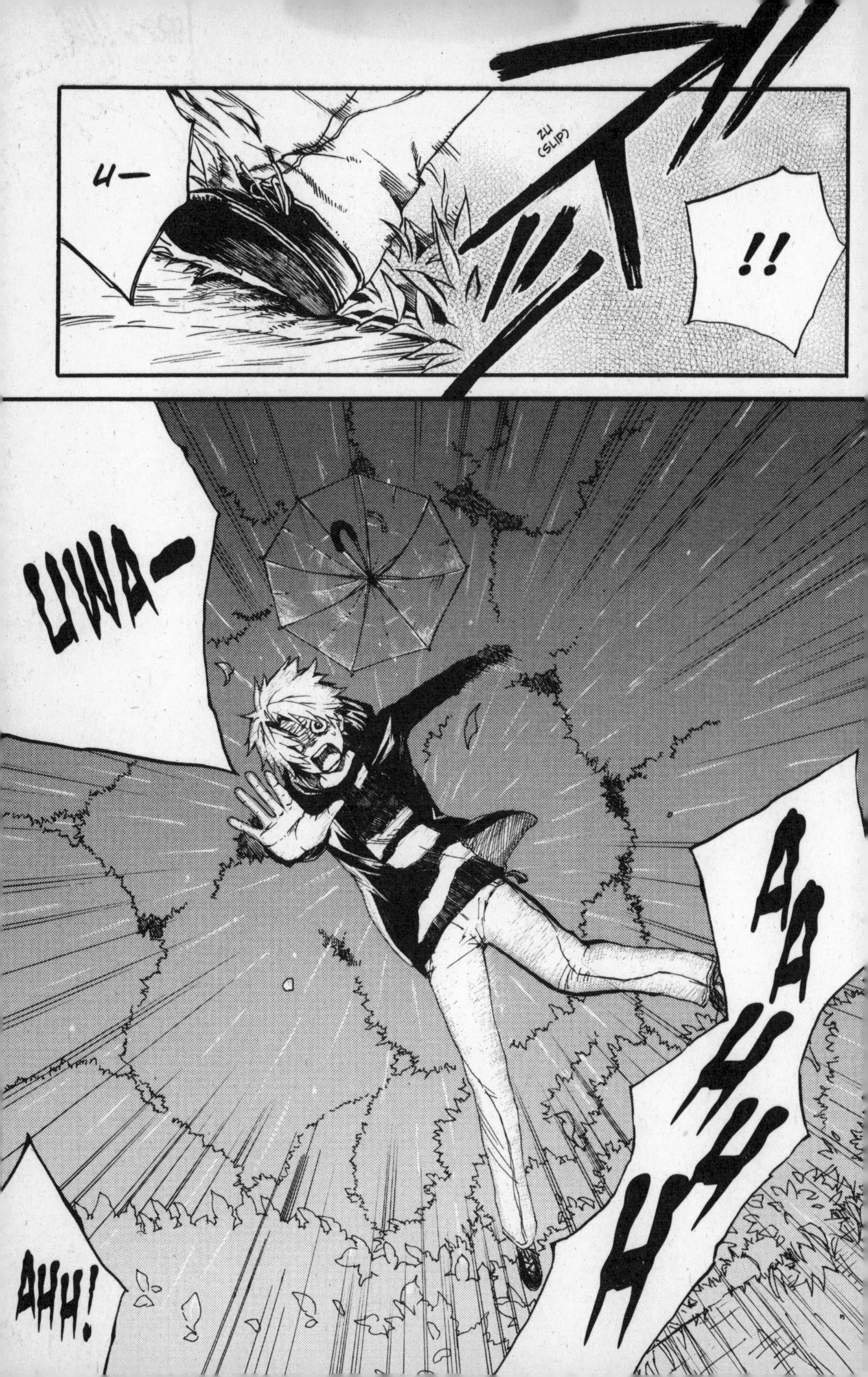
!!
ZU
(SLIP)
U–
UWA-
AAHHHH
AHH!

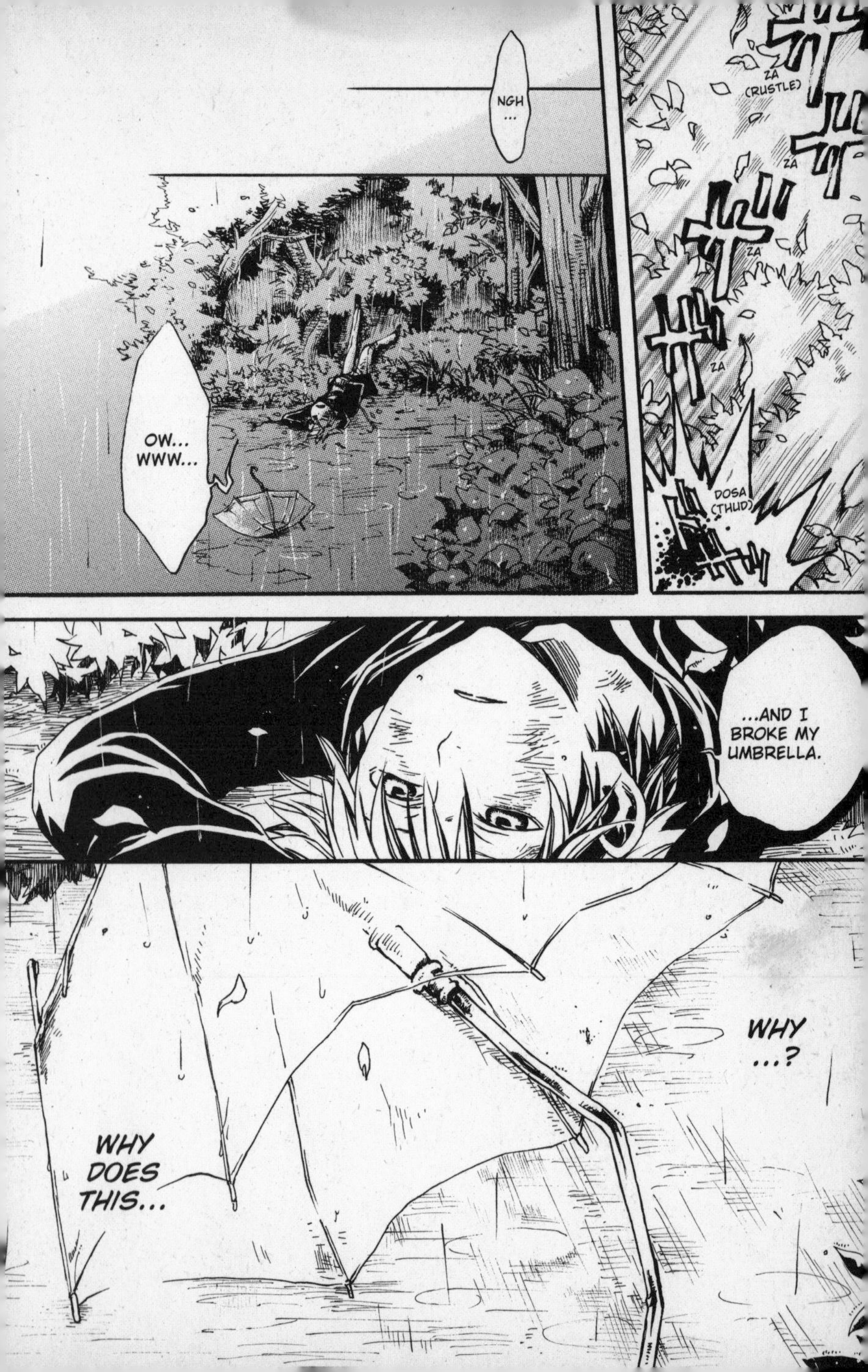
ZA (RUSTLE)
ZA
ZA
ZA
DOSA (THUD)
NGH ...
OW... WWW...
...AND I BROKE MY UMBRELLA.
WHY ...?
WHY DOES THIS...

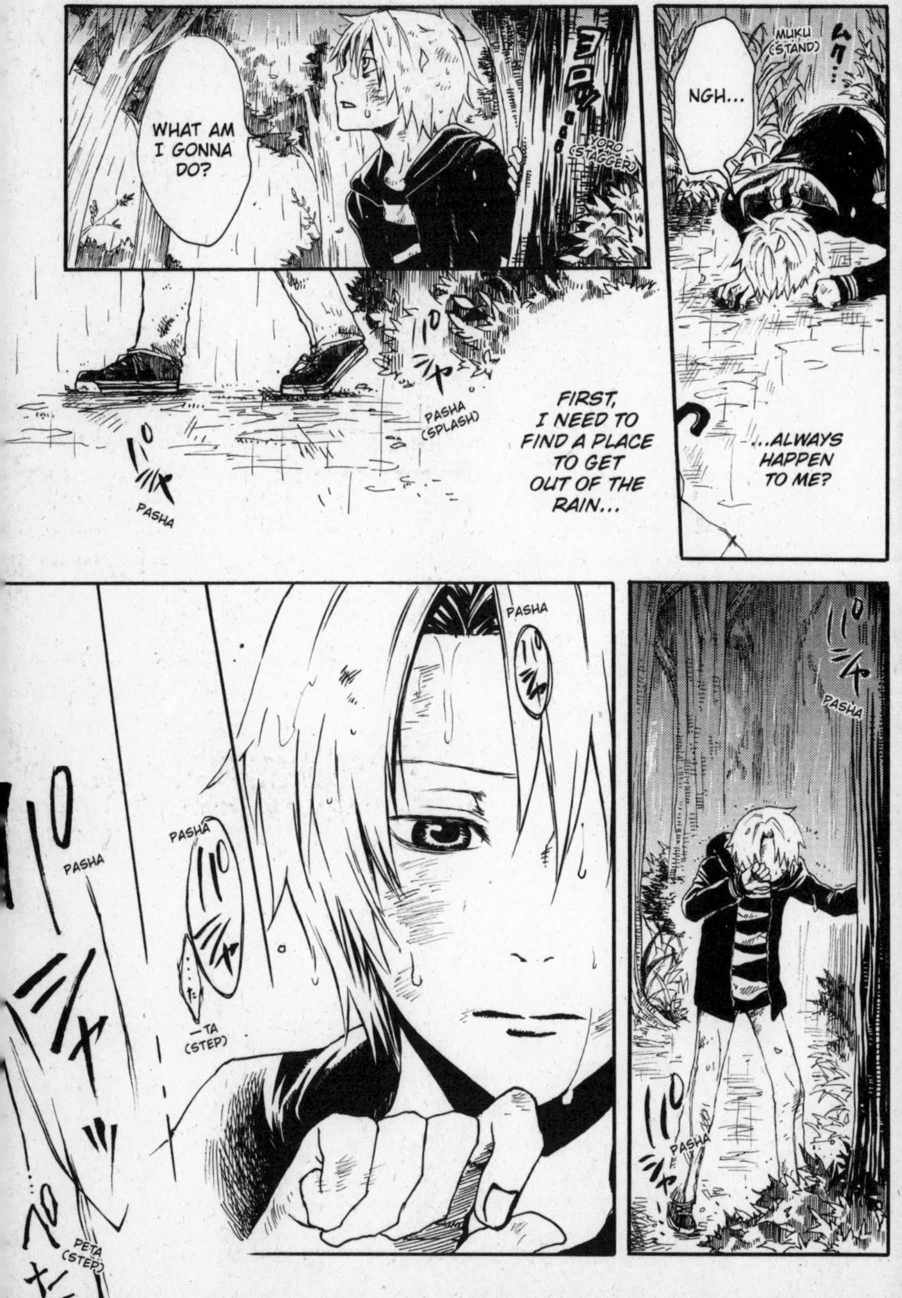
MUKU (STAND)
NGH...
...ALWAYS HAPPEN TO ME?
YORO (STAGGER)
WHAT AM I GONNA DO?
PASHA (SPLASH)
PASHA
FIRST, I NEED TO FIND A PLACE TO GET OUT OF THE RAIN...
PASHA
PASHA
PASHA
PASHA
PASHA
—TA (STEP)
PETA (STEP)

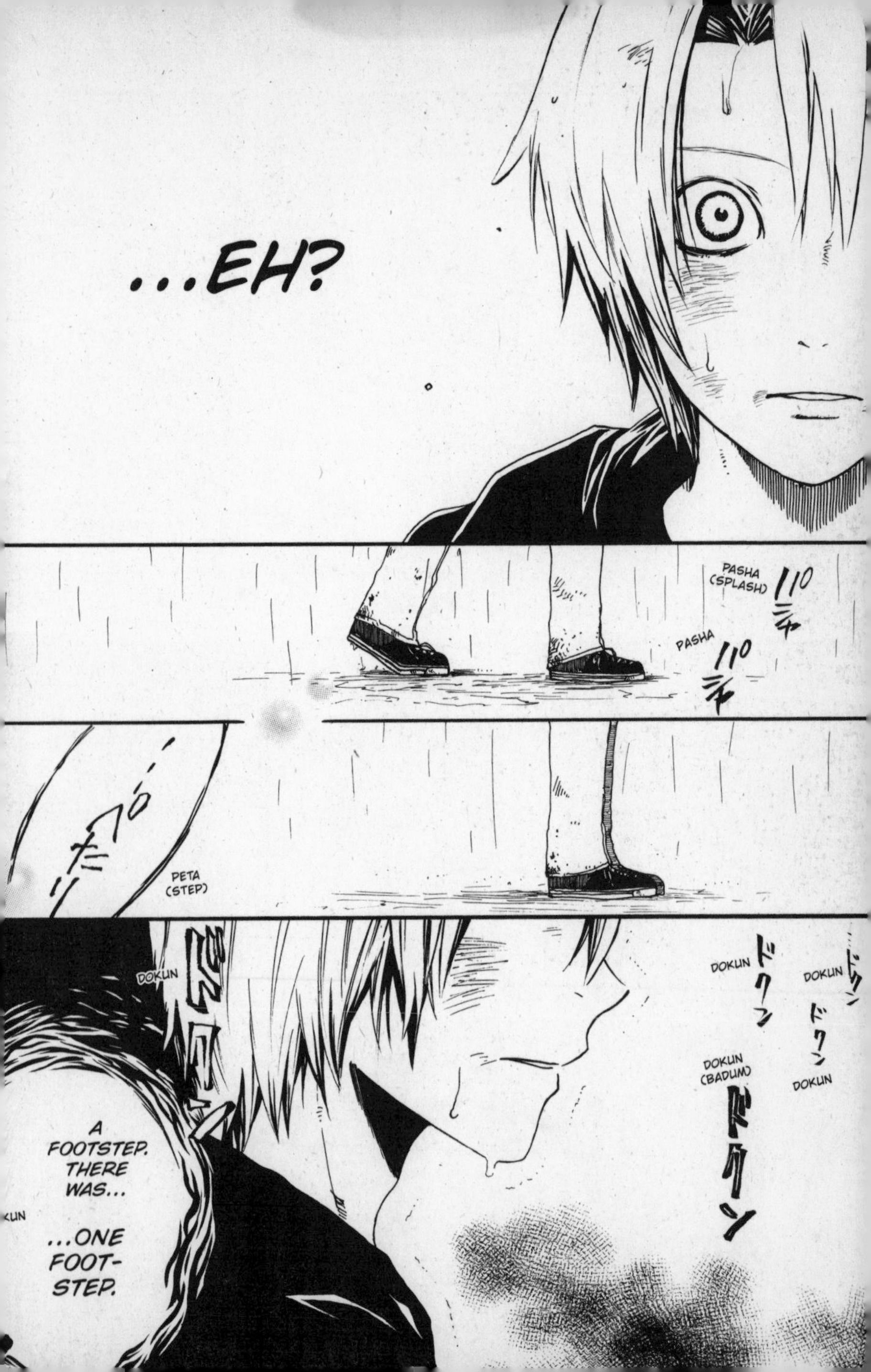
...EH?
PASHA (SPLASH)
PASHA
PETA (STEP)
DOKUN
DOKUN
DOKUN
DOKUN (BADUM)
DOKUN
A FOOTSTEP. THERE WAS...
...ONE FOOT-STEP.

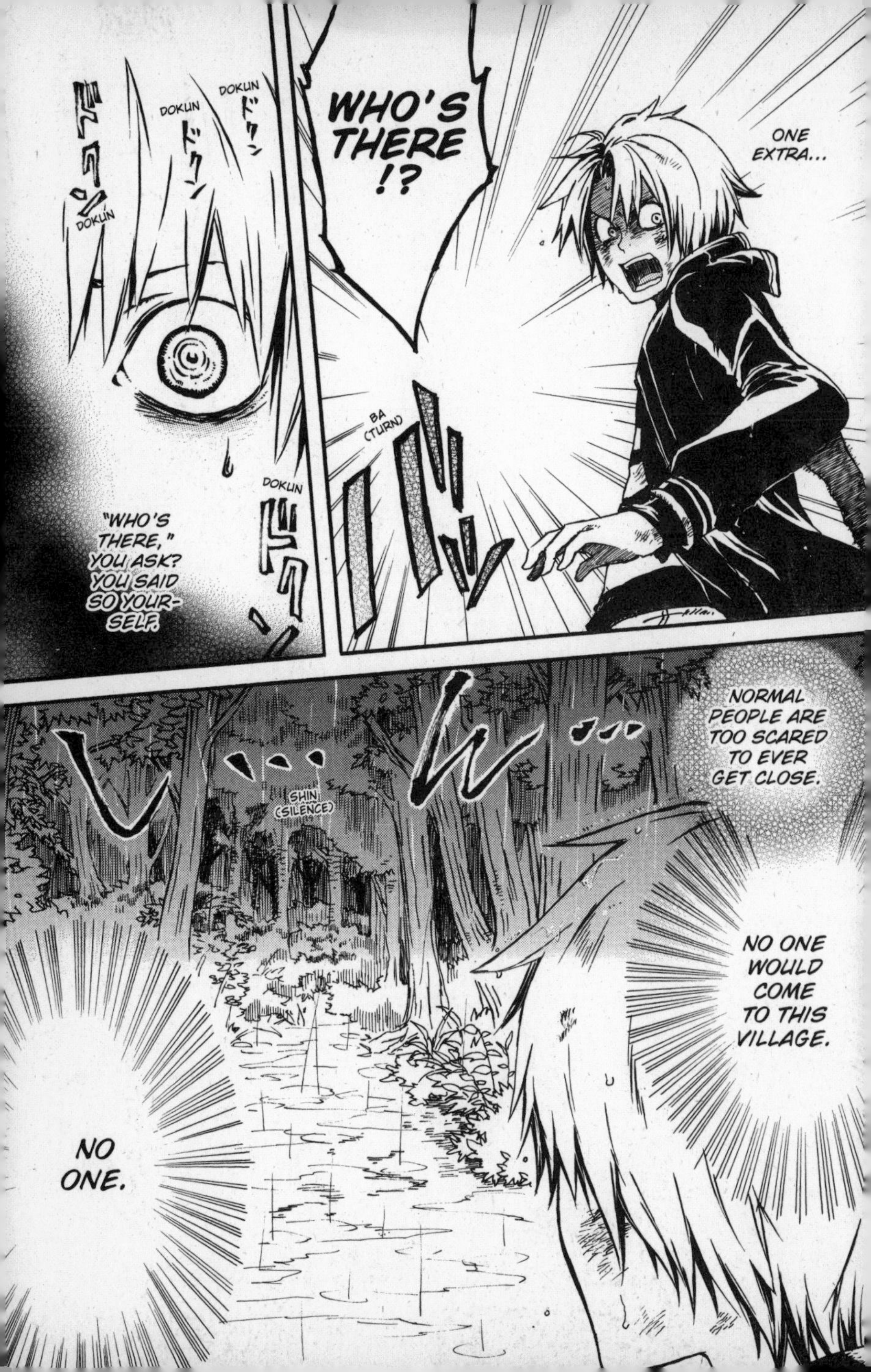
ONE EXTRA...
WHO'S THERE !?
BA (TURN)
DOKUN
DOKUN
DOKUN
DOKUN
"WHO'S THERE," YOU ASK? YOU SAID SO YOUR-SELF.
NORMAL PEOPLE ARE TOO SCARED TO EVER GET CLOSE.
NO ONE WOULD COME TO THIS VILLAGE.
SHIN (SILENCE)
NO ONE.

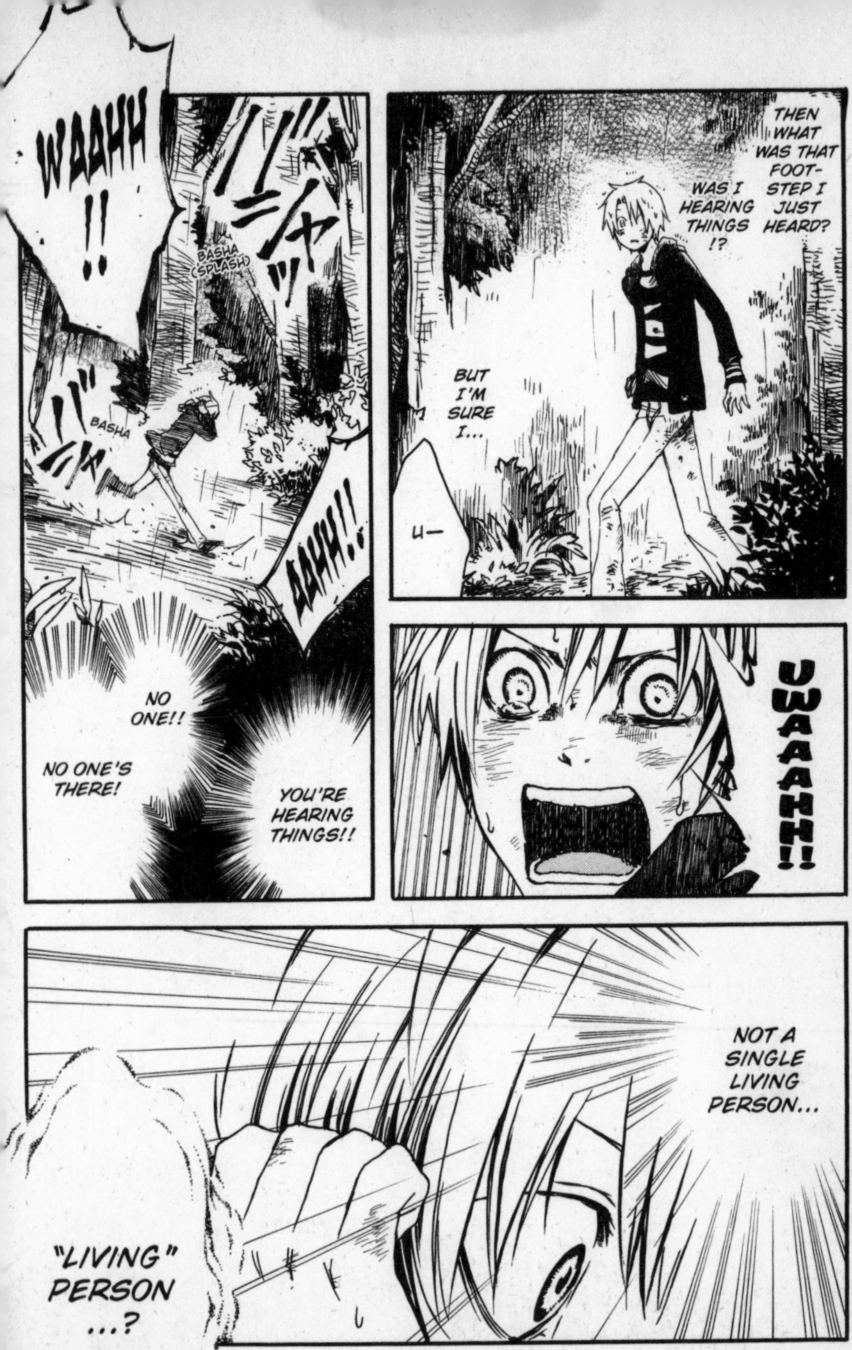
THEN WHAT WAS THAT FOOT-STEP I JUST HEARD?
WAS I HEARING THINGS !?
BUT I'M SURE I...
U—
UWAAAAHH!!
BASHA (SPLASH)
WAAHH !!
AAHH!!
BASHA
YOU'RE HEARING THINGS!!
NO ONE!!
NO ONE'S THERE!
NOT A SINGLE LIVING PERSON...
"LIVING" PERSON ...?

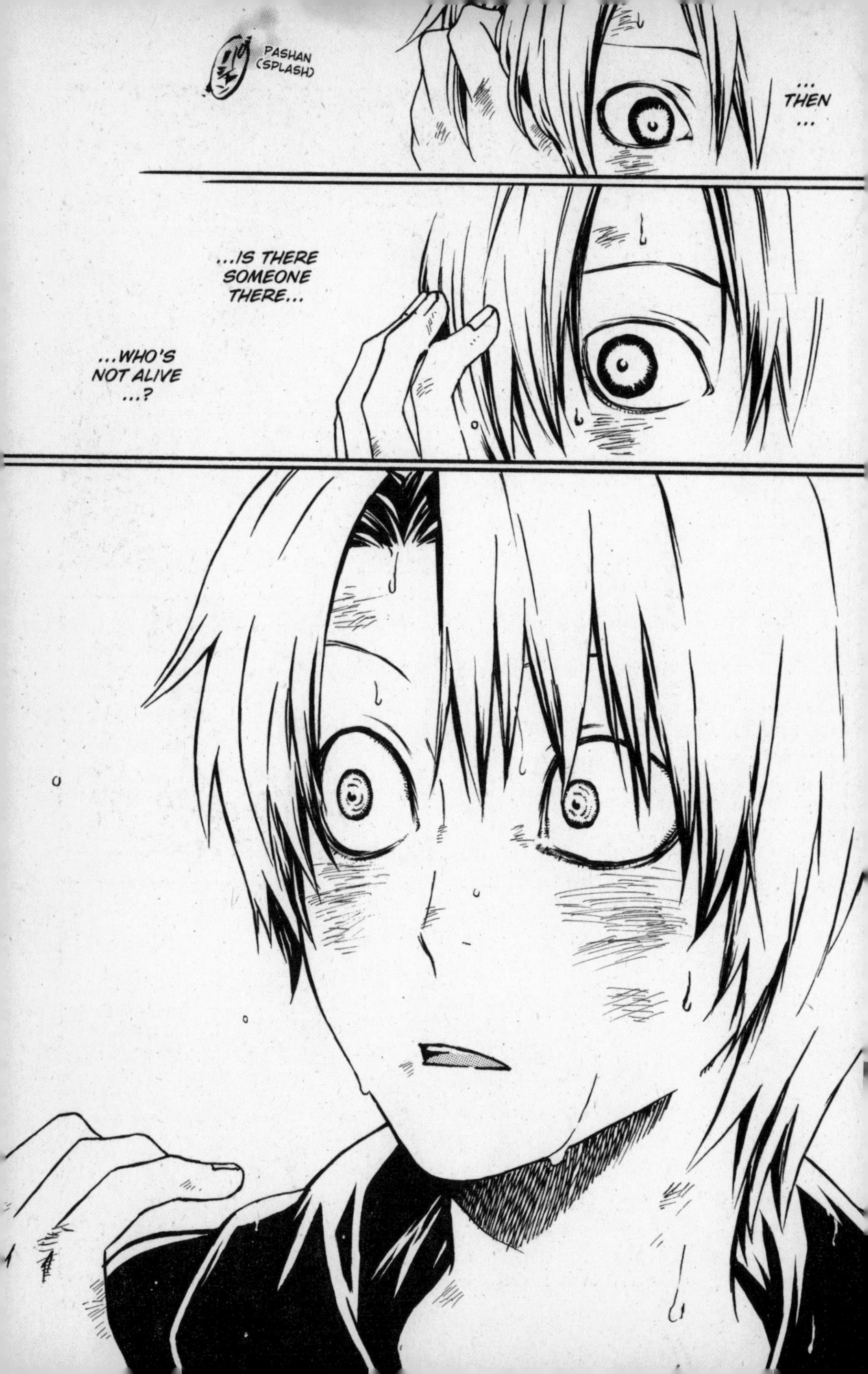
... THEN ...
PASHAN (SPLASH)
...IS THERE SOMEONE THERE...
...WHO'S NOT ALIVE ...?

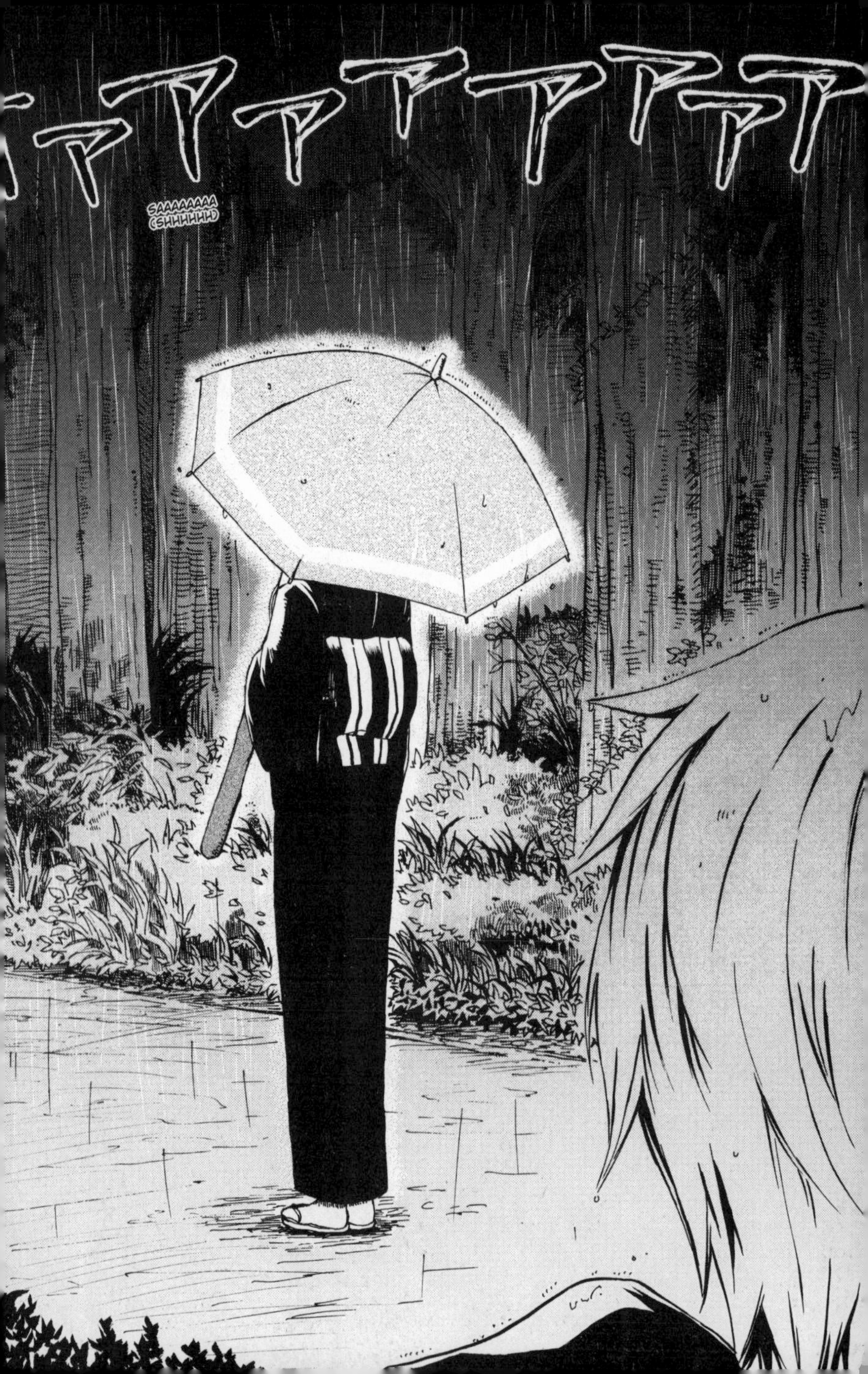
ザァァァァァァァァ
SAAAAAAAA
(SHHHHHH)

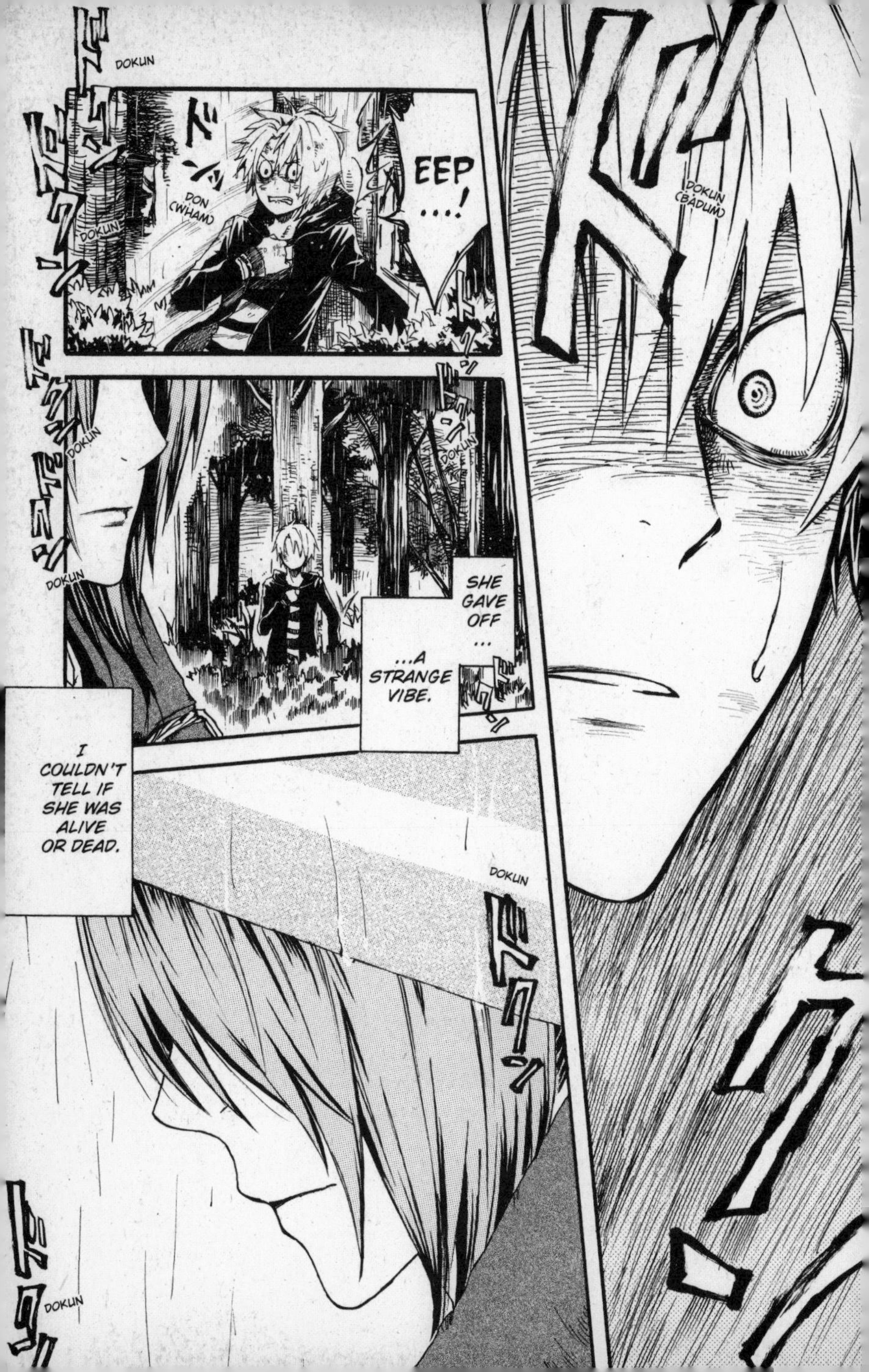
DOKUN (BADUM)
DOKUN
EEP ...!
DON (WHAM)
DOKUN
DOKUN
SHE GAVE OFF ...
...A STRANGE VIBE.
DOKUN
DOKUN
I COULDN'T TELL IF SHE WAS ALIVE OR DEAD.
DOKUN

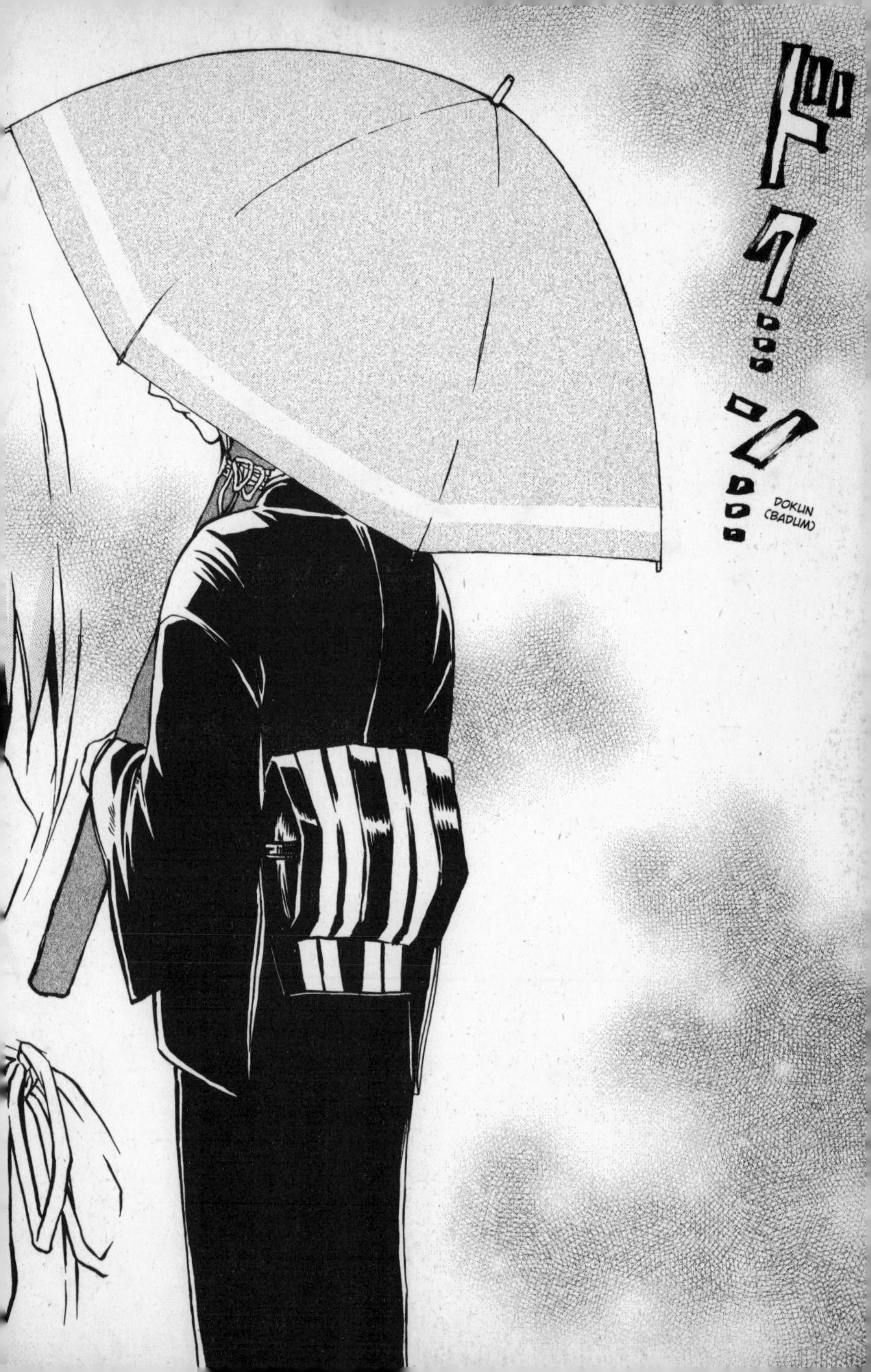
ドク…ン…
DOKUN (BADUM)

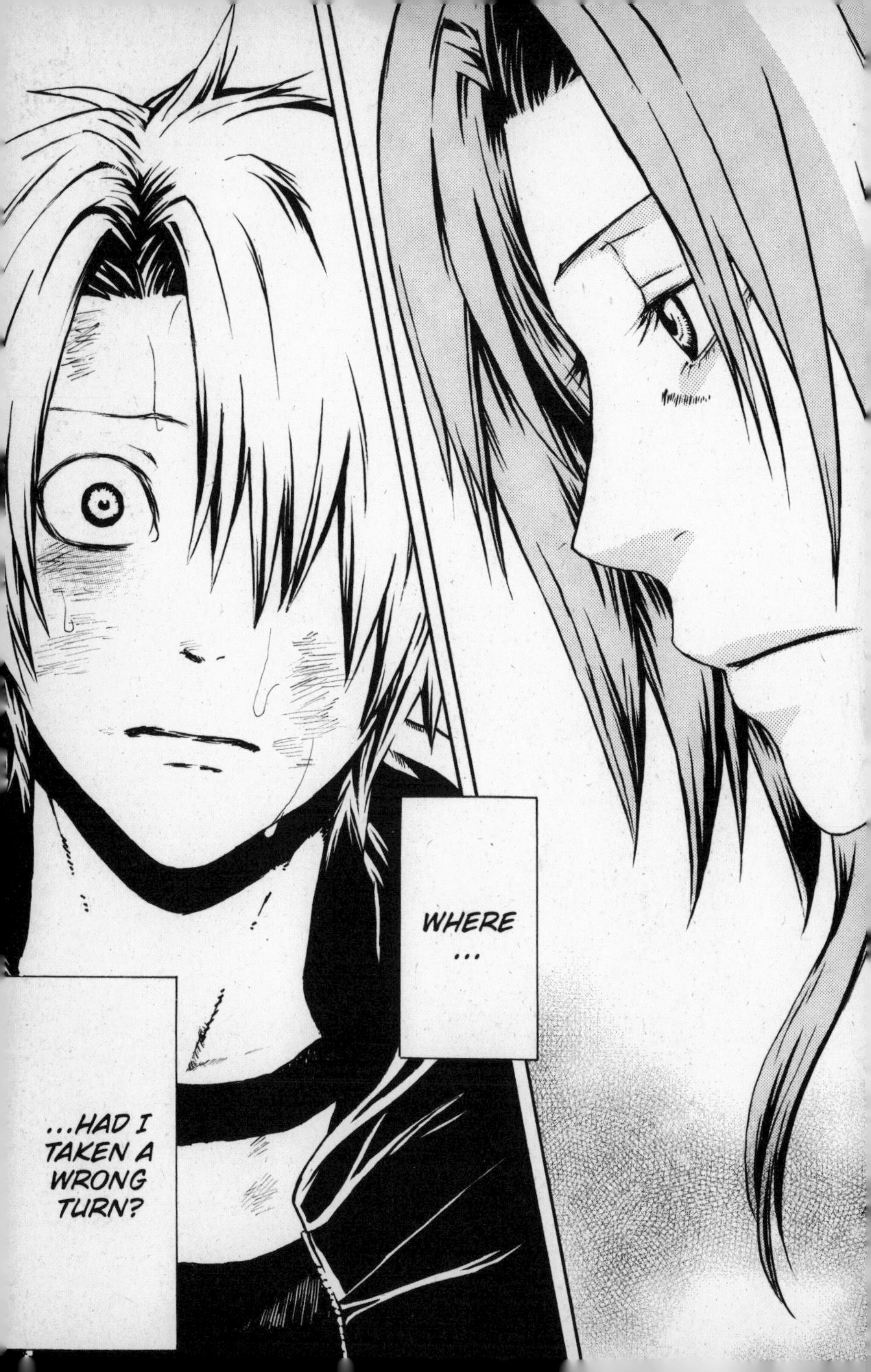
WHERE ...
...HAD I TAKEN A WRONG TURN?

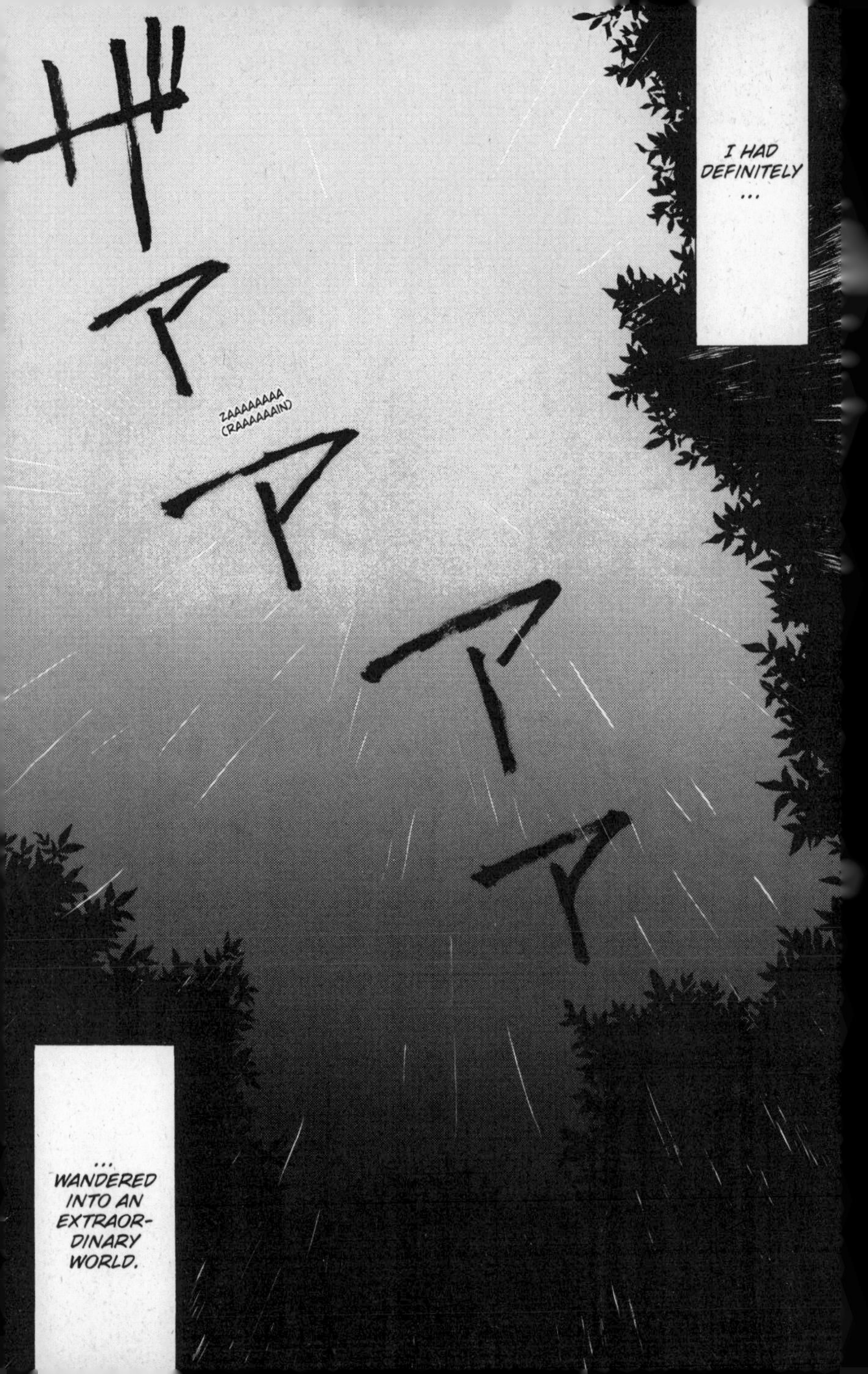
I HAD DEFINITELY ...
ザアアアア
ZAAAAAAAA (RAAAAAAAIN)
... WANDERED INTO AN EXTRAOR-DINARY WORLD.

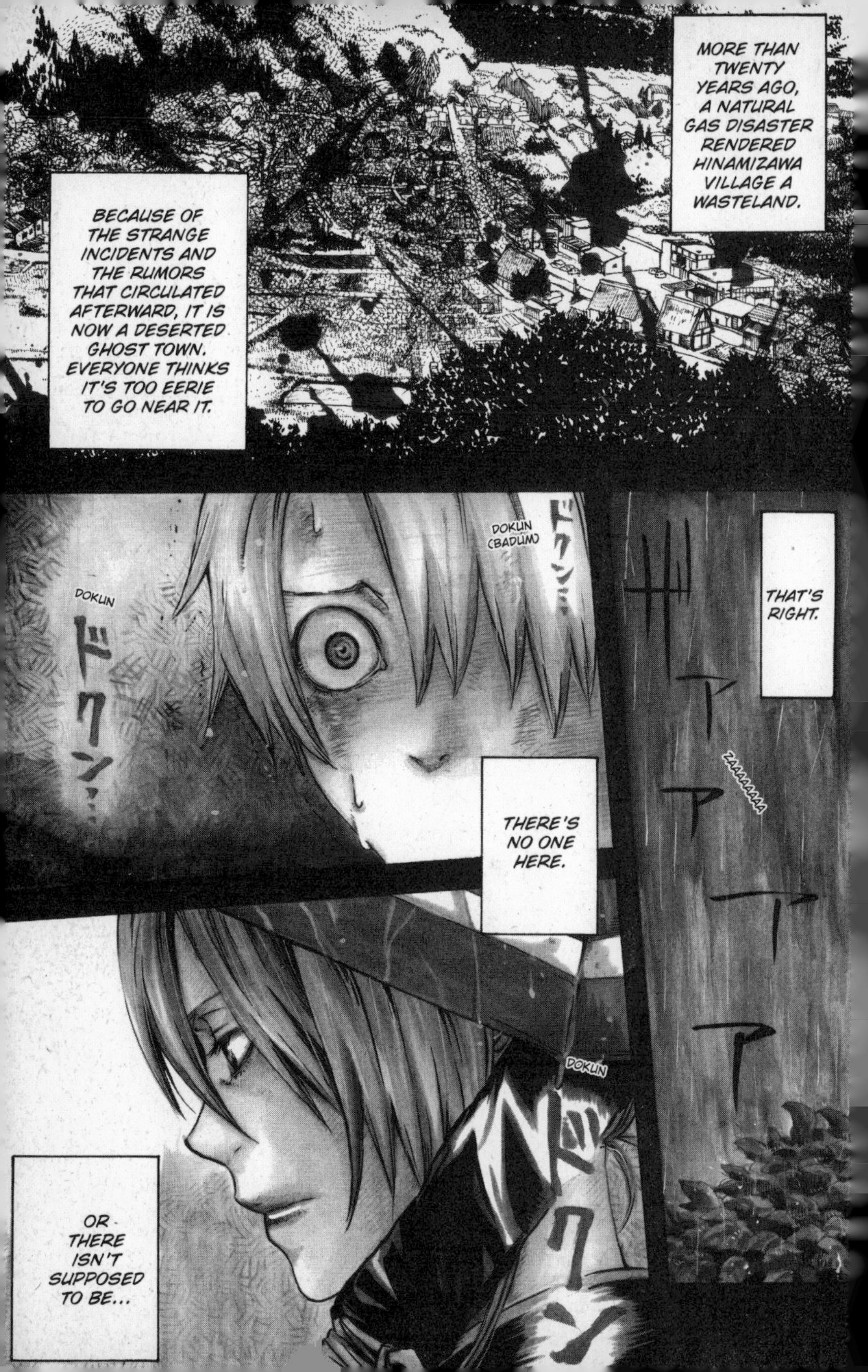
MORE THAN TWENTY YEARS AGO, A NATURAL GAS DISASTER RENDERED HINAMIZAWA VILLAGE A WASTELAND.
BECAUSE OF THE STRANGE INCIDENTS AND THE RUMORS THAT CIRCULATED AFTERWARD, IT IS NOW A DESERTED GHOST TOWN. EVERYONE THINKS IT'S TOO EERIE TO GO NEAR IT.
THAT'S RIGHT.
ZAAAAAAAA
DOKUN (BADUM)
DOKUN
THERE'S NO ONE HERE.
DOKUN
OR THERE ISN'T SUPPOSED TO BE...

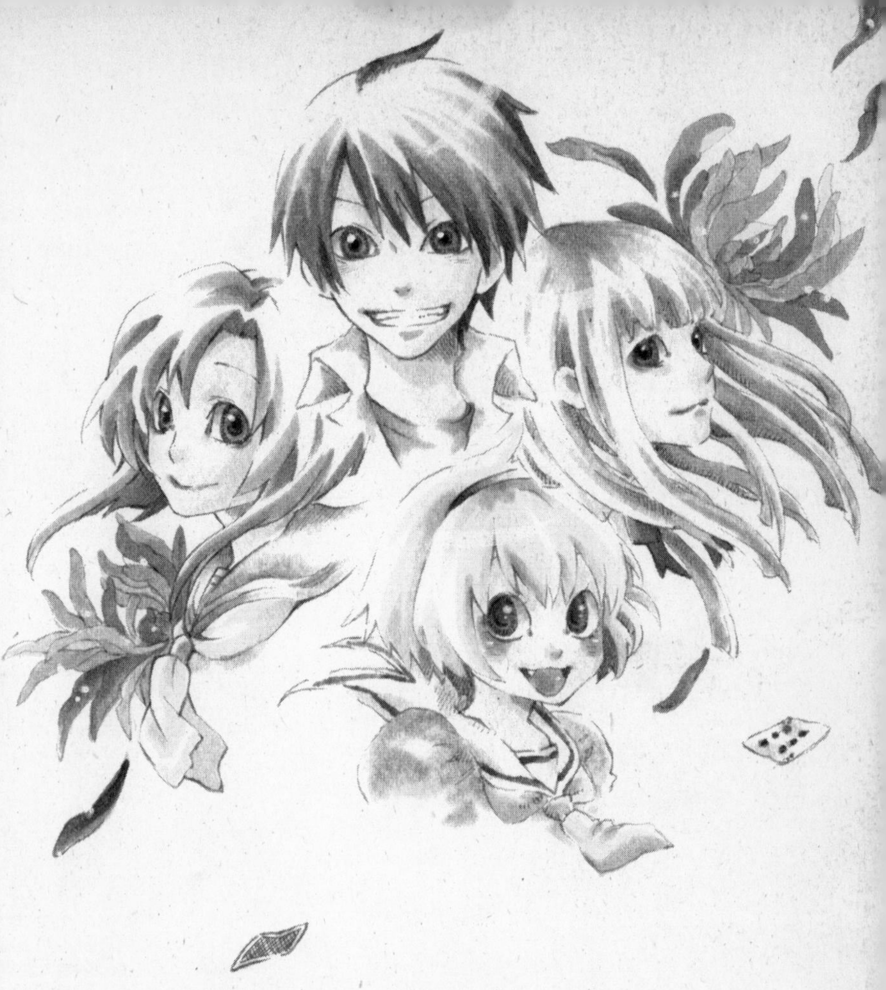

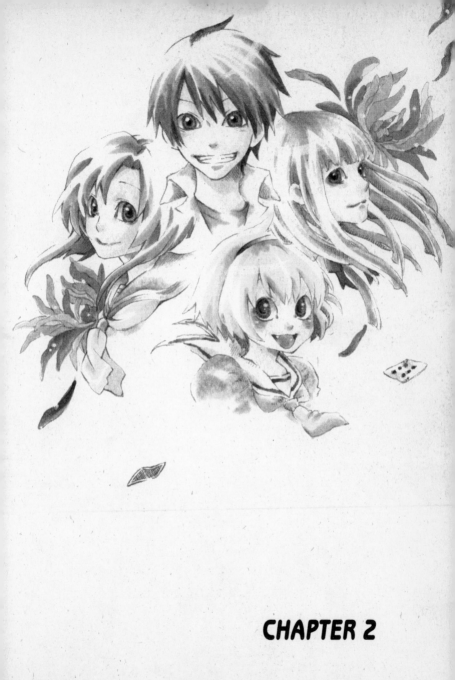

CHAPTER 2

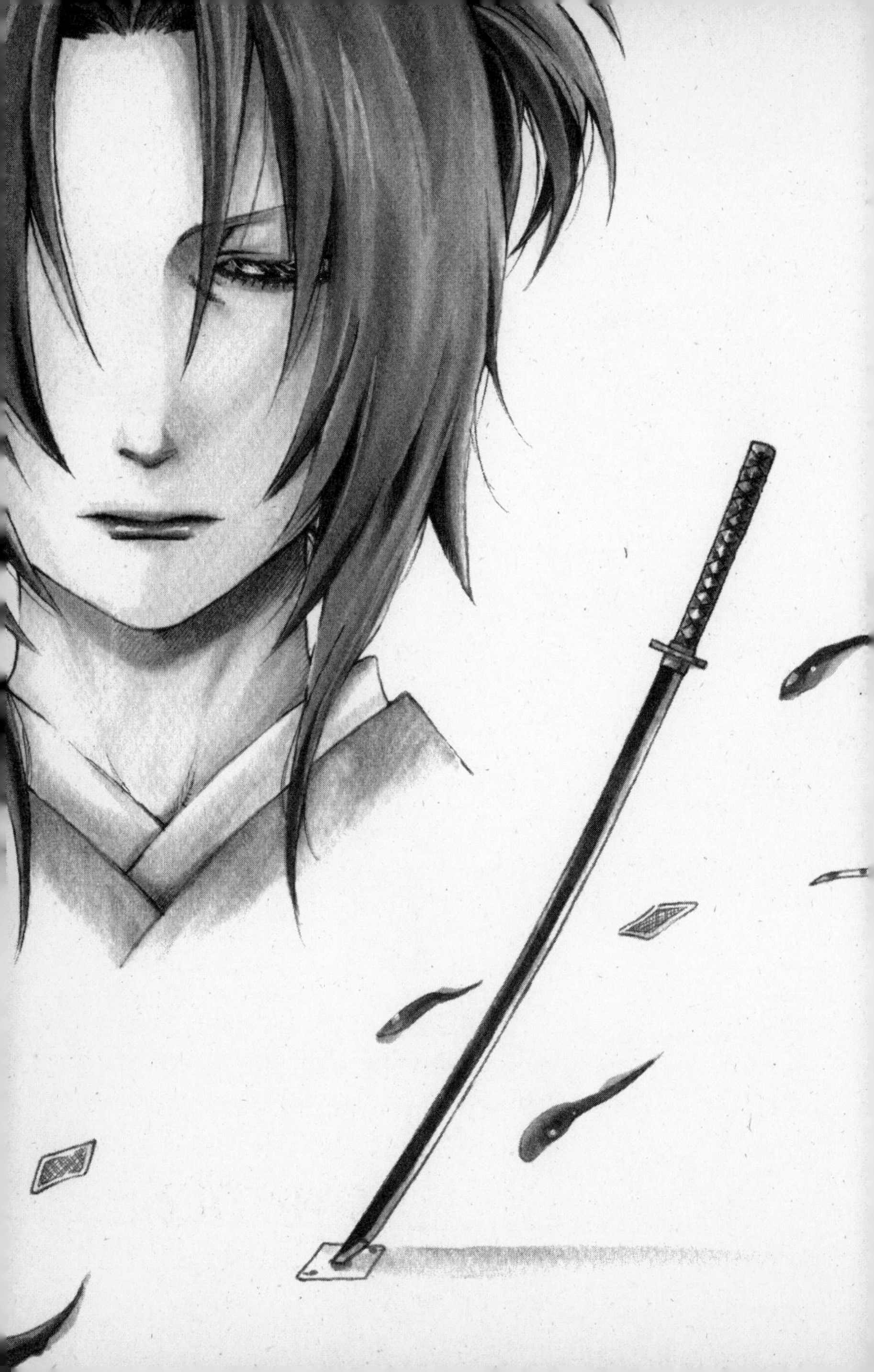

Special Thanks

Ryukishi07-sama
Mochizuki-sama
Koizumi-sama

Morinaga-san
Naitou-san

Higashi-san

Everyone in
my family

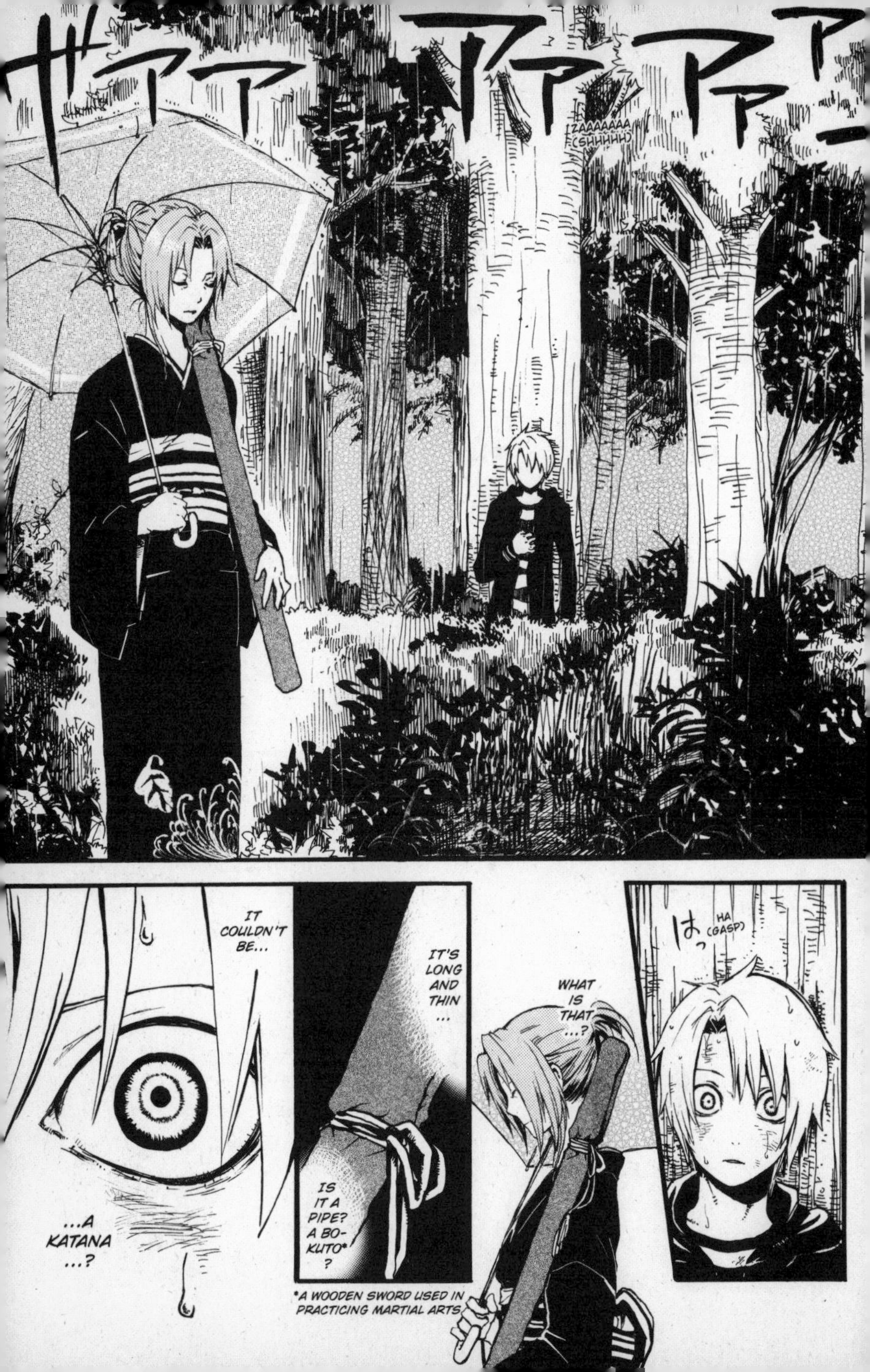
ザアアアアアアアー
ZAAAAAAA (SHHHHH)
はっ
HA (GASP)
WHAT IS THAT ...?
IT'S LONG AND THIN ...
IS IT A PIPE? A BO-KUTO*?
IT COULDN'T BE...
...A KATANA ...?
*A WOODEN SWORD USED IN PRACTICING MARTIAL ARTS

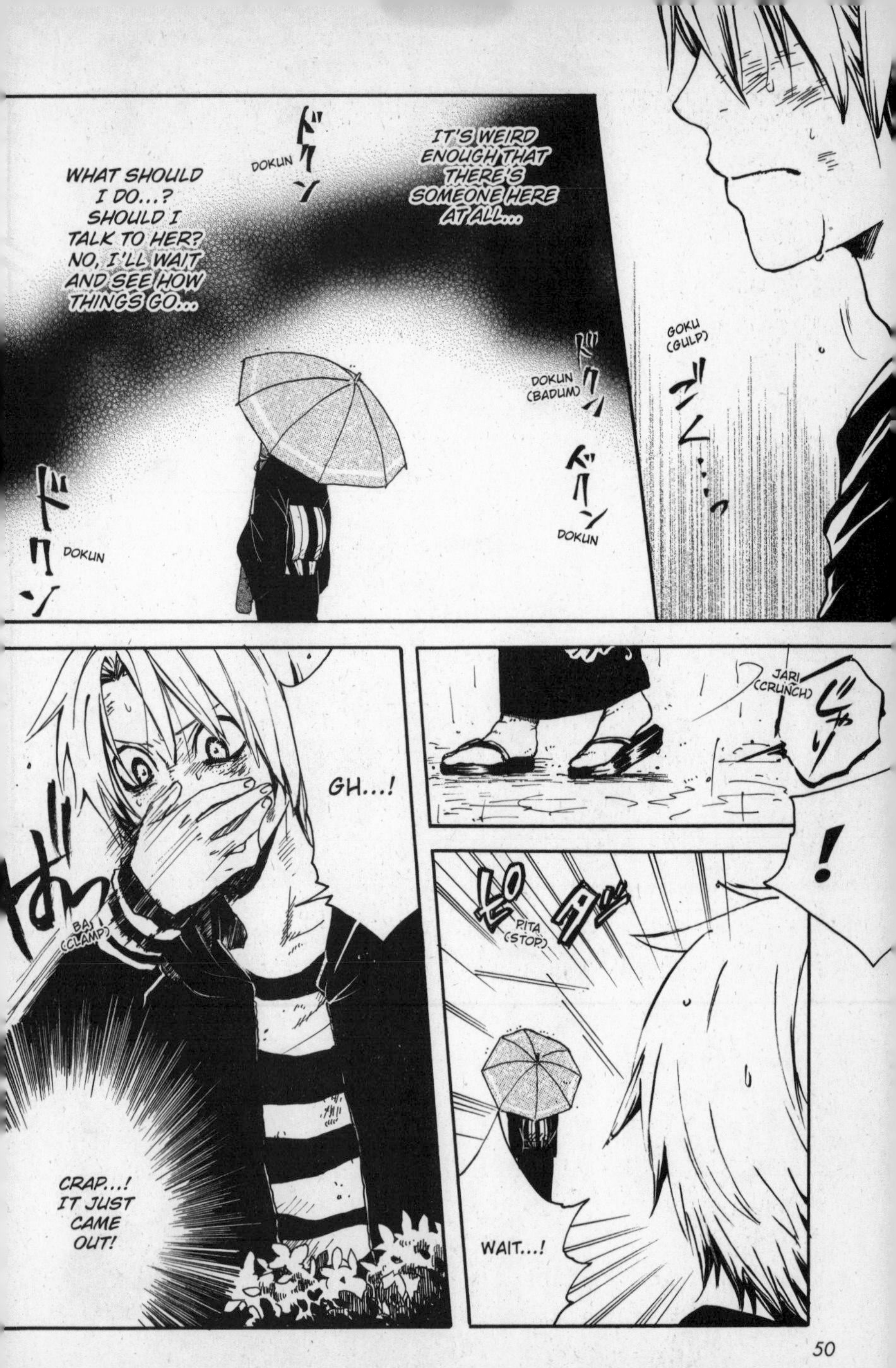
GOKU (GULP)
IT'S WEIRD ENOUGH THAT THERE'S SOMEONE HERE AT ALL...
DOKUN
WHAT SHOULD I DO...? SHOULD I TALK TO HER? NO, I'LL WAIT AND SEE HOW THINGS GO...
DOKUN (BADUM)
DOKUN
DOKUN
JARI (CRUNCH)
!
PITA (STOP)
WAIT...!
GH...!
BA! (CLAMP)
CRAP...! IT JUST CAME OUT!

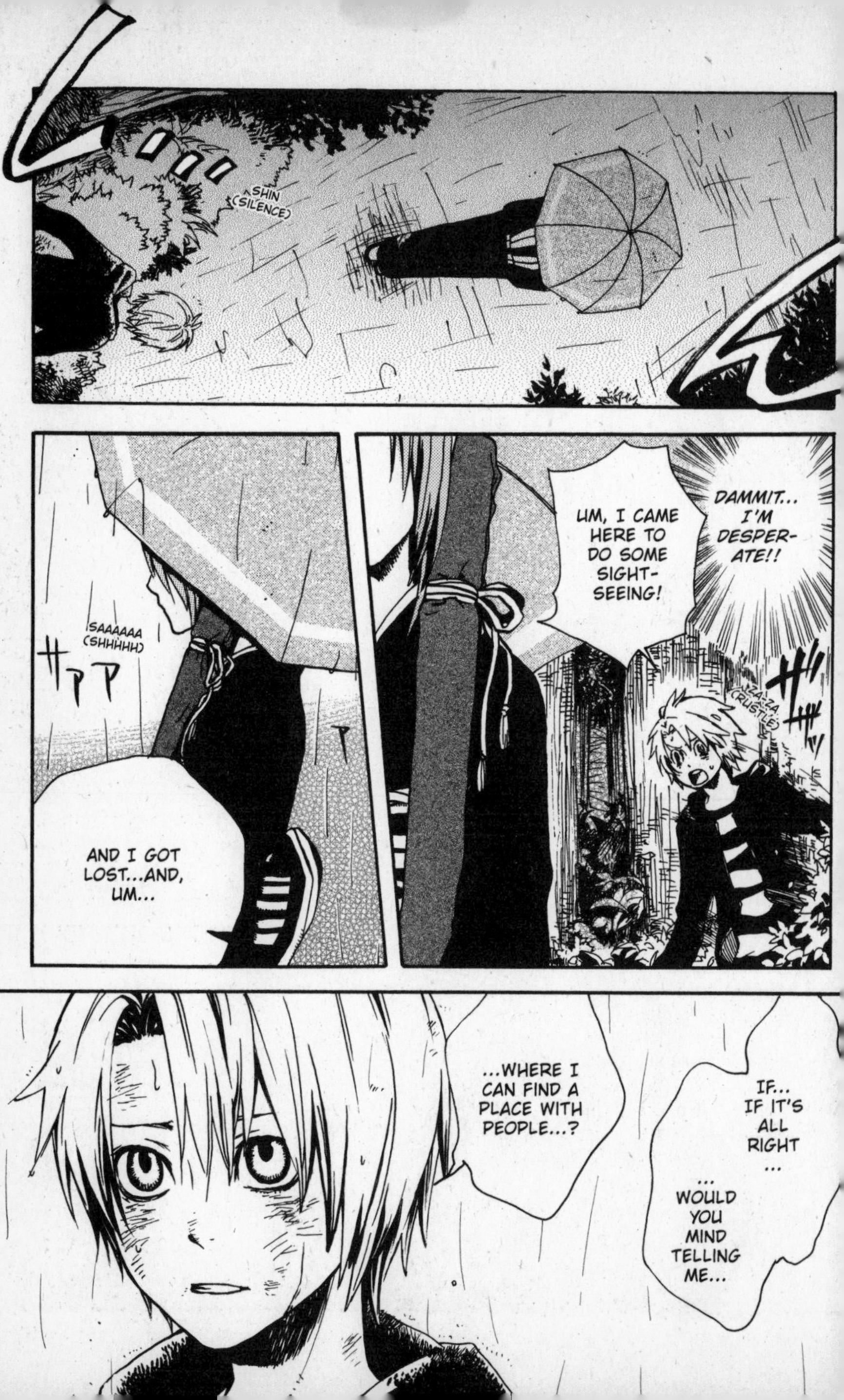
SHIN (SILENCE)
DAMMIT... I'M DESPER-ATE!!
UM, I CAME HERE TO DO SOME SIGHT-SEEING!
ZA-ZA (RUSTLE)
SAAAAAA (SHHHHH)
AND I GOT LOST...AND, UM...
IF... IF IT'S ALL RIGHT ...
... WOULD YOU MIND TELLING ME...
...WHERE I CAN FIND A PLACE WITH PEOPLE...?

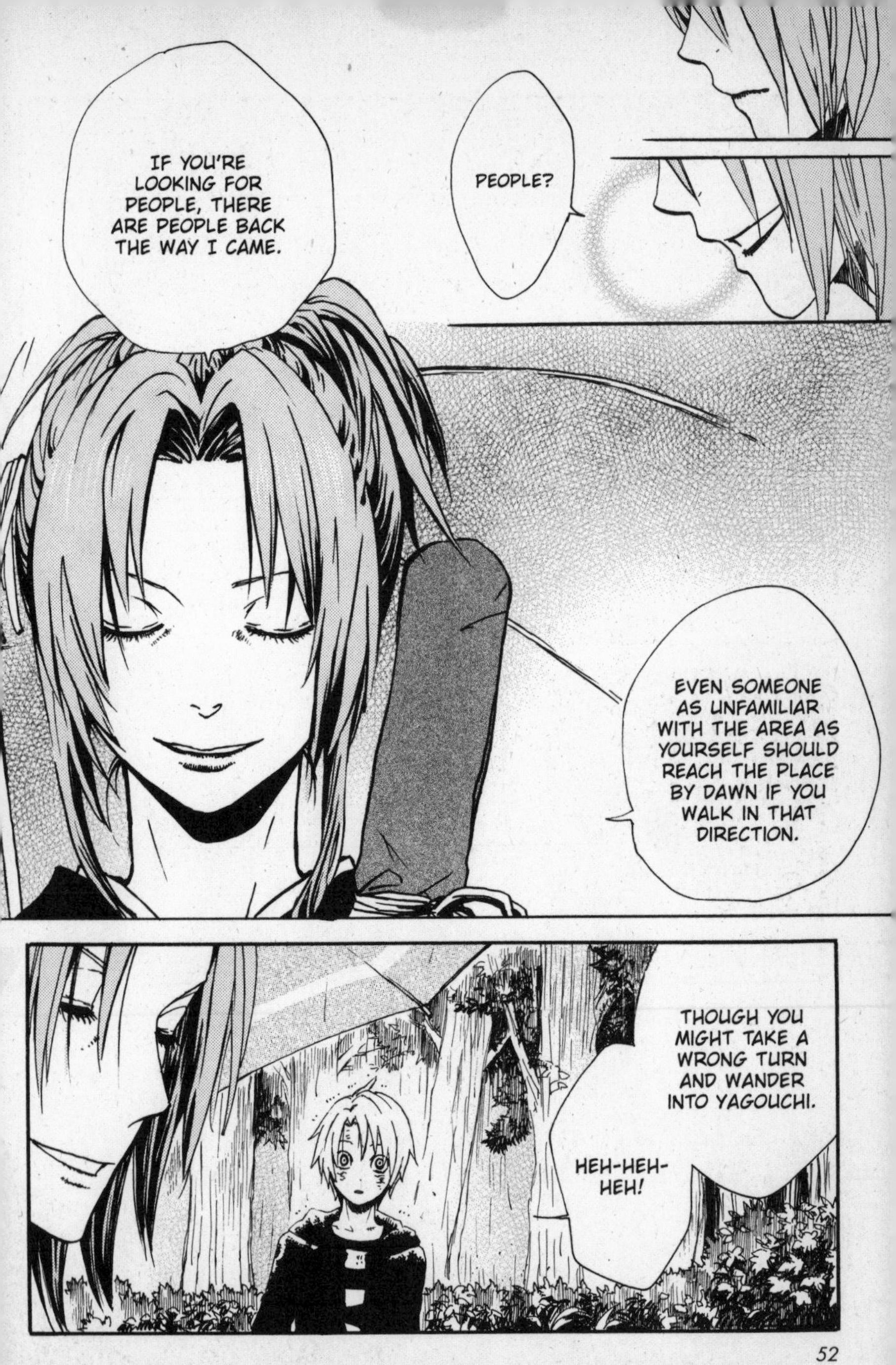
PEOPLE?
IF YOU'RE LOOKING FOR PEOPLE, THERE ARE PEOPLE BACK THE WAY I CAME.
EVEN SOMEONE AS UNFAMILIAR WITH THE AREA AS YOURSELF SHOULD REACH THE PLACE BY DAWN IF YOU WALK IN THAT DIRECTION.
THOUGH YOU MIGHT TAKE A WRONG TURN AND WANDER INTO YAGOUCHI.
HEH-HEH-HEH!

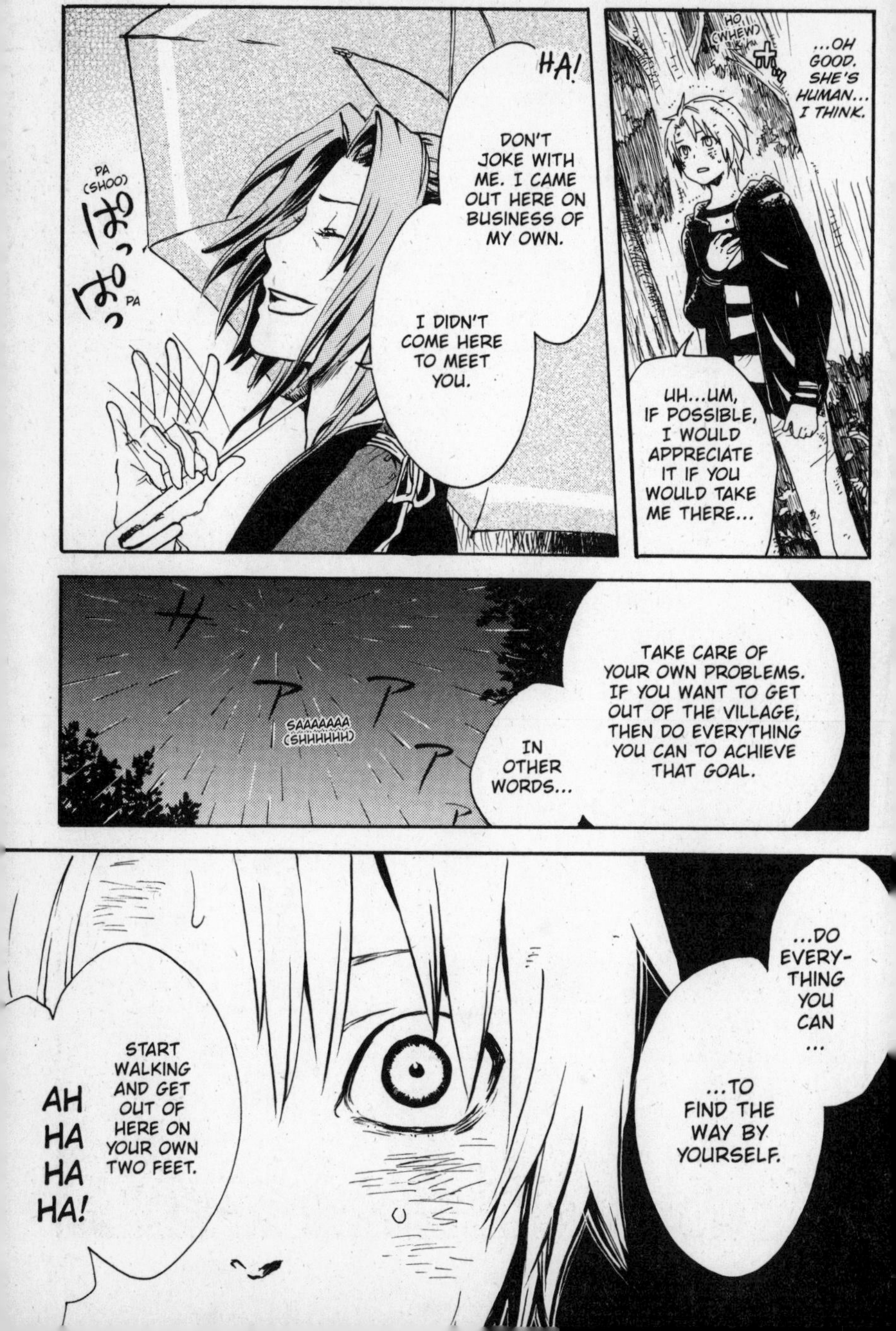
HO (WHEW)
...OH GOOD. SHE'S HUMAN... I THINK.
UH...UM, IF POSSIBLE, I WOULD APPRECIATE IT IF YOU WOULD TAKE ME THERE...
HA!
DON'T JOKE WITH ME. I CAME OUT HERE ON BUSINESS OF MY OWN.
I DIDN'T COME HERE TO MEET YOU.
PA (SHOO)
ぱっぱっ
PA
TAKE CARE OF YOUR OWN PROBLEMS. IF YOU WANT TO GET OUT OF THE VILLAGE, THEN DO EVERYTHING YOU CAN TO ACHIEVE THAT GOAL.
IN OTHER WORDS...
SAAAAAAA (SHHHHHH)
...DO EVERY-THING YOU CAN ...
...TO FIND THE WAY BY YOURSELF.
START WALKING AND GET OUT OF HERE ON YOUR OWN TWO FEET.
AH HA HA HA!

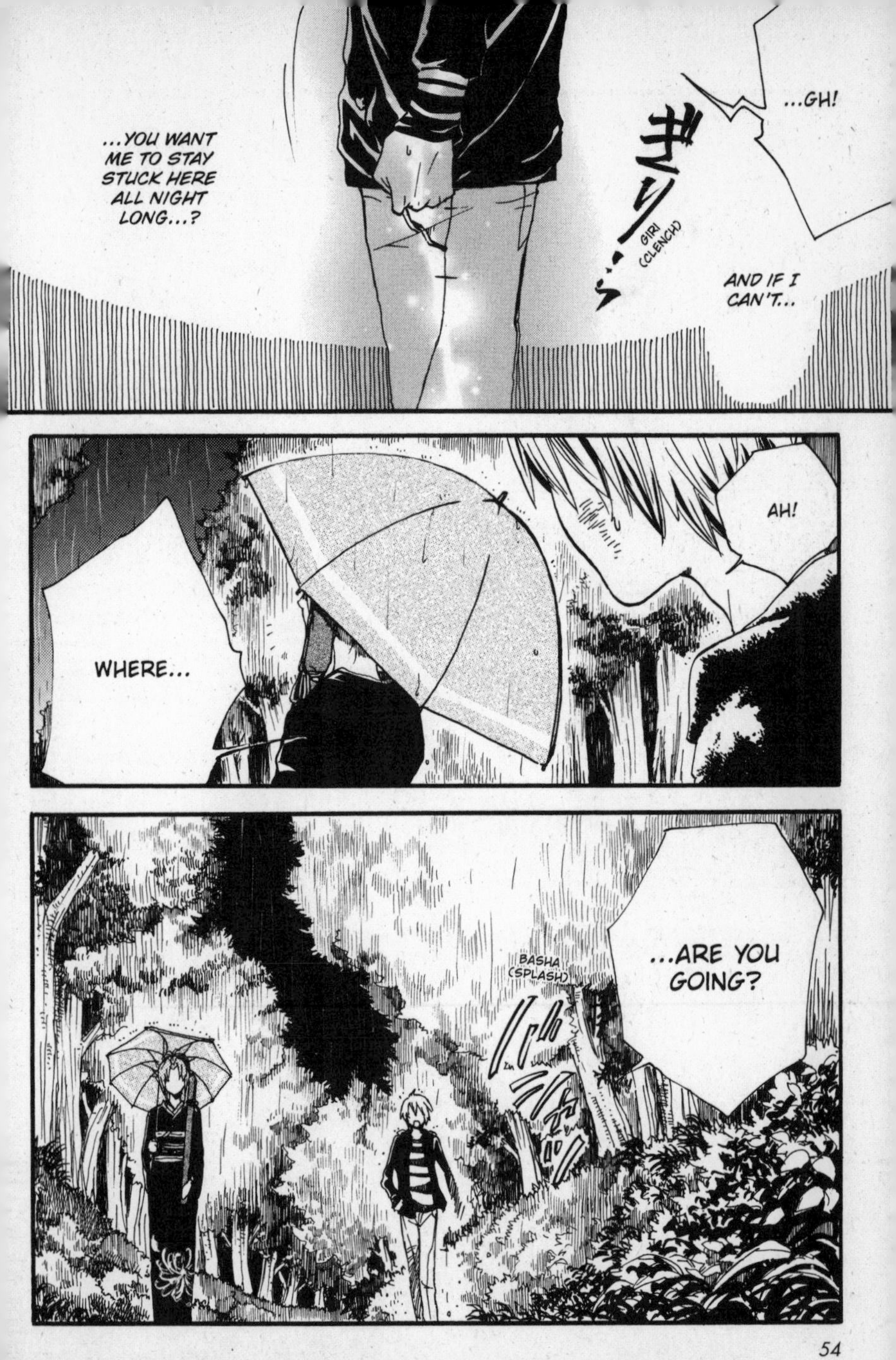
...GH!
AND IF I CAN'T...
ギリ
GIRI (CLENCH)
...YOU WANT ME TO STAY STUCK HERE ALL NIGHT LONG...?
AH!
WHERE...
...ARE YOU GOING?
BASHA (SPLASH)

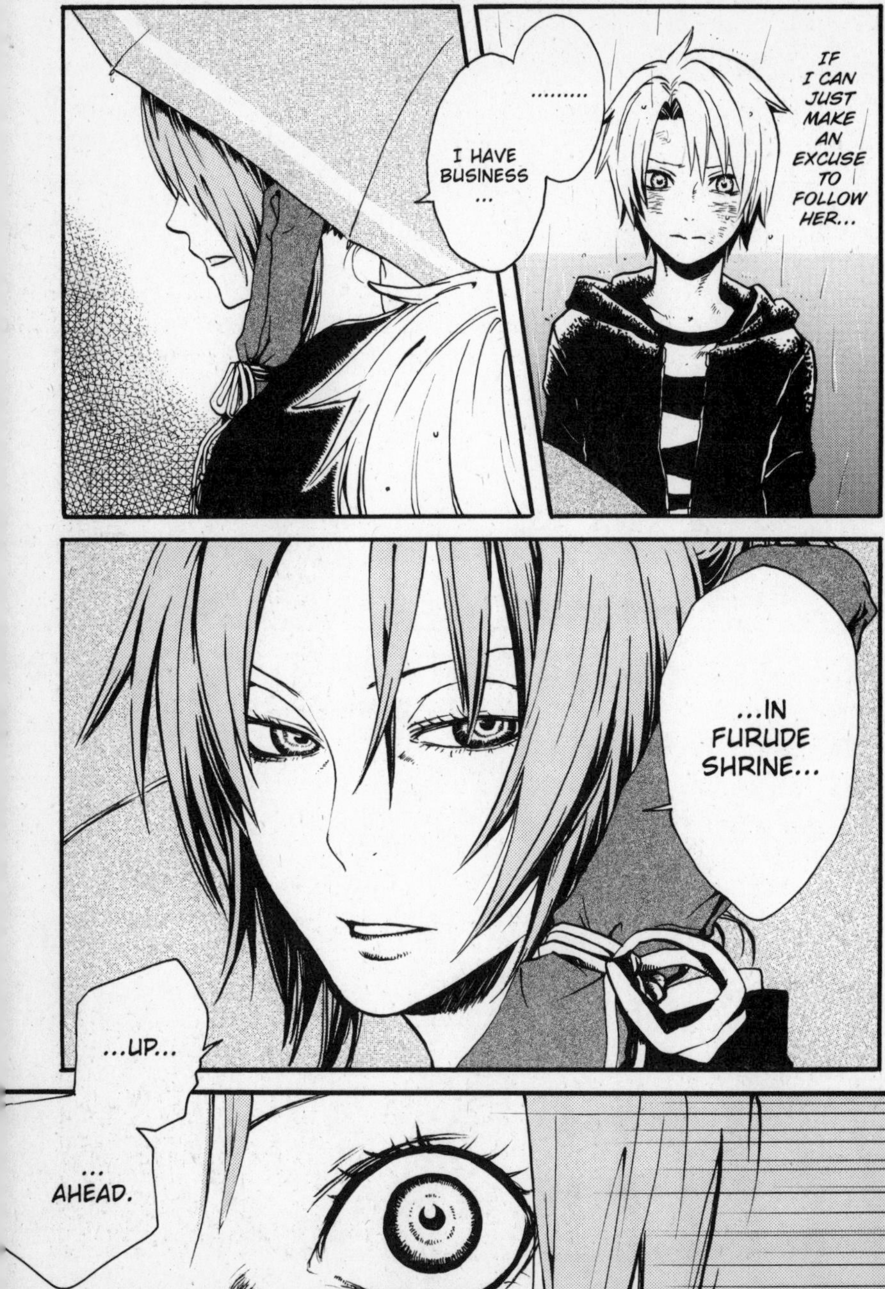
IF I CAN JUST MAKE AN EXCUSE TO FOLLOW HER...
....
I HAVE BUSINESS ...
...IN FURUDE SHRINE...
...UP...
... AHEAD.

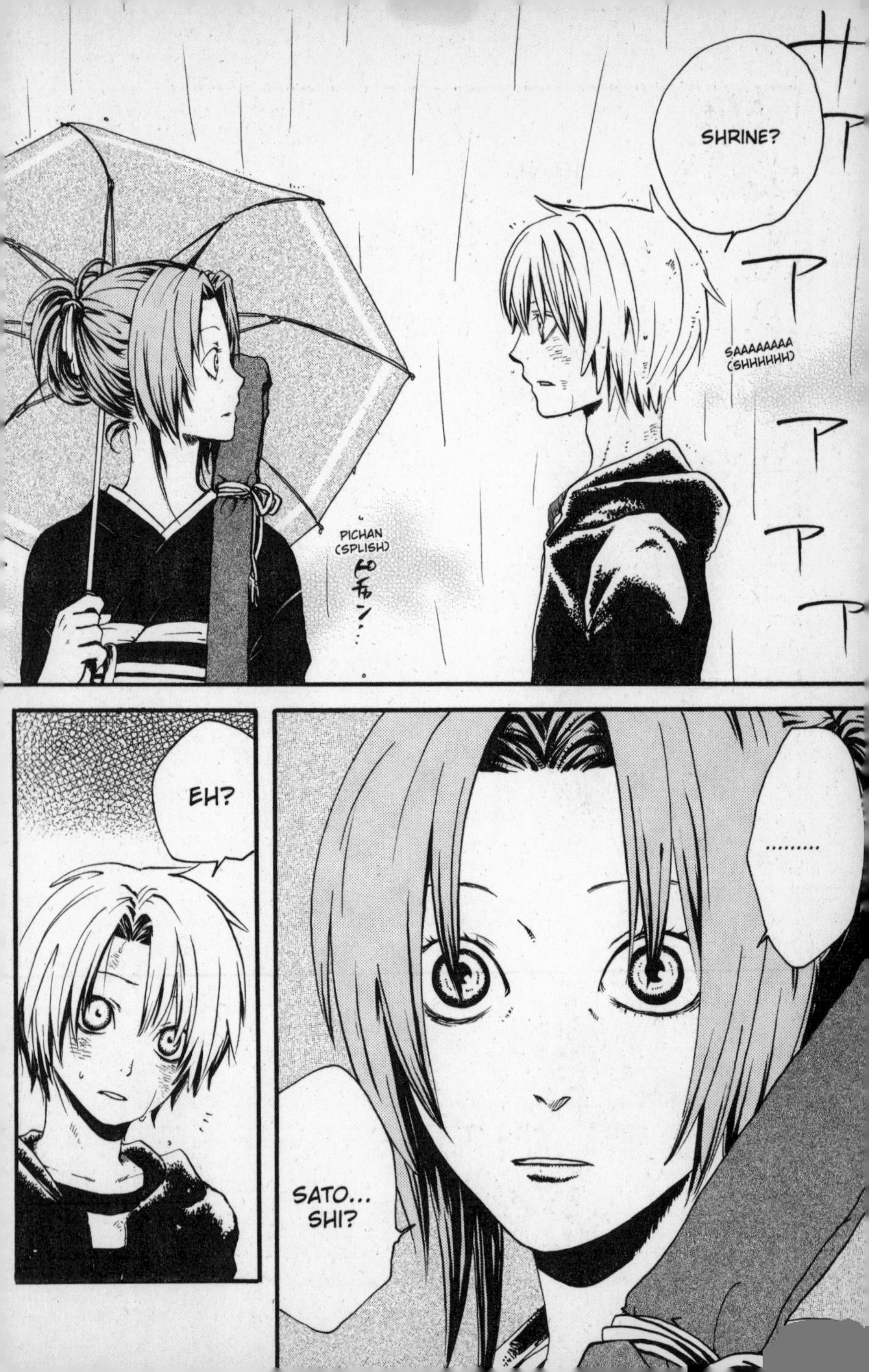
SHRINE?
SAAAAAAAA (SHHHHHHH)
PICHAN (SPLISH)
....
SATO... SHI?
EH?

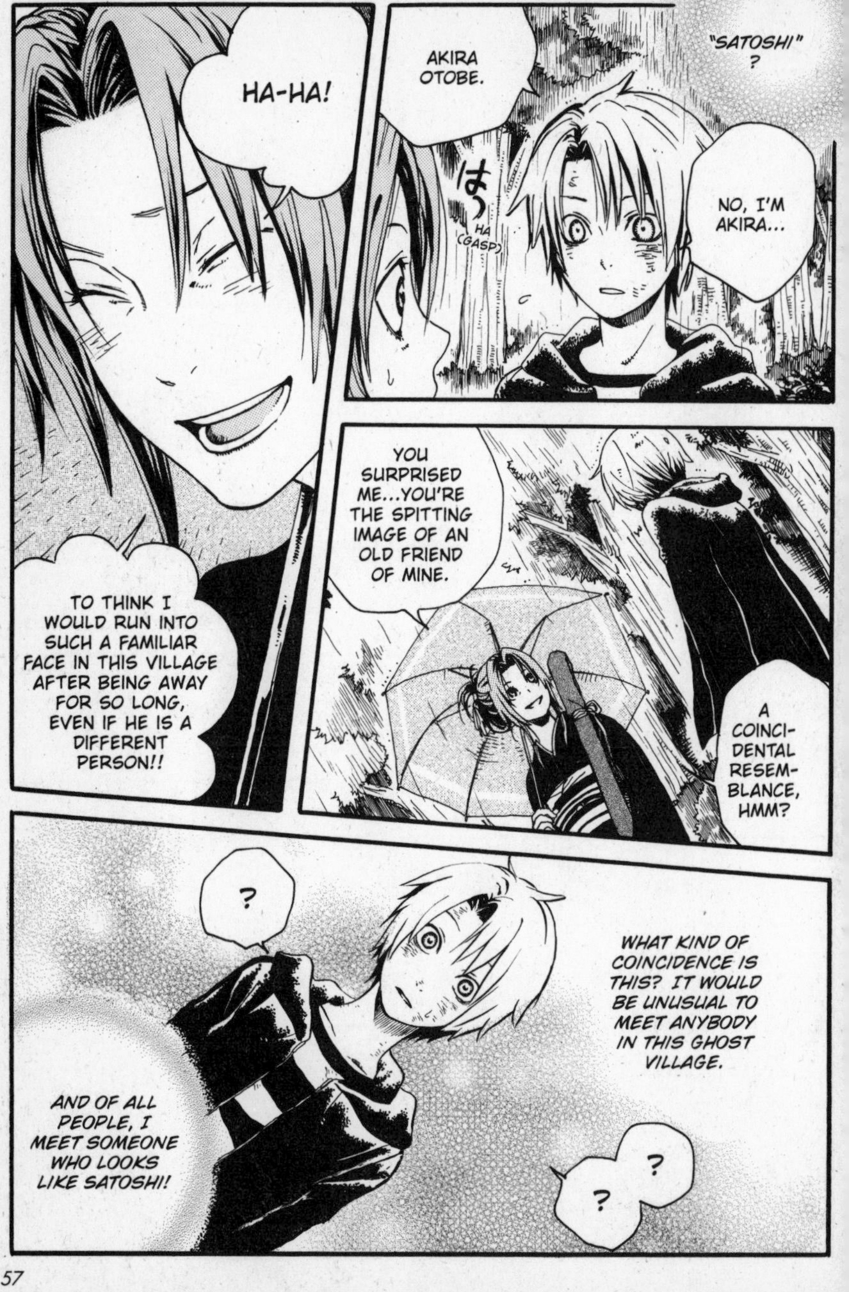
"SATOSHI" ?
NO, I'M AKIRA...
AKIRA OTOBE.
はっ
HA (GASP)
YOU SURPRISED ME...YOU'RE THE SPITTING IMAGE OF AN OLD FRIEND OF MINE.
A COINCI-DENTAL RESEM-BLANCE, HMM?
HA-HA!
TO THINK I WOULD RUN INTO SUCH A FAMILIAR FACE IN THIS VILLAGE AFTER BEING AWAY FOR SO LONG, EVEN IF HE IS A DIFFERENT PERSON!!
WHAT KIND OF COINCIDENCE IS THIS? IT WOULD BE UNUSUAL TO MEET ANYBODY IN THIS GHOST VILLAGE.
?
AND OF ALL PEOPLE, I MEET SOMEONE WHO LOOKS LIKE SATOSHI!
? ?

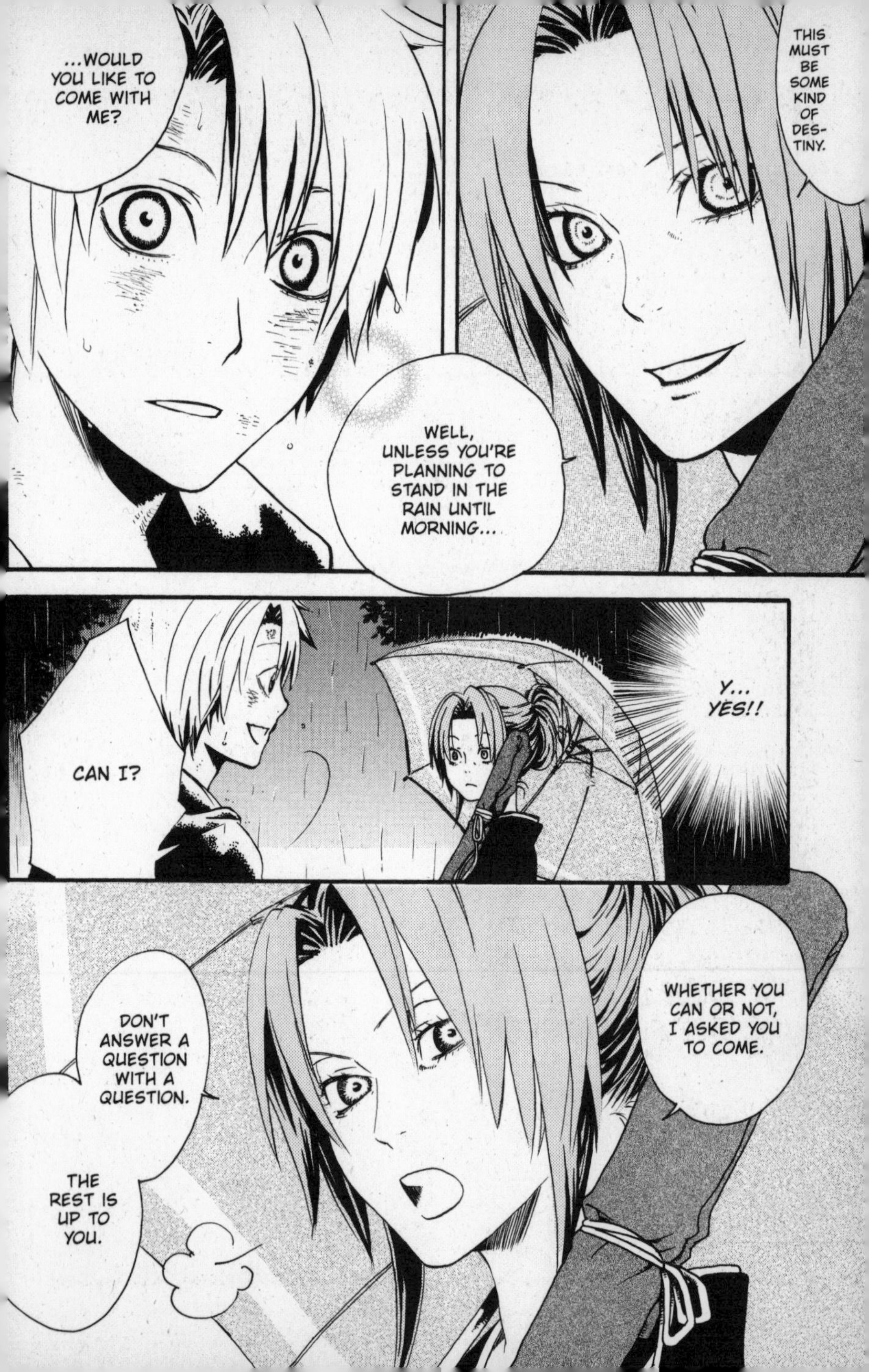
THIS MUST BE SOME KIND OF DES-TINY.
WELL, UNLESS YOU'RE PLANNING TO STAND IN THE RAIN UNTIL MORNING...
...WOULD YOU LIKE TO COME WITH ME?
Y... YES!!
CAN I?
WHETHER YOU CAN OR NOT, I ASKED YOU TO COME.
DON'T ANSWER A QUESTION WITH A QUESTION.
THE REST IS UP TO YOU.

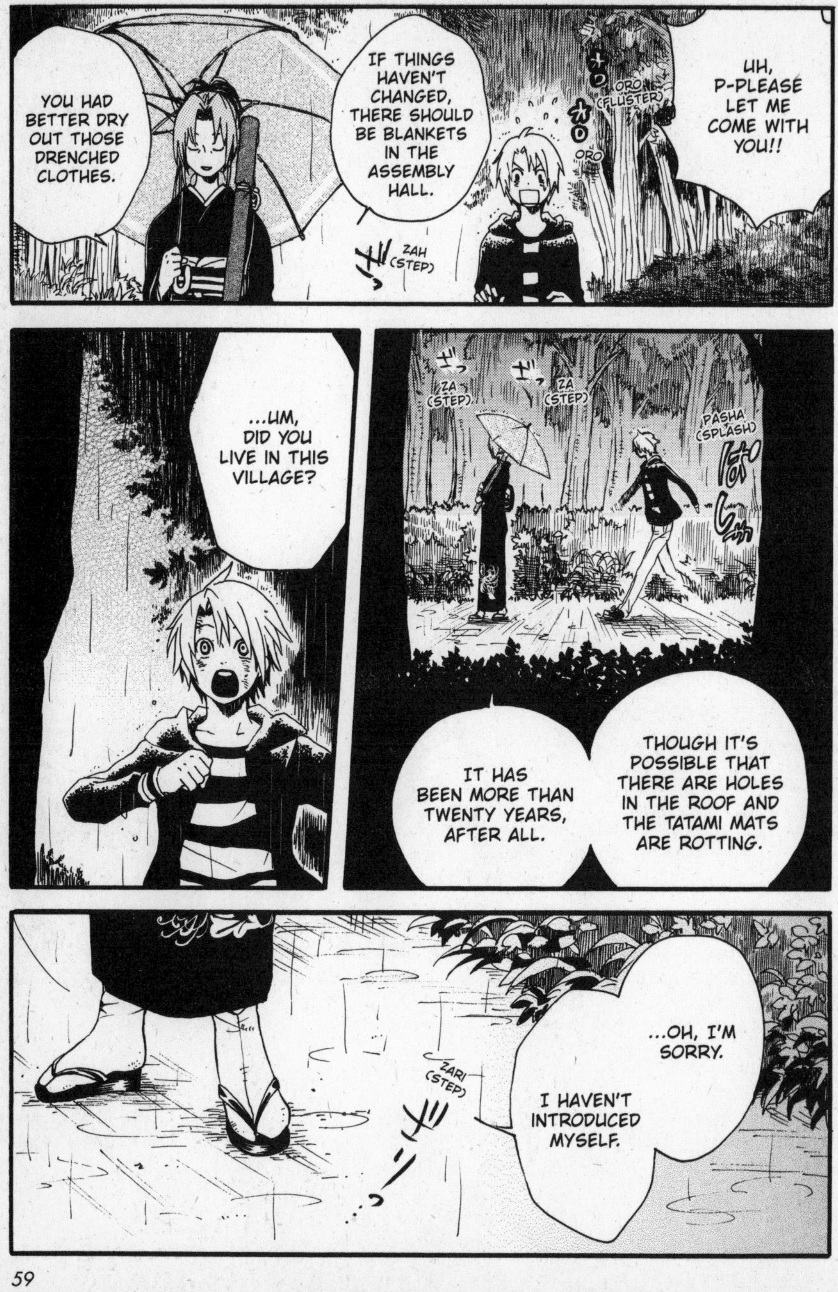
UH, P-PLEASE LET ME COME WITH YOU!!
ORO (FLUSTER)
ORO
IF THINGS HAVEN'T CHANGED, THERE SHOULD BE BLANKETS IN THE ASSEMBLY HALL.
ZAH (STEP)
YOU HAD BETTER DRY OUT THOSE DRENCHED CLOTHES.
ZA (STEP)
ZA (STEP)
PASHA (SPLASH)
THOUGH IT'S POSSIBLE THAT THERE ARE HOLES IN THE ROOF AND THE TATAMI MATS ARE ROTTING.
IT HAS BEEN MORE THAN TWENTY YEARS, AFTER ALL.
...UM, DID YOU LIVE IN THIS VILLAGE?
...OH, I'M SORRY.
I HAVEN'T INTRODUCED MYSELF.
ZARI (STEP)

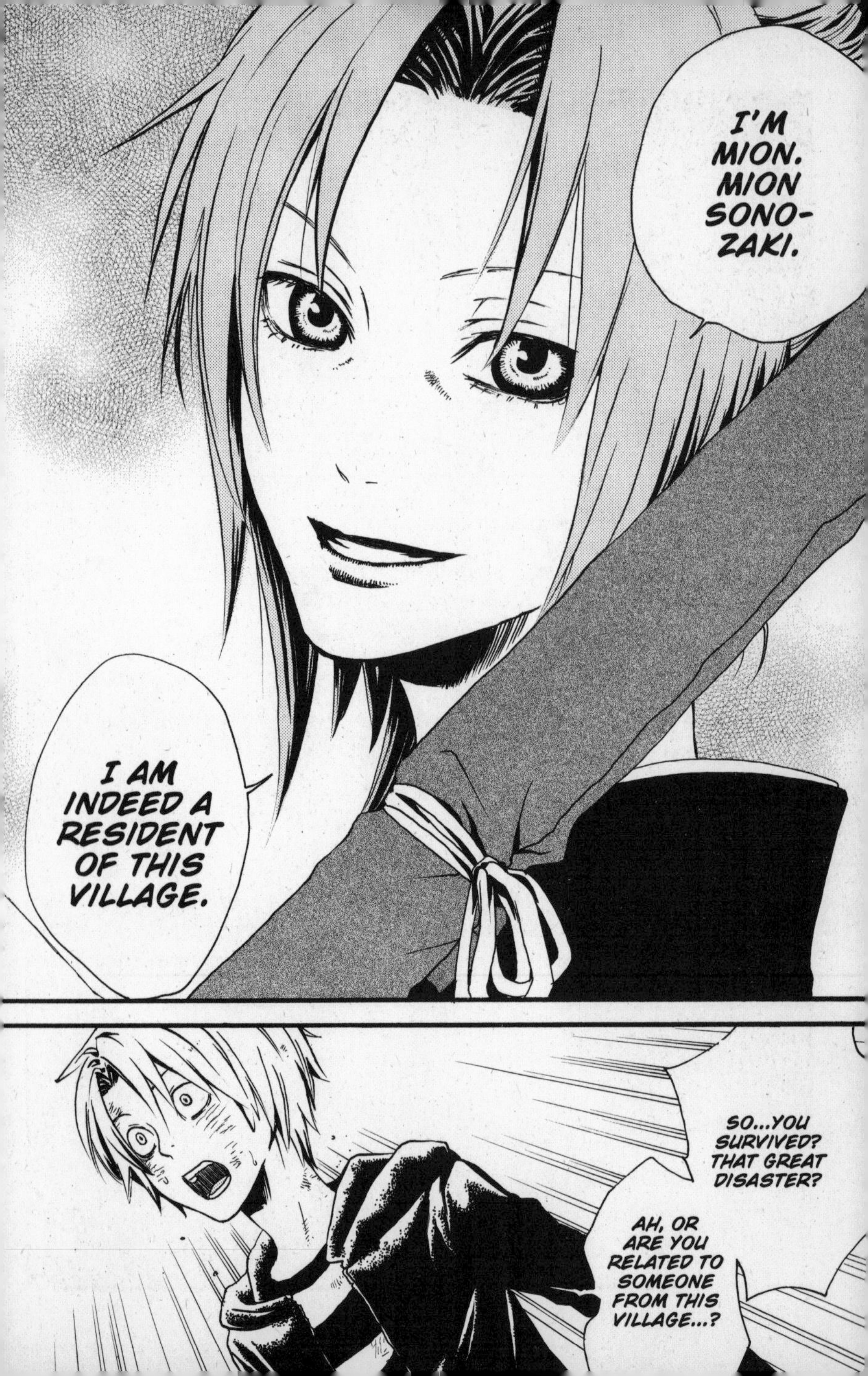
I'M MION. MION SONO-ZAKI.
I AM INDEED A RESIDENT OF THIS VILLAGE.
SO...YOU SURVIVED? THAT GREAT DISASTER?
AH, OR ARE YOU RELATED TO SOMEONE FROM THIS VILLAGE...?

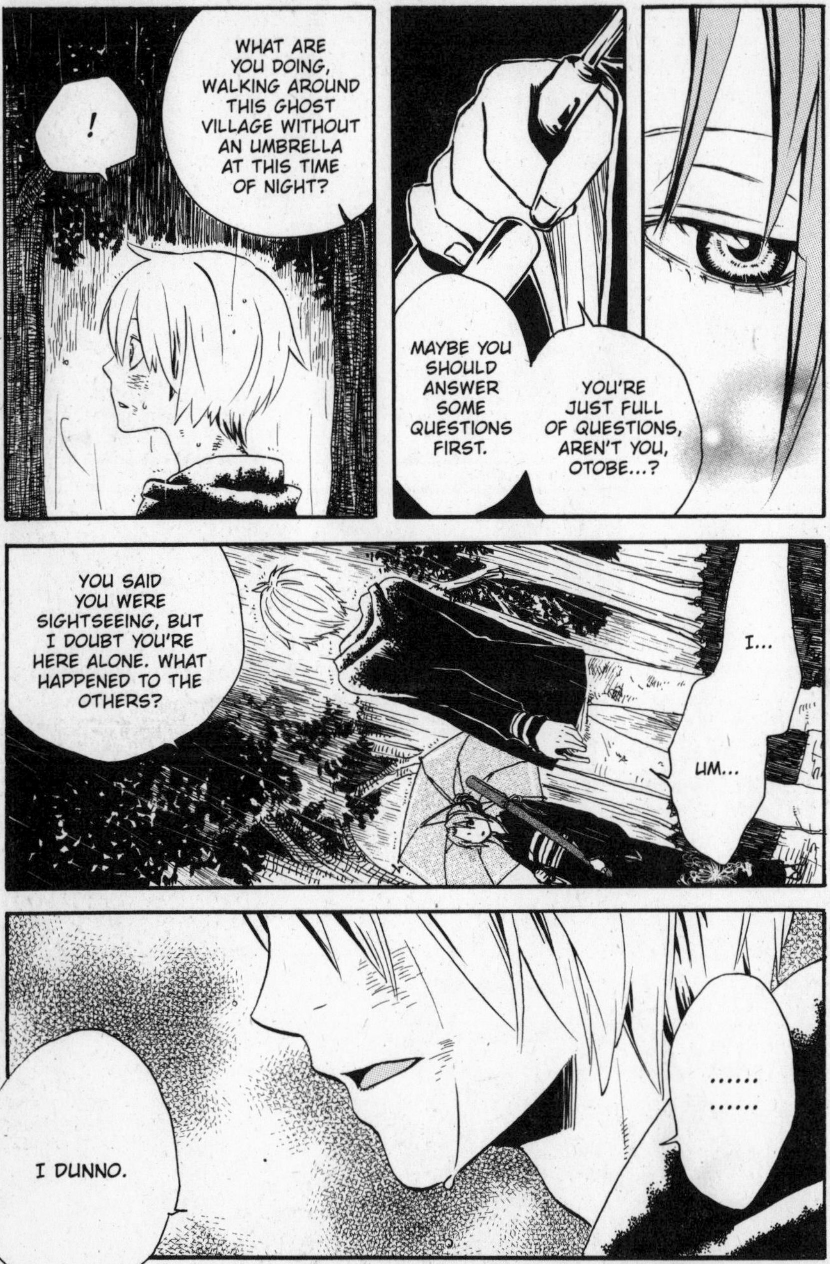
!
WHAT ARE YOU DOING, WALKING AROUND THIS GHOST VILLAGE WITHOUT AN UMBRELLA AT THIS TIME OF NIGHT?
MAYBE YOU SHOULD ANSWER SOME QUESTIONS FIRST.
YOU'RE JUST FULL OF QUESTIONS, AREN'T YOU, OTOBE...?
YOU SAID YOU WERE SIGHTSEEING, BUT I DOUBT YOU'RE HERE ALONE. WHAT HAPPENED TO THE OTHERS?
I...
UM...
I DUNNO.
......
......

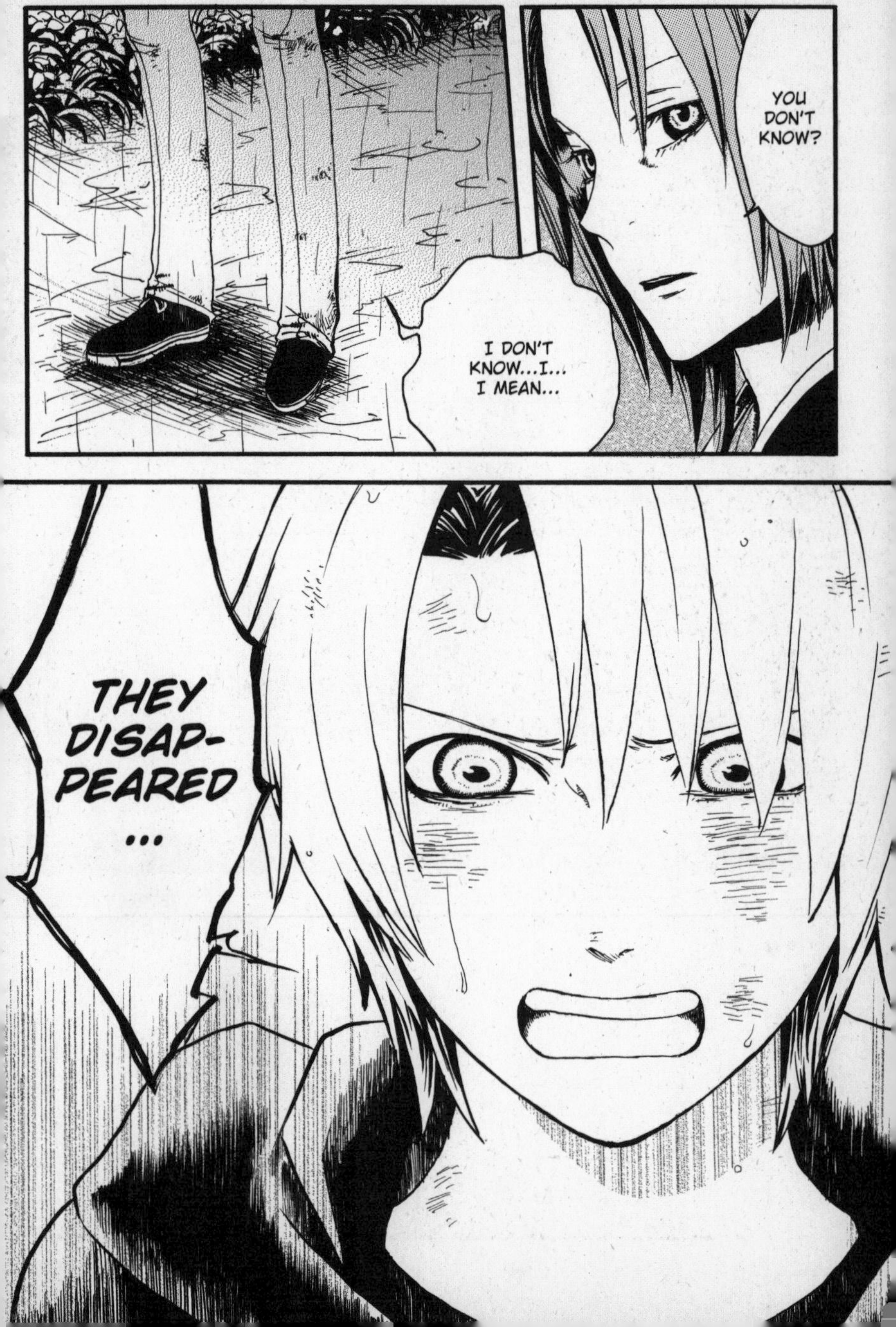
YOU DON'T KNOW?
I DON'T KNOW...I... I MEAN...
THEY DISAP-PEARED ...

IT STARTED WITH A MAGAZINE.

IT TALKED ABOUT THIS VILLAGE, SO MY FRIENDS AND I THOUGHT IT SOUNDED INTERESTING AND CAME FOR SOME SIGHTSEEING.

ON THE WAY, I NEEDED TO USE THE BATHROOM...

BATAN (SHUT)

...SO I GOT OUT OF THE CAR BY MYSELF.

BUT IT WAS PITCH-BLACK OUTSIDE. I COULDN'T SEE ANYTHING, AND I FIGURED I WOULDN'T GET VERY FAR LIKE THAT.

SO I WAS GOING TO GO BACK FOR A FLASHLIGHT.

WHEN I TURNED AROUND ...

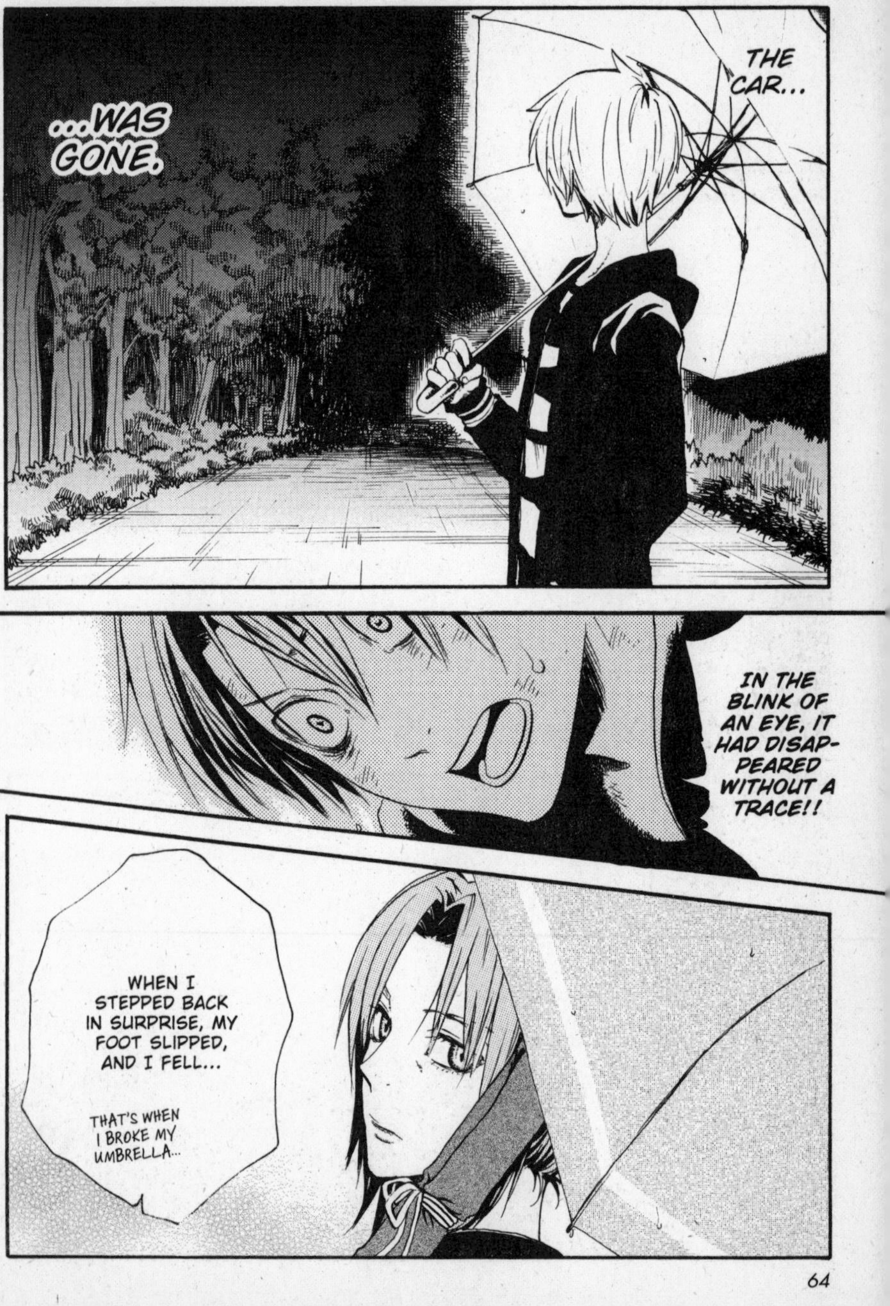
THE CAR...
...WAS GONE.
IN THE BLINK OF AN EYE, IT HAD DISAP-PEARED WITHOUT A TRACE!!
WHEN I STEPPED BACK IN SURPRISE, MY FOOT SLIPPED, AND I FELL...
THAT'S WHEN I BROKE MY UMBRELLA...

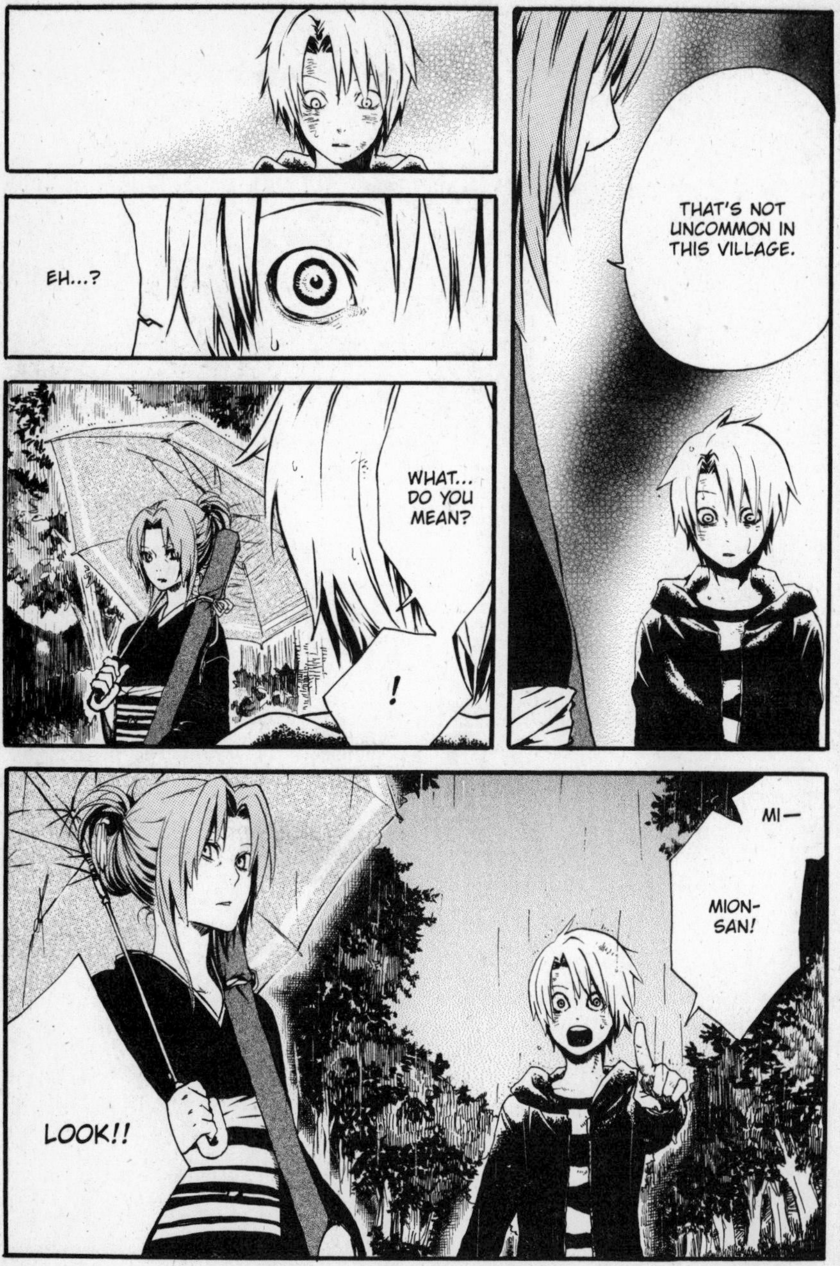

THAT'S NOT UNCOMMON IN THIS VILLAGE.
EH...?
WHAT... DO YOU MEAN?
!
MI—
MION-SAN!
LOOK!!

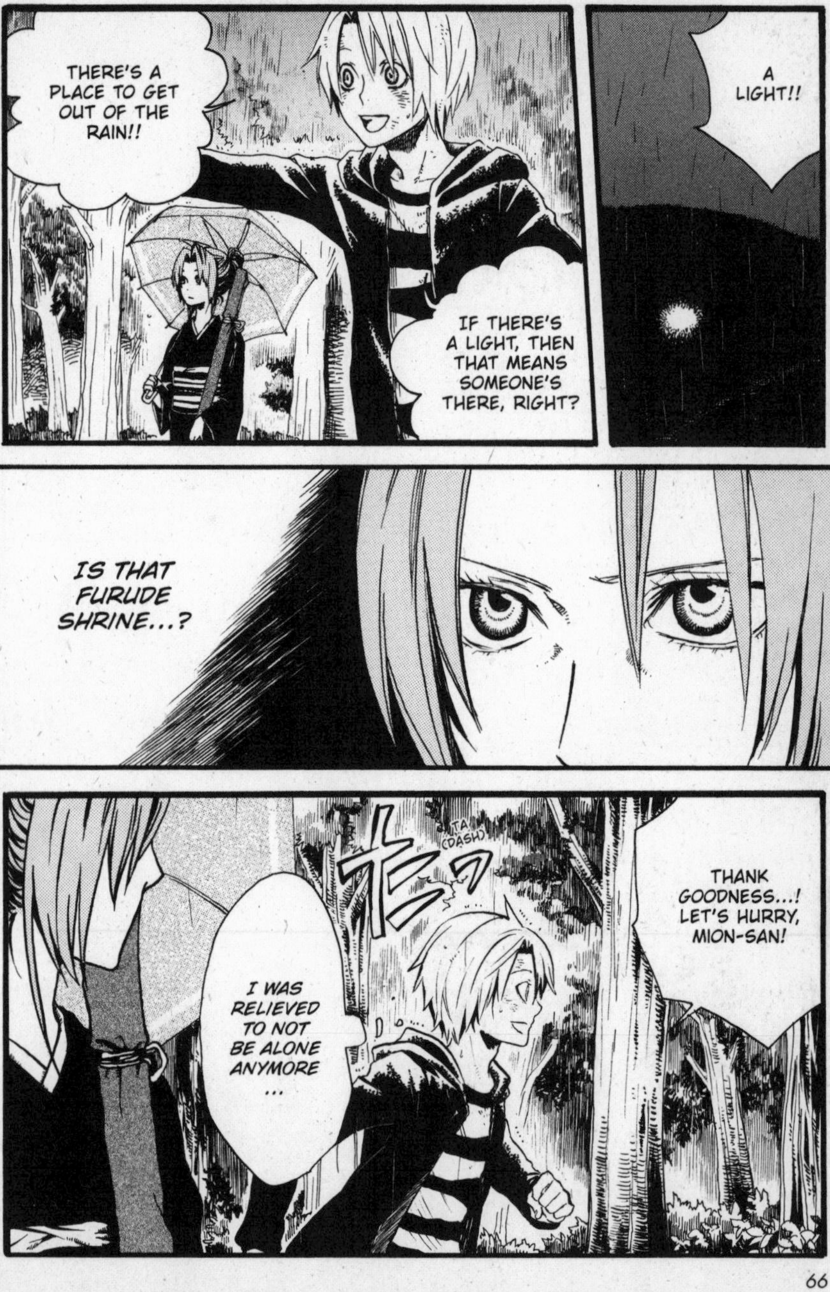
A LIGHT!!
THERE'S A PLACE TO GET OUT OF THE RAIN!!
IF THERE'S A LIGHT, THEN THAT MEANS SOMEONE'S THERE, RIGHT?
IS THAT FURUDE SHRINE...?
THANK GOODNESS...! LET'S HURRY, MION-SAN!
TA (DASH)
I WAS RELIEVED TO NOT BE ALONE ANYMORE ...

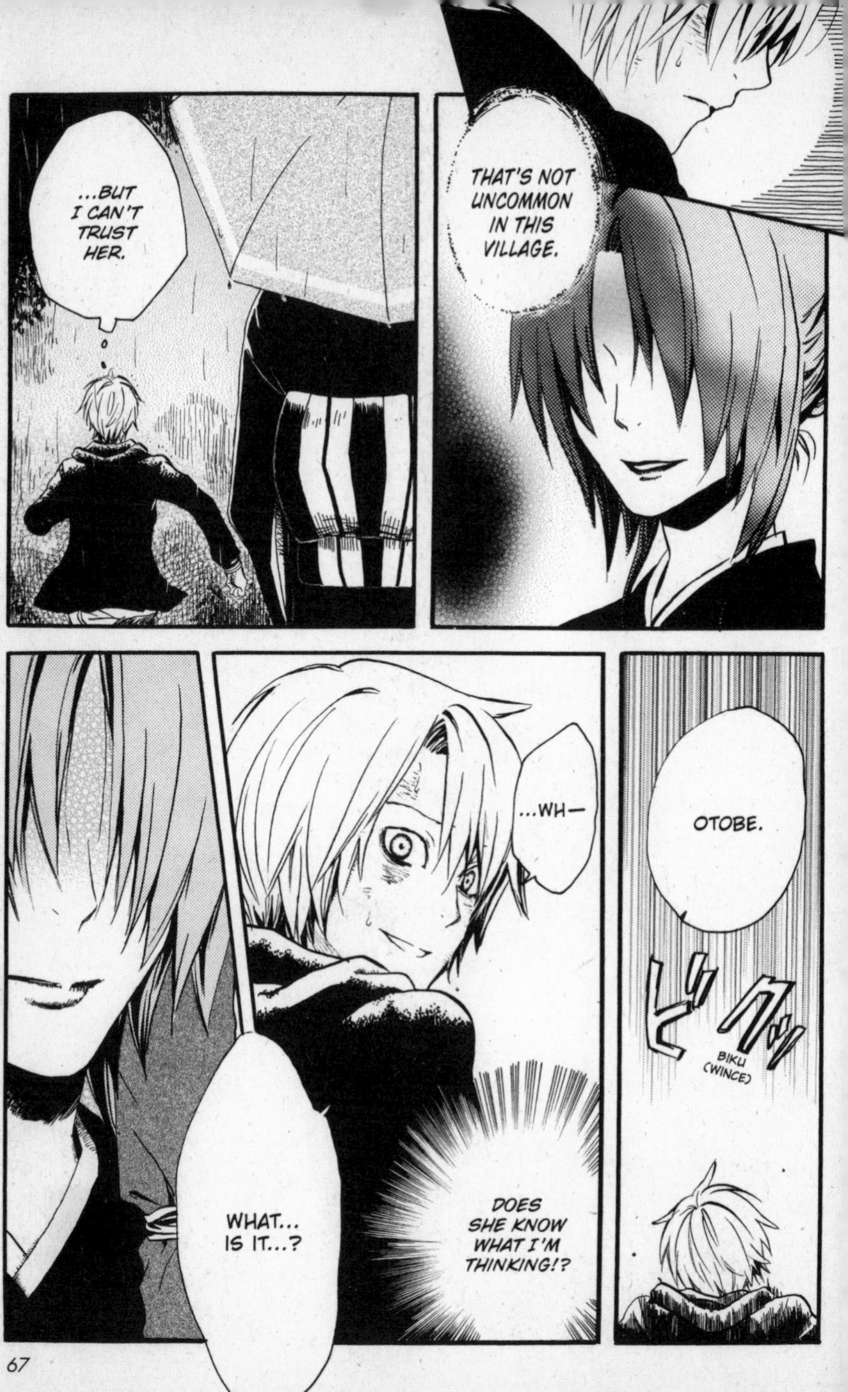
THAT'S NOT UNCOMMON IN THIS VILLAGE.
...BUT I CAN'T TRUST HER.
OTOBE.
ビクッ
BIKU (WINCE)
...WH—
DOES SHE KNOW WHAT I'M THINKING!?
WHAT... IS IT...?

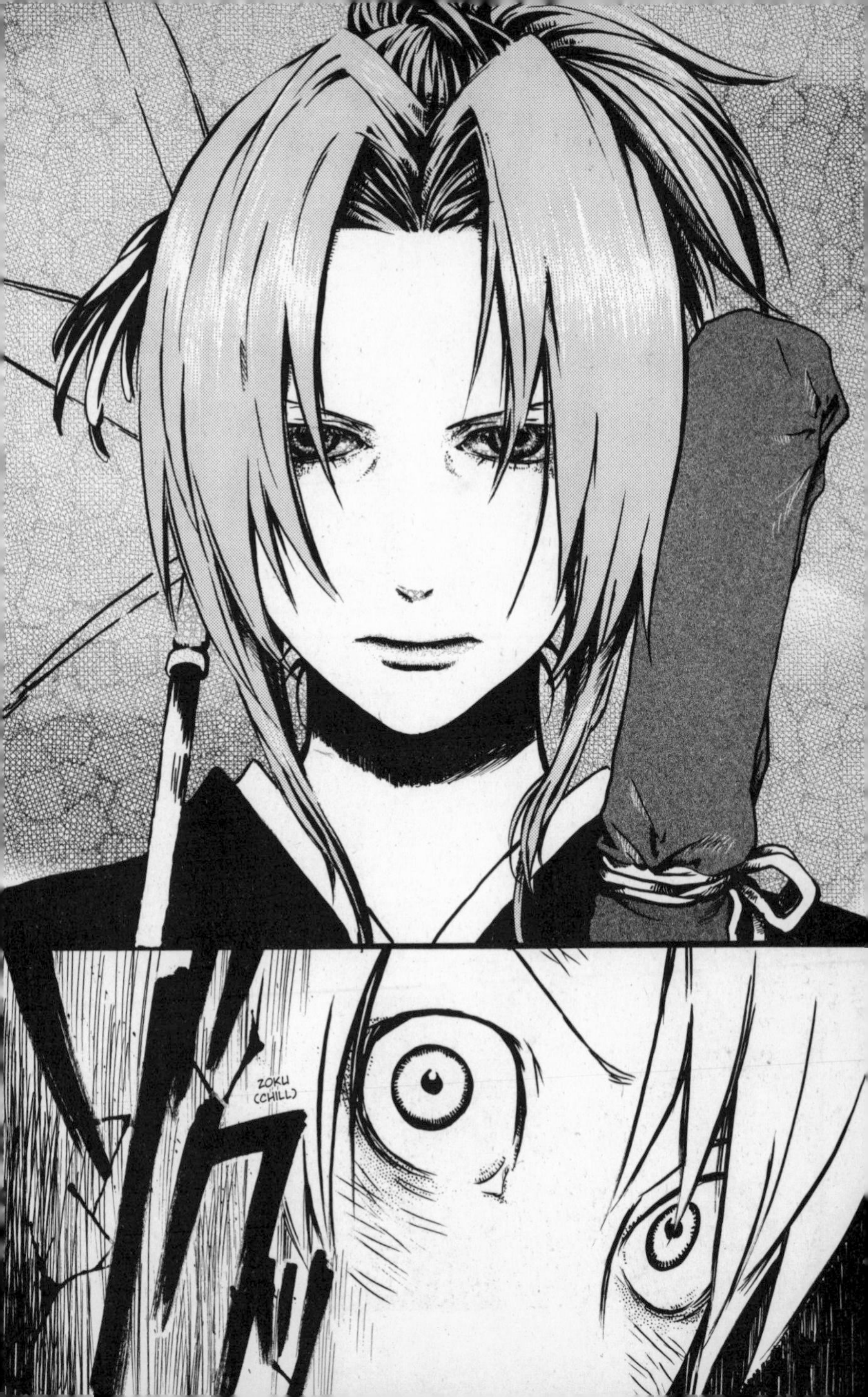
ZOKU
(CHILL)

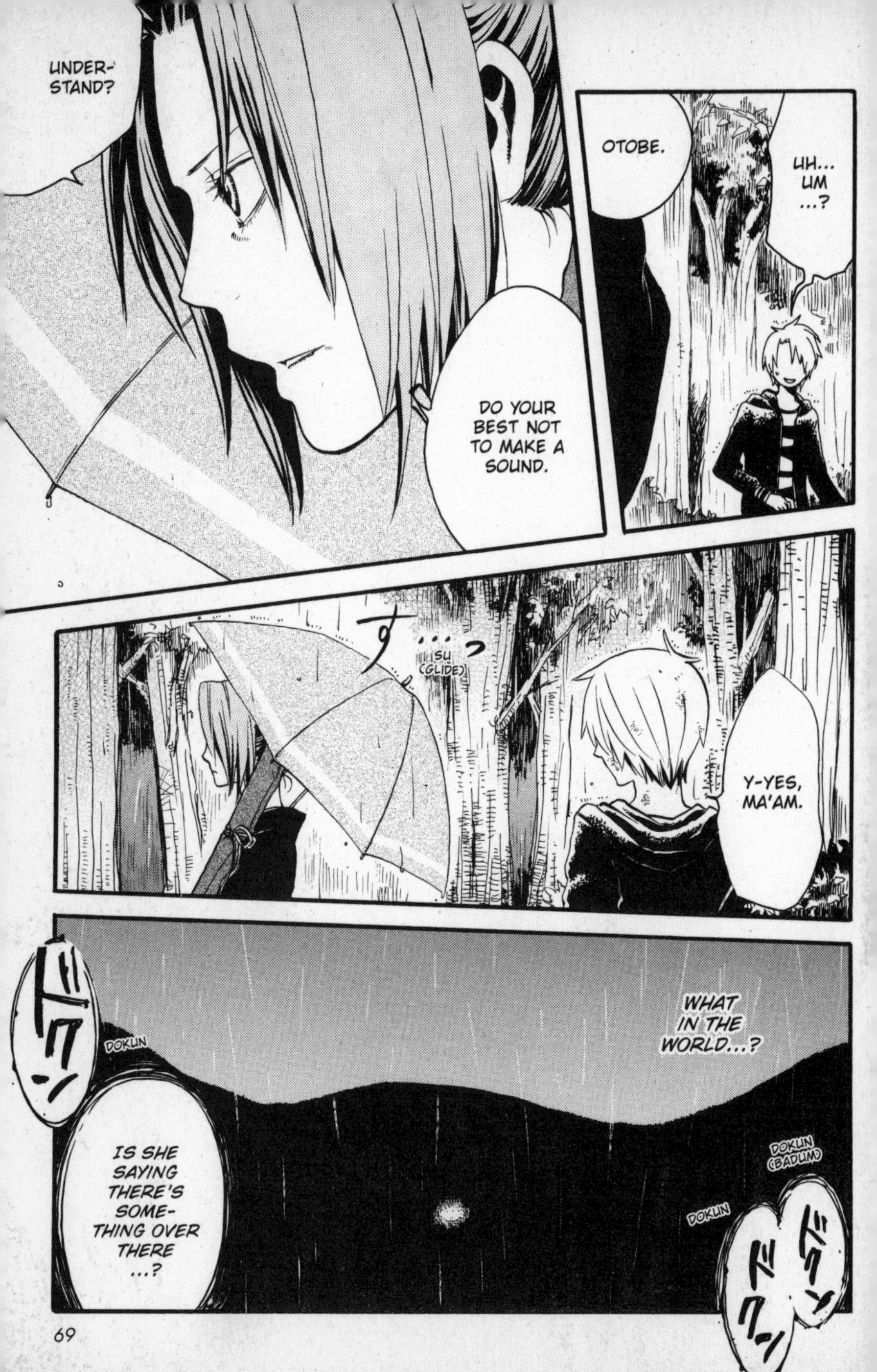
OTOBE.
UH... UM ...?
DO YOUR BEST NOT TO MAKE A SOUND.
UNDER-STAND?
Y-YES, MA'AM.
SU (GLIDE)
WHAT IN THE WORLD...?
DOKUN (BADUM)
DOKUN
DOKUN
IS SHE SAYING THERE'S SOME-THING OVER THERE ...?

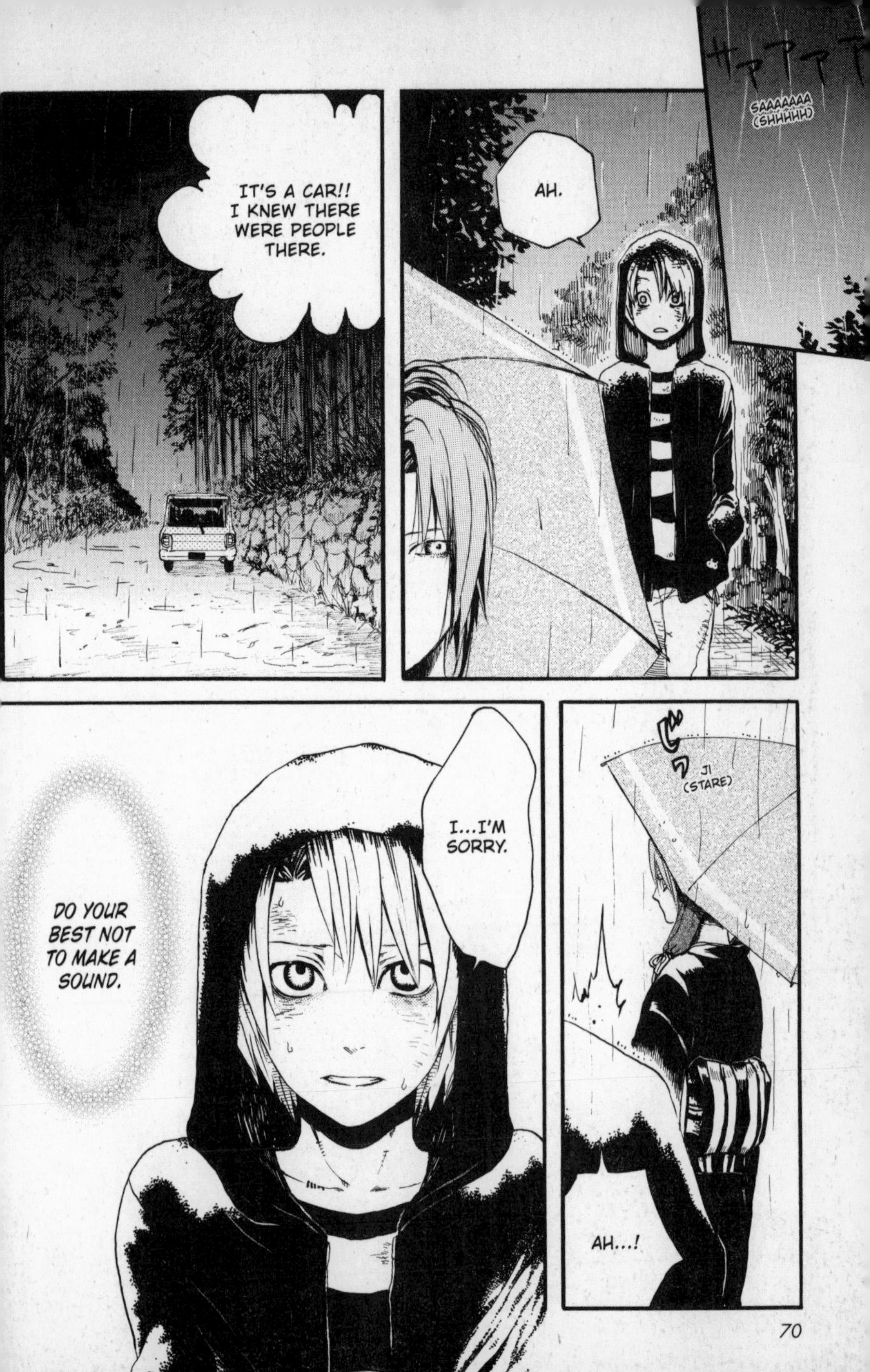
SAAAAAAA (SHHHHH)
AH.
IT'S A CAR!! I KNEW THERE WERE PEOPLE THERE.
JI (STARE)
AH...!
I...I'M SORRY.
DO YOUR BEST NOT TO MAKE A SOUND.

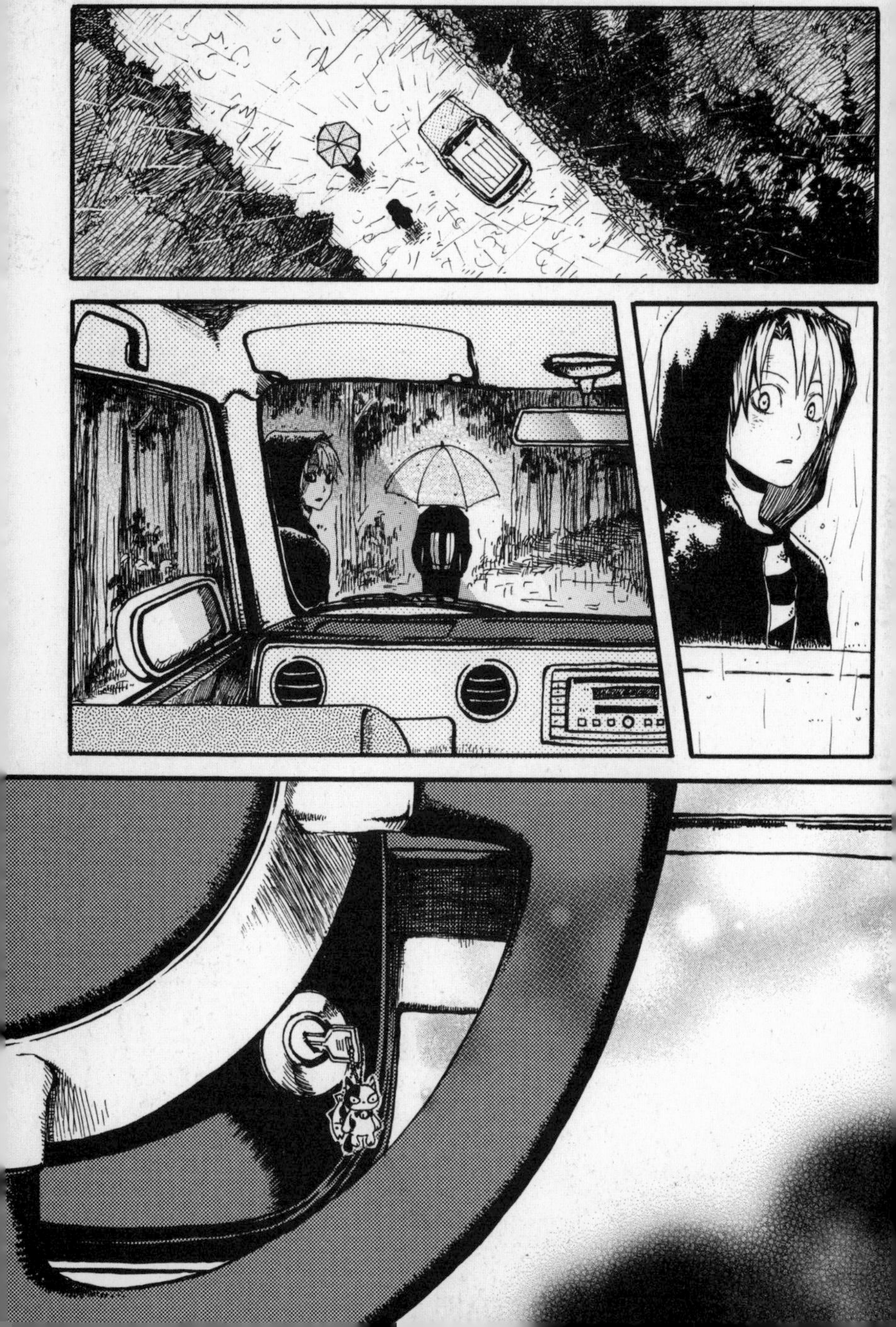

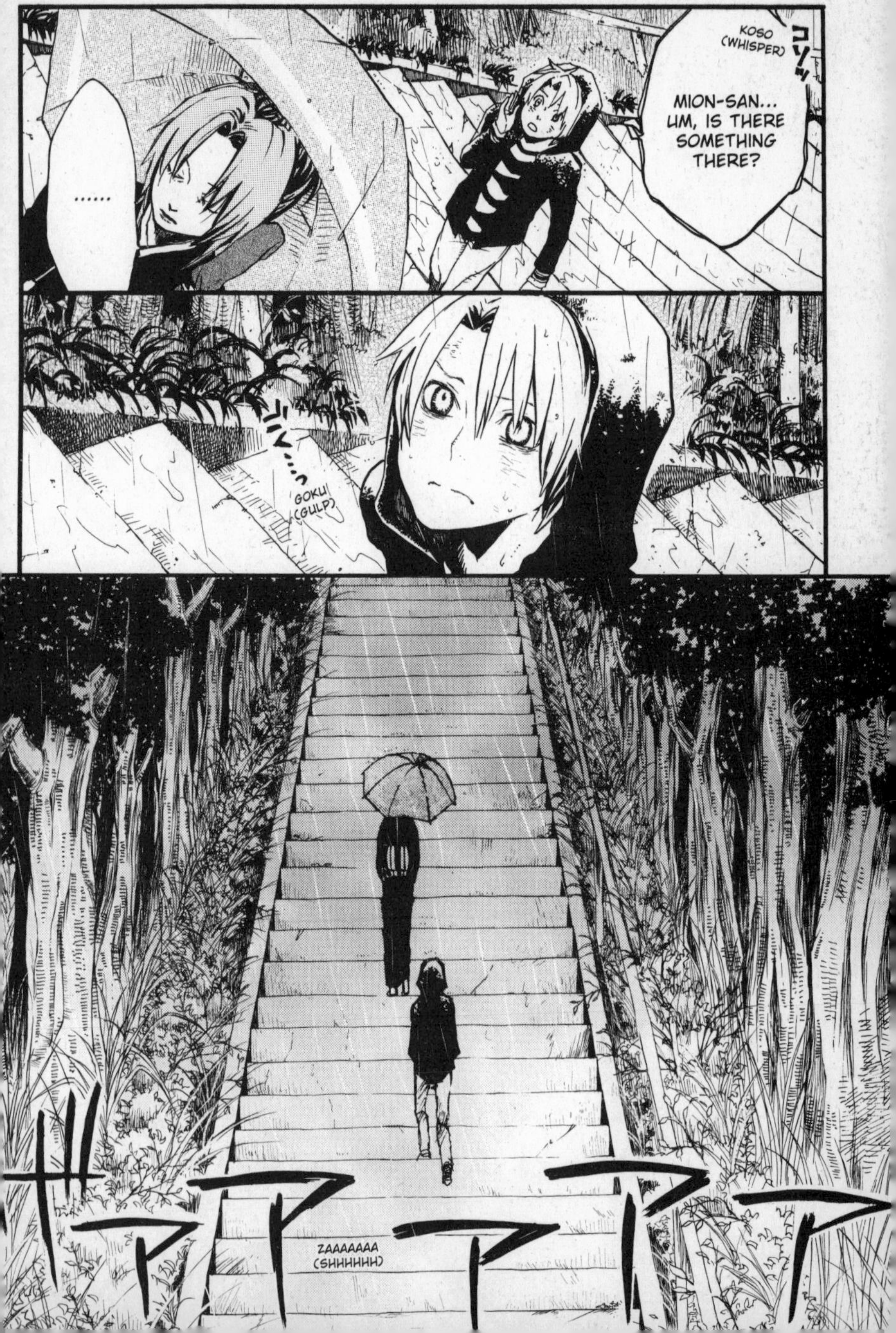
KOSO (WHISPER)
MION-SAN... UM, IS THERE SOMETHING THERE?
......
GOKU (GULP)
ZAAAAAAA (SHHHHHH)

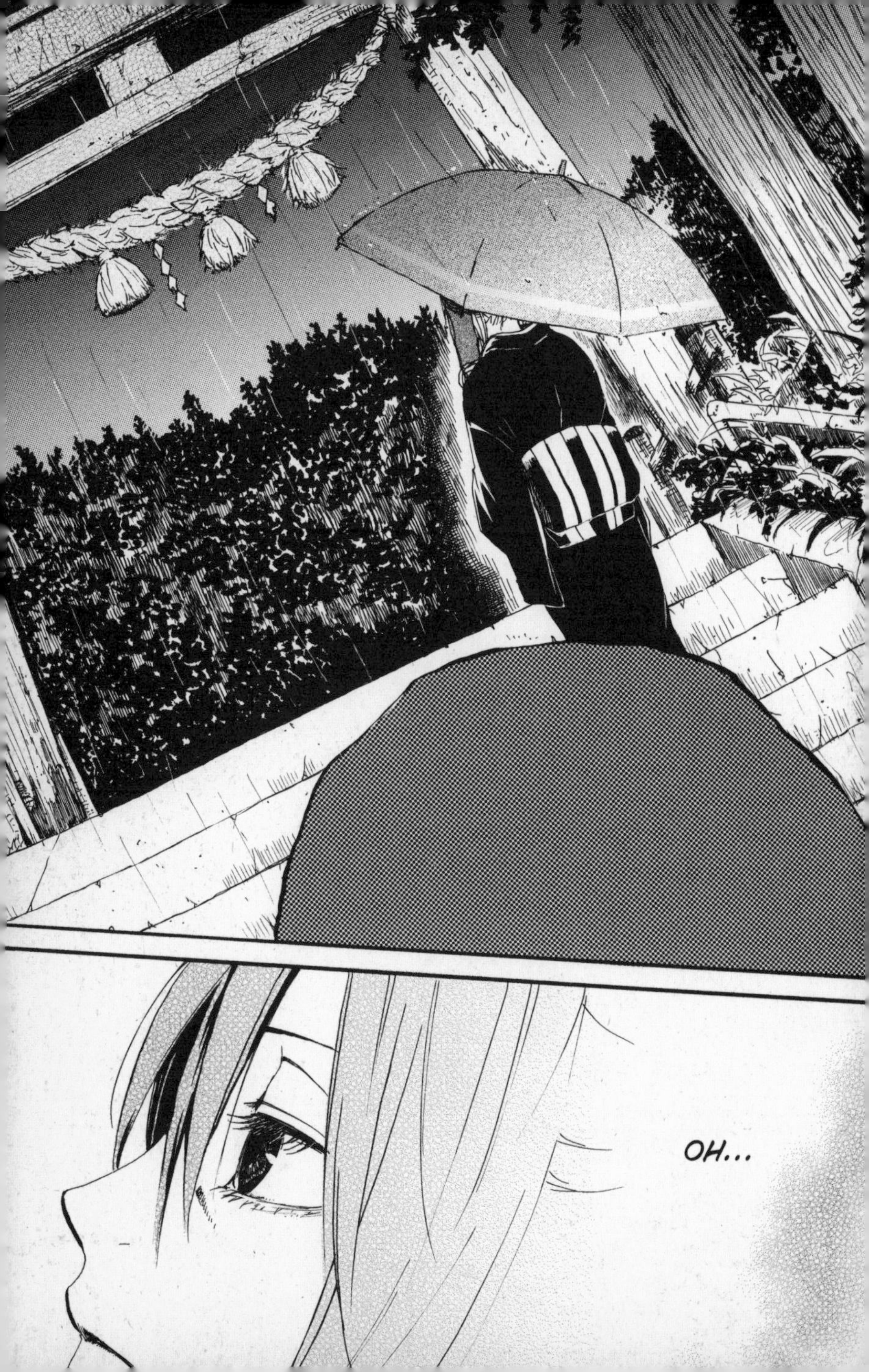
OH...

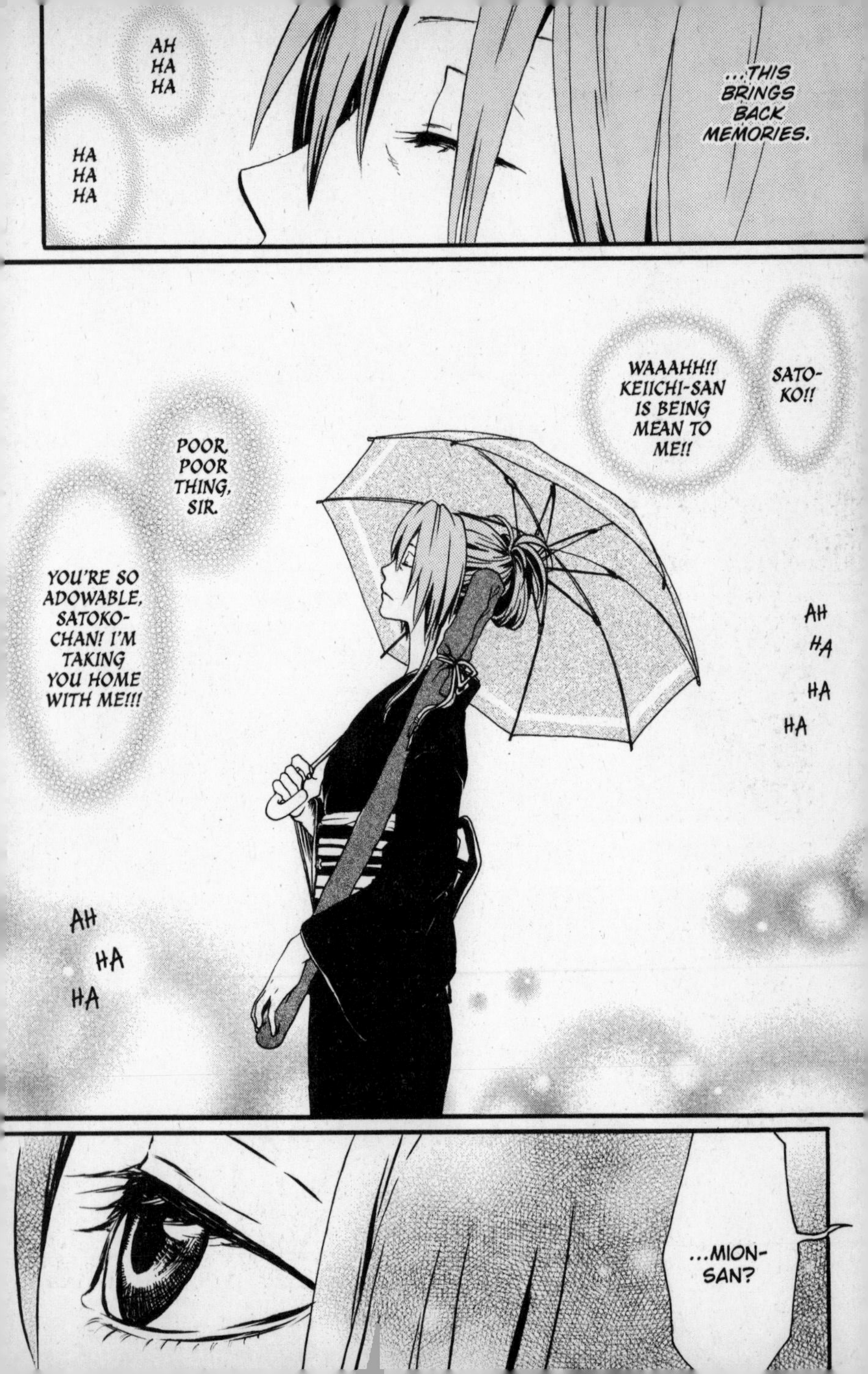
...THIS BRINGS BACK MEMORIES.
AH HA HA
HA HA HA
SATO-KO!!
WAAAHH!! KEIICHI-SAN IS BEING MEAN TO ME!!
AH HA HA HA
POOR, POOR THING, SIR.
YOU'RE SO ADOWABLE, SATOKO-CHAN! I'M TAKING YOU HOME WITH ME!!!
AH HA HA
...MION-SAN?

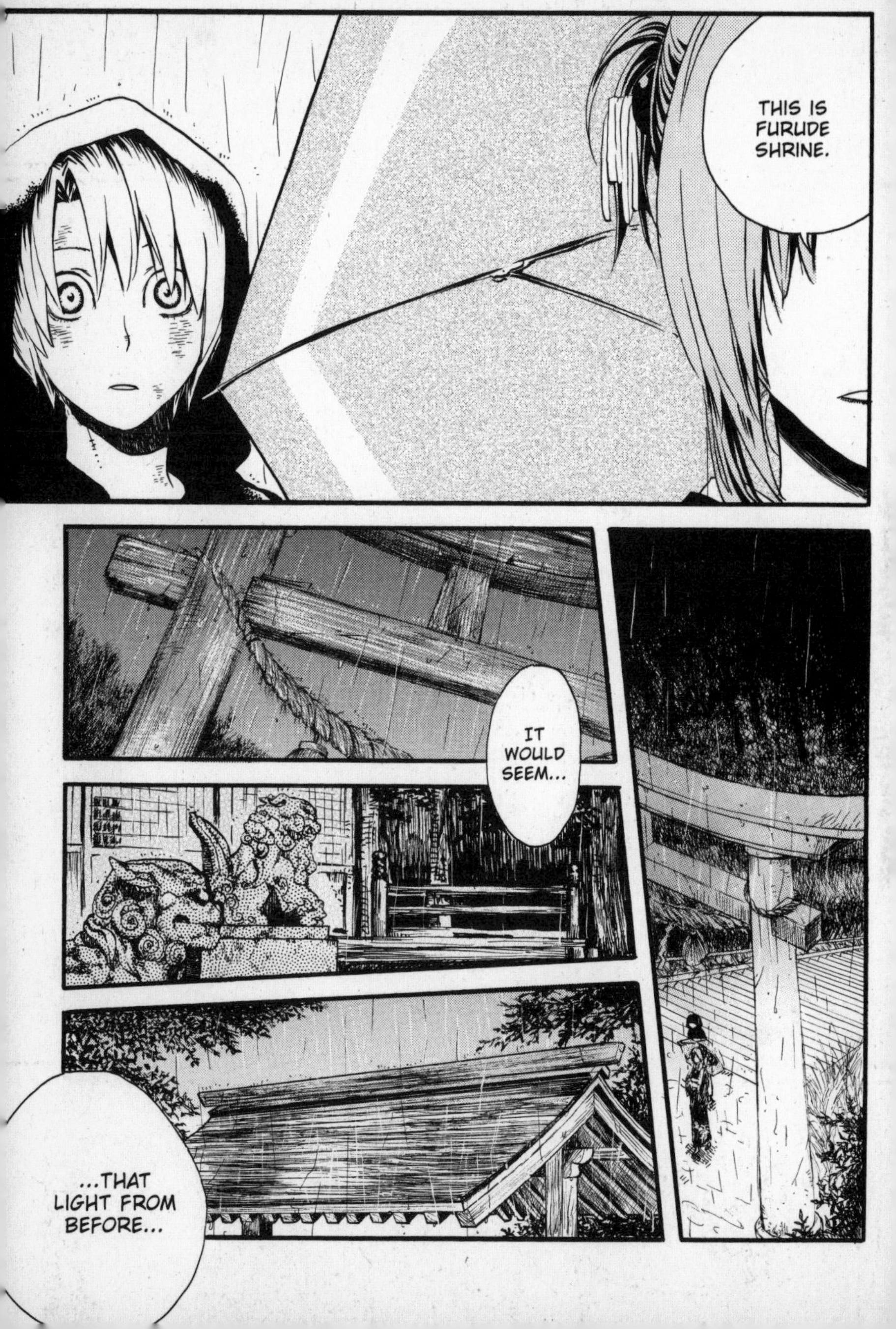
THIS IS FURUDE SHRINE.
IT WOULD SEEM...
...THAT LIGHT FROM BEFORE...

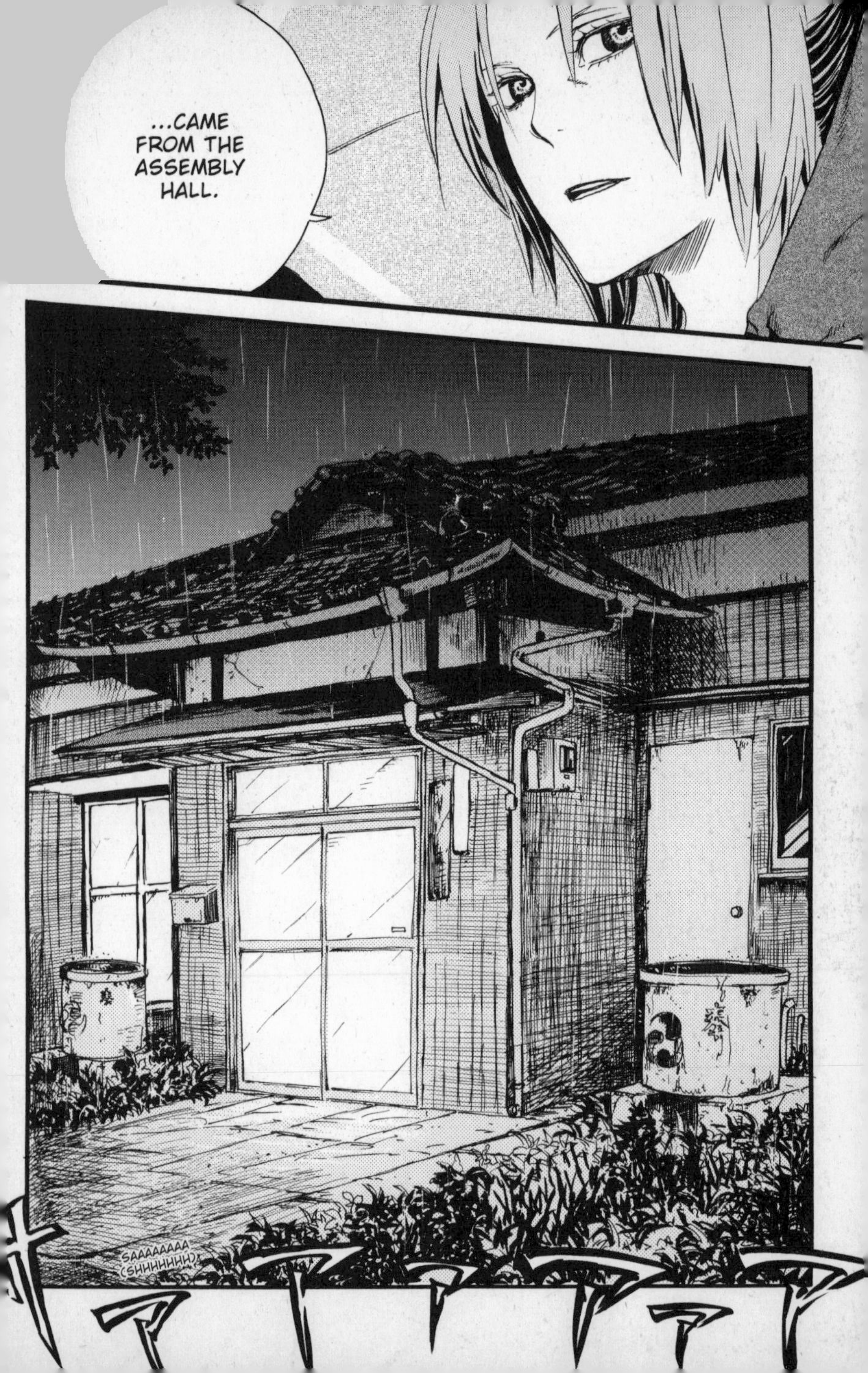
...CAME FROM THE ASSEMBLY HALL.
SAAAAAAAA (SHHHHHHHH)

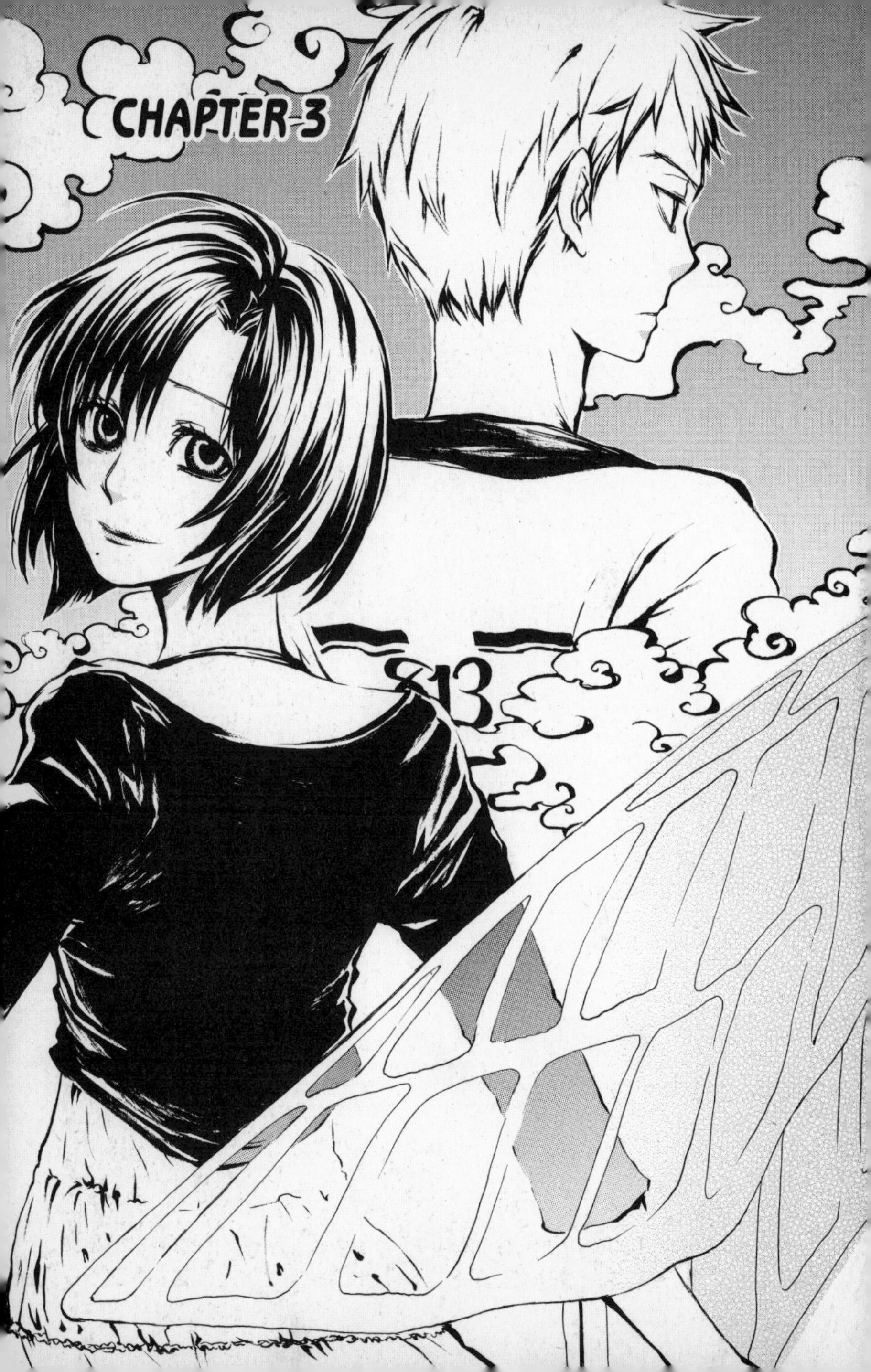
CHAPTER 3
13

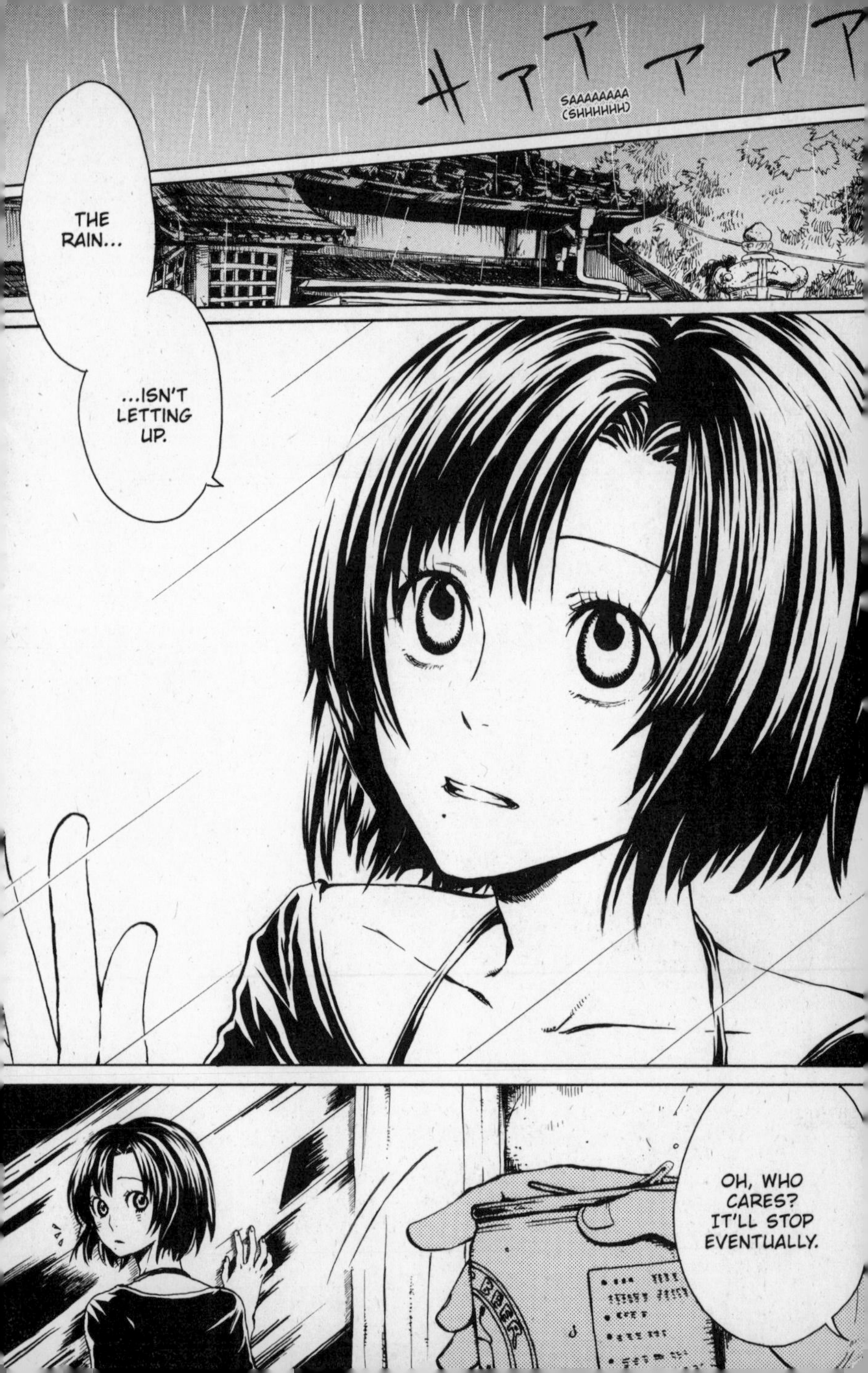
SAAAAAAAA (SHHHHHH)
THE RAIN...
...ISN'T LETTING UP.
OH, WHO CARES? IT'LL STOP EVENTUALLY.

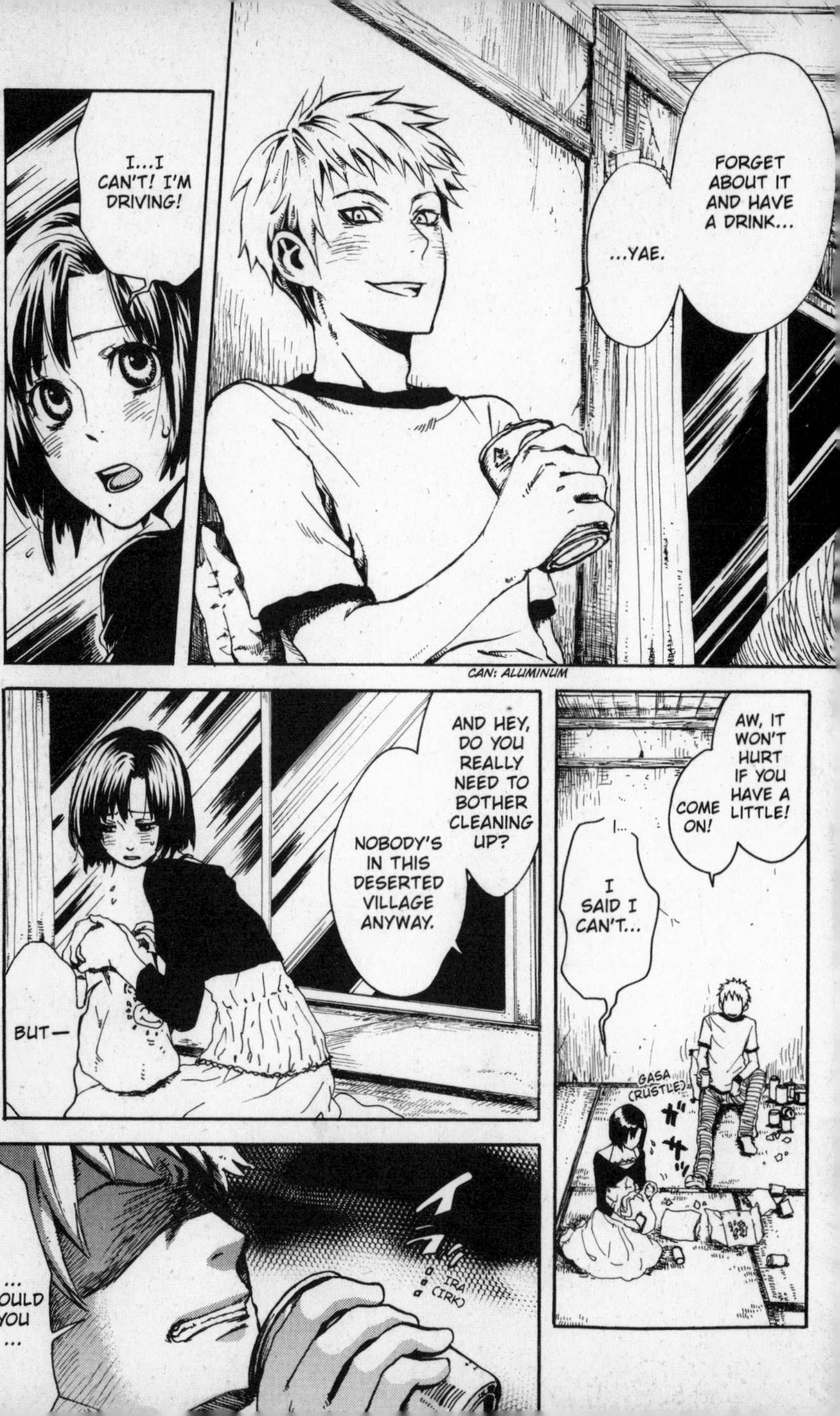
FORGET ABOUT IT AND HAVE A DRINK...
...YAE.
CAN: ALUMINUM
I...I CAN'T! I'M DRIVING!
AW, IT WON'T HURT IF YOU HAVE A LITTLE!
COME ON!
I...
I SAID I CAN'T...
GASA (RUSTLE)
AND HEY, DO YOU REALLY NEED TO BOTHER CLEANING UP?
NOBODY'S IN THIS DESERTED VILLAGE ANYWAY.
BUT—
IRA (IRK)
...WOULD YOU...

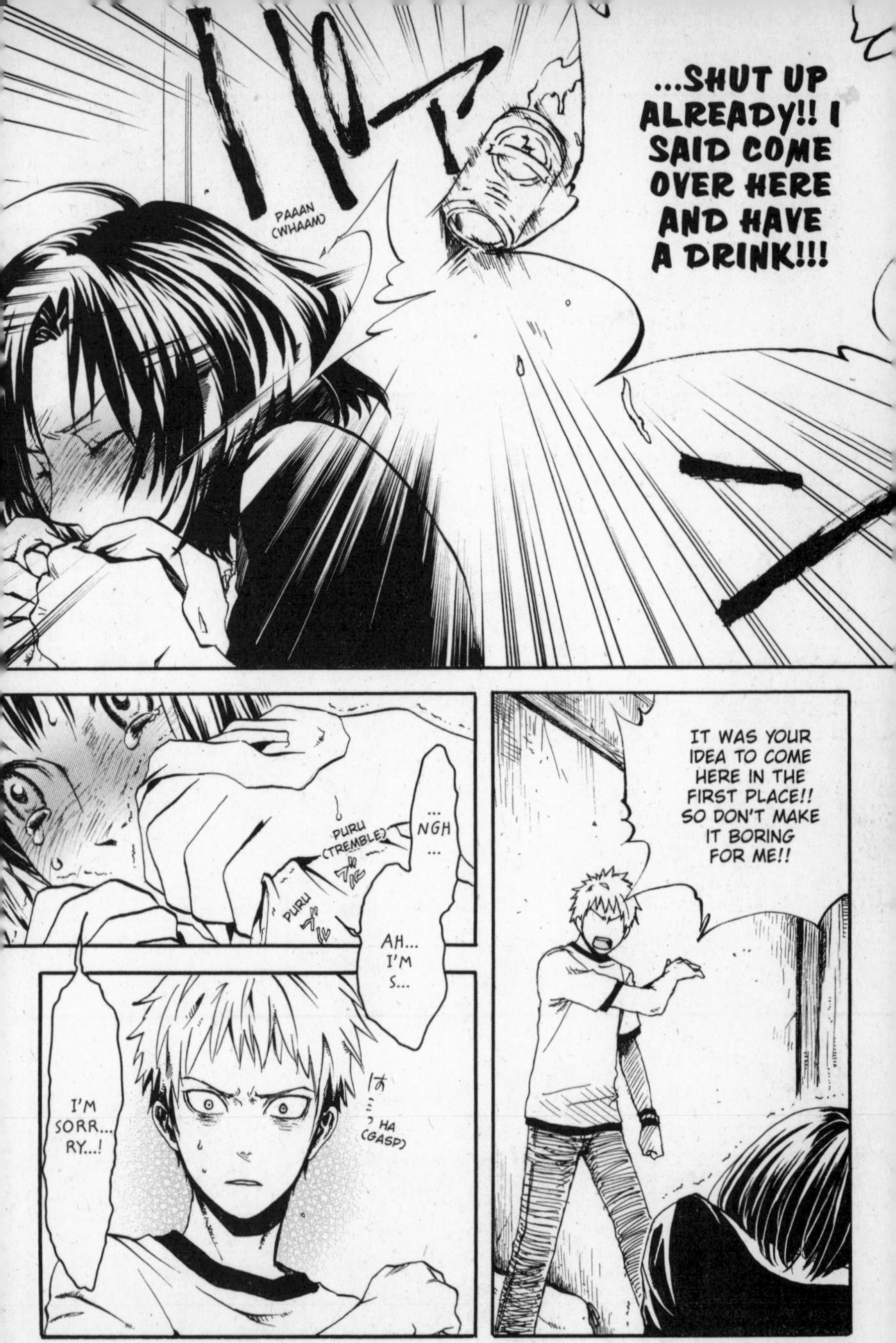
...SHUT UP ALREADY!! I SAID COME OVER HERE AND HAVE A DRINK!!!
PAAAN (WHAAM)
IT WAS YOUR IDEA TO COME HERE IN THE FIRST PLACE!! SO DON'T MAKE IT BORING FOR ME!!
...
... NGH ...
PURU (TREMBLE)
PURU
AH... I'M S...
HA (GASP)
I'M SORRR... RY...!

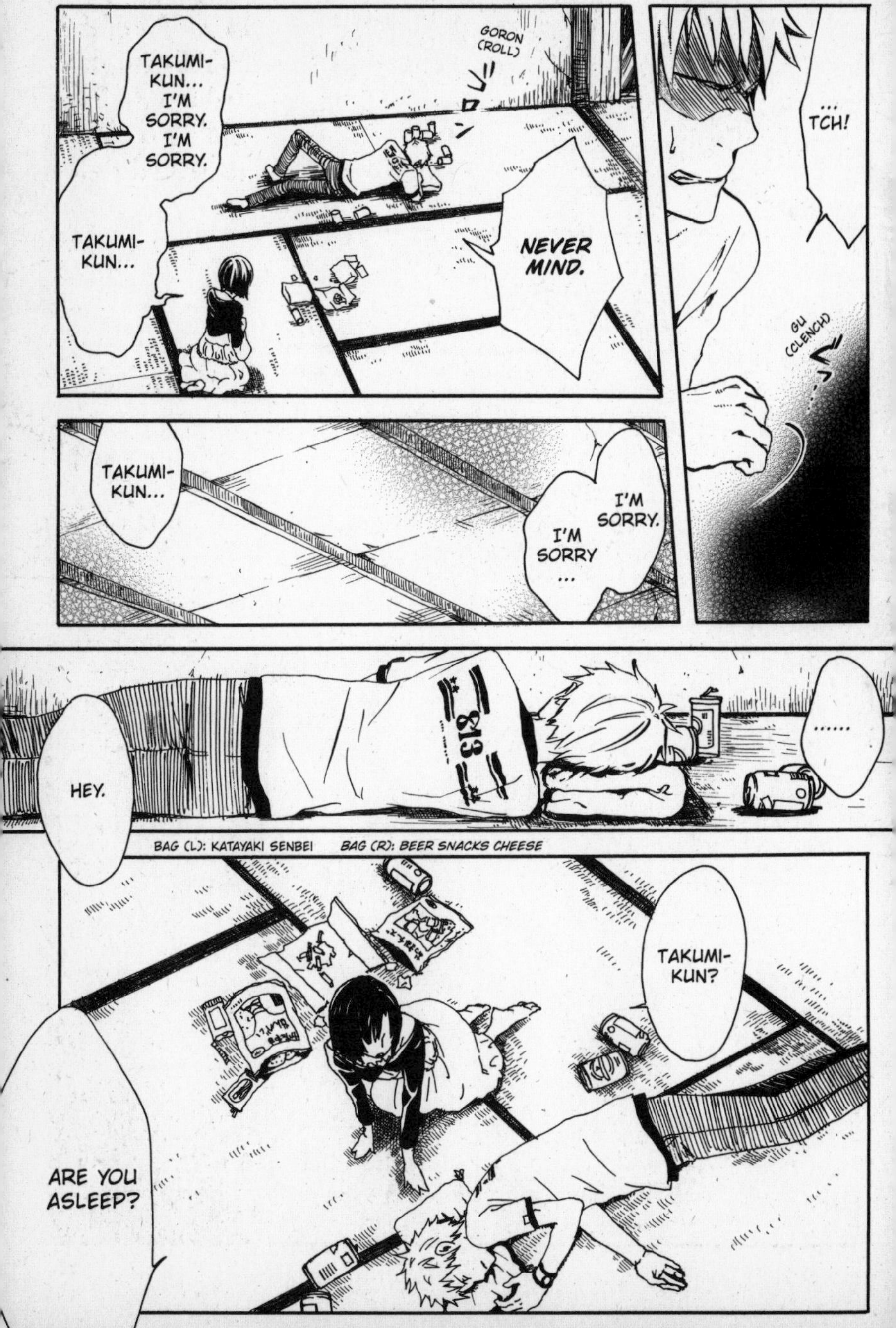
...TCH!
GU (CLENCH)
GORON (ROLL)
TAKUMI-KUN... I'M SORRY. I'M SORRY.
NEVER MIND.
TAKUMI-KUN...
I'M SORRY.
I'M SORRY ...
TAKUMI-KUN...
......
HEY.
BAG (L): KATAYAKI SENBEI
BAG (R): BEER SNACKS CHEESE
TAKUMI-KUN?
ARE YOU ASLEEP?

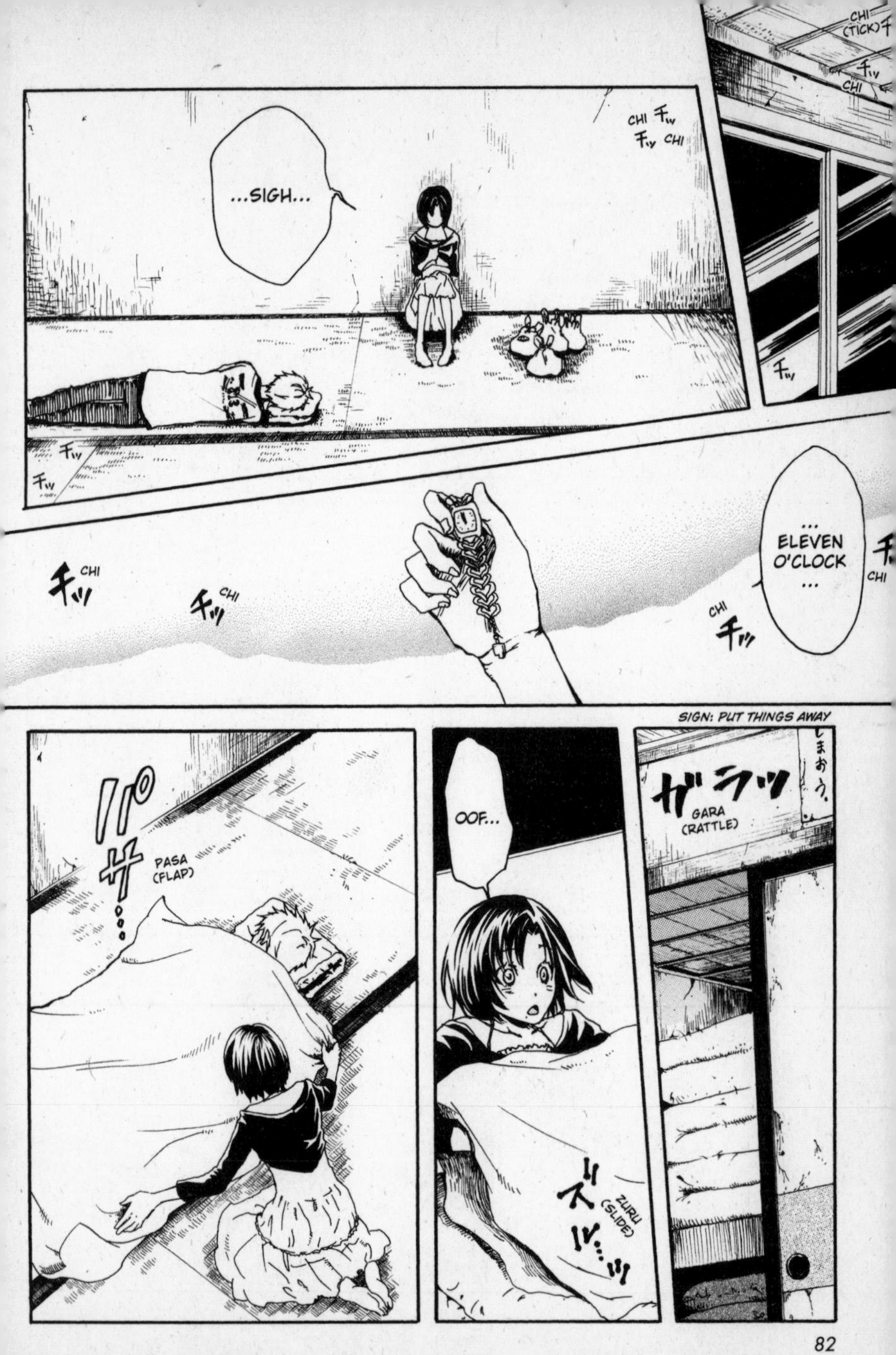
CHI (TICK) チ
チッ CHI
チッ
CHI チッ
チッ CHI
...SIGH...
チッ
チッ
CHI
...ELEVEN O'CLOCK...
CHI チッ
CHI チッ
CHI チッ
SIGN: PUT THINGS AWAY
しまおう。
ガラッ
GARA (RATTLE)
OOF...
ZURU (SLIDE)
パサ
PASA (FLAP)

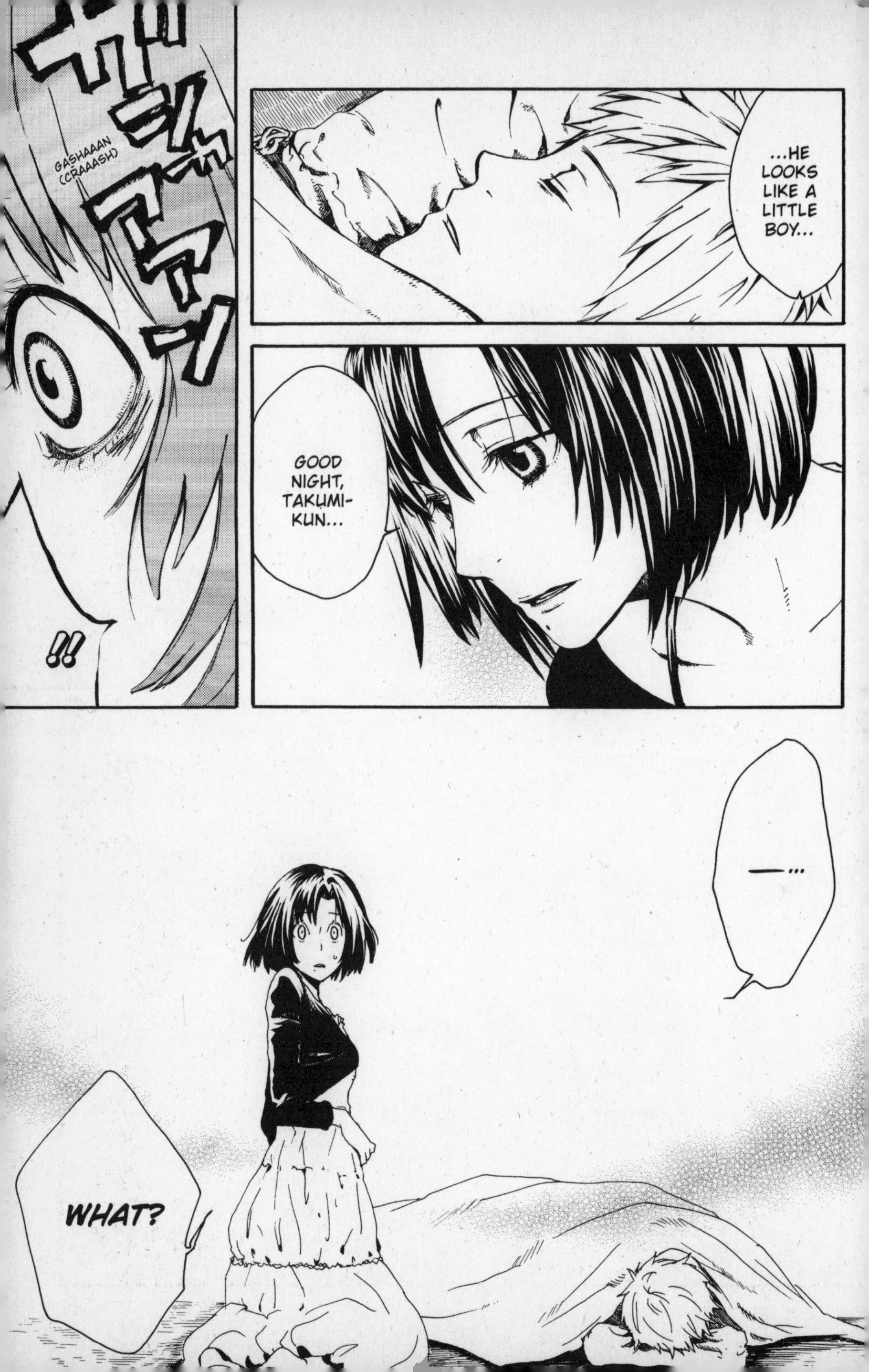
...HE LOOKS LIKE A LITTLE BOY...
GOOD NIGHT, TAKUMI-KUN...
GASHAAAN (CRAAASH)
!!
—...
WHAT?

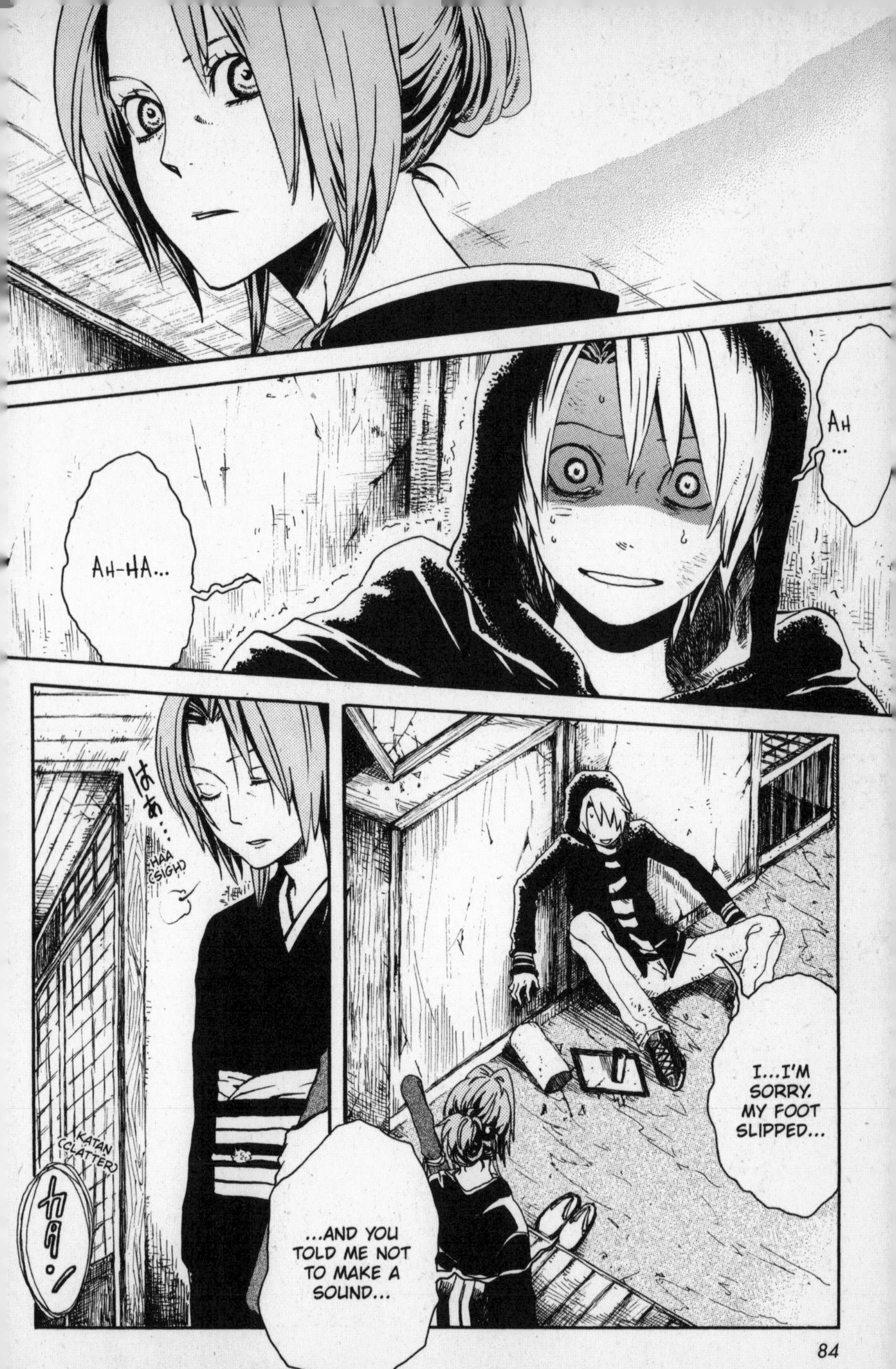
AH ...
AH-HA...
I...I'M SORRY. MY FOOT SLIPPED...
...AND YOU TOLD ME NOT TO MAKE A SOUND...
はぁ…
HAA (SIGH)
カタン。!
KATAN (CLATTER)

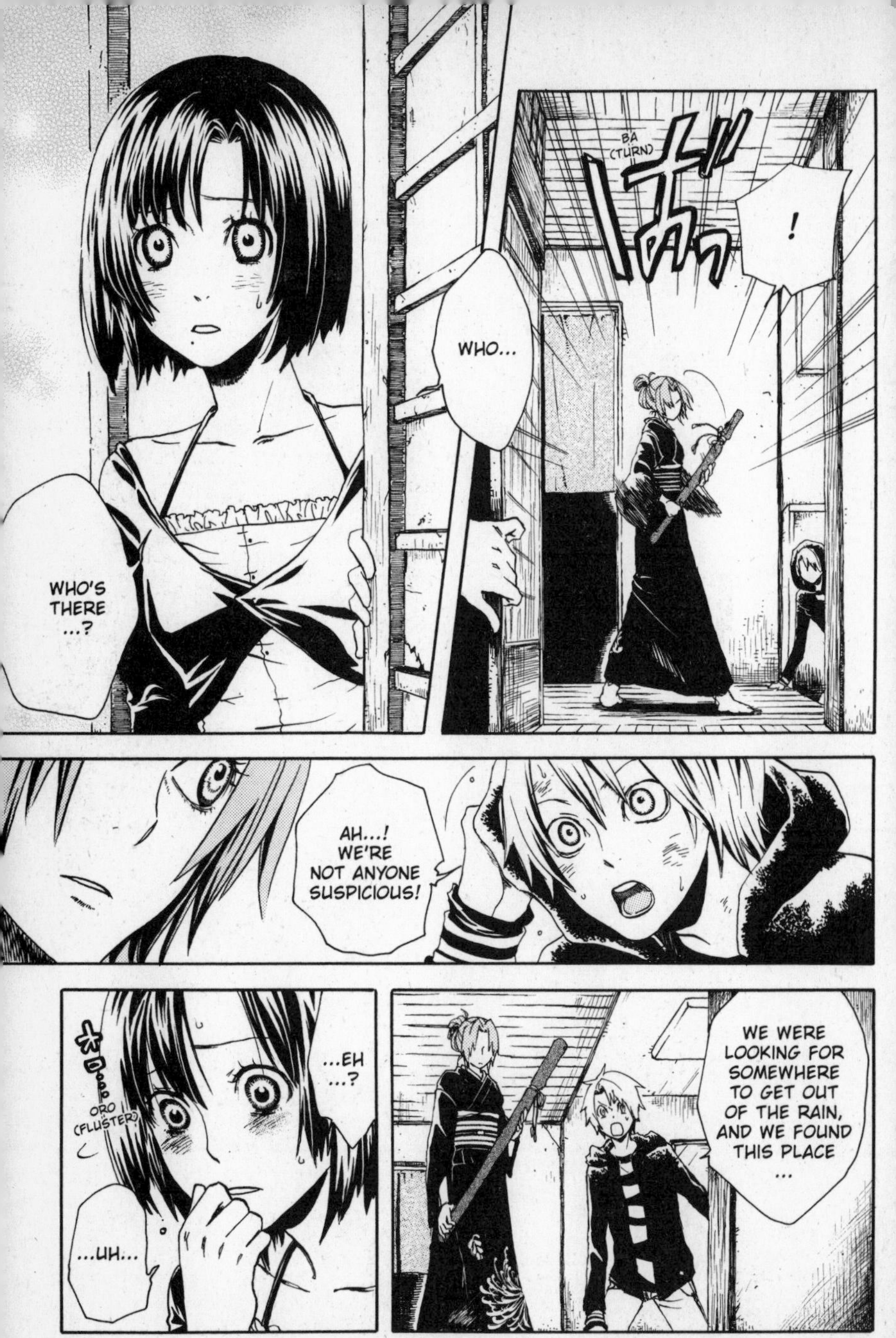
BA (TURN)
!
WHO...
WHO'S THERE ...?
AH...! WE'RE NOT ANYONE SUSPICIOUS!
WE WERE LOOKING FOR SOMEWHERE TO GET OUT OF THE RAIN, AND WE FOUND THIS PLACE ...
...EH ...?
ORO (FLUSTER)
...UH...

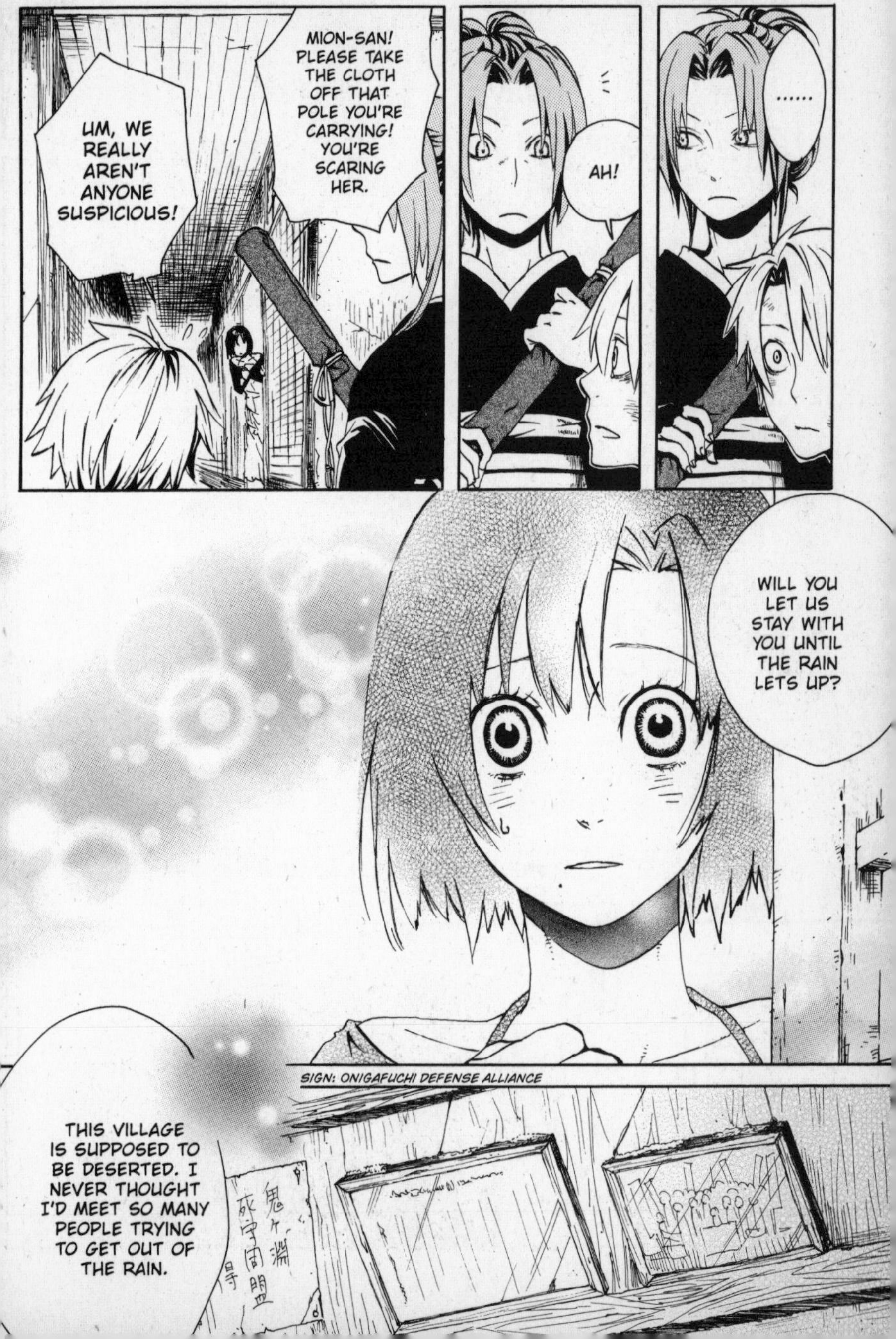
......
AH!
MION-SAN! PLEASE TAKE THE CLOTH OFF THAT POLE YOU'RE CARRYING! YOU'RE SCARING HER.
UM, WE REALLY AREN'T ANYONE SUSPICIOUS!
WILL YOU LET US STAY WITH YOU UNTIL THE RAIN LETS UP?
SIGN: ONIGAFUCHI DEFENSE ALLIANCE
THIS VILLAGE IS SUPPOSED TO BE DESERTED. I NEVER THOUGHT I'D MEET SO MANY PEOPLE TRYING TO GET OUT OF THE RAIN.

BAGS (R-L): SEAWEED SALT, COVERED IN SEAWEED / KAKI AND P! NUTS, ¥100

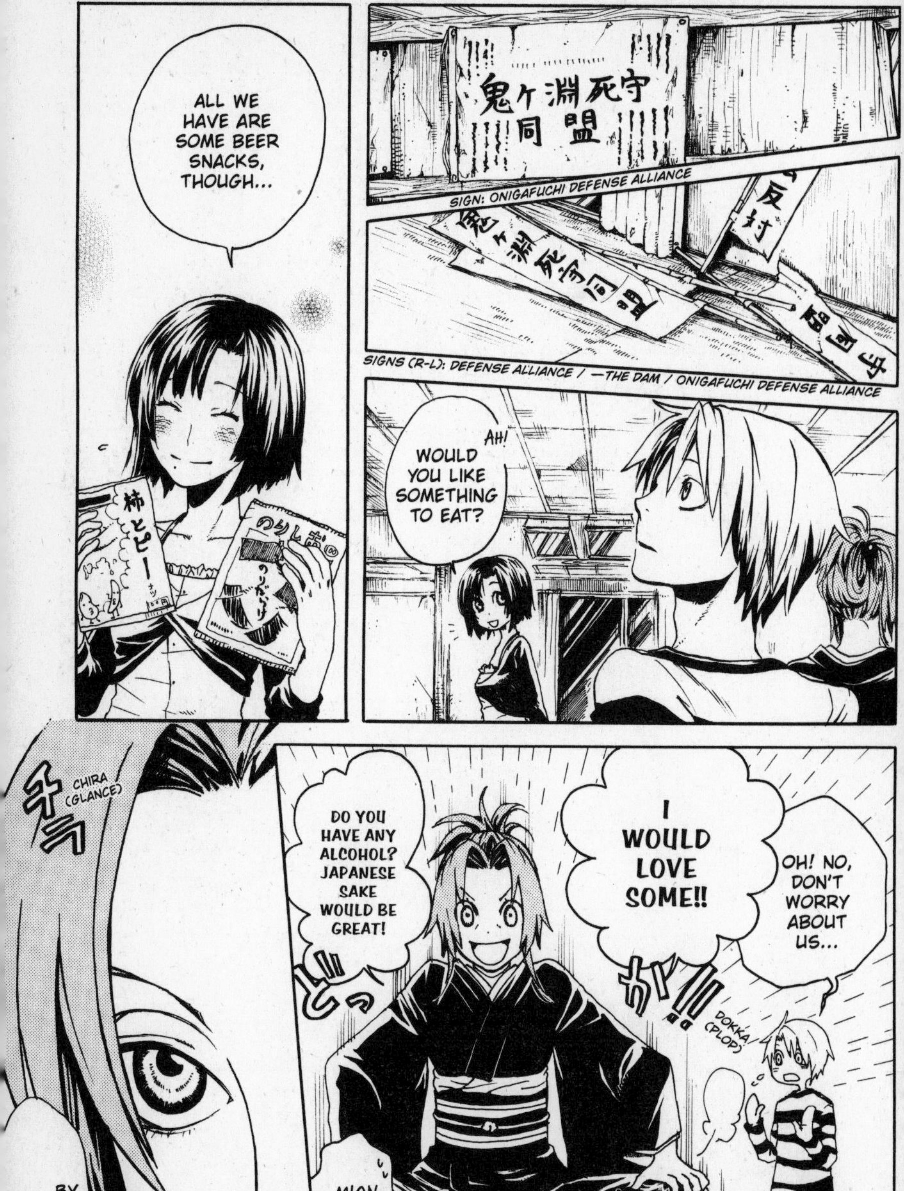
鬼ヶ淵死守同盟
SIGN: ONIGAFUCHI DEFENSE ALLIANCE
反対
鬼ヶ淵死守同盟
SIGNS (R-L): DEFENSE ALLIANCE / —THE DAM / ONIGAFUCHI DEFENSE ALLIANCE
AH!
WOULD YOU LIKE SOMETHING TO EAT?
ALL WE HAVE ARE SOME BEER SNACKS, THOUGH...
OH! NO, DON'T WORRY ABOUT US...
I WOULD LOVE SOME!!
DO YOU HAVE ANY ALCOHOL? JAPANESE SAKE WOULD BE GREAT!
DOKKA (PLOP)
...MION-SAN...
CHIRA (GLANCE)
BY THE WAY...

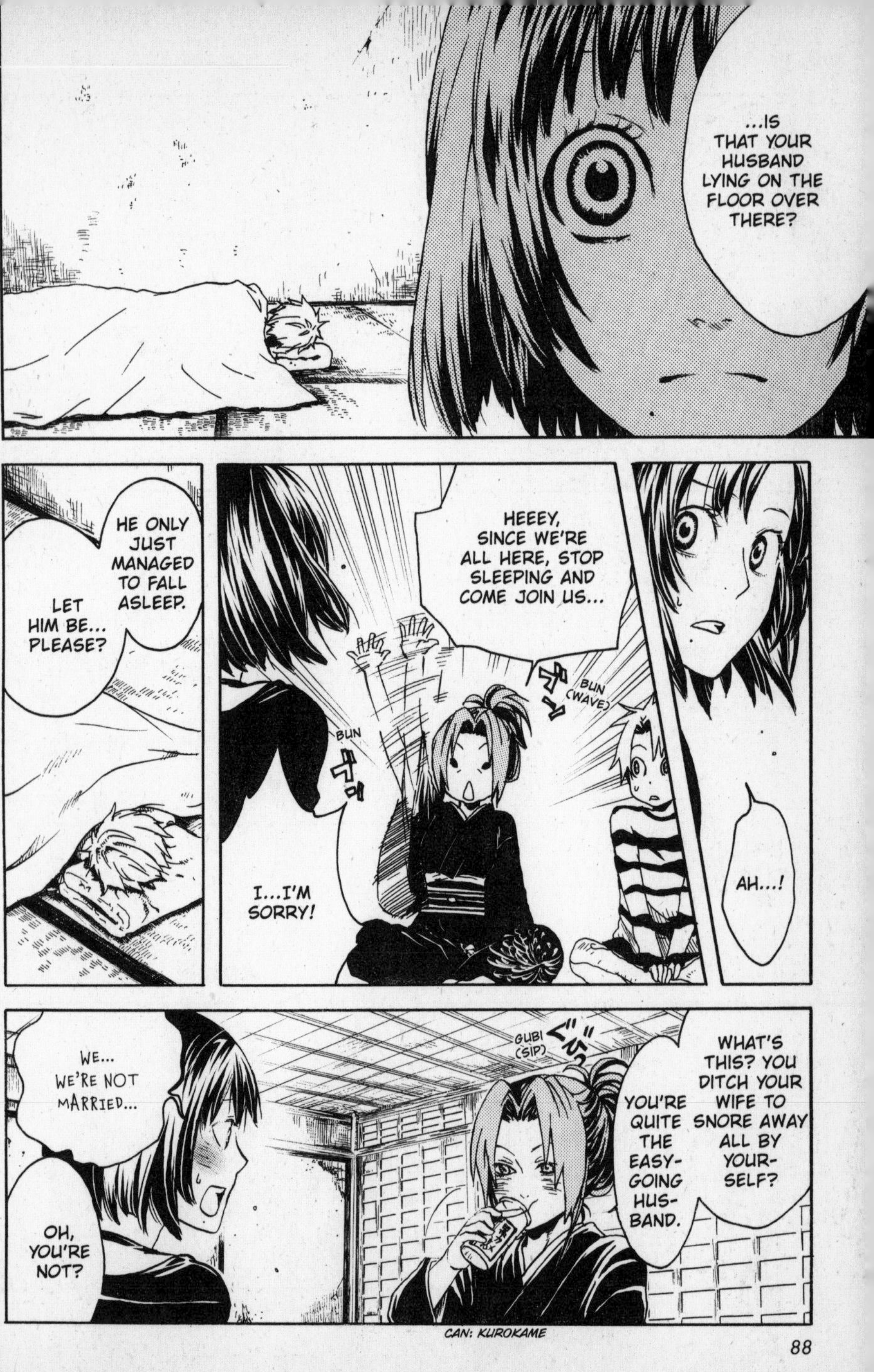

...IS THAT YOUR HUSBAND LYING ON THE FLOOR OVER THERE?
AH...!
HEEEY, SINCE WE'RE ALL HERE, STOP SLEEPING AND COME JOIN US...
BUN (WAVE)
BUN
I...I'M SORRY!
HE ONLY JUST MANAGED TO FALL ASLEEP.
LET HIM BE... PLEASE?
GUBI (SIP)
WHAT'S THIS? YOU DITCH YOUR WIFE TO SNORE AWAY ALL BY YOUR-SELF?
YOU'RE QUITE THE EASY-GOING HUS-BAND.
WE... WE'RE NOT MARRIED...
OH, YOU'RE NOT?

CAN: KUROKAME

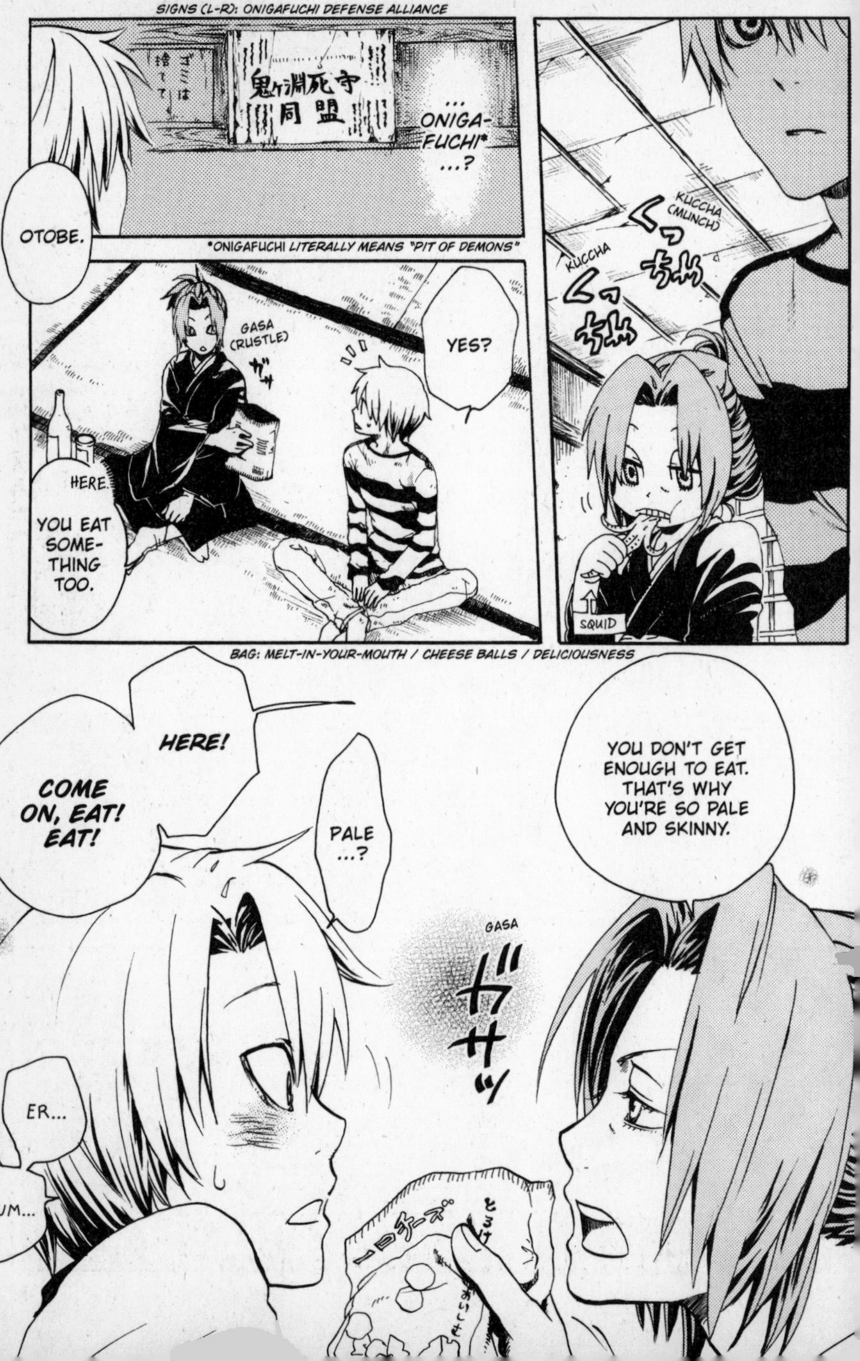

KUCCHA (MUNCH)
KUCCHA
SQUID
SIGNS (L-R): ONIGAFUCHI DEFENSE ALLIANCE
鬼ヶ淵死守同盟
ゴミは捨てて
...ONIGA-FUCHI* ...?
OTOBE.
*ONIGAFUCHI LITERALLY MEANS "PIT OF DEMONS"
YES?
GASA (RUSTLE)
HERE.
YOU EAT SOME-THING TOO.
BAG: MELT-IN-YOUR-MOUTH / CHEESE BALLS / DELICIOUSNESS
YOU DON'T GET ENOUGH TO EAT. THAT'S WHY YOU'RE SO PALE AND SKINNY.
GASA
ガサッ
PALE ...?
HERE!
COME ON, EAT! EAT!
ER...
UM...

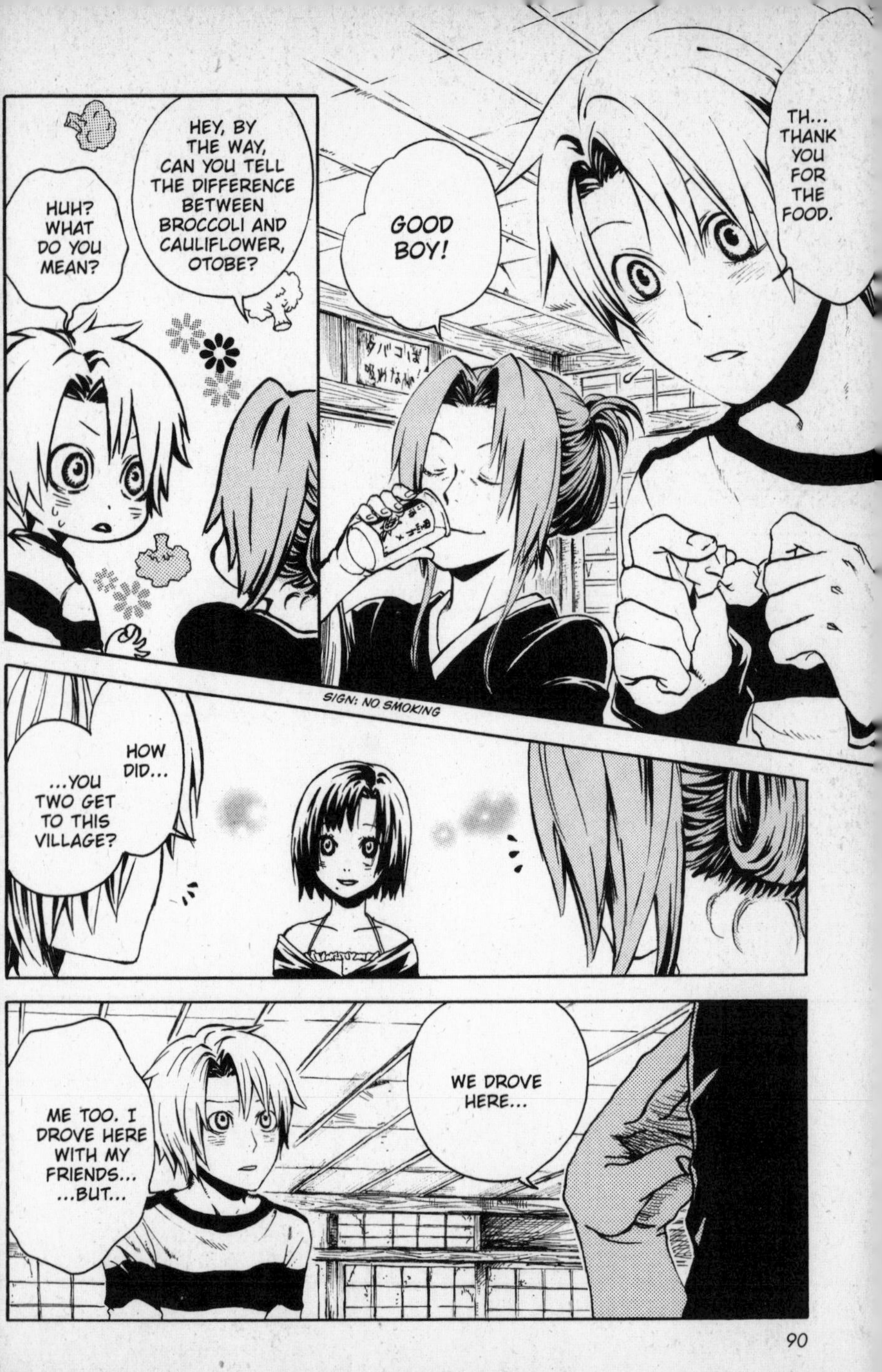
TH... THANK YOU FOR THE FOOD.
GOOD BOY!
SIGN: NO SMOKING
HEY, BY THE WAY, CAN YOU TELL THE DIFFERENCE BETWEEN BROCCOLI AND CAULIFLOWER, OTOBE?
HUH? WHAT DO YOU MEAN?
HOW DID...
...YOU TWO GET TO THIS VILLAGE?
WE DROVE HERE...
ME TOO. I DROVE HERE WITH MY FRIENDS... ...BUT...

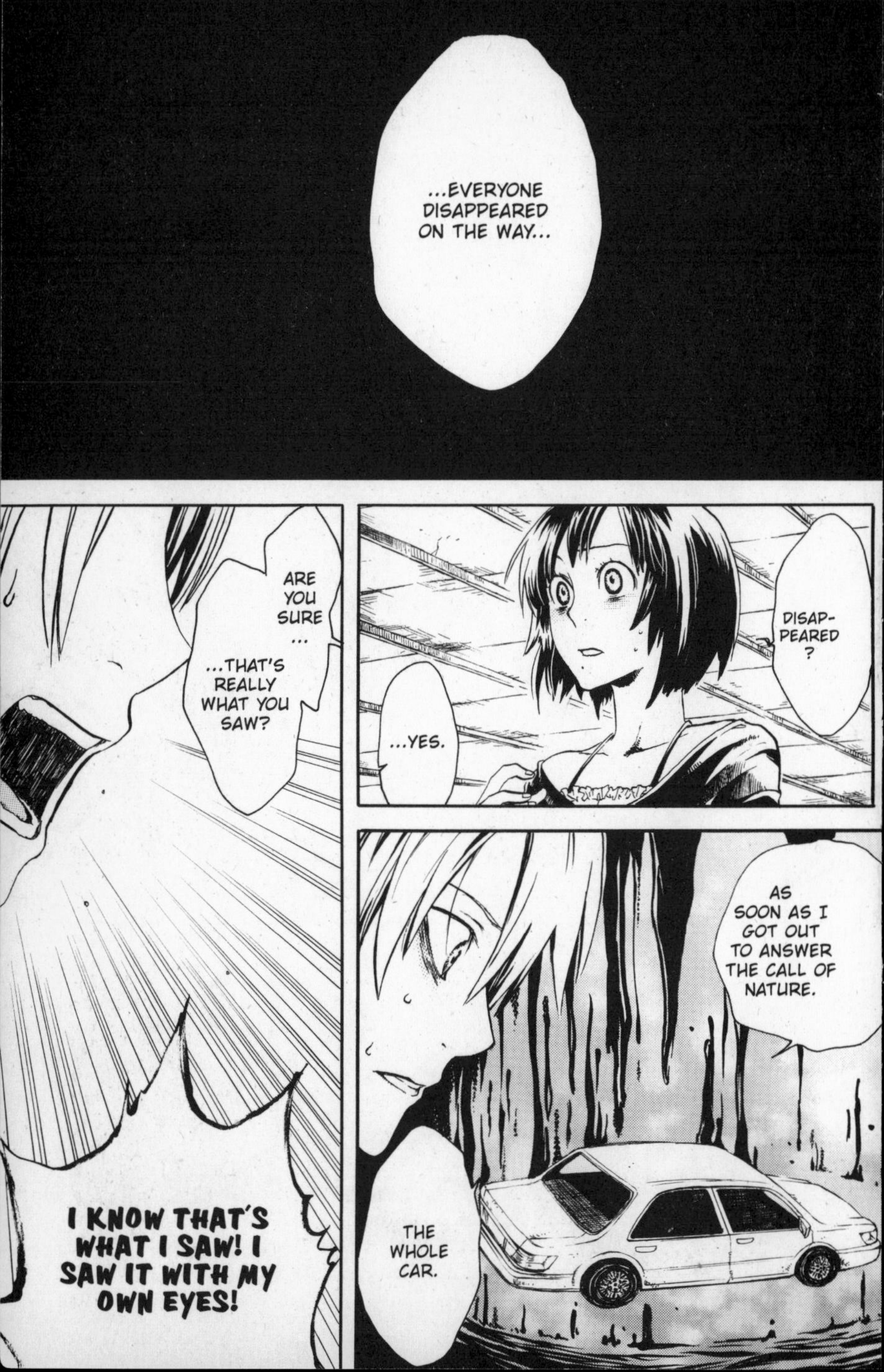
...EVERYONE DISAPPEARED ON THE WAY...
DISAP-PEARED?
...YES.
AS SOON AS I GOT OUT TO ANSWER THE CALL OF NATURE.
THE WHOLE CAR.
ARE YOU SURE...
...THAT'S REALLY WHAT YOU SAW?
I KNOW THAT'S WHAT I SAW! I SAW IT WITH MY OWN EYES!

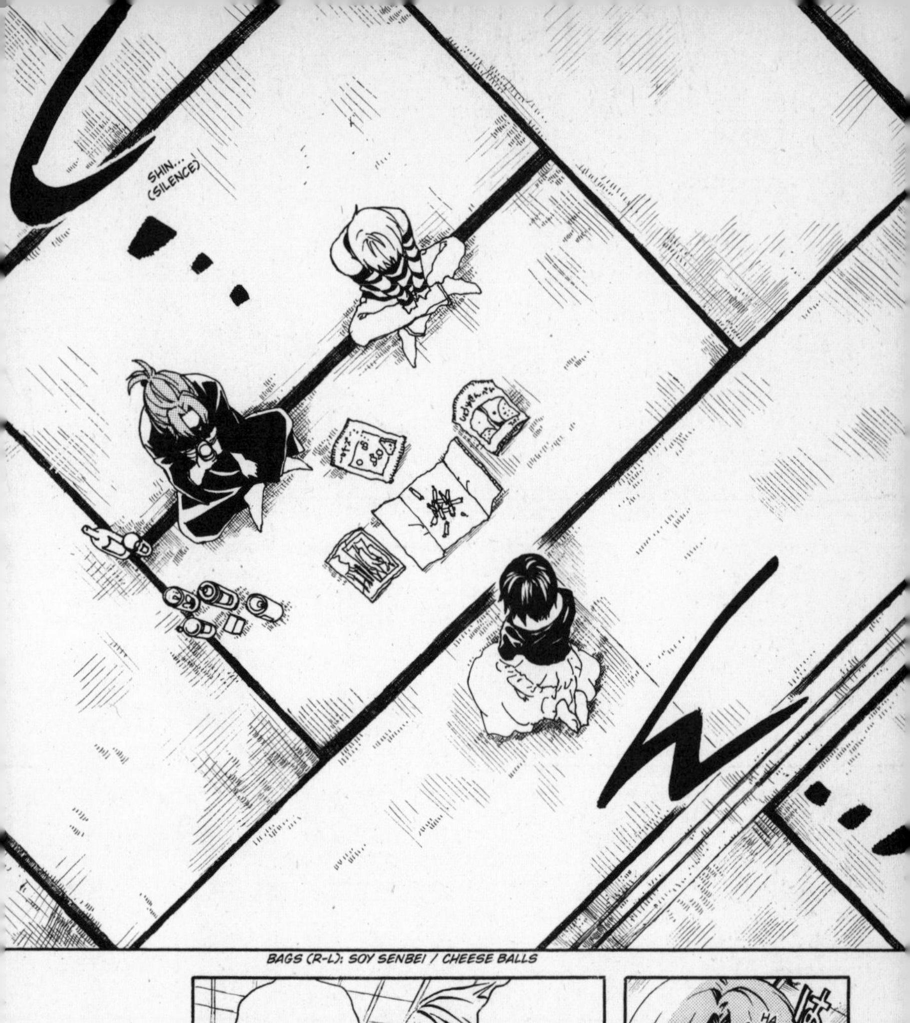
SHIN... (SILENCE)

BAGS (R-L): SOY SENBEI / CHEESE BALLS

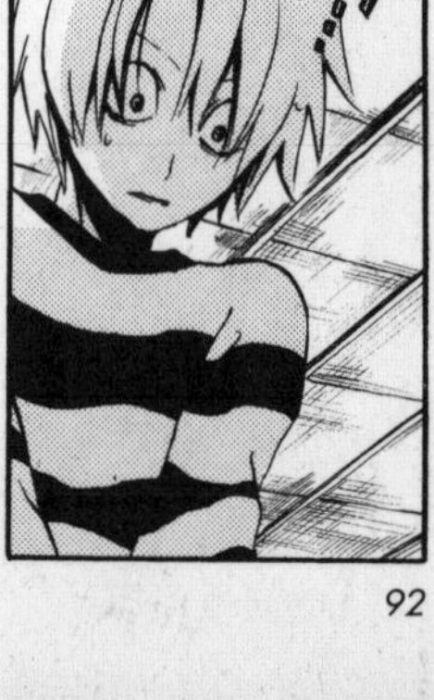
HA (GASP)

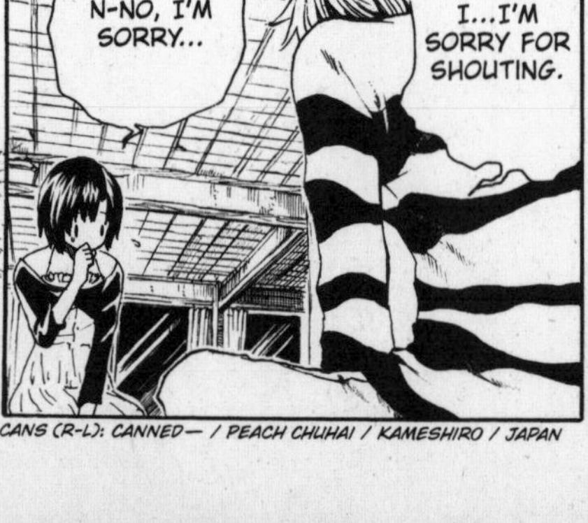
I...I'M SORRY FOR SHOUTING.
N-NO, I'M SORRY...

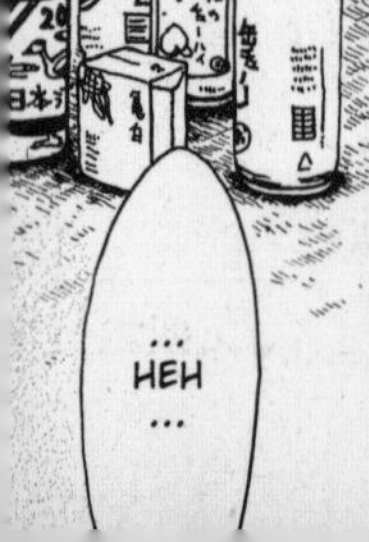
...HEH...

CANS (R-L): CANNED— / PEACH CHUHAI / KAMESHIRO / JAPAN

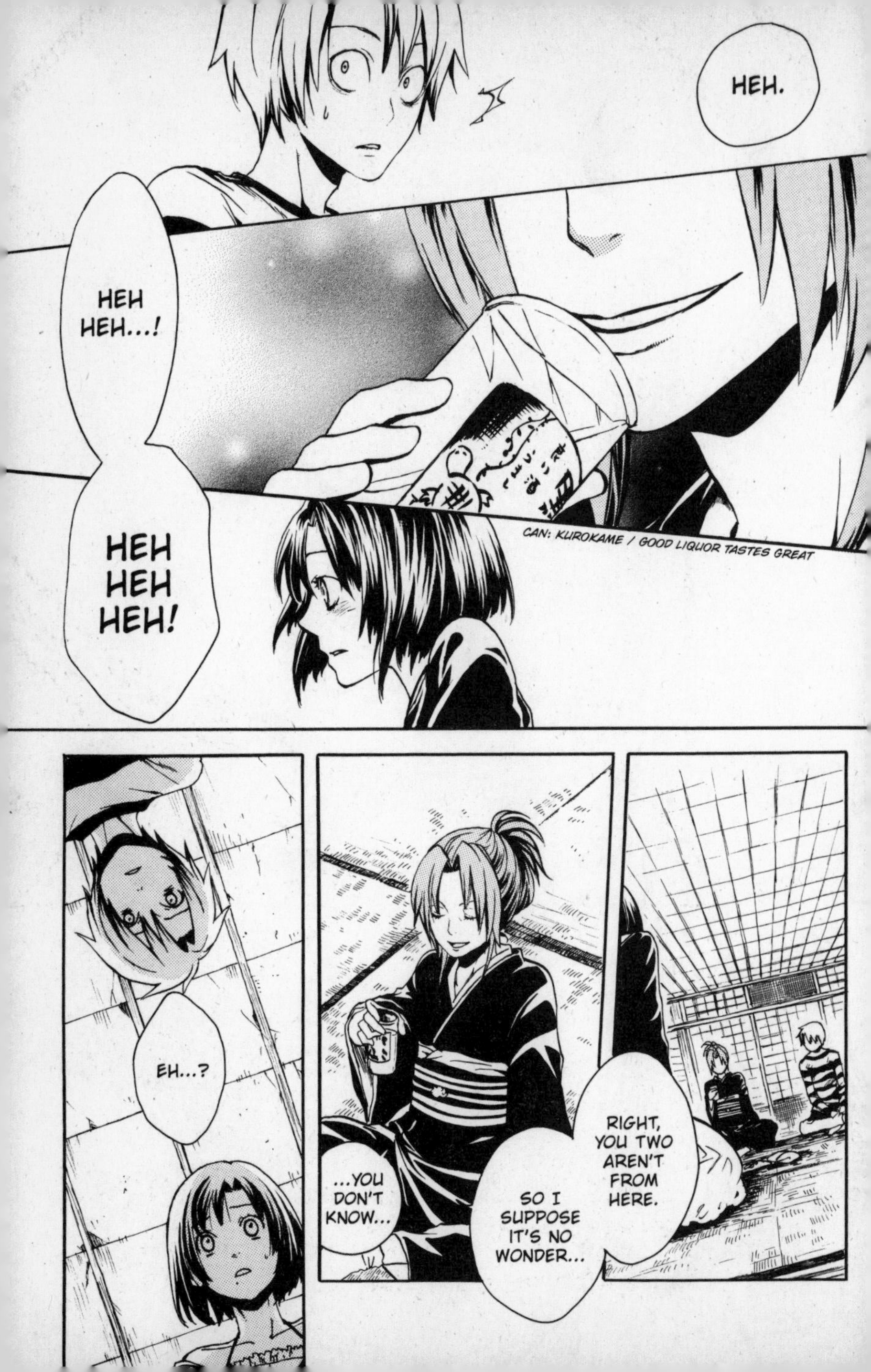
HEH.
HEH HEH...!
CAN: KUROKAME / GOOD LIQUOR TASTES GREAT
HEH HEH HEH!
RIGHT, YOU TWO AREN'T FROM HERE.
SO I SUPPOSE IT'S NO WONDER...
...YOU DON'T KNOW...
EH...?

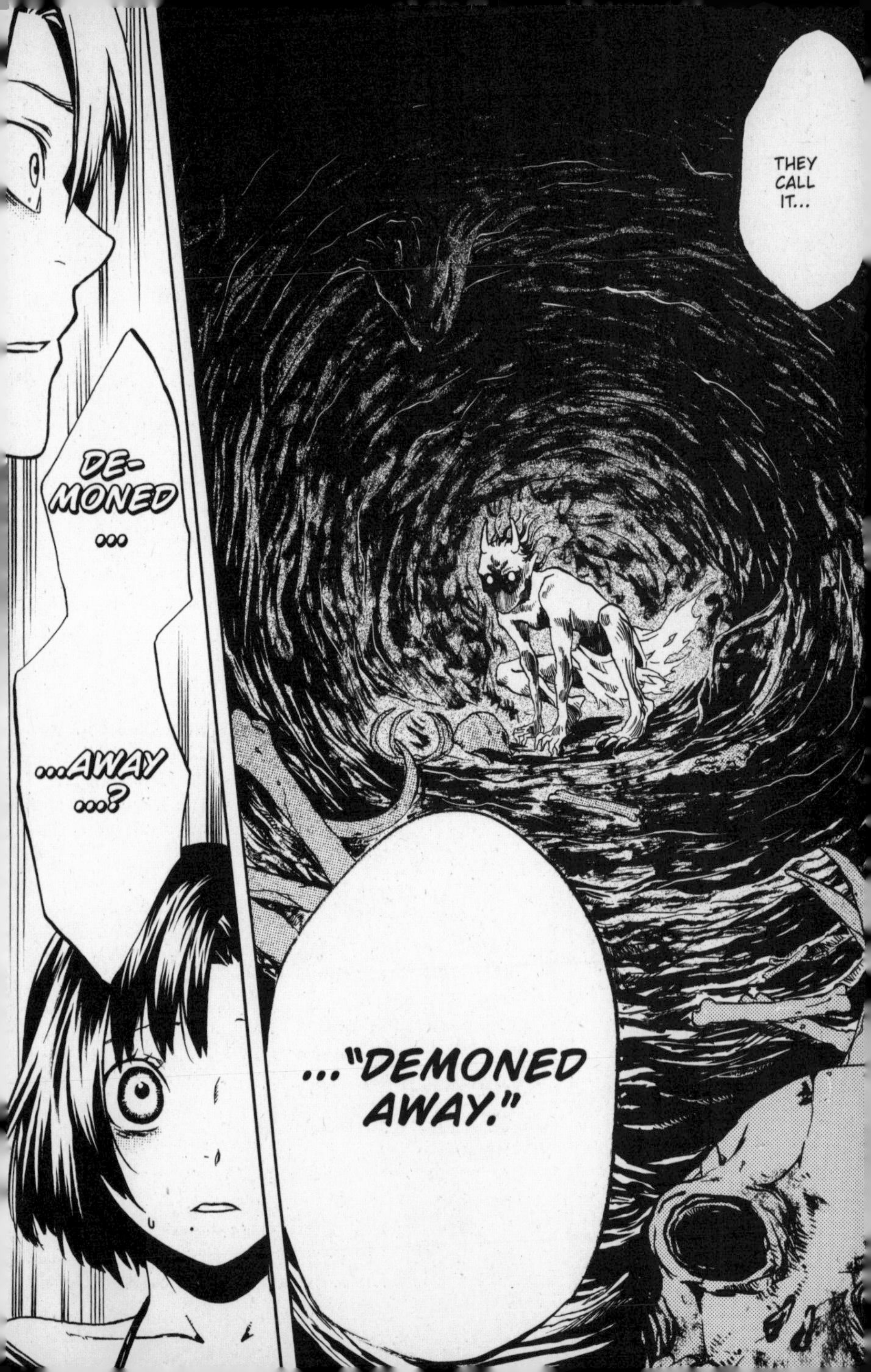
THEY CALL IT...
..."DEMONED AWAY."
DE-MONED ...
...AWAY ...?

BAG (R): MELT-IN-YOUR-MOUTH DELICIOUSNESS / CHEESE BALLS

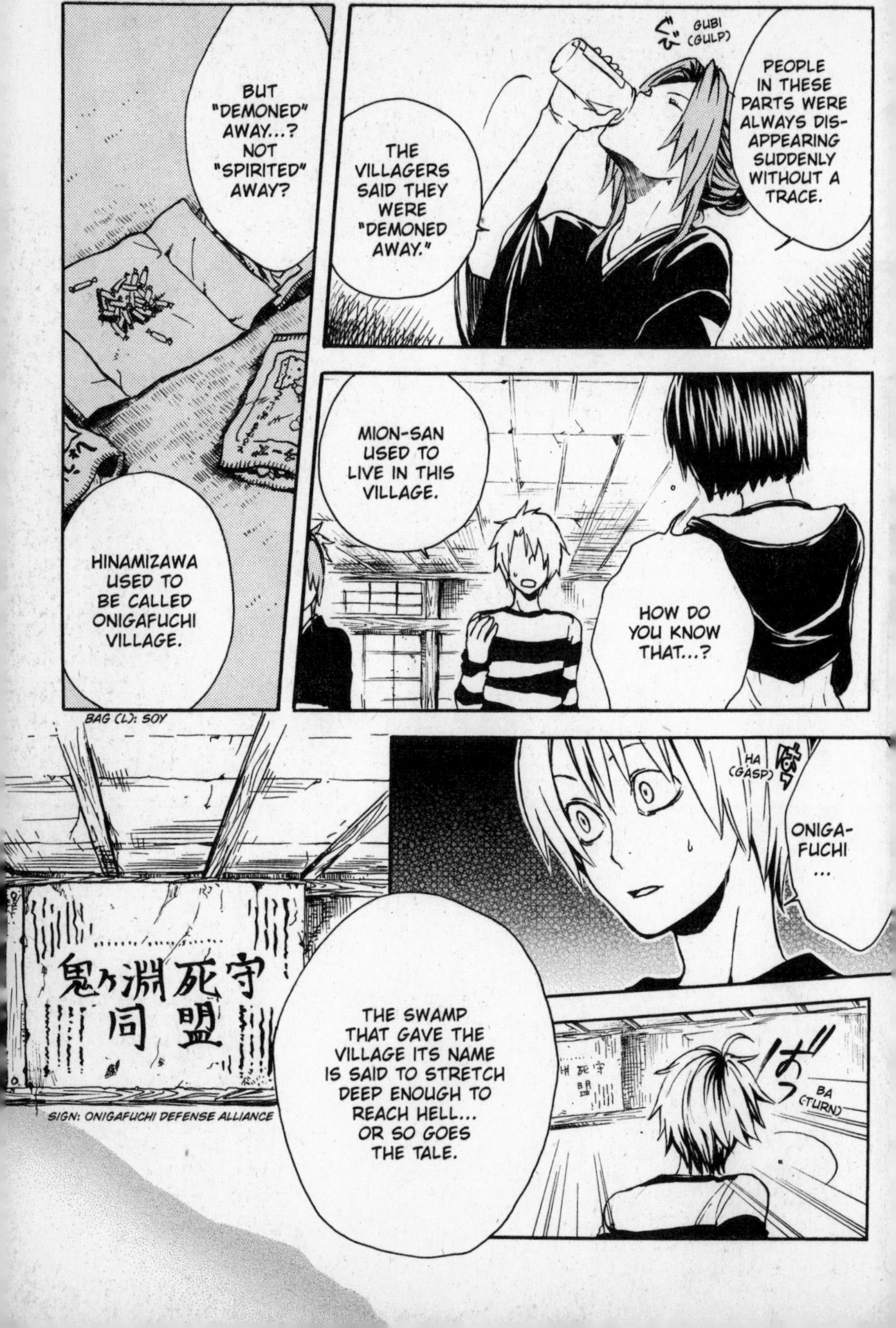
ぐび
GUBI (GULP)
PEOPLE IN THESE PARTS WERE ALWAYS DIS-APPEARING SUDDENLY WITHOUT A TRACE.
THE VILLAGERS SAID THEY WERE "DEMONED AWAY."
HOW DO YOU KNOW THAT...?
MION-SAN USED TO LIVE IN THIS VILLAGE.
BUT "DEMONED" AWAY...? NOT "SPIRITED" AWAY?
HINAMIZAWA USED TO BE CALLED ONIGAFUCHI VILLAGE.
BAG (L): SOY
はっ
HA (GASP)
ONIGA-FUCHI ...
ばっ
BA (TURN)
THE SWAMP THAT GAVE THE VILLAGE ITS NAME IS SAID TO STRETCH DEEP ENOUGH TO REACH HELL... OR SO GOES THE TALE.
鬼ヶ淵死守同盟
SIGN: ONIGAFUCHI DEFENSE ALLIANCE

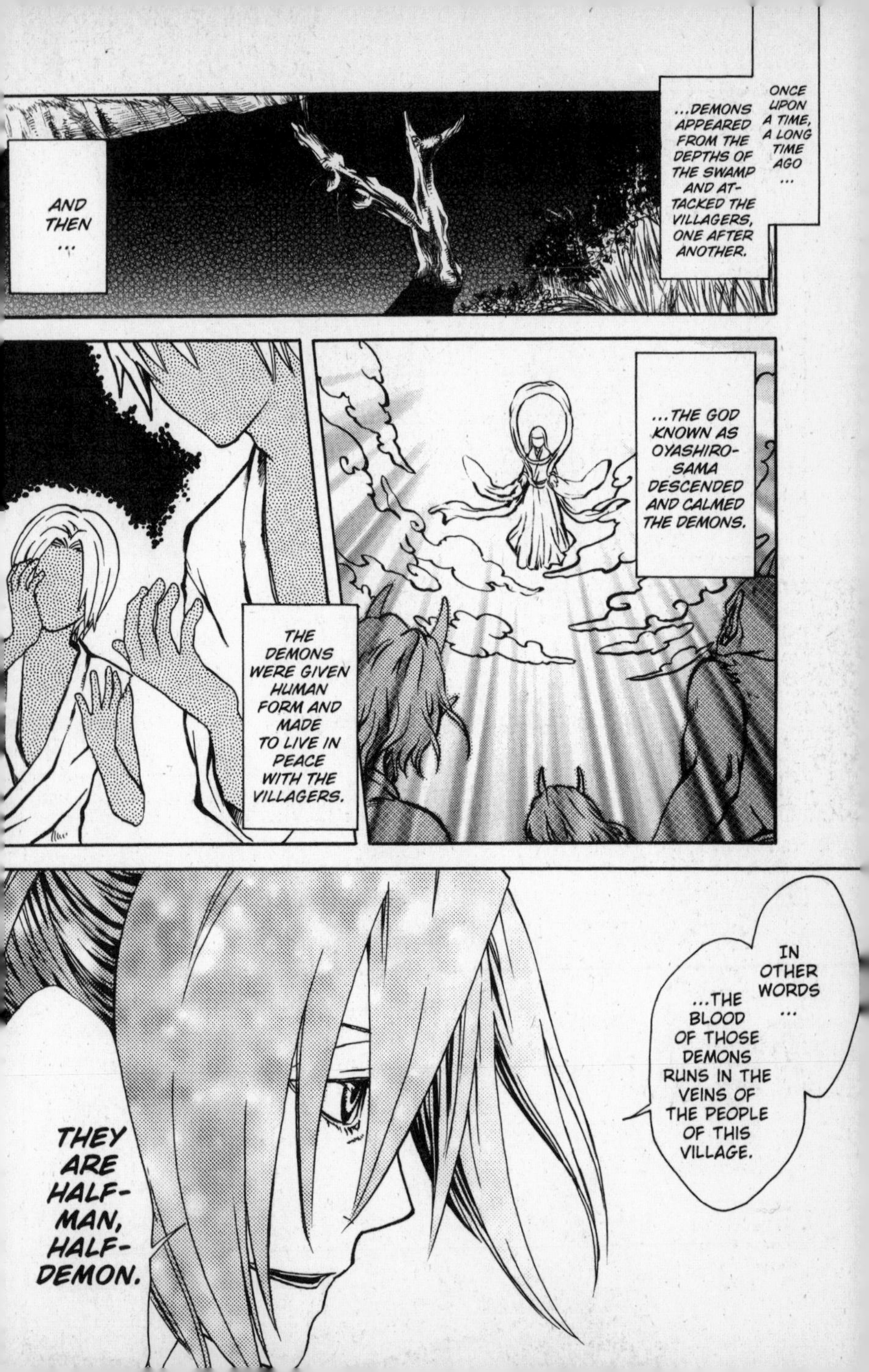

ONCE UPON A TIME, A LONG TIME AGO ...
...DEMONS APPEARED FROM THE DEPTHS OF THE SWAMP AND AT-TACKED THE VILLAGERS, ONE AFTER ANOTHER.
AND THEN ...
...THE GOD KNOWN AS OYASHIRO-SAMA DESCENDED AND CALMED THE DEMONS.
THE DEMONS WERE GIVEN HUMAN FORM AND MADE TO LIVE IN PEACE WITH THE VILLAGERS.
IN OTHER WORDS ...
...THE BLOOD OF THOSE DEMONS RUNS IN THE VEINS OF THE PEOPLE OF THIS VILLAGE.
THEY ARE HALF-MAN, HALF-DEMON.

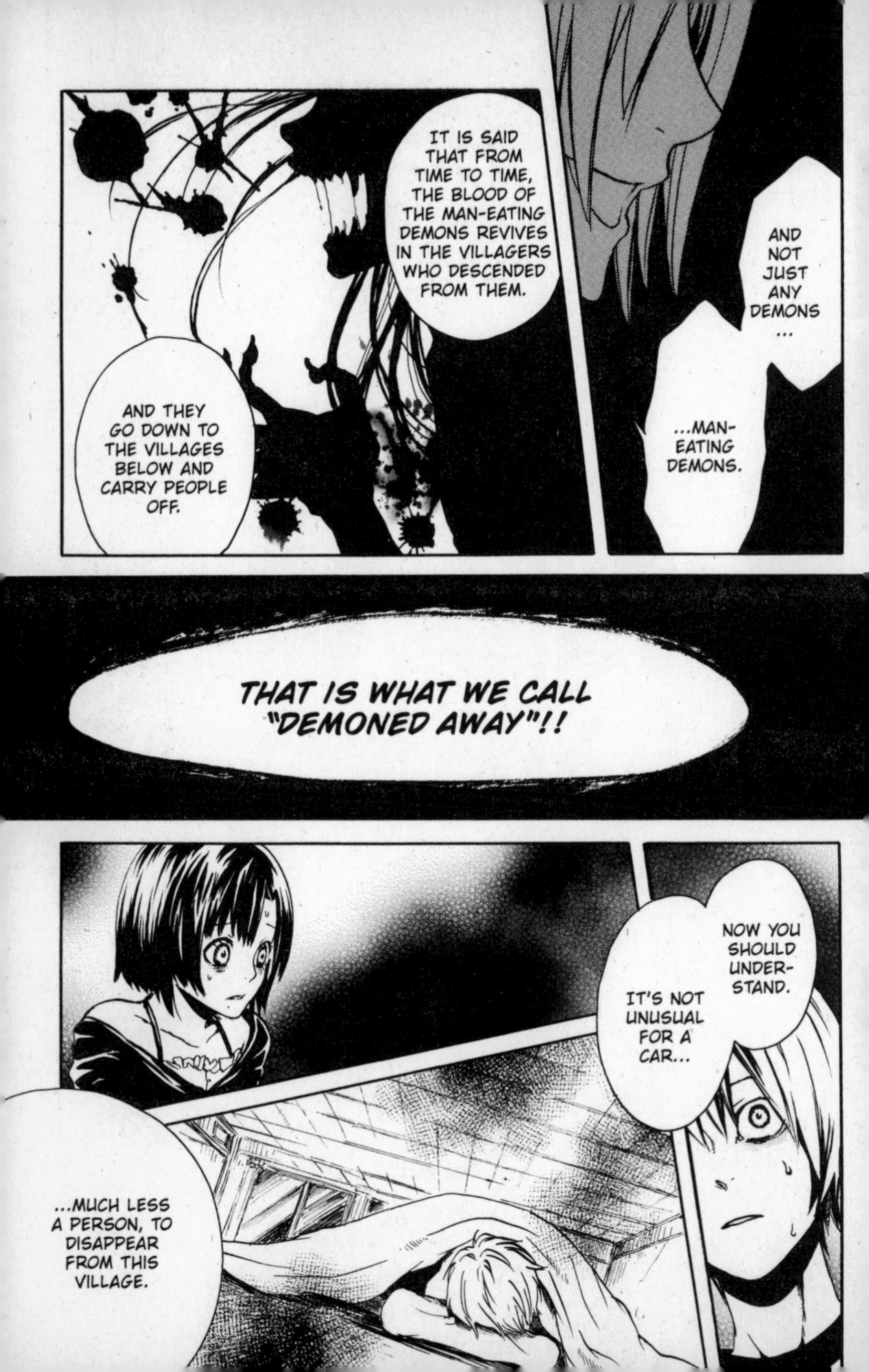
AND NOT JUST ANY DEMONS ...
...MAN-EATING DEMONS.
IT IS SAID THAT FROM TIME TO TIME, THE BLOOD OF THE MAN-EATING DEMONS REVIVES IN THE VILLAGERS WHO DESCENDED FROM THEM.
AND THEY GO DOWN TO THE VILLAGES BELOW AND CARRY PEOPLE OFF.
THAT IS WHAT WE CALL "DEMONED AWAY"!!
NOW YOU SHOULD UNDERSTAND.
IT'S NOT UNUSUAL FOR A CAR...
...MUCH LESS A PERSON, TO DISAPPEAR FROM THIS VILLAGE.

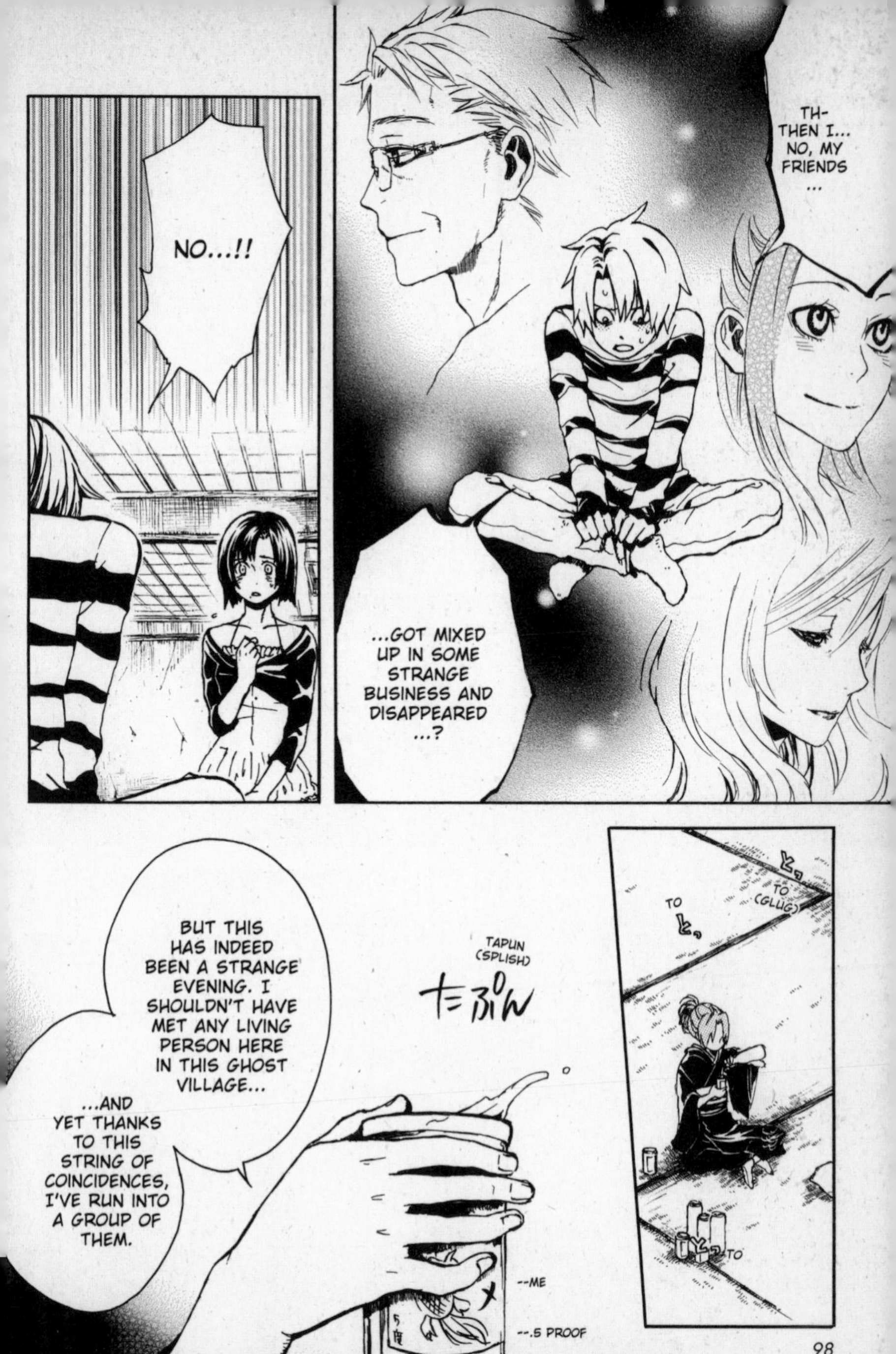

TH- THEN I... NO, MY FRIENDS ...
...GOT MIXED UP IN SOME STRANGE BUSINESS AND DISAPPEARED ...?
NO...!!
とっ TO (GLUG)
TO とっ
とっ TO
BUT THIS HAS INDEED BEEN A STRANGE EVENING. I SHOULDN'T HAVE MET ANY LIVING PERSON HERE IN THIS GHOST VILLAGE...
...AND YET THANKS TO THIS STRING OF COINCIDENCES, I'VE RUN INTO A GROUP OF THEM.
TAPUN (SPLISH)
たぷん
--ME
--.5 PROOF

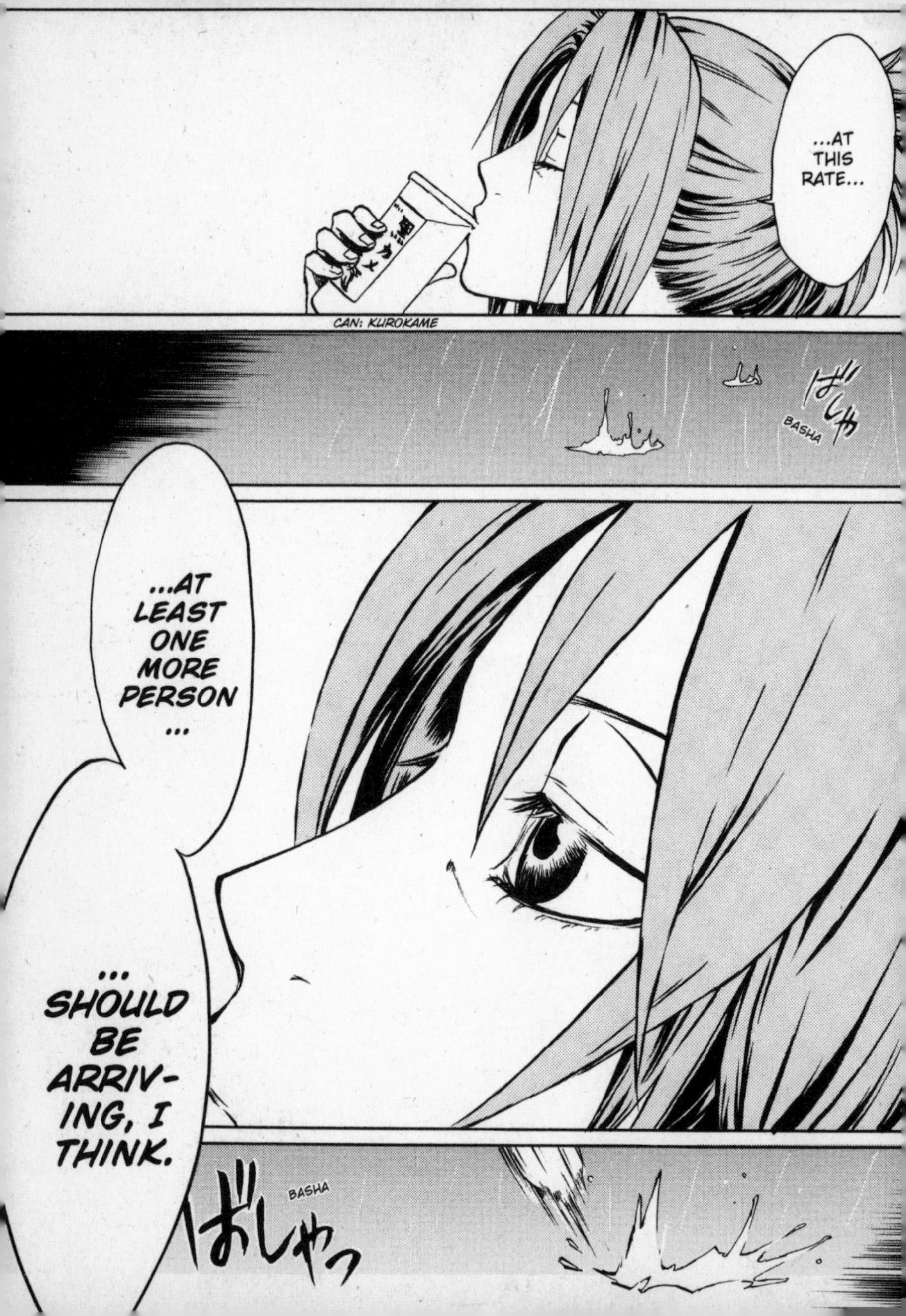
...AT THIS RATE...
CAN: KUROKAME
ばしゃ
BASHA
...AT LEAST ONE MORE PERSON ...
... SHOULD BE ARRIV- ING, I THINK.
ばしゃっ
BASHA

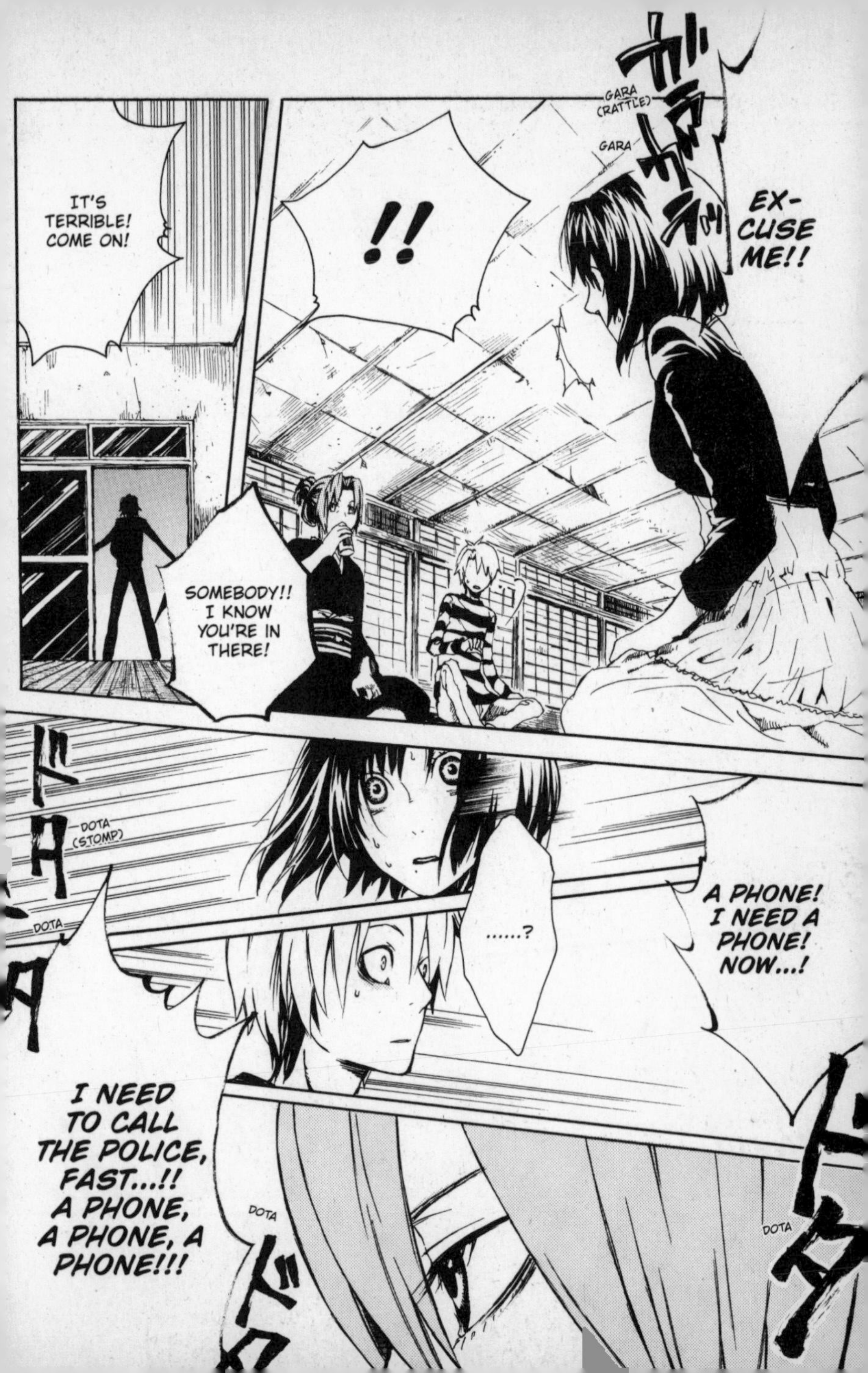
GARA (RATTLE)
GARA
EX-CUSE ME!!
!!
SOMEBODY!! I KNOW YOU'RE IN THERE!
IT'S TERRIBLE! COME ON!
A PHONE! I NEED A PHONE! NOW...!
DOTA (STOMP)
DOTA
......?
DOTA
I NEED TO CALL THE POLICE, FAST...!! A PHONE, A PHONE, A PHONE!!!
DOTA

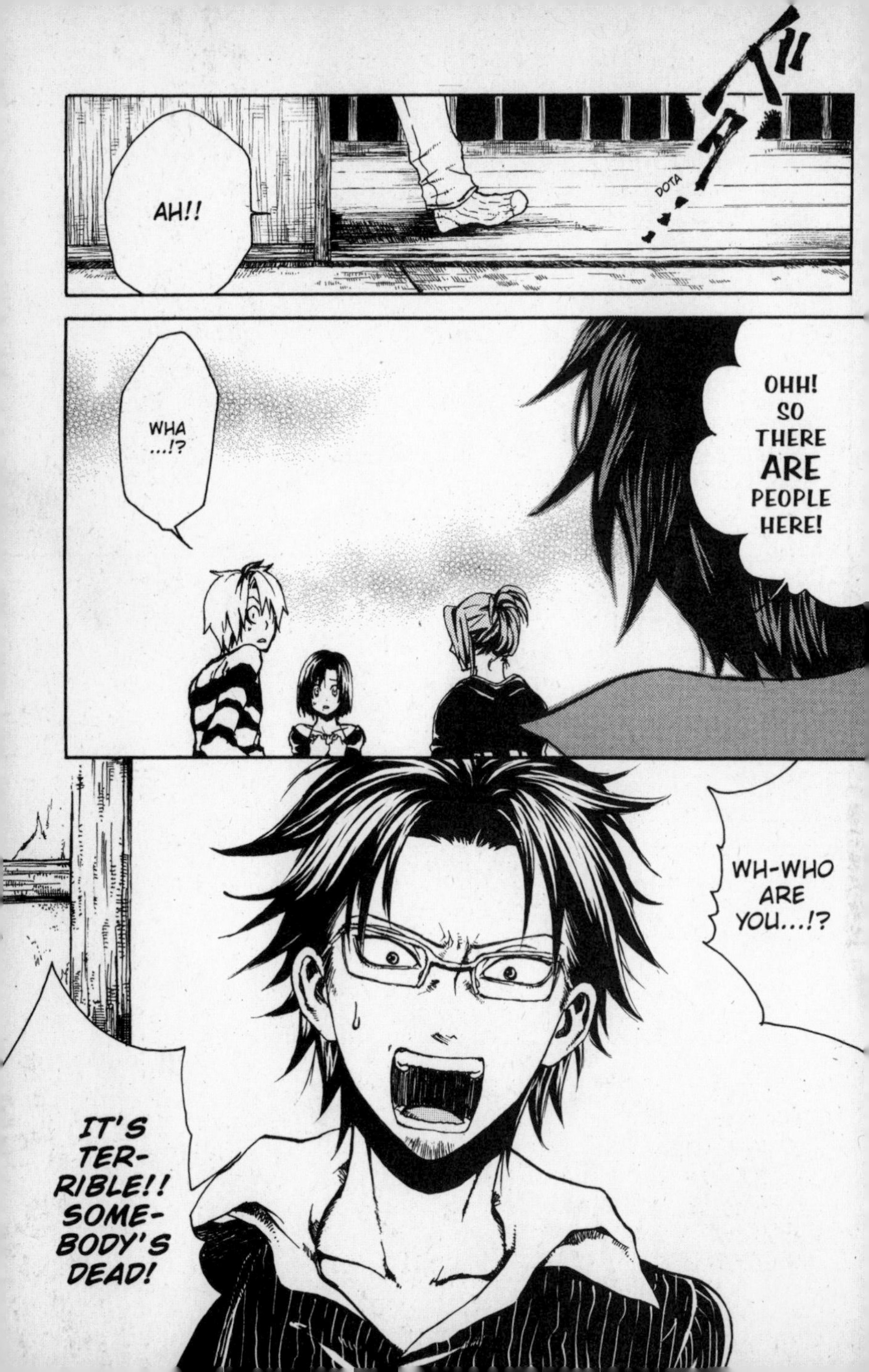
DOTA
AH!!
OHH! SO THERE ARE PEOPLE HERE!
WHA...!?
WH-WHO ARE YOU...!?
IT'S TERRIBLE!! SOMEBODY'S DEAD!

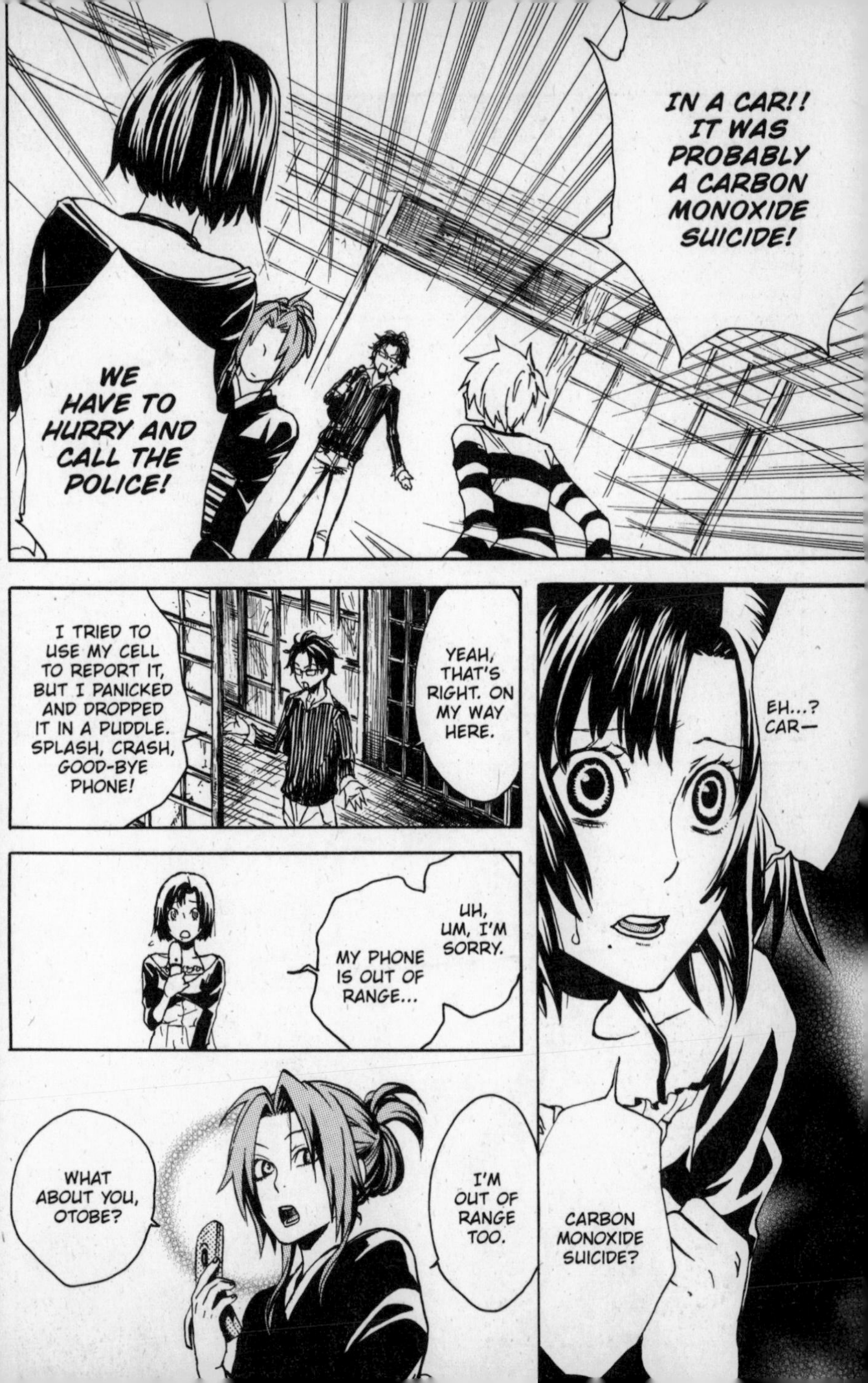
IN A CAR!! IT WAS PROBABLY A CARBON MONOXIDE SUICIDE!
WE HAVE TO HURRY AND CALL THE POLICE!
EH...? CAR—
CARBON MONOXIDE SUICIDE?
YEAH, THAT'S RIGHT. ON MY WAY HERE.
I TRIED TO USE MY CELL TO REPORT IT, BUT I PANICKED AND DROPPED IT IN A PUDDLE. SPLASH, CRASH, GOOD-BYE PHONE!
UH, UM, I'M SORRY.
MY PHONE IS OUT OF RANGE...
I'M OUT OF RANGE TOO.
WHAT ABOUT YOU, OTOBE?

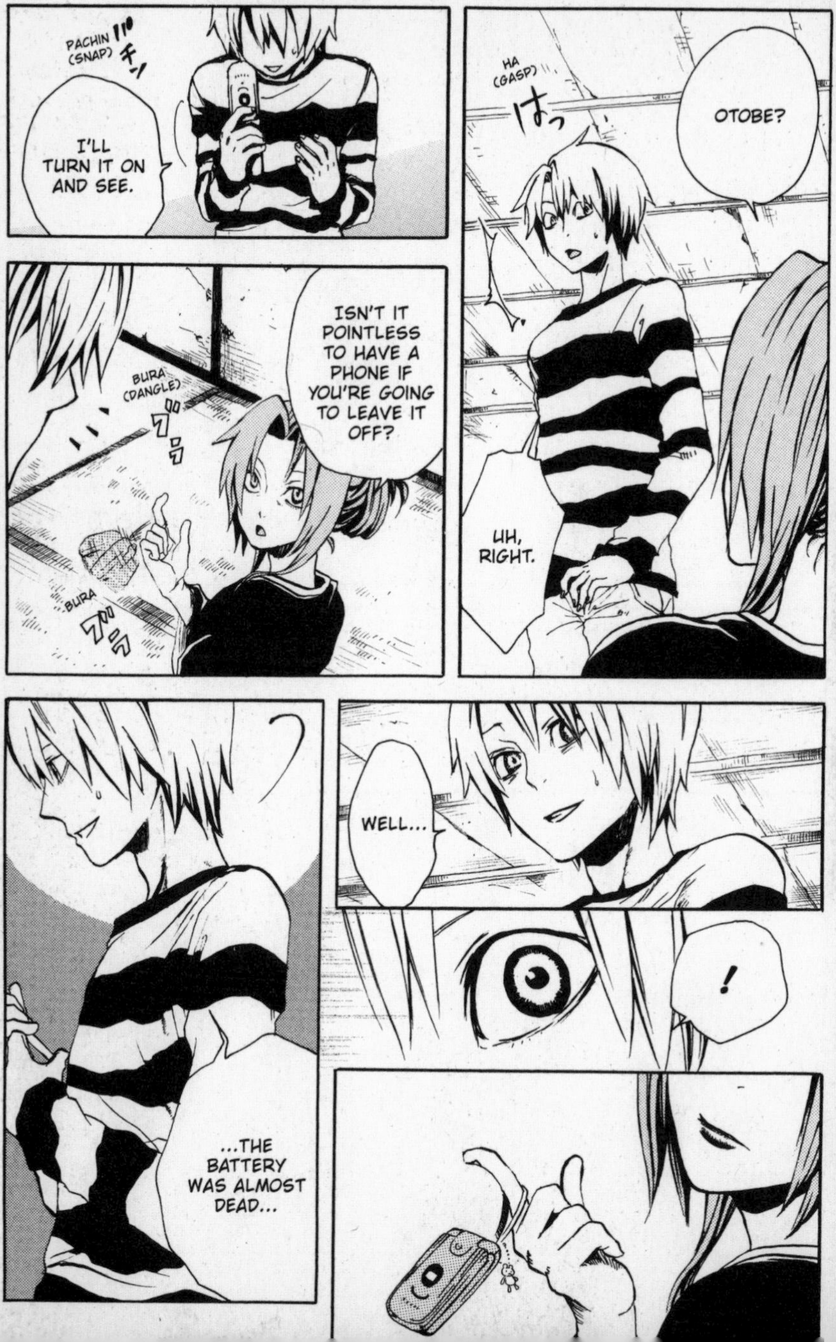
HA (GASP)
はっ
OTOBE?
UH, RIGHT.
PACHIN (SNAP)
パチッ
I'LL TURN IT ON AND SEE.
ISN'T IT POINTLESS TO HAVE A PHONE IF YOU'RE GOING TO LEAVE IT OFF?
BURA (DANGLE)
ブラ
BURA
ブラ
WELL...
!
...THE BATTERY WAS ALMOST DEAD...

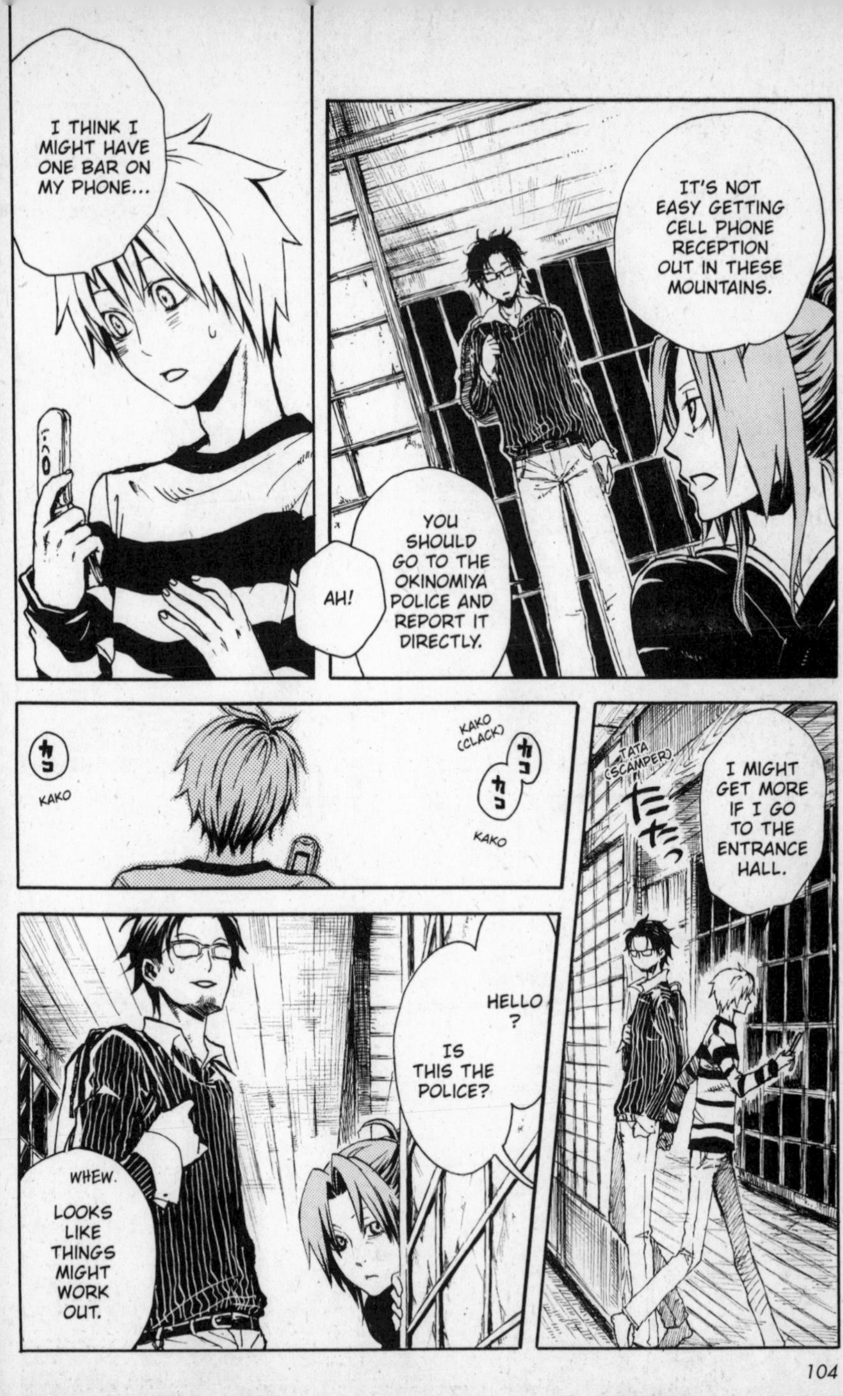
IT'S NOT EASY GETTING CELL PHONE RECEPTION OUT IN THESE MOUNTAINS.
YOU SHOULD GO TO THE OKINOMIYA POLICE AND REPORT IT DIRECTLY.
AH!
I THINK I MIGHT HAVE ONE BAR ON MY PHONE...
I MIGHT GET MORE IF I GO TO THE ENTRANCE HALL.
TATA (SCAMPER)
たたっ
KAKO (CLACK)
カコ
カコ
KAKO
カコ
KAKO
HELLO?
IS THIS THE POLICE?
WHEW.
LOOKS LIKE THINGS MIGHT WORK OUT.

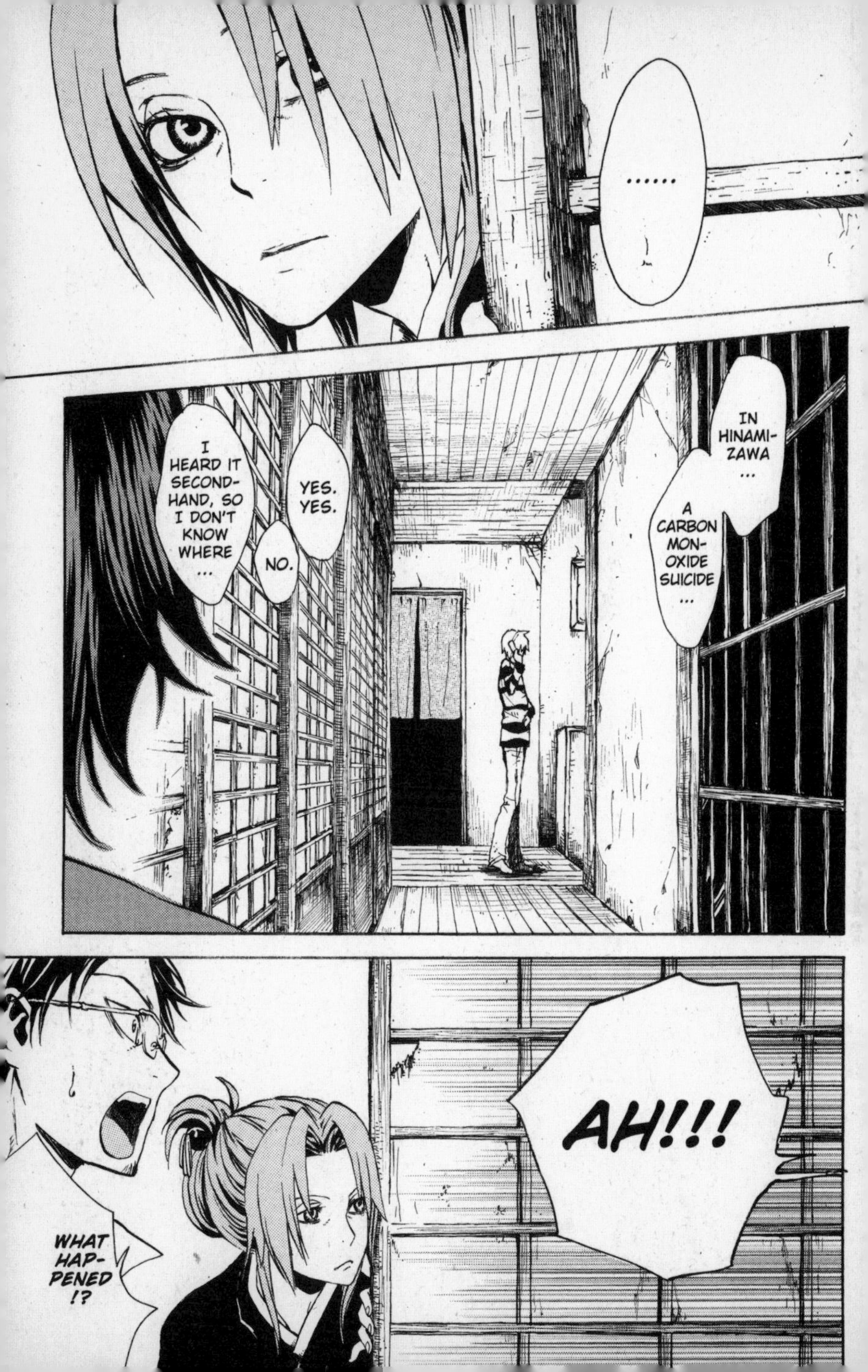
……
IN HINAMI-ZAWA …
A CARBON MON-OXIDE SUICIDE …
YES. YES.
NO.
I HEARD IT SECOND-HAND, SO I DON'T KNOW WHERE …
AH!!!
WHAT HAP-PENED !?

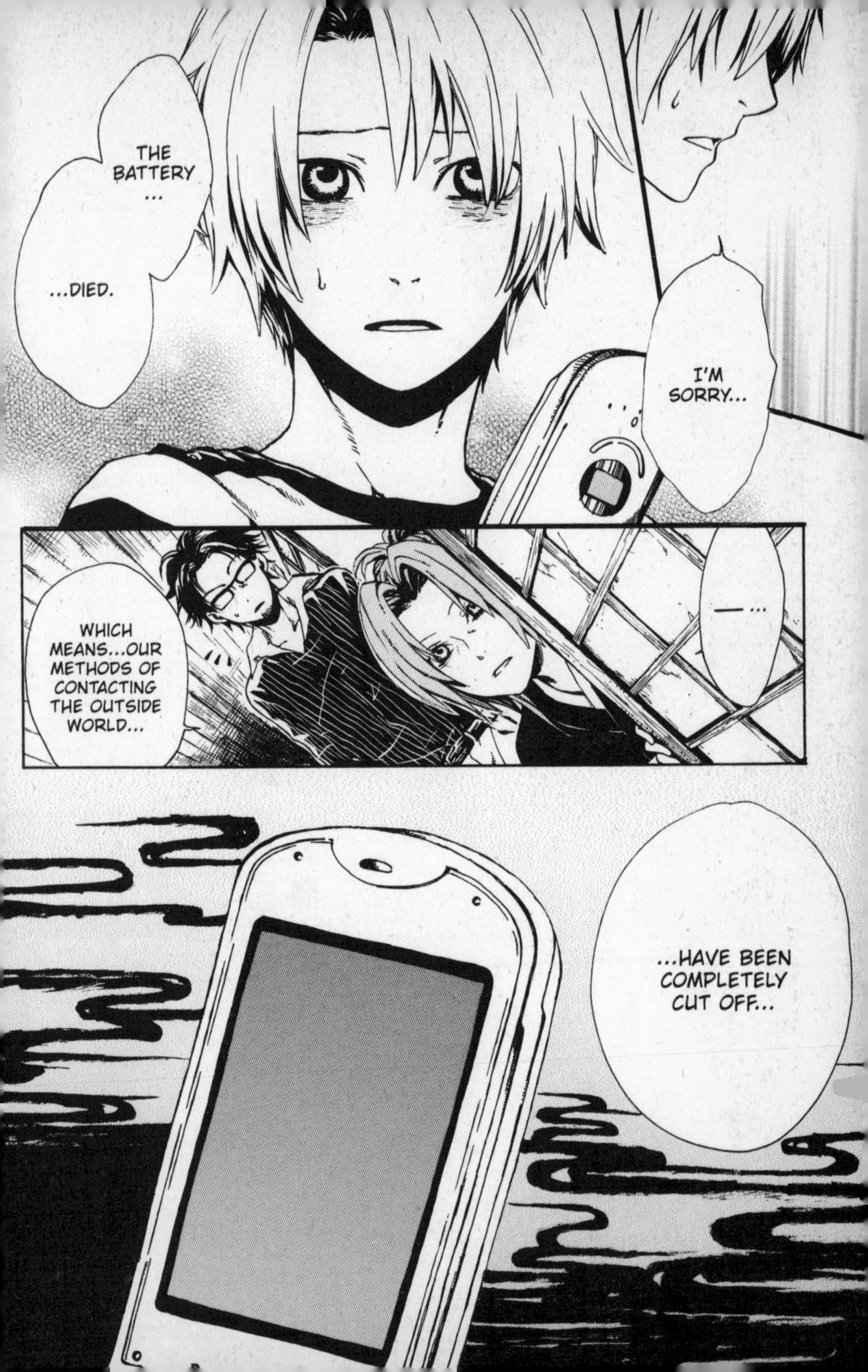
THE BATTERY ... ...DIED.
I'M SORRY...
—...
WHICH MEANS...OUR METHODS OF CONTACTING THE OUTSIDE WORLD...
...HAVE BEEN COMPLETELY CUT OFF...

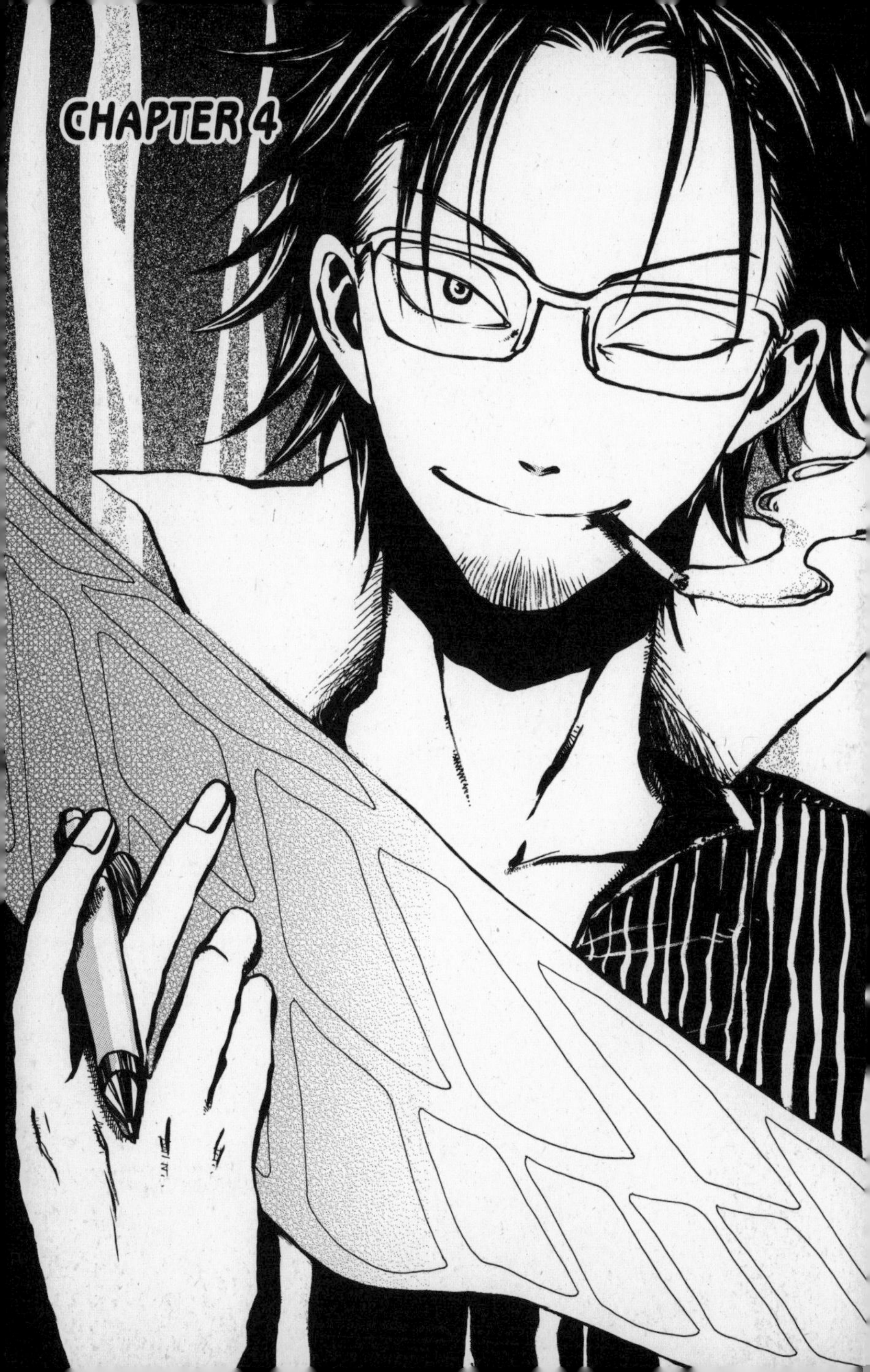
CHAPTER 4

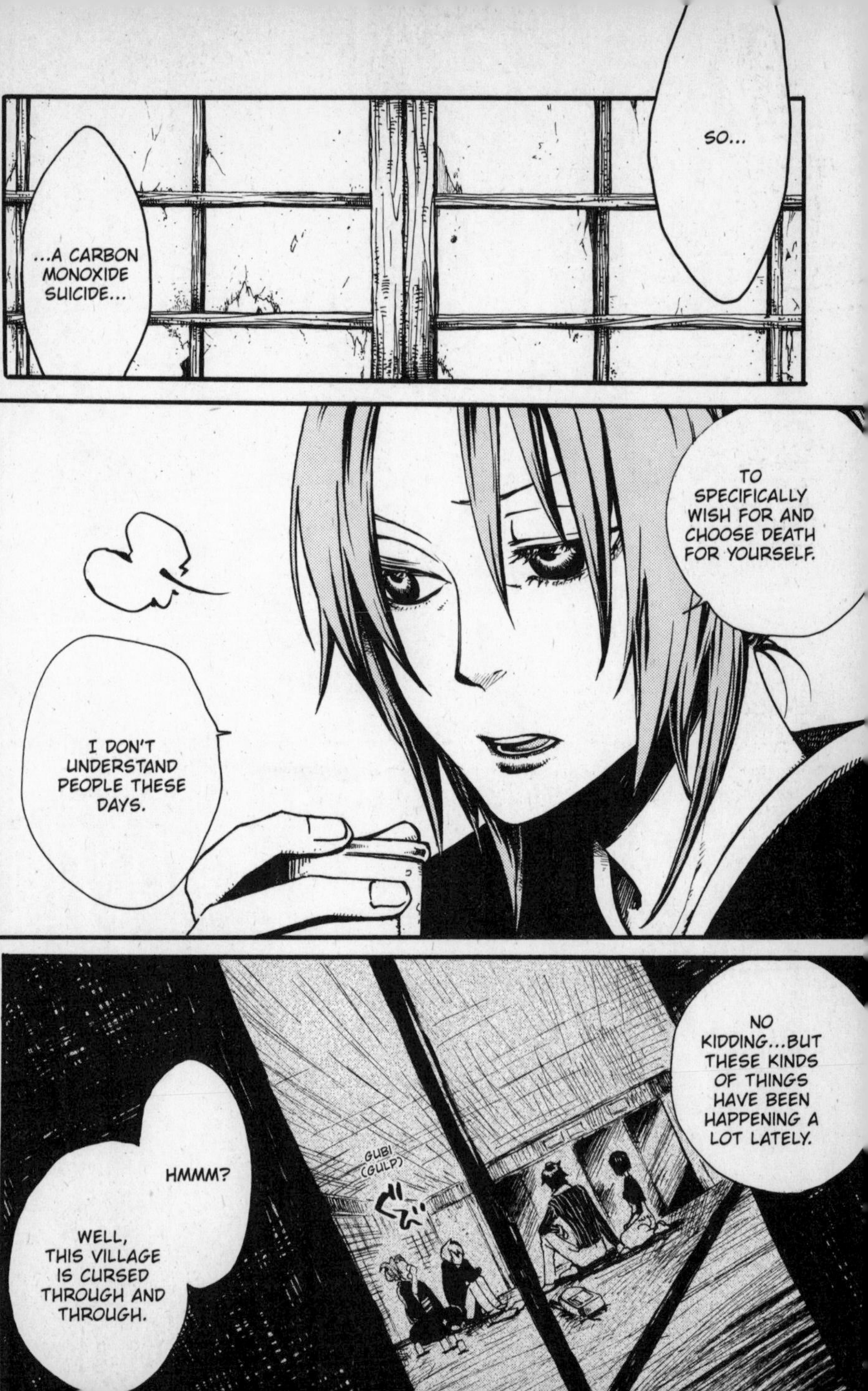
SO...
...A CARBON MONOXIDE SUICIDE...
TO SPECIFICALLY WISH FOR AND CHOOSE DEATH FOR YOURSELF.
I DON'T UNDERSTAND PEOPLE THESE DAYS.
NO KIDDING...BUT THESE KINDS OF THINGS HAVE BEEN HAPPENING A LOT LATELY.
GUBI (GULP)
HMMM?
WELL, THIS VILLAGE IS CURSED THROUGH AND THROUGH.

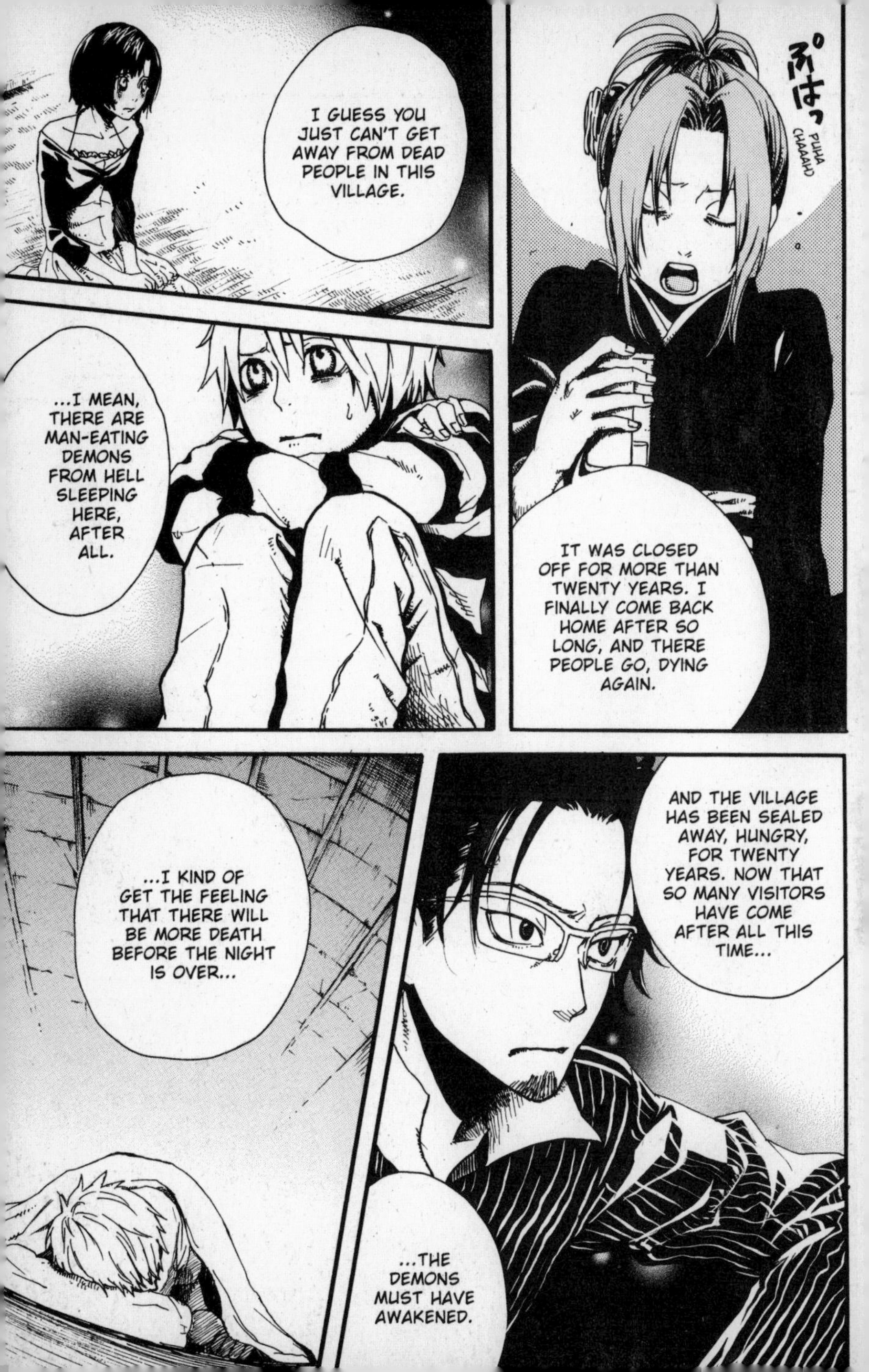
ぷはっ
PUHA CHAAAAH
IT WAS CLOSED OFF FOR MORE THAN TWENTY YEARS. I FINALLY COME BACK HOME AFTER SO LONG, AND THERE PEOPLE GO, DYING AGAIN.
I GUESS YOU JUST CAN'T GET AWAY FROM DEAD PEOPLE IN THIS VILLAGE.
...I MEAN, THERE ARE MAN-EATING DEMONS FROM HELL SLEEPING HERE, AFTER ALL.
AND THE VILLAGE HAS BEEN SEALED AWAY, HUNGRY, FOR TWENTY YEARS. NOW THAT SO MANY VISITORS HAVE COME AFTER ALL THIS TIME...
...THE DEMONS MUST HAVE AWAKENED.
...I KIND OF GET THE FEELING THAT THERE WILL BE MORE DEATH BEFORE THE NIGHT IS OVER...

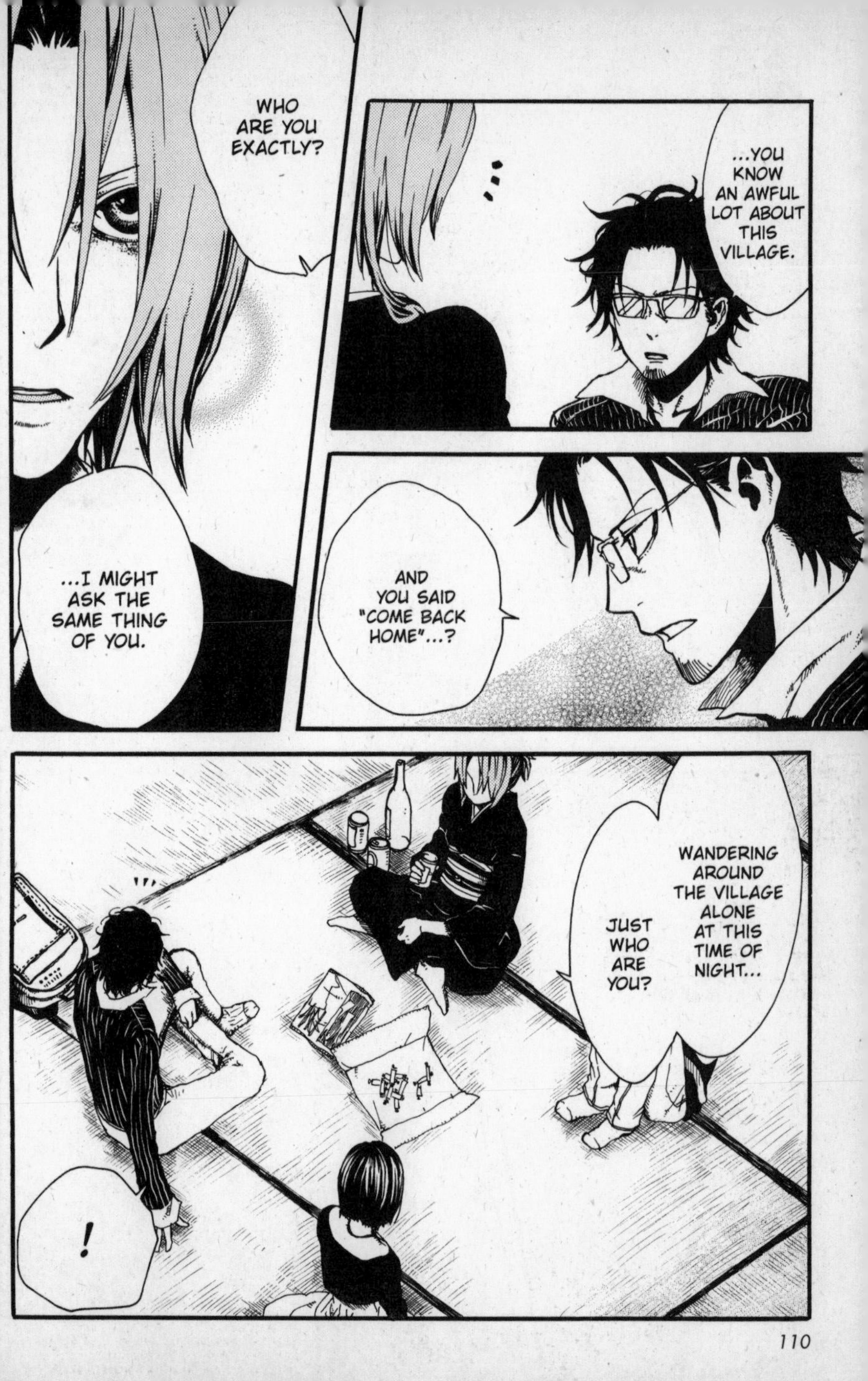
...YOU KNOW AN AWFUL LOT ABOUT THIS VILLAGE.
AND YOU SAID "COME BACK HOME"...?
WHO ARE YOU EXACTLY?
...I MIGHT ASK THE SAME THING OF YOU.
WANDERING AROUND THE VILLAGE ALONE AT THIS TIME OF NIGHT...
JUST WHO ARE YOU?
!

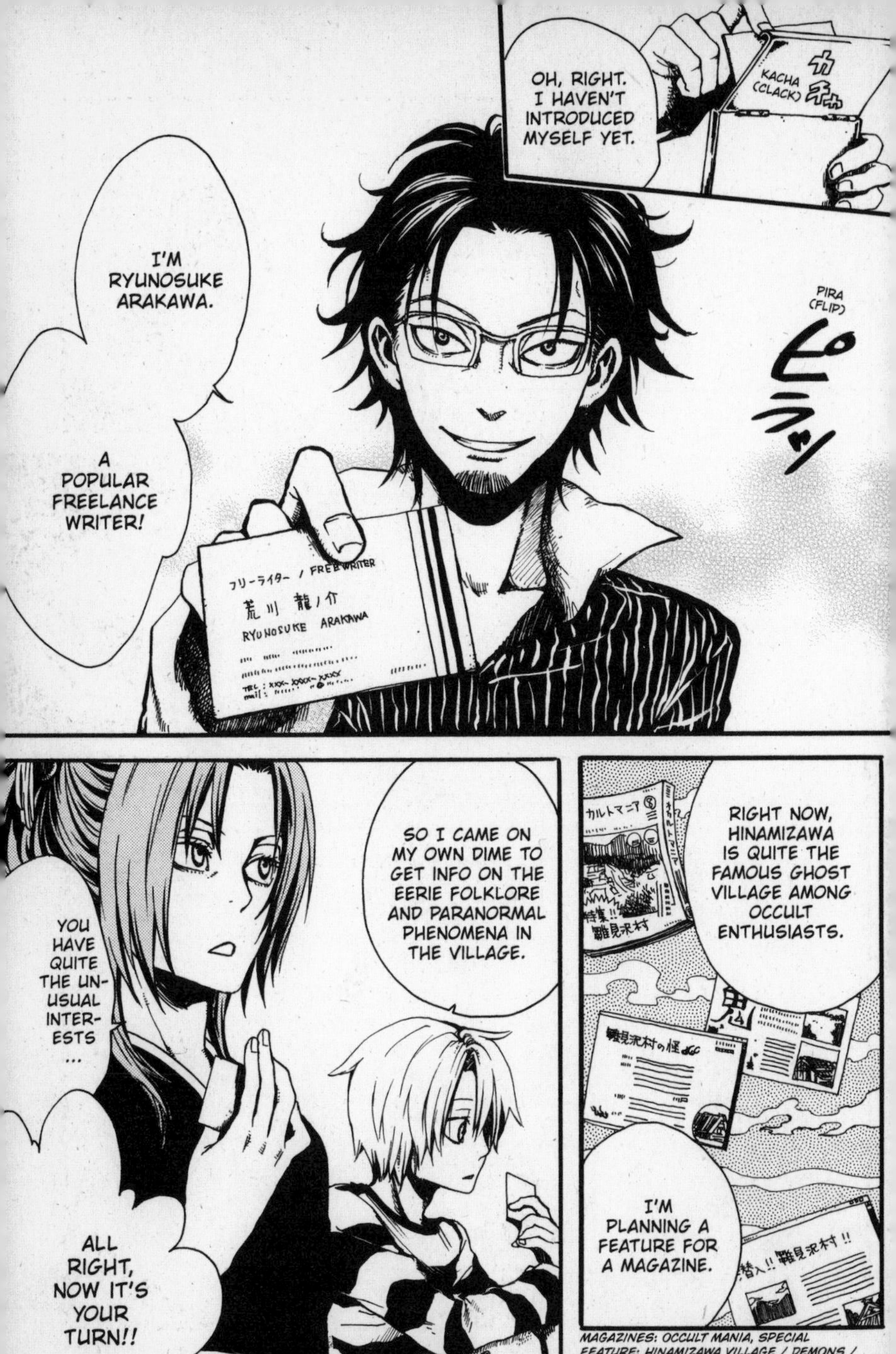
OH, RIGHT. I HAVEN'T INTRODUCED MYSELF YET.
KACHA (CLACK)
カチャ
I'M RYUNOSUKE ARAKAWA.
A POPULAR FREELANCE WRITER!
PIRA (FLIP)
ピラッ
フリーライター / FREE WRITER
荒川 龍ノ介
RYUNOSUKE ARAKAWA
RIGHT NOW, HINAMIZAWA IS QUITE THE FAMOUS GHOST VILLAGE AMONG OCCULT ENTHUSIASTS.
カルトマニア
特集!! 雛見沢村
鬼
雛見沢村の怪
潜入!! 雛見沢村!!
I'M PLANNING A FEATURE FOR A MAGAZINE.
SO I CAME ON MY OWN DIME TO GET INFO ON THE EERIE FOLKLORE AND PARANORMAL PHENOMENA IN THE VILLAGE.
YOU HAVE QUITE THE UN-USUAL INTER-ESTS ...
ALL RIGHT, NOW IT'S YOUR TURN!!

MAGAZINES: OCCULT MANIA, SPECIAL FEATURE: HINAMIZAWA VILLAGE / DEMONS / THE MYSTERIES OF HINAMIZAWA / INFILTRATION!! HINAMIZAWA VILLAGE!!

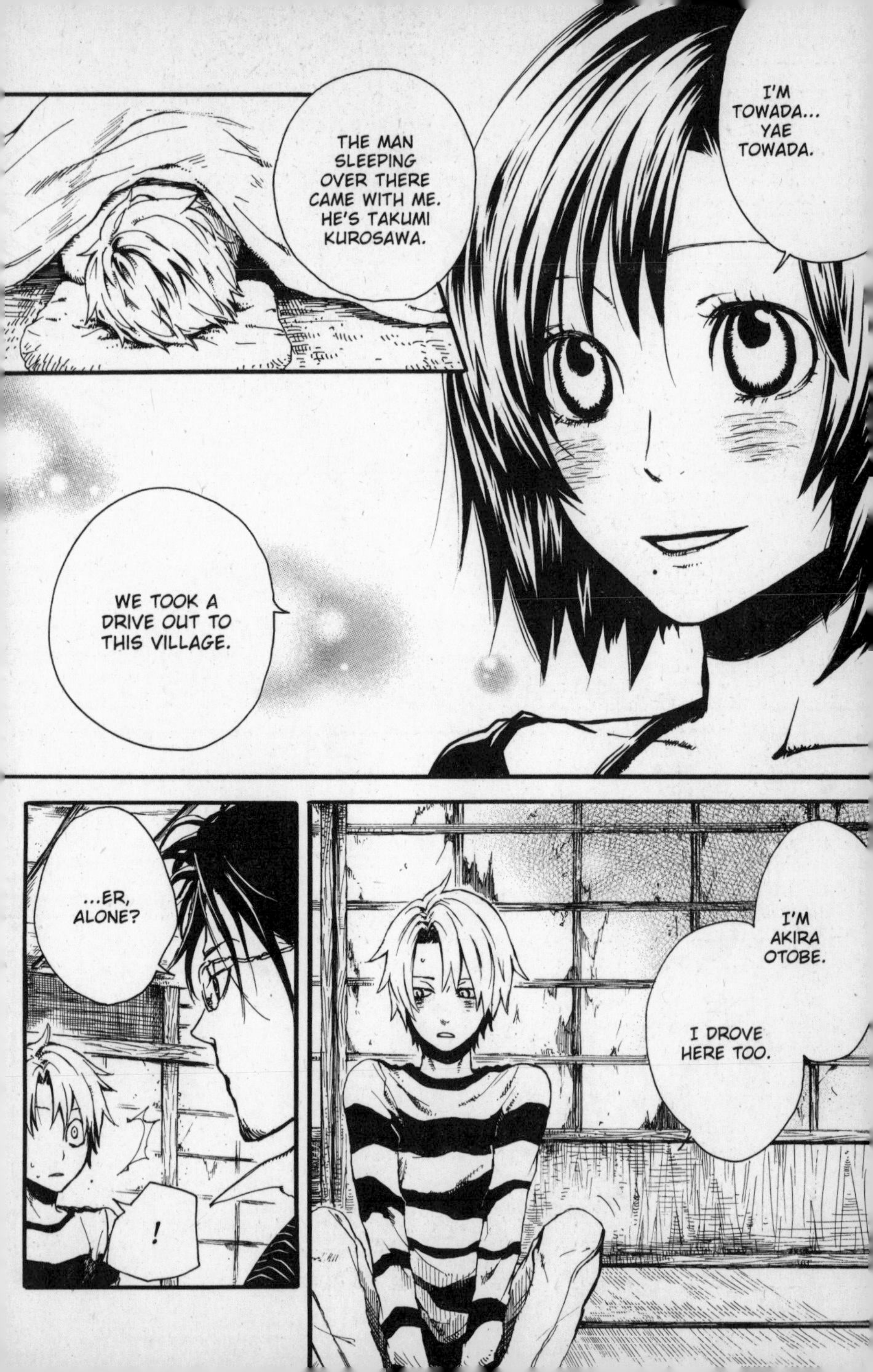
I'M TOWADA... YAE TOWADA.
THE MAN SLEEPING OVER THERE CAME WITH ME. HE'S TAKUMI KUROSAWA.
WE TOOK A DRIVE OUT TO THIS VILLAGE.
I'M AKIRA OTOBE.
I DROVE HERE TOO.
...ER, ALONE?
!

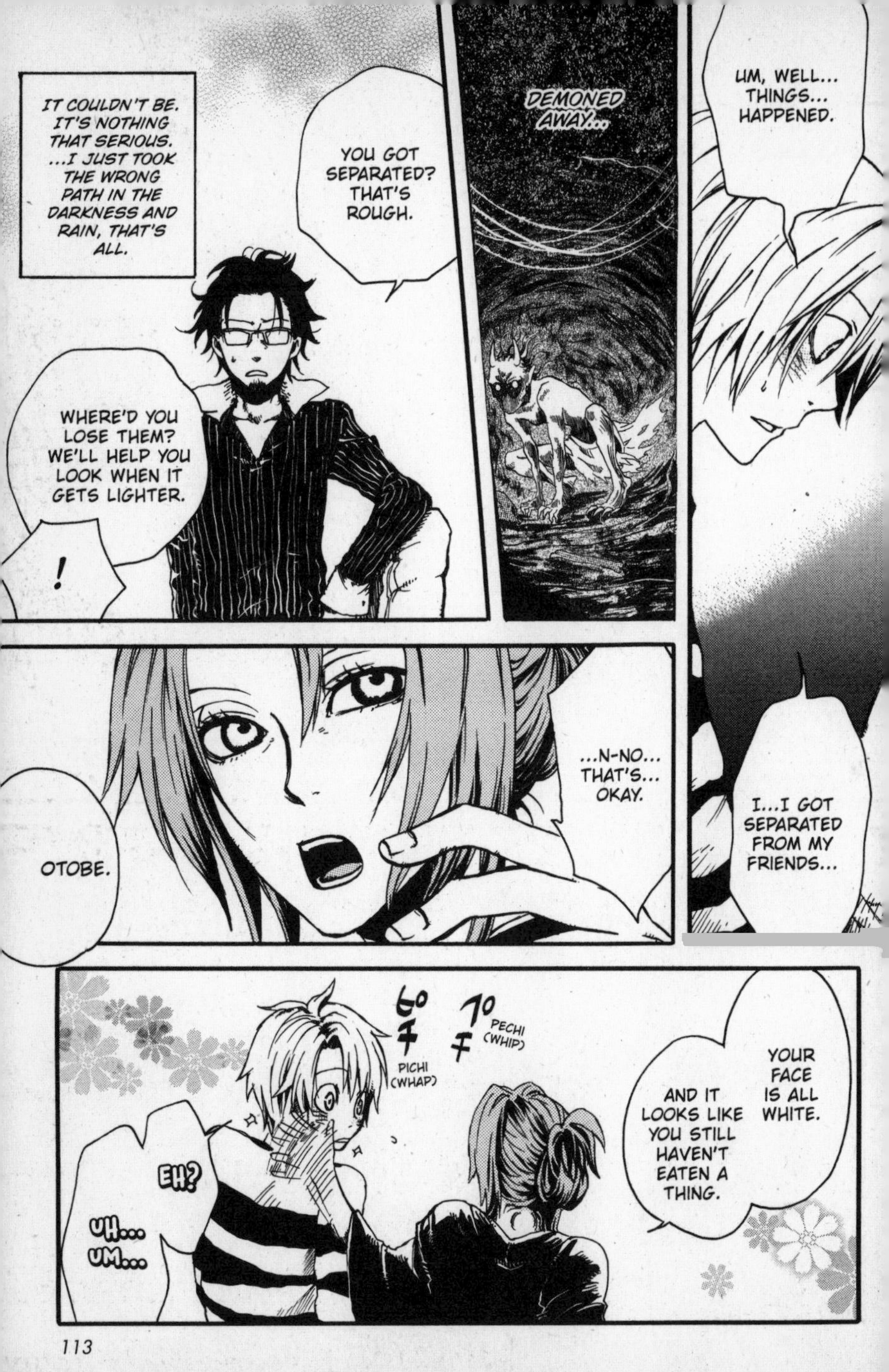
UM, WELL... THINGS... HAPPENED.
I...I GOT SEPARATED FROM MY FRIENDS...
DEMONED AWAY...
YOU GOT SEPARATED? THAT'S ROUGH.
IT COULDN'T BE. IT'S NOTHING THAT SERIOUS. ...I JUST TOOK THE WRONG PATH IN THE DARKNESS AND RAIN, THAT'S ALL.
WHERE'D YOU LOSE THEM? WE'LL HELP YOU LOOK WHEN IT GETS LIGHTER.
!
...N-NO... THAT'S... OKAY.
OTOBE.
YOUR FACE IS ALL WHITE.
AND IT LOOKS LIKE YOU STILL HAVEN'T EATEN A THING.
ペチ
PECHI (WHIP)
ピチ
PICHI (WHAP)
EH?
UH... UM...

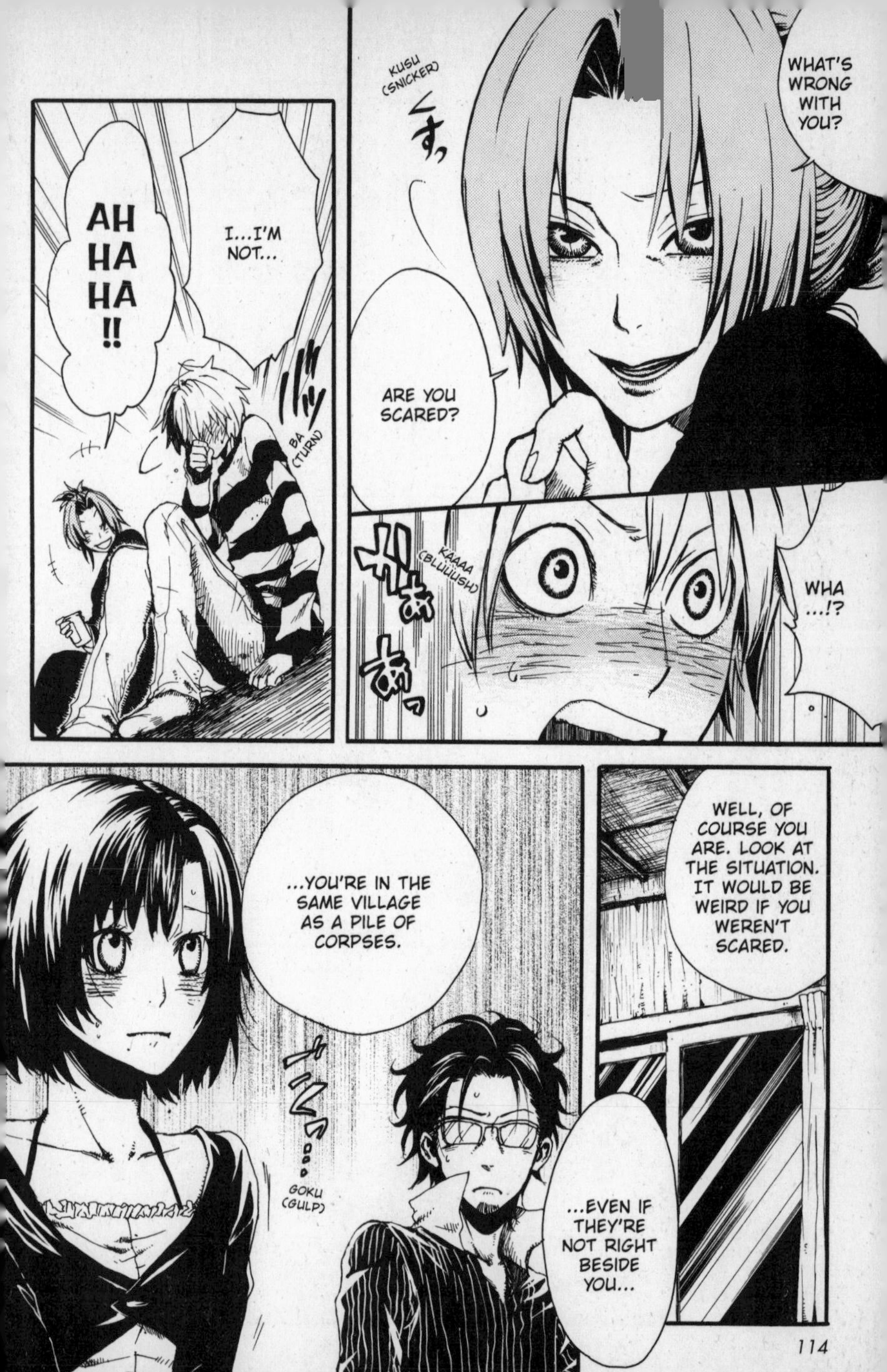
KUSU (SNICKER)
くすっ
WHAT'S WRONG WITH YOU?
ARE YOU SCARED?
KAAAA (BLUUUSH)
WHA ...!?
BA (TURN)
I...I'M NOT...
AH HA HA!!
WELL, OF COURSE YOU ARE. LOOK AT THE SITUATION. IT WOULD BE WEIRD IF YOU WEREN'T SCARED.
...YOU'RE IN THE SAME VILLAGE AS A PILE OF CORPSES.
GOKU (GULP)
...EVEN IF THEY'RE NOT RIGHT BESIDE YOU...

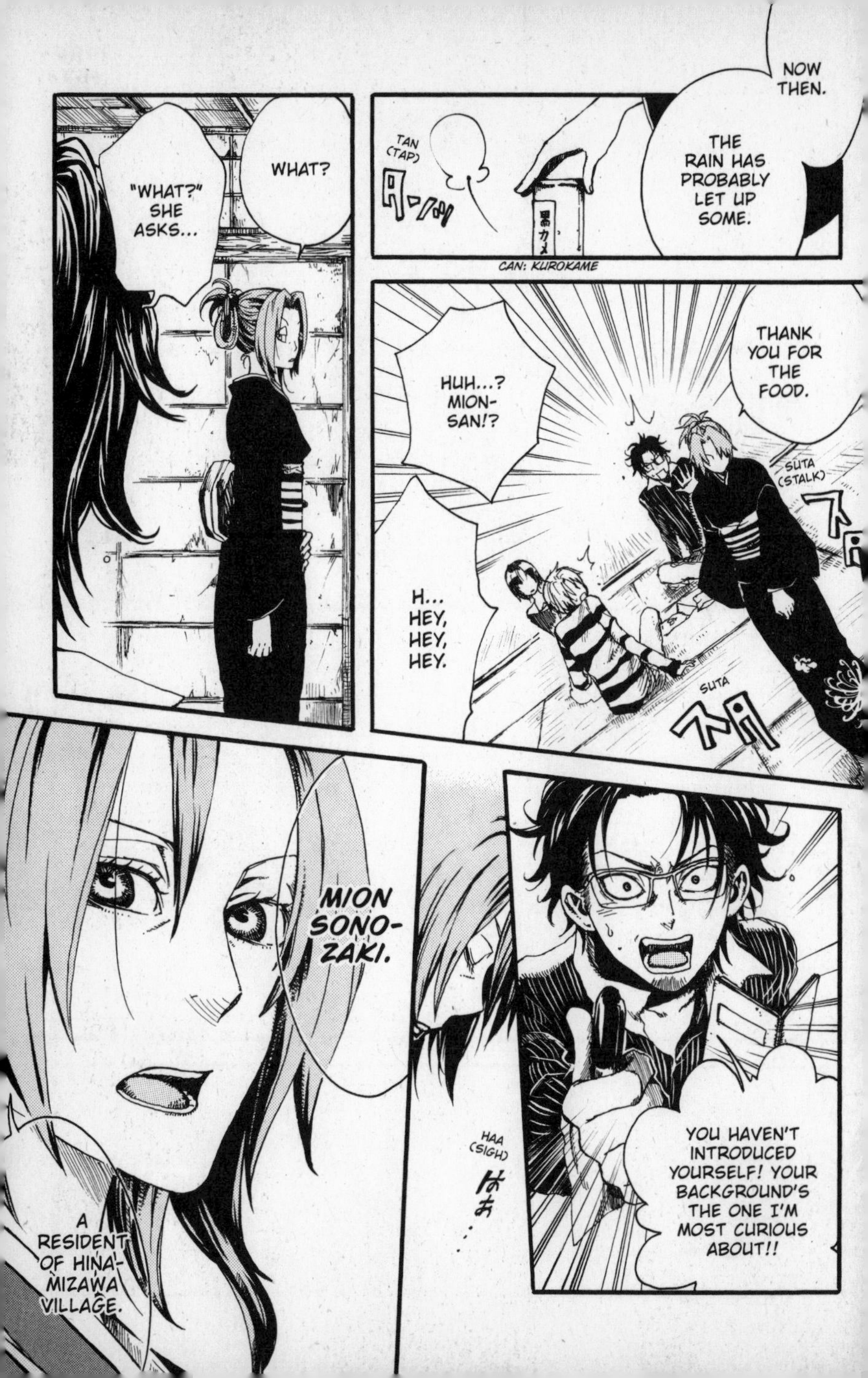
NOW THEN.
THE RAIN HAS PROBABLY LET UP SOME.
TAN (TAP)
CAN: KUROKAME
THANK YOU FOR THE FOOD.
SUTA (STALK)
HUH...? MION-SAN!?
H... HEY, HEY, HEY.
SUTA
WHAT?
"WHAT?" SHE ASKS...
YOU HAVEN'T INTRODUCED YOURSELF! YOUR BACKGROUND'S THE ONE I'M MOST CURIOUS ABOUT!!
HAA (SIGH)
MION SONO-ZAKI.
A RESIDENT OF HINA-MIZAWA VILLAGE.

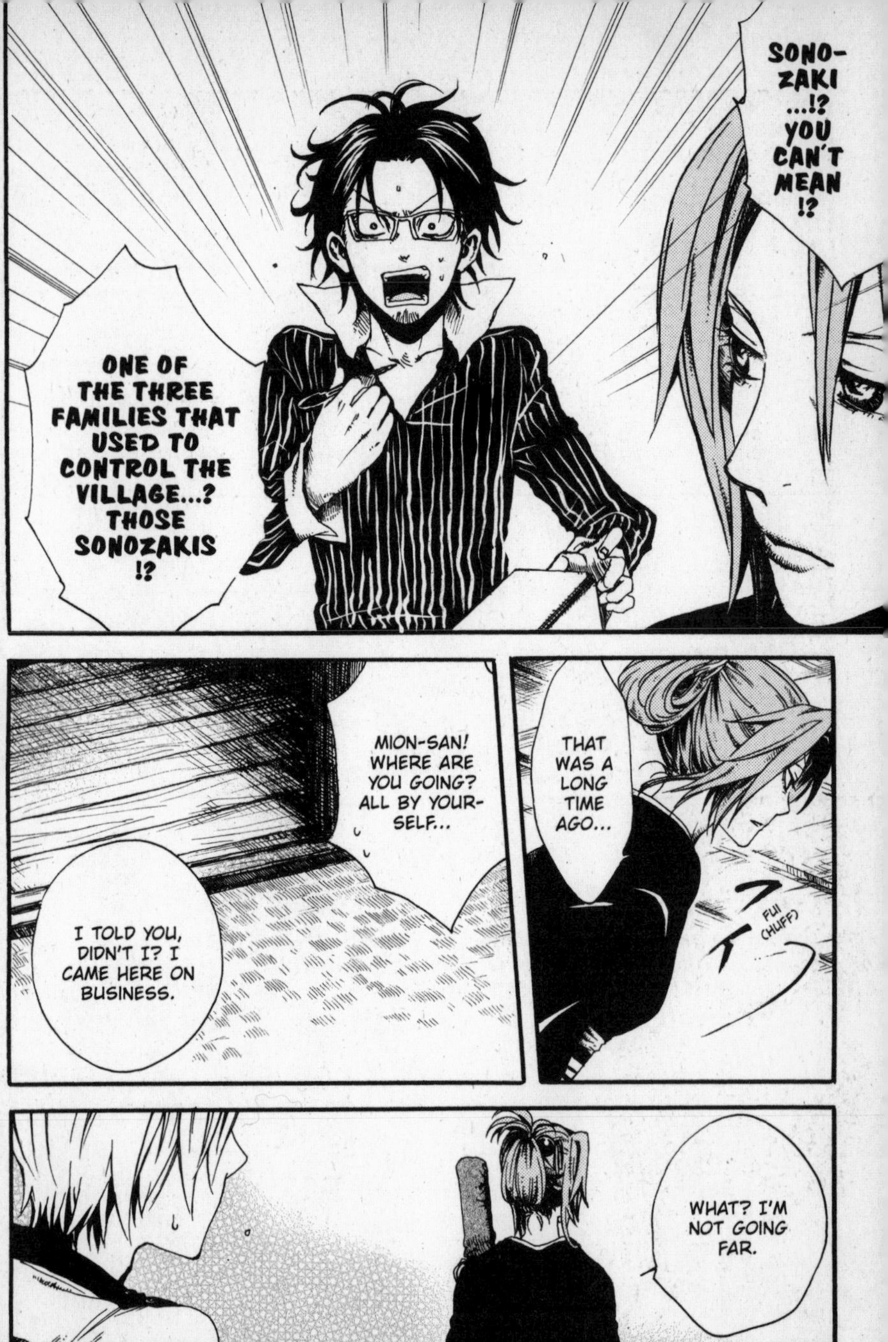
SONO-ZAKI ...!? YOU CAN'T MEAN !?
ONE OF THE THREE FAMILIES THAT USED TO CONTROL THE VILLAGE...? THOSE SONOZAKIS !?
THAT WAS A LONG TIME AGO...
FUI (HUFF)
MION-SAN! WHERE ARE YOU GOING? ALL BY YOURSELF...
I TOLD YOU, DIDN'T I? I CAME HERE ON BUSINESS.
WHAT? I'M NOT GOING FAR.

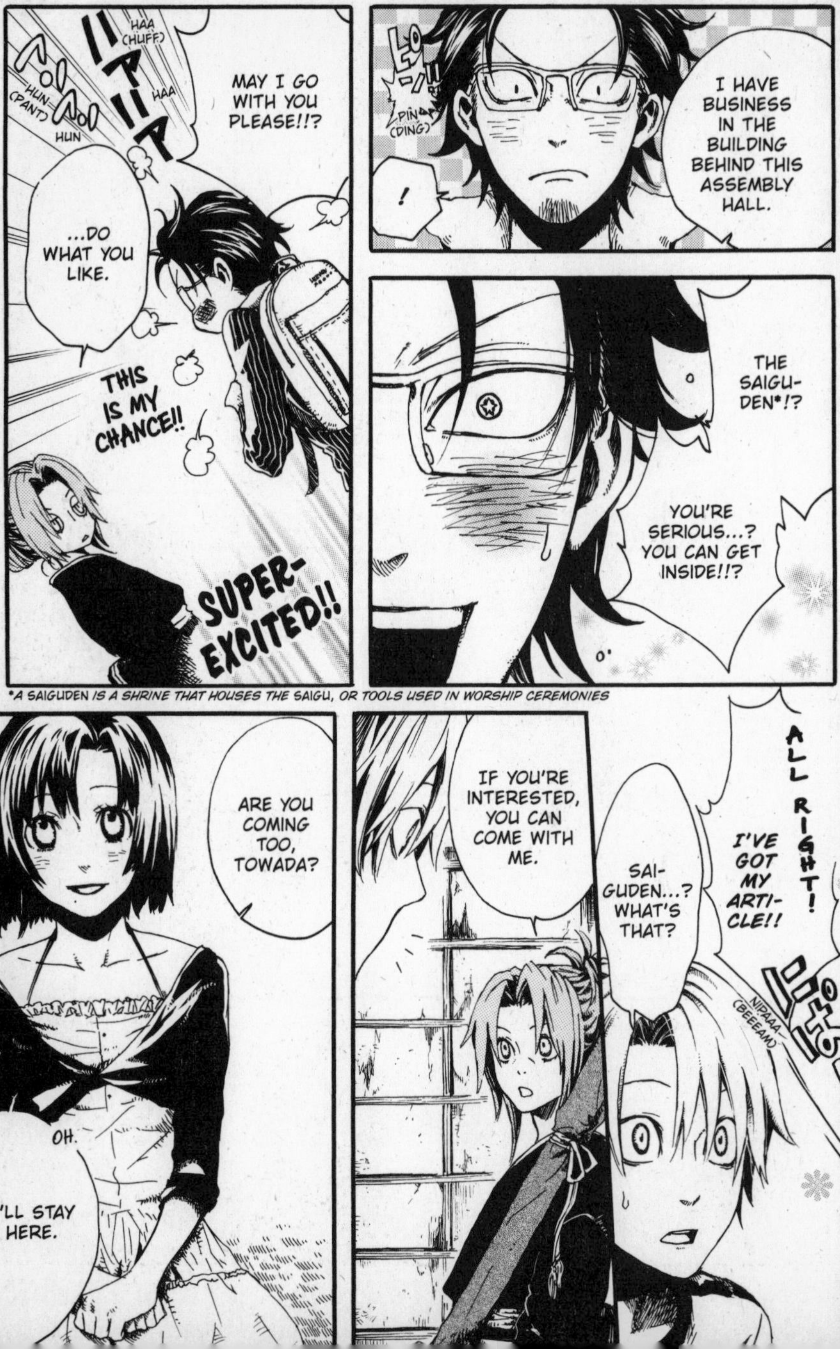
PIN (DING)
!
I HAVE BUSINESS IN THE BUILDING BEHIND THIS ASSEMBLY HALL.
THE SAIGU-DEN*!?
YOU'RE SERIOUS...? YOU CAN GET INSIDE!!?
HAA (HUFF) HAA
HUN (PANT) HUN
MAY I GO WITH YOU PLEASE!!?
...DO WHAT YOU LIKE.
THIS IS MY CHANCE!!
SUPER-EXCITED!!
IF YOU'RE INTERESTED, YOU CAN COME WITH ME.
SAI-GUDEN...? WHAT'S THAT?
ALL RIGHT! I'VE GOT MY ARTI-CLE!!
NIPAAA (BEEEAM)
ARE YOU COMING TOO, TOWADA?
OH.
I'LL STAY HERE.

*A SAIGUDEN IS A SHRINE THAT HOUSES THE SAIGU, OR TOOLS USED IN WORSHIP CEREMONIES

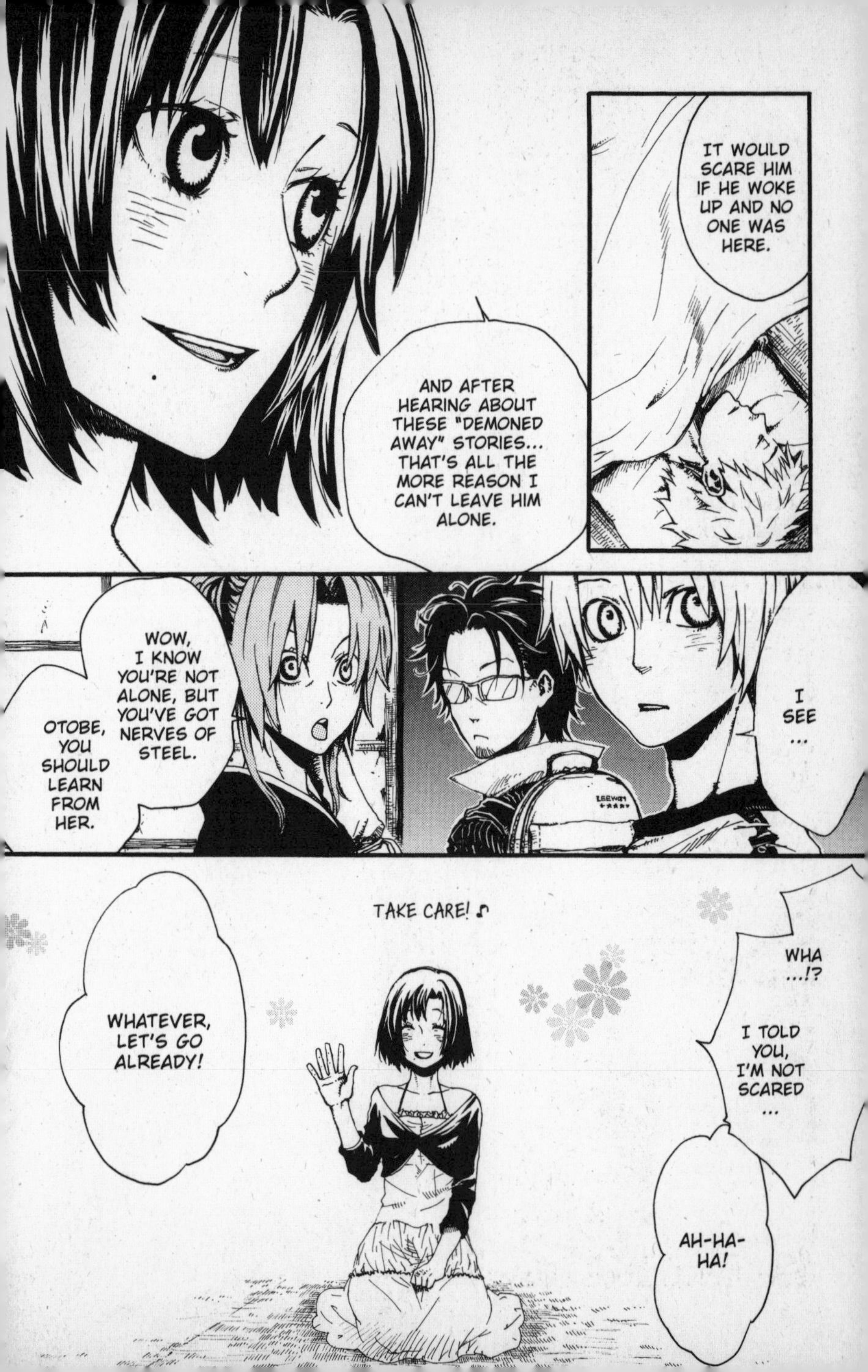
IT WOULD SCARE HIM IF HE WOKE UP AND NO ONE WAS HERE.
AND AFTER HEARING ABOUT THESE "DEMONED AWAY" STORIES... THAT'S ALL THE MORE REASON I CAN'T LEAVE HIM ALONE.
I SEE ...
WOW, I KNOW YOU'RE NOT ALONE, BUT YOU'VE GOT NERVES OF STEEL.
OTOBE, YOU SHOULD LEARN FROM HER.
WHA ...!?
I TOLD YOU, I'M NOT SCARED ...
TAKE CARE! ♪
AH-HA-HA!
WHATEVER, LET'S GO ALREADY!

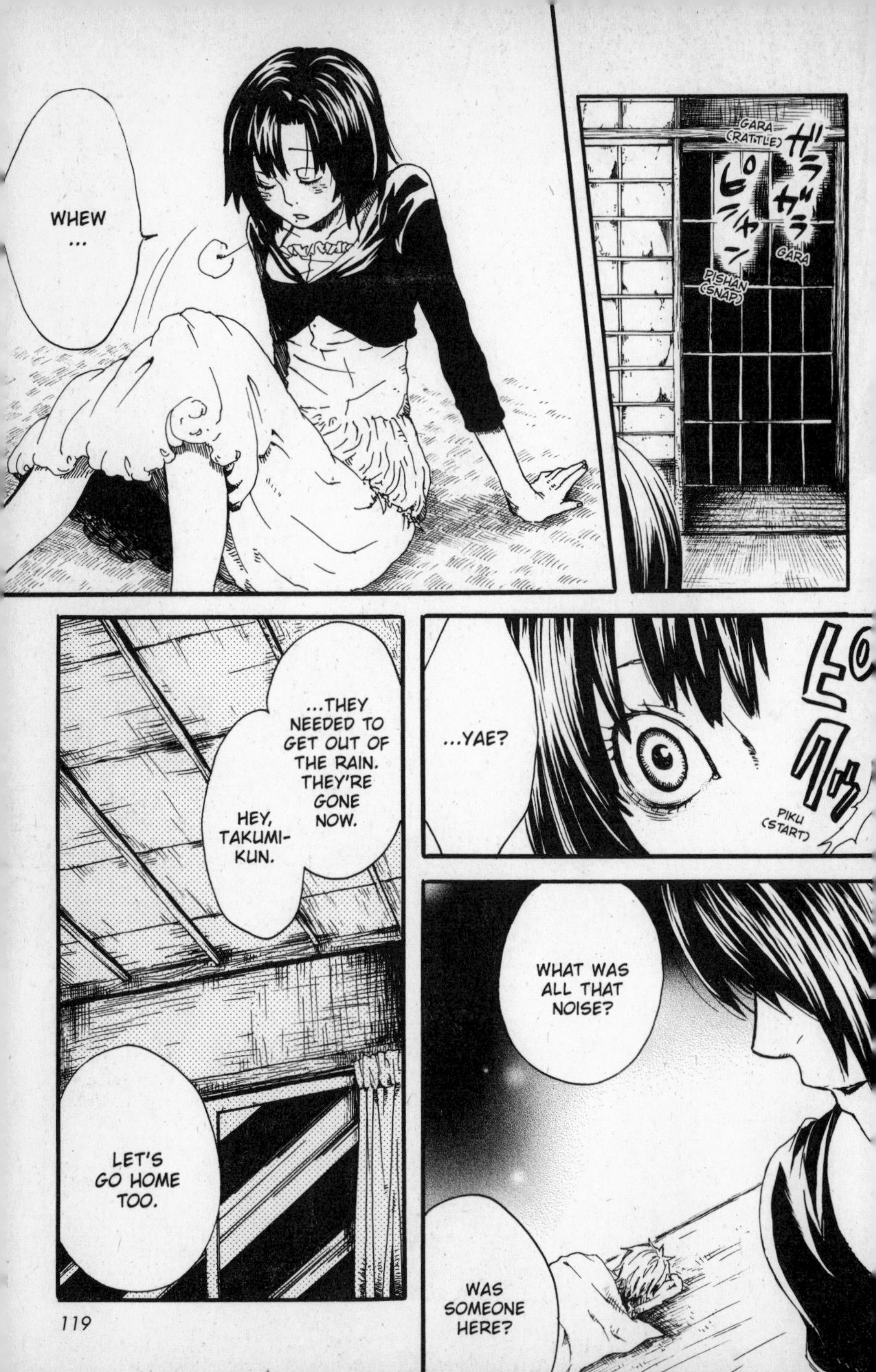

GARA (RATTLE)
GARA
PISHAN (SNAP)
WHEW …
PIKU (START)
…YAE?
WHAT WAS ALL THAT NOISE?
WAS SOMEONE HERE?
…THEY NEEDED TO GET OUT OF THE RAIN. THEY'RE GONE NOW.
HEY, TAKUMI-KUN.
LET'S GO HOME TOO.

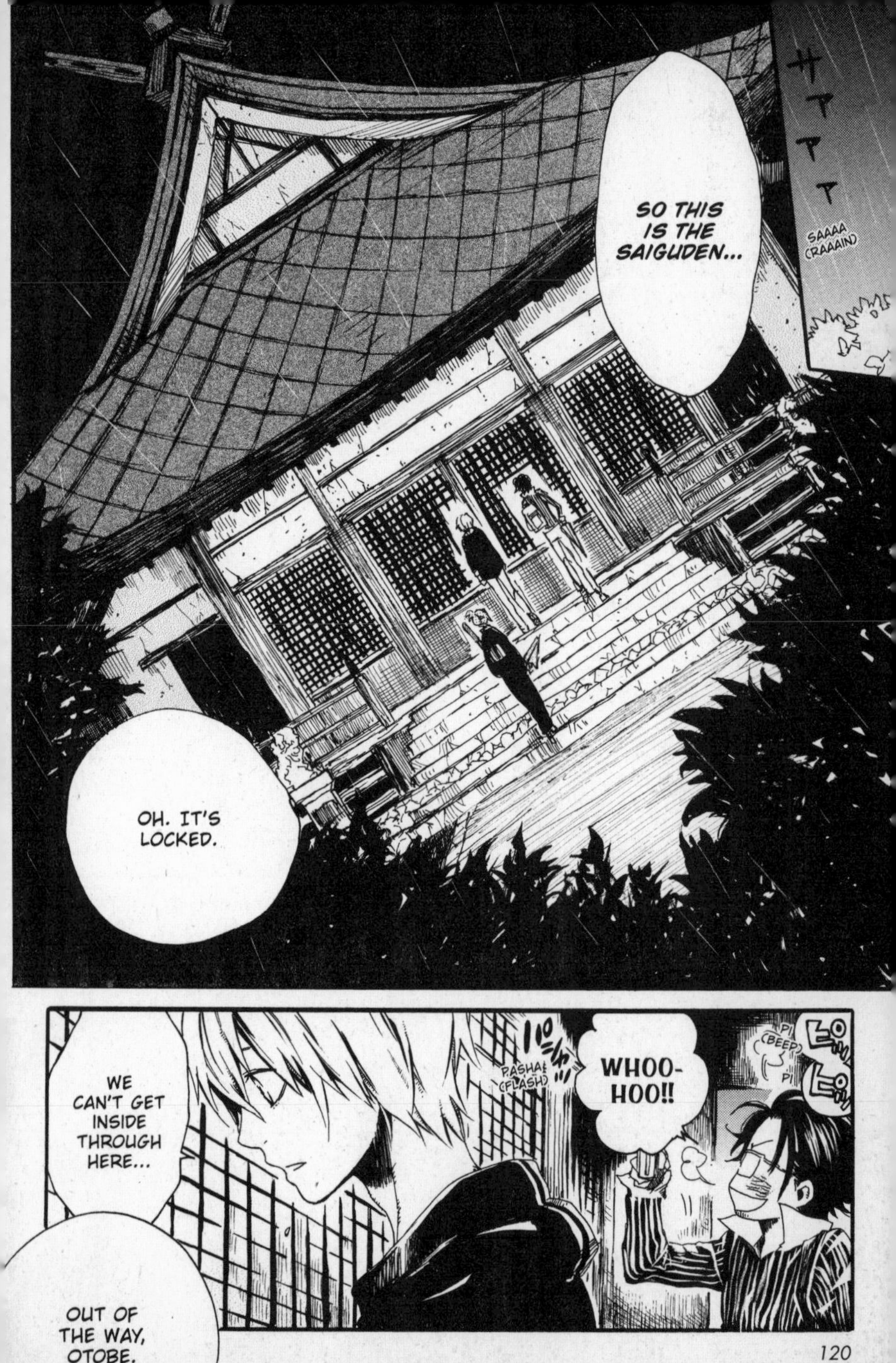
SO THIS IS THE SAIGUDEN...
SAAAA (RAAAIN)
OH. IT'S LOCKED.
PI (BEEP) PI
WHOO-HOO!!
PASHA (FLASH)
WE CAN'T GET INSIDE THROUGH HERE...
OUT OF THE WAY, OTOBE.

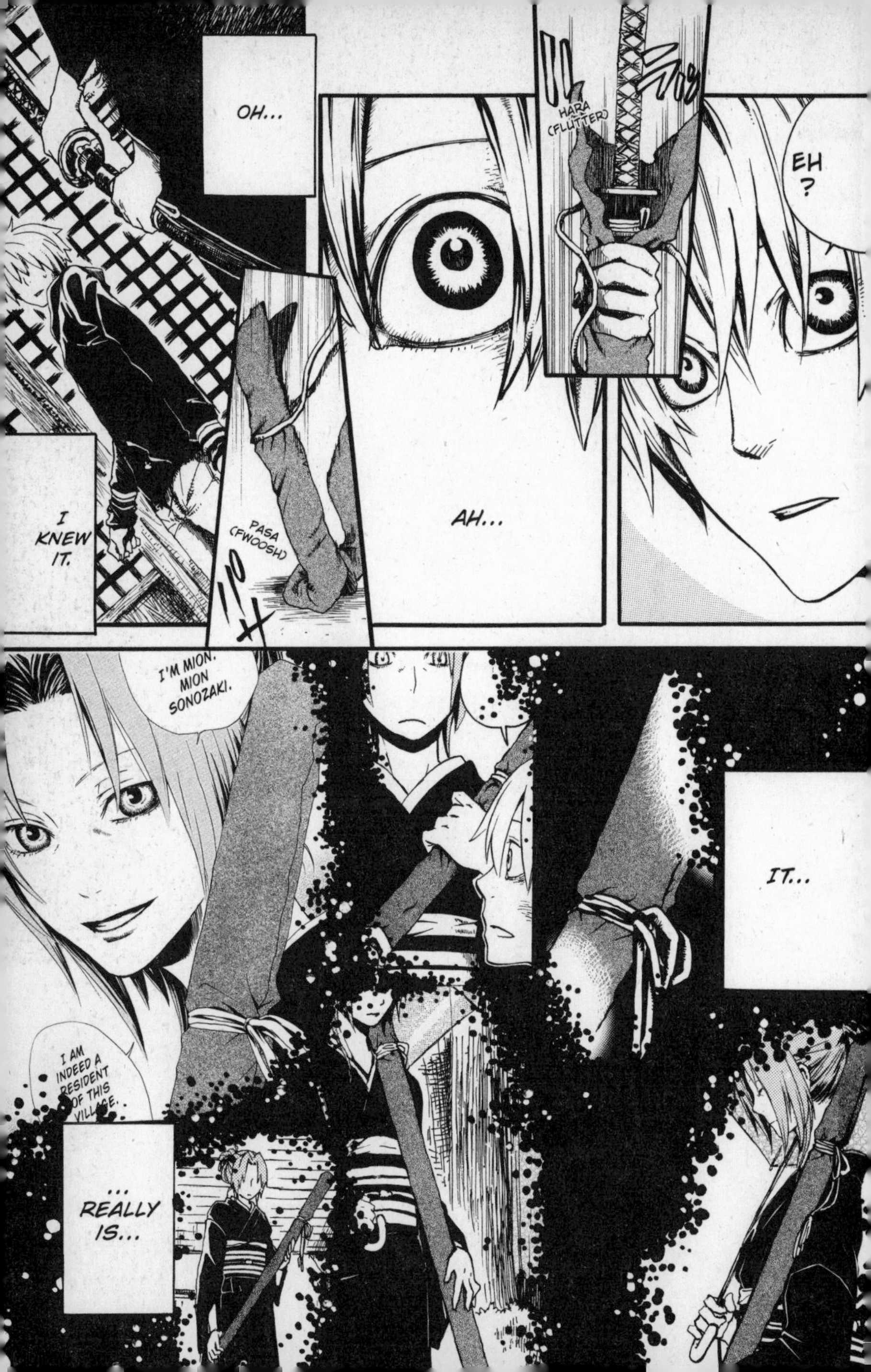
EH?
HARA (FLUTTER)
AH...
PASA (FWOOSH)
OH...
I KNEW IT.
IT...
I'M MION. MION SONOZAKI.
I AM INDEED A RESIDENT OF THIS VILLAGE.
... REALLY IS...

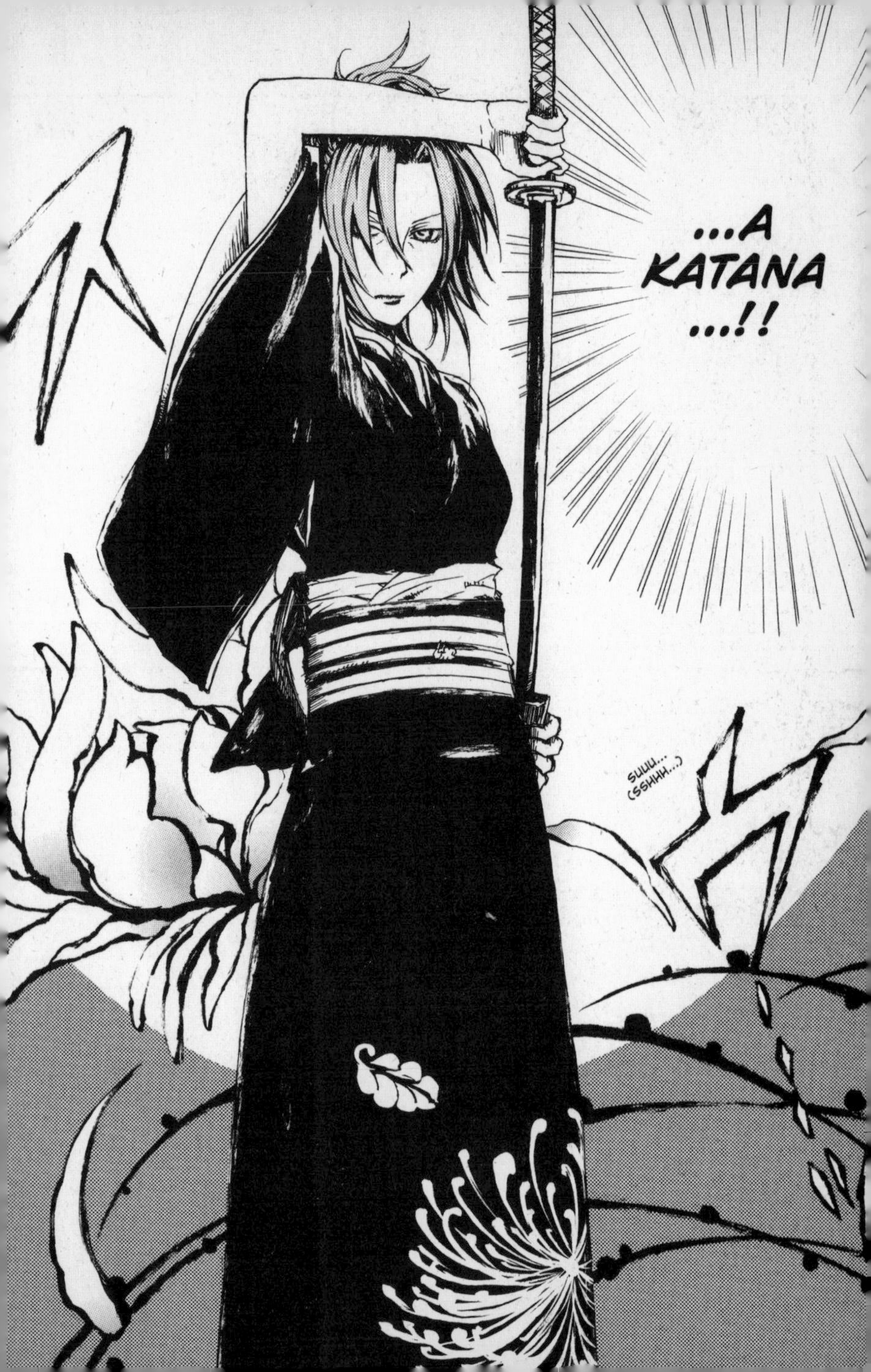
...A KATANA ...!!
SUUU... (SSHHH...)

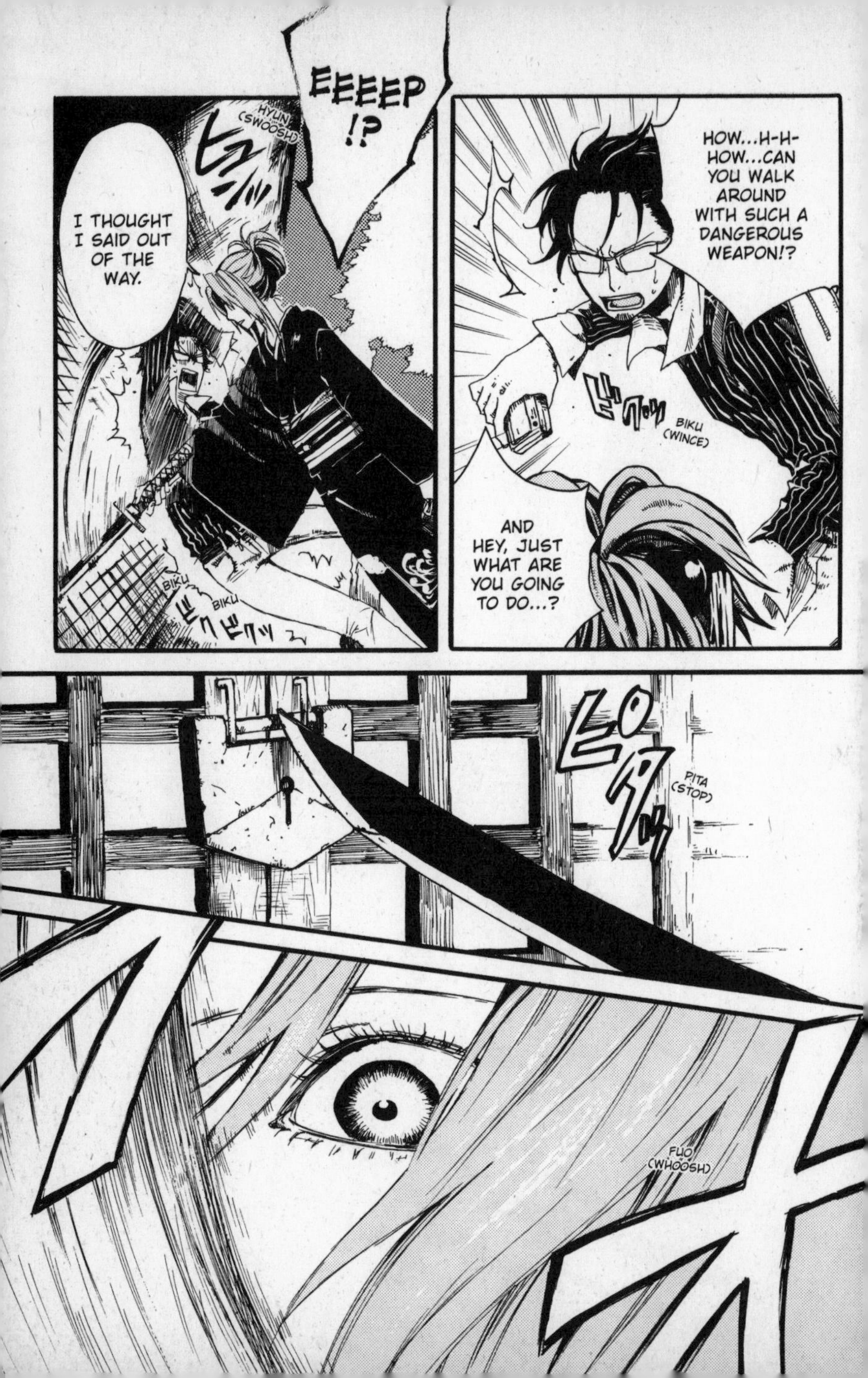
HOW...H-H-HOW...CAN YOU WALK AROUND WITH SUCH A DANGEROUS WEAPON!?
BIKU (WINCE)
AND HEY, JUST WHAT ARE YOU GOING TO DO...?
EEEEP !?
HYUN (SWOOSH)
I THOUGHT I SAID OUT OF THE WAY.
BIKU BIKU
PITA (STOP)
FUO (WHOOSH)

KIIIN
(KLING)

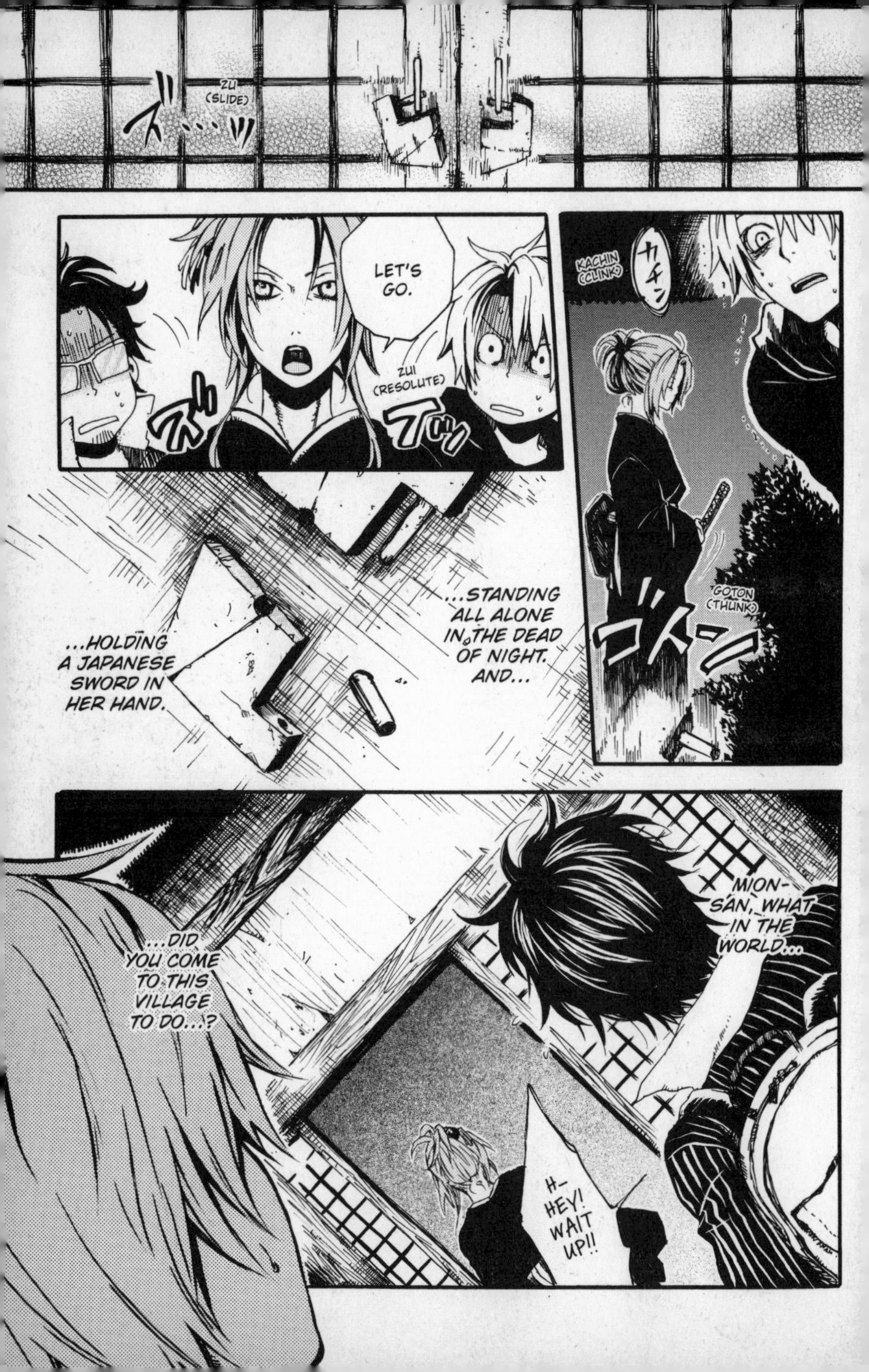
ZU (SLIDE)
KACHIN (CLINK)
GOTON (THUNK)
LET'S GO.
ZUI (RESOLUTE)
...STANDING ALL ALONE IN THE DEAD OF NIGHT. AND...
...HOLDING A JAPANESE SWORD IN HER HAND.
MION-SAN, WHAT IN THE WORLD...
...DID YOU COME TO THIS VILLAGE TO DO...?
H-HEY! WAIT UP!!

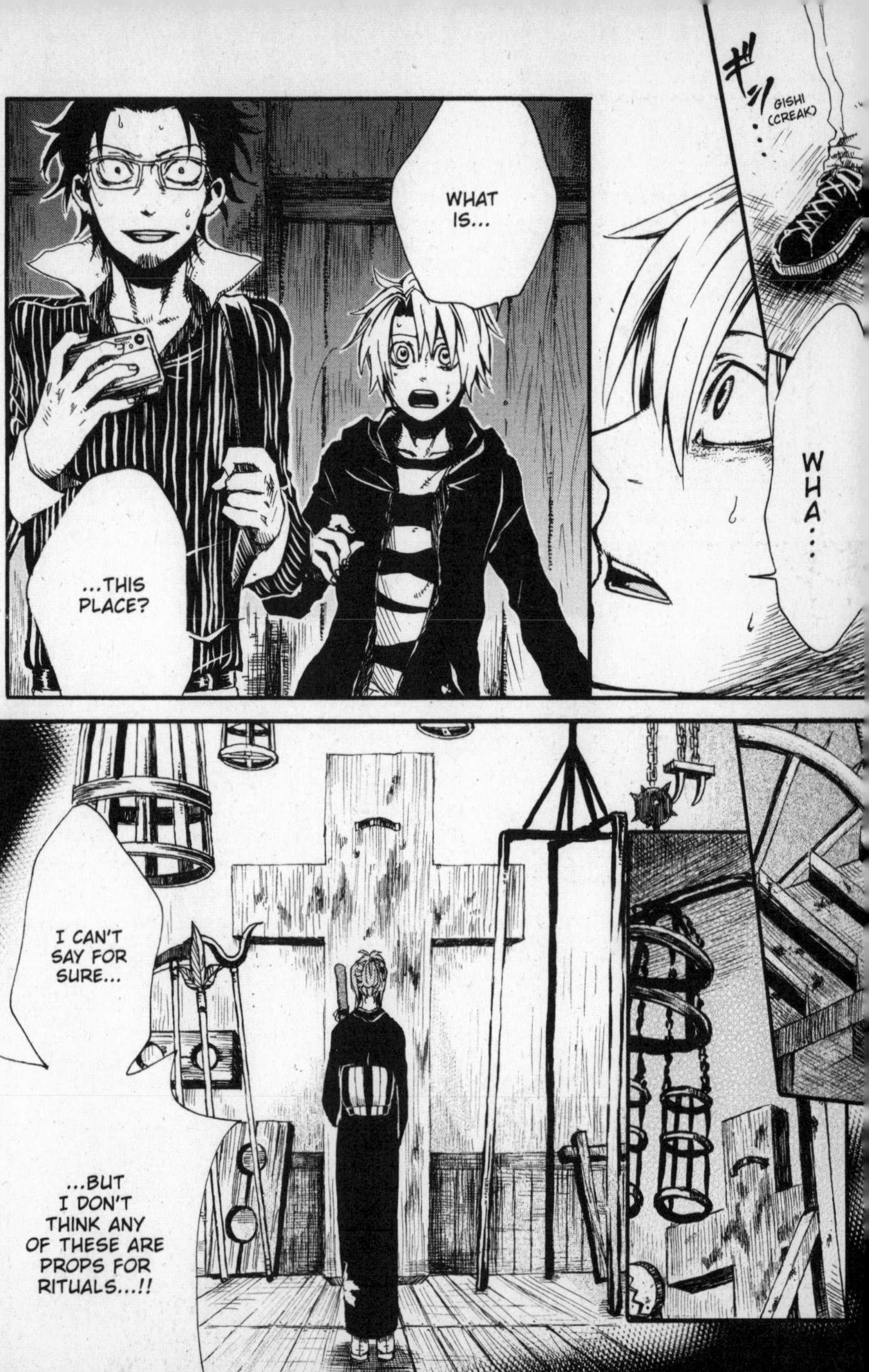
ギシ
GISHI (CREAK)
WHA...
WHAT IS...
...THIS PLACE?
I CAN'T SAY FOR SURE...
...BUT I DON'T THINK ANY OF THESE ARE PROPS FOR RITUALS...!!

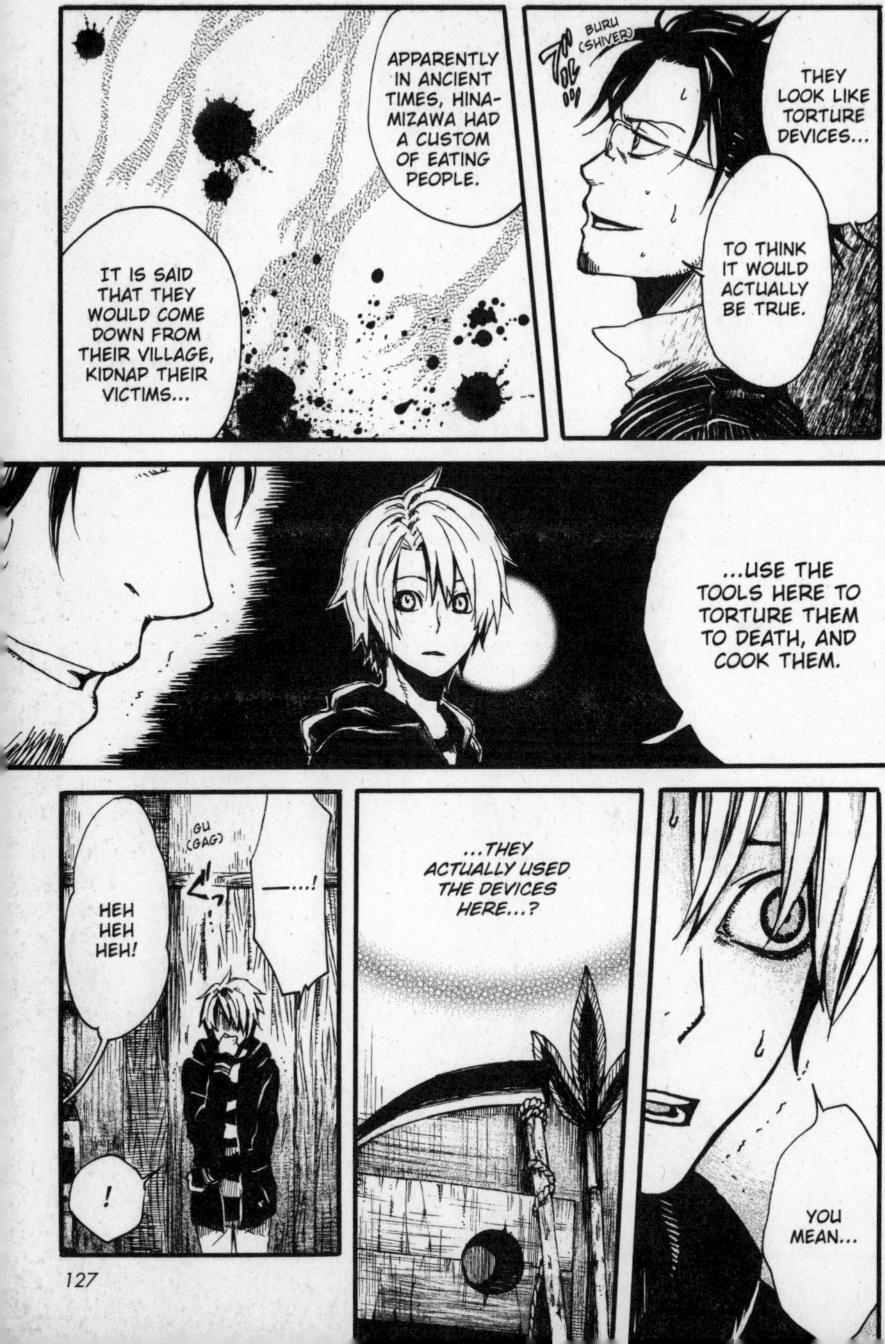
BURU (SHIVER)
THEY LOOK LIKE TORTURE DEVICES...
TO THINK IT WOULD ACTUALLY BE TRUE.
APPARENTLY IN ANCIENT TIMES, HINA-MIZAWA HAD A CUSTOM OF EATING PEOPLE.
IT IS SAID THAT THEY WOULD COME DOWN FROM THEIR VILLAGE, KIDNAP THEIR VICTIMS...
...USE THE TOOLS HERE TO TORTURE THEM TO DEATH, AND COOK THEM.
YOU MEAN...
...THEY ACTUALLY USED THE DEVICES HERE...?
—...!
GU (GAG)
HEH HEH HEH!
!

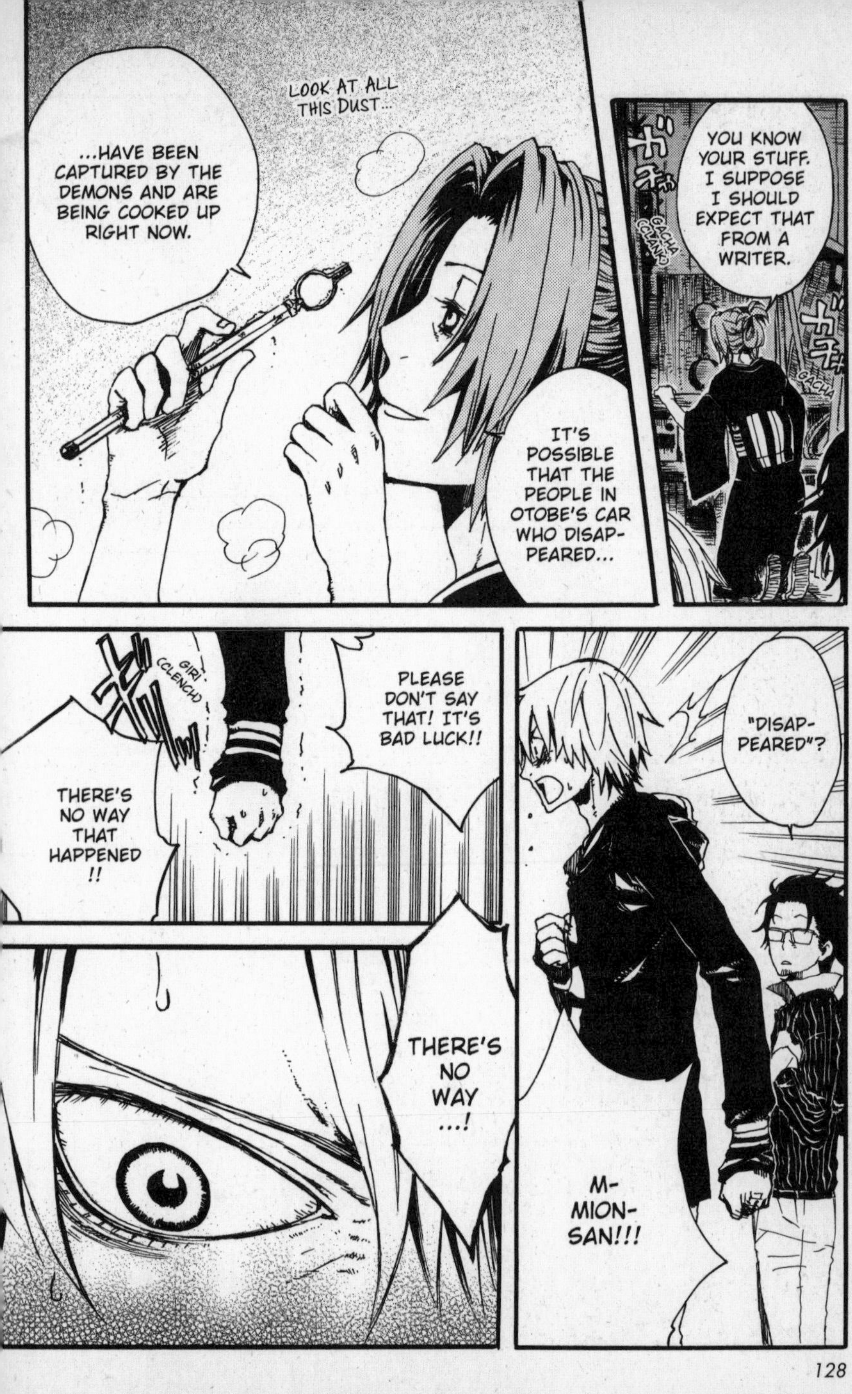
YOU KNOW YOUR STUFF. I SUPPOSE I SHOULD EXPECT THAT FROM A WRITER.
GACHA (CLANK)
GACHA
LOOK AT ALL THIS DUST...
IT'S POSSIBLE THAT THE PEOPLE IN OTOBE'S CAR WHO DISAP-PEARED...
...HAVE BEEN CAPTURED BY THE DEMONS AND ARE BEING COOKED UP RIGHT NOW.
"DISAP-PEARED"?
M-MION-SAN!!!
PLEASE DON'T SAY THAT! IT'S BAD LUCK!!
GIRI (CLENCH)
THERE'S NO WAY THAT HAPPENED!!
THERE'S NO WAY ...!

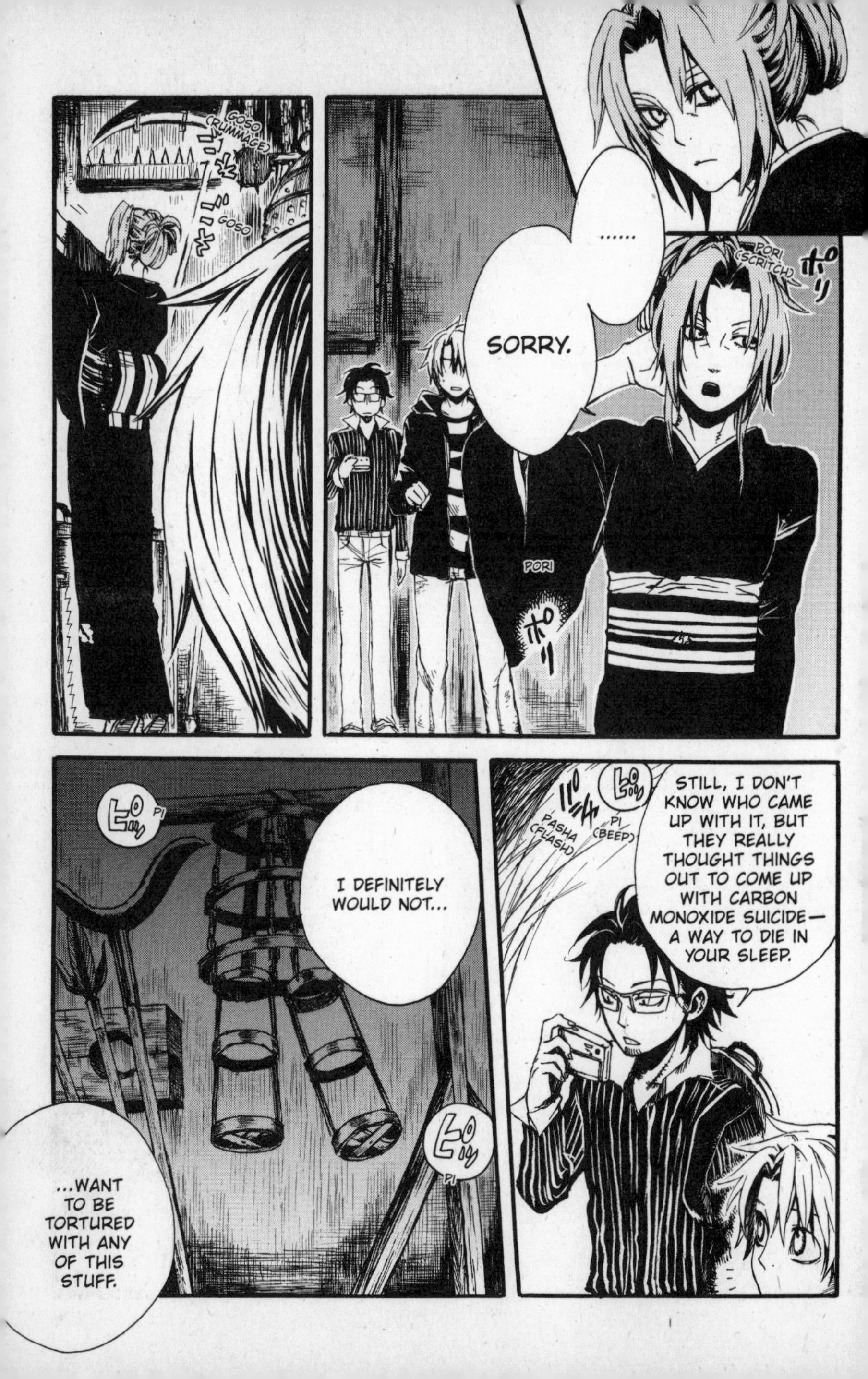
......
PORI (SCRITCH)
SORRY.
PORI
GOSO (RUMMAGE)
GOSO
PI (BEEP)
PASHA (FLASH)
STILL, I DON'T KNOW WHO CAME UP WITH IT, BUT THEY REALLY THOUGHT THINGS OUT TO COME UP WITH CARBON MONOXIDE SUICIDE—A WAY TO DIE IN YOUR SLEEP.
PI
I DEFINITELY WOULD NOT...
PI
...WANT TO BE TORTURED WITH ANY OF THIS STUFF.

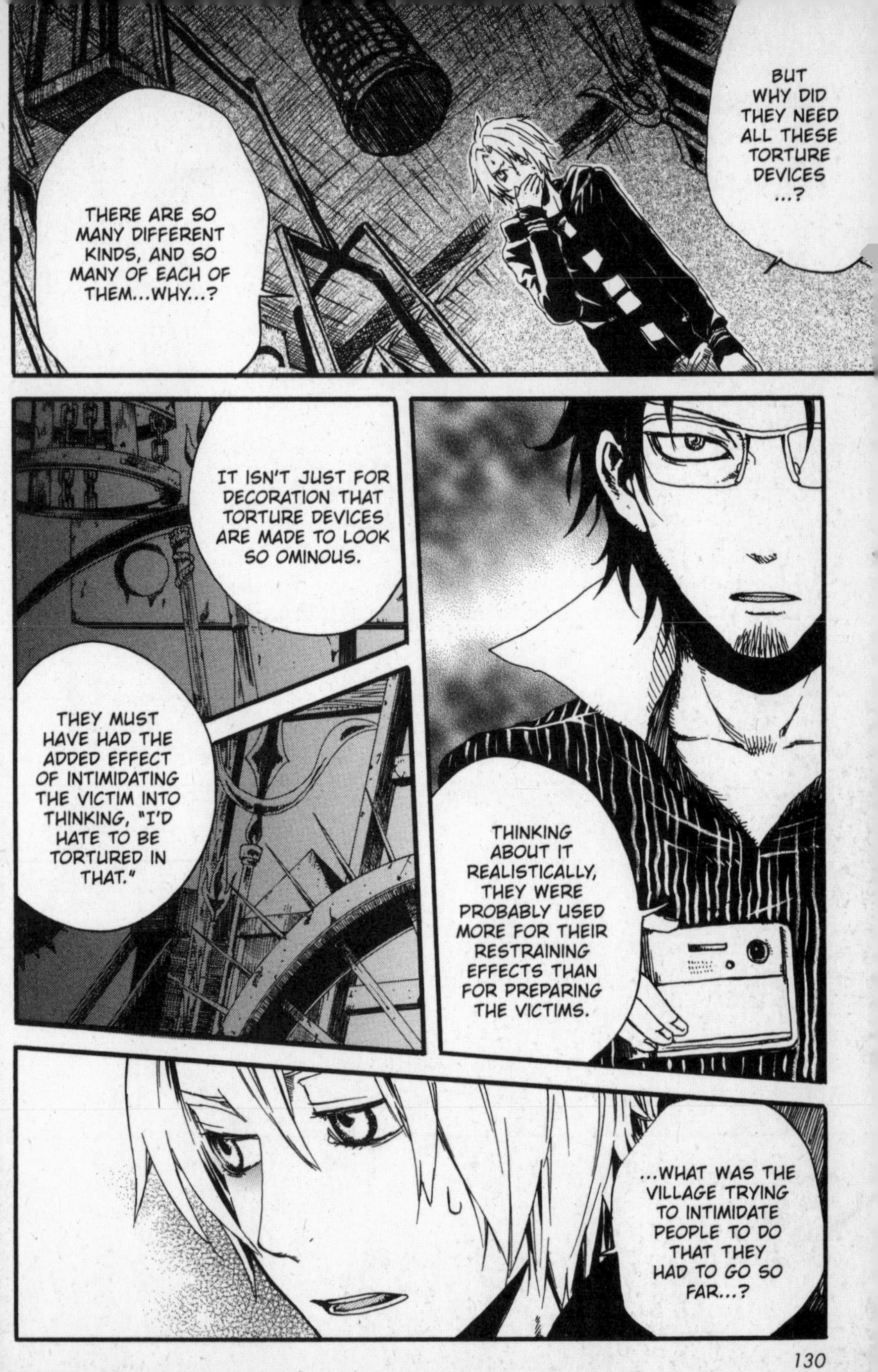
BUT WHY DID THEY NEED ALL THESE TORTURE DEVICES ...?
THERE ARE SO MANY DIFFERENT KINDS, AND SO MANY OF EACH OF THEM...WHY...?
THINKING ABOUT IT REALISTICALLY, THEY WERE PROBABLY USED MORE FOR THEIR RESTRAINING EFFECTS THAN FOR PREPARING THE VICTIMS.
IT ISN'T JUST FOR DECORATION THAT TORTURE DEVICES ARE MADE TO LOOK SO OMINOUS.
THEY MUST HAVE HAD THE ADDED EFFECT OF INTIMIDATING THE VICTIM INTO THINKING, "I'D HATE TO BE TORTURED IN THAT."
...WHAT WAS THE VILLAGE TRYING TO INTIMIDATE PEOPLE TO DO THAT THEY HAD TO GO SO FAR...?

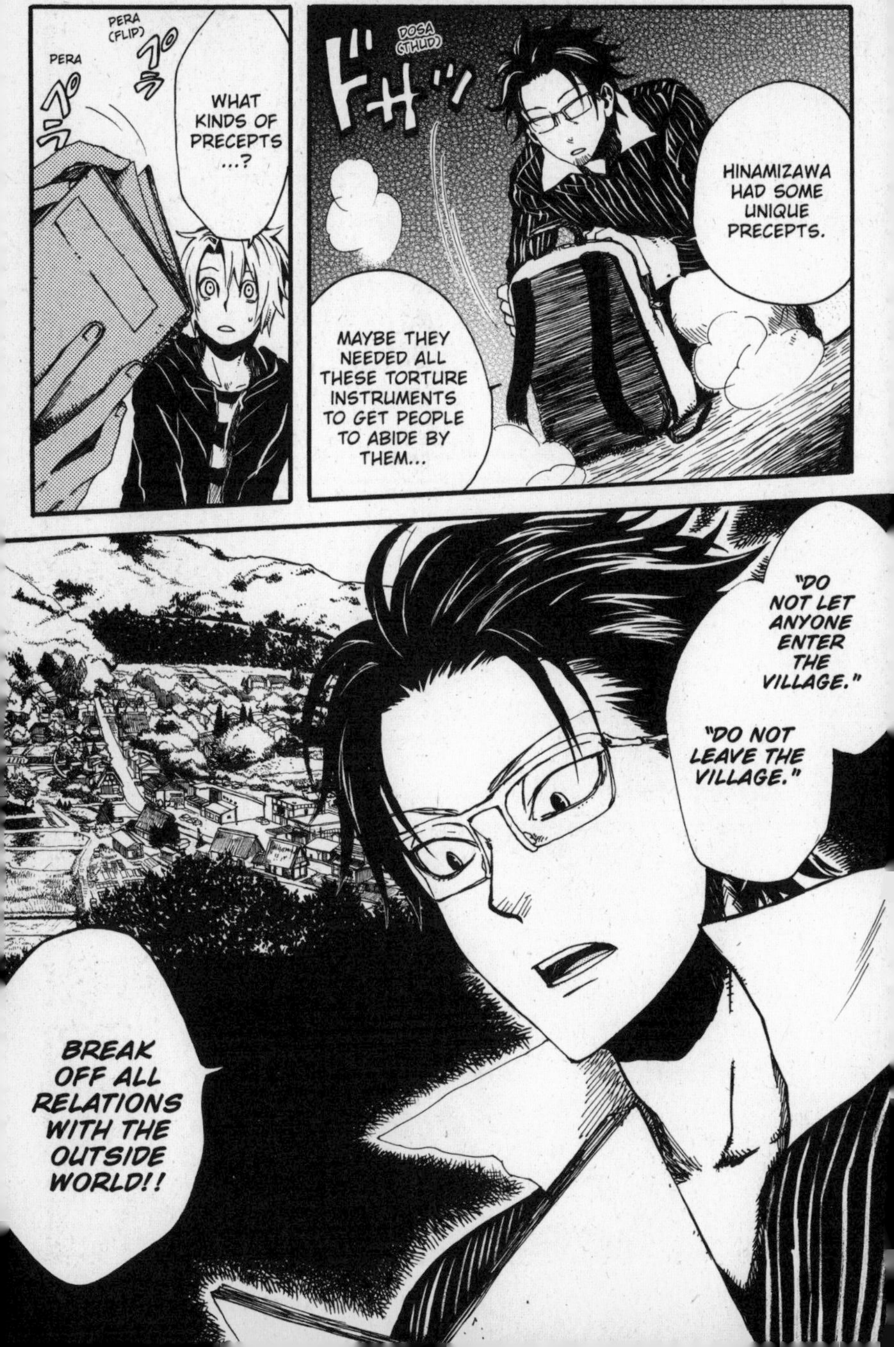

ドサッ
DOSA (THUD)
HINAMIZAWA HAD SOME UNIQUE PRECEPTS.
MAYBE THEY NEEDED ALL THESE TORTURE INSTRUMENTS TO GET PEOPLE TO ABIDE BY THEM...
ペラ
PERA (FLIP)
ペラ
PERA
WHAT KINDS OF PRECEPTS ...?
"DO NOT LET ANYONE ENTER THE VILLAGE."
"DO NOT LEAVE THE VILLAGE."
BREAK OFF ALL RELATIONS WITH THE OUTSIDE WORLD!!

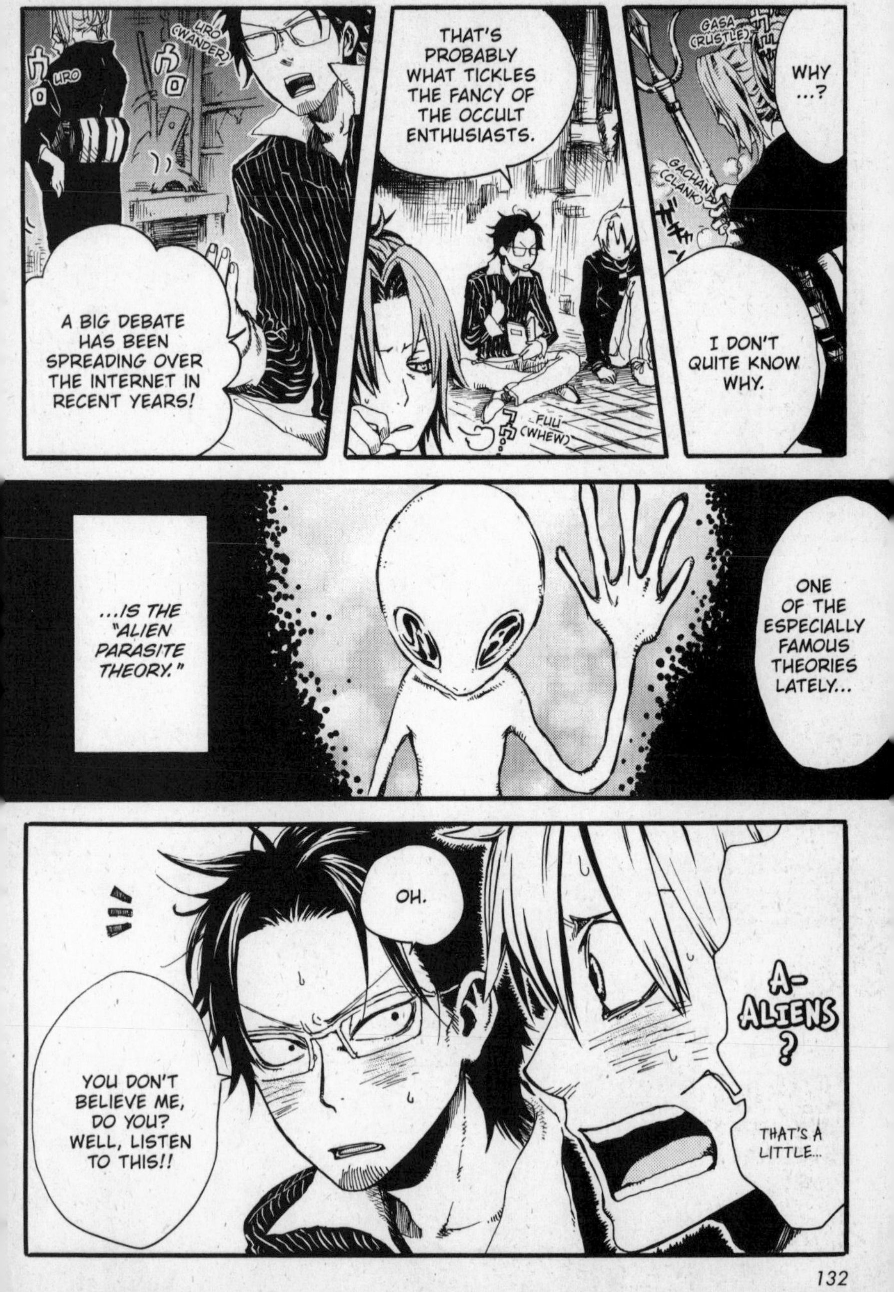
GASA (RUSTLE)
WHY ...?
GACHAN (CLANK)
I DON'T QUITE KNOW WHY.
THAT'S PROBABLY WHAT TICKLES THE FANCY OF THE OCCULT ENTHUSIASTS.
FUU (WHEW)
URO (WANDER)
URO
A BIG DEBATE HAS BEEN SPREADING OVER THE INTERNET IN RECENT YEARS!
ONE OF THE ESPECIALLY FAMOUS THEORIES LATELY...
...IS THE "ALIEN PARASITE THEORY."
A-ALIENS?
THAT'S A LITTLE...
OH.
YOU DON'T BELIEVE ME, DO YOU? WELL, LISTEN TO THIS!!

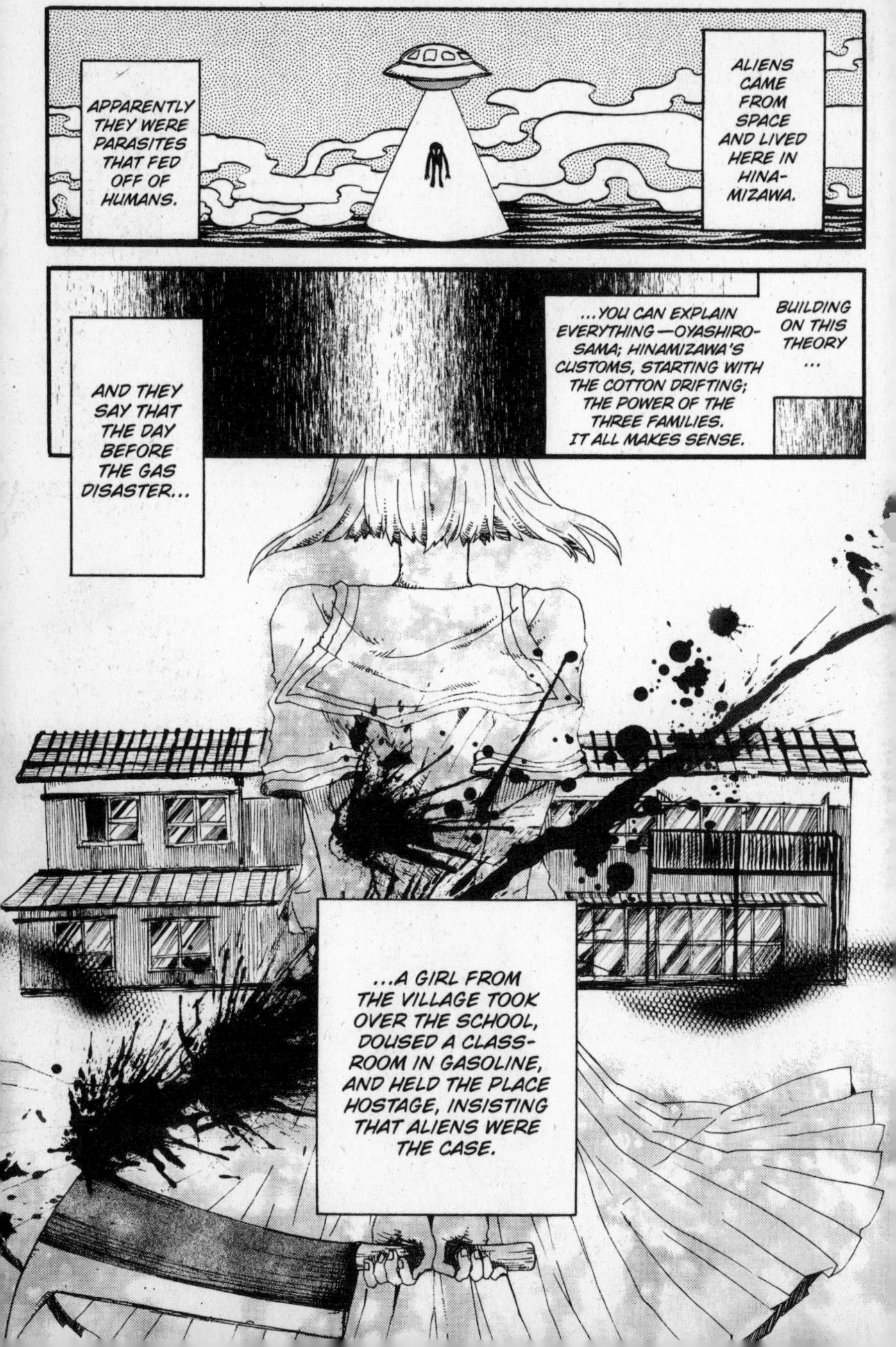
ALIENS CAME FROM SPACE AND LIVED HERE IN HINA-MIZAWA.
APPARENTLY THEY WERE PARASITES THAT FED OFF OF HUMANS.
BUILDING ON THIS THEORY...
...YOU CAN EXPLAIN EVERYTHING—OYASHIRO-SAMA; HINAMIZAWA'S CUSTOMS, STARTING WITH THE COTTON DRIFTING; THE POWER OF THE THREE FAMILIES. IT ALL MAKES SENSE.
AND THEY SAY THAT THE DAY BEFORE THE GAS DISASTER...
...A GIRL FROM THE VILLAGE TOOK OVER THE SCHOOL, DOUSED A CLASS-ROOM IN GASOLINE, AND HELD THE PLACE HOSTAGE, INSISTING THAT ALIENS WERE THE CASE.

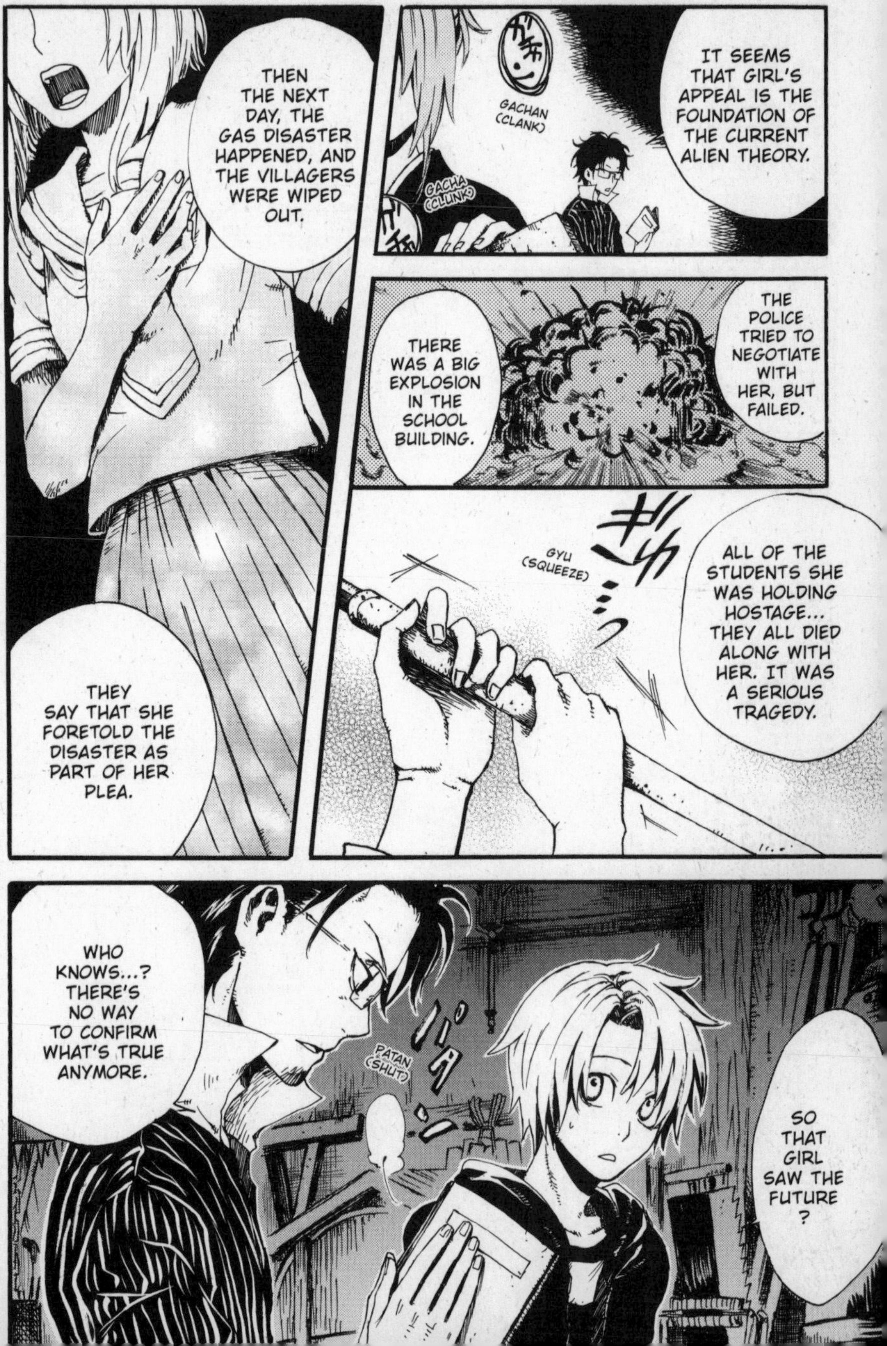
IT SEEMS THAT GIRL'S APPEAL IS THE FOUNDATION OF THE CURRENT ALIEN THEORY.
GACHAN (CLANK)
GACHA (CLUNK)
THE POLICE TRIED TO NEGOTIATE WITH HER, BUT FAILED.
THERE WAS A BIG EXPLOSION IN THE SCHOOL BUILDING.
ALL OF THE STUDENTS SHE WAS HOLDING HOSTAGE... THEY ALL DIED ALONG WITH HER. IT WAS A SERIOUS TRAGEDY.
GYU (SQUEEZE)
THEN THE NEXT DAY, THE GAS DISASTER HAPPENED, AND THE VILLAGERS WERE WIPED OUT.
THEY SAY THAT SHE FORETOLD THE DISASTER AS PART OF HER PLEA.
SO THAT GIRL SAW THE FUTURE?
PATAN (SHUT)
WHO KNOWS...? THERE'S NO WAY TO CONFIRM WHAT'S TRUE ANYMORE.

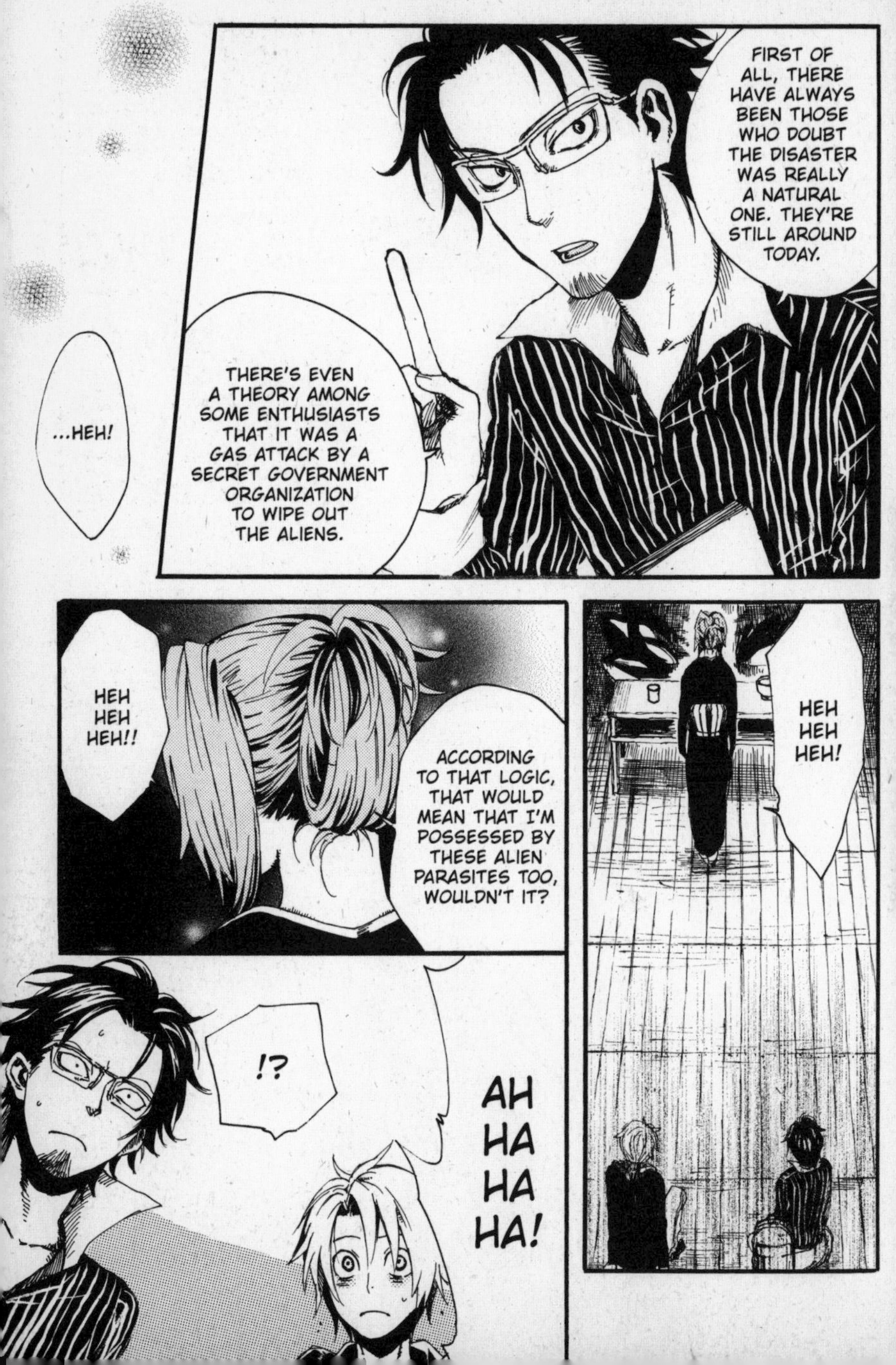
FIRST OF ALL, THERE HAVE ALWAYS BEEN THOSE WHO DOUBT THE DISASTER WAS REALLY A NATURAL ONE. THEY'RE STILL AROUND TODAY.
THERE'S EVEN A THEORY AMONG SOME ENTHUSIASTS THAT IT WAS A GAS ATTACK BY A SECRET GOVERNMENT ORGANIZATION TO WIPE OUT THE ALIENS.
...HEH!
HEH HEH HEH!
ACCORDING TO THAT LOGIC, THAT WOULD MEAN THAT I'M POSSESSED BY THESE ALIEN PARASITES TOO, WOULDN'T IT?
HEH HEH HEH!!
AH HA HA HA!
!?

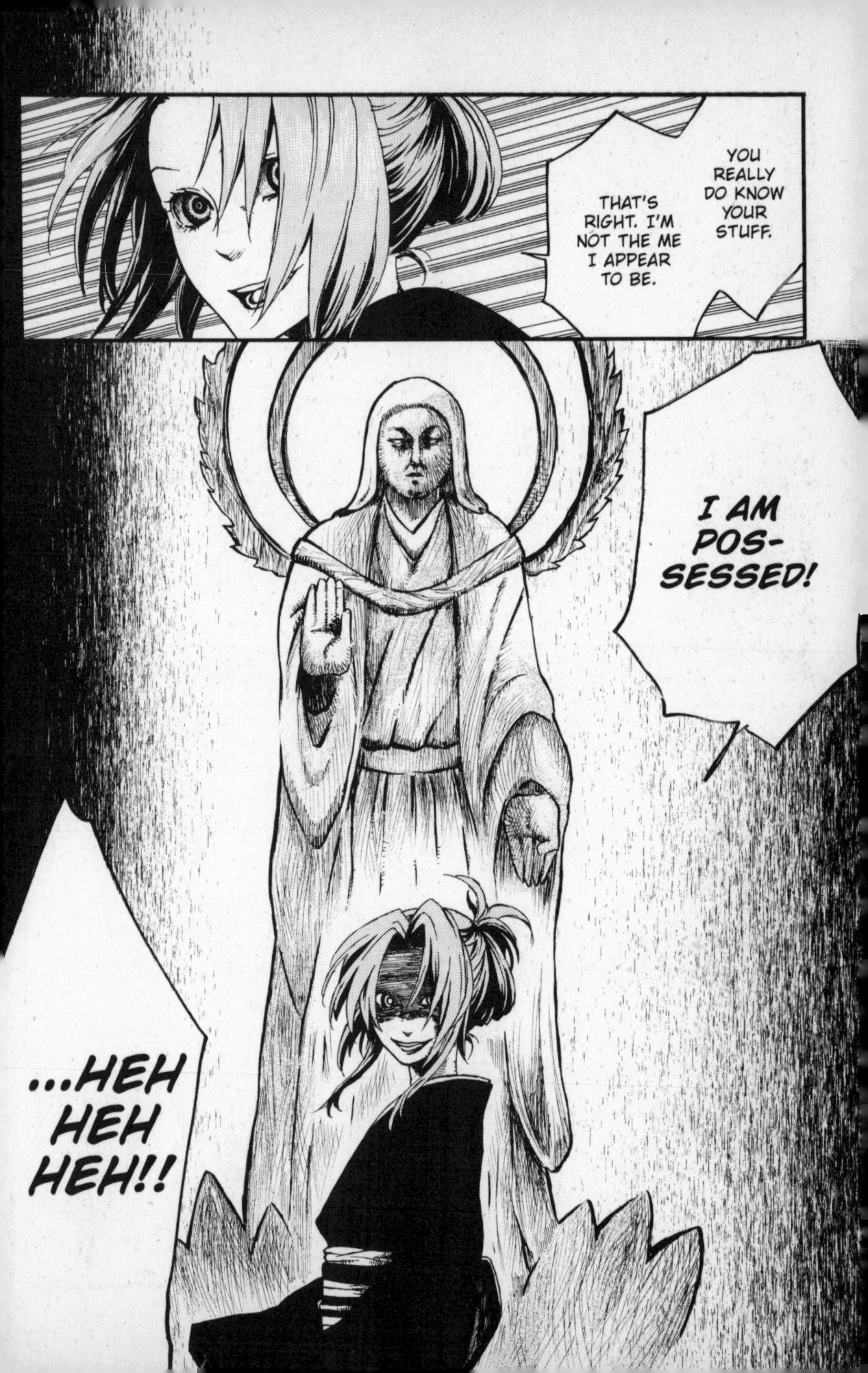
YOU REALLY DO KNOW YOUR STUFF.
THAT'S RIGHT. I'M NOT THE ME I APPEAR TO BE.
I AM POS-SESSED!
...HEH HEH HEH!!

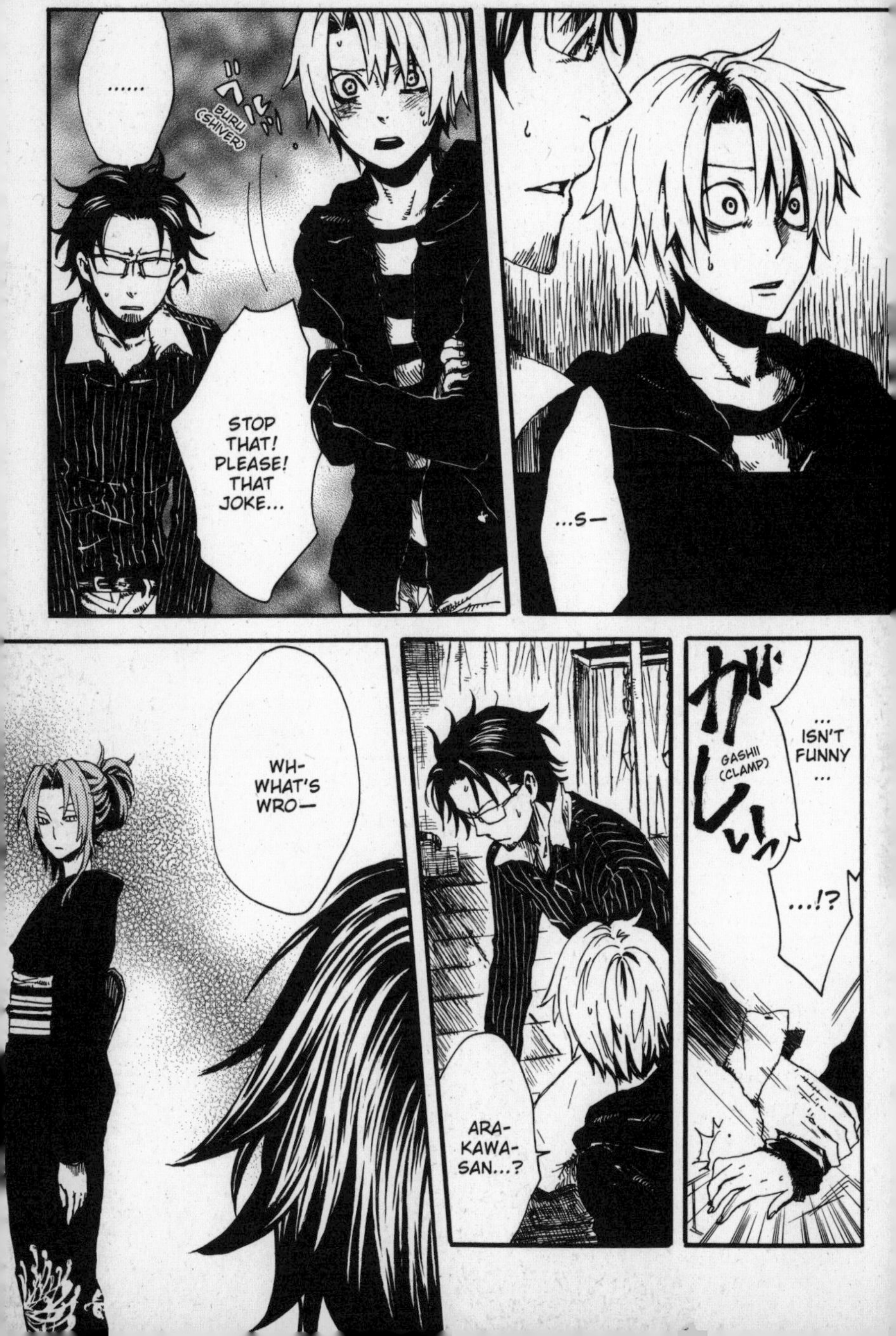
...S—
......
BURU (SHIVER)
STOP THAT! PLEASE! THAT JOKE...
GASHII (CLAMP)
...ISN'T FUNNY...
...!?
ARA-KAWA-SAN...?
WH-WHAT'S WRO—

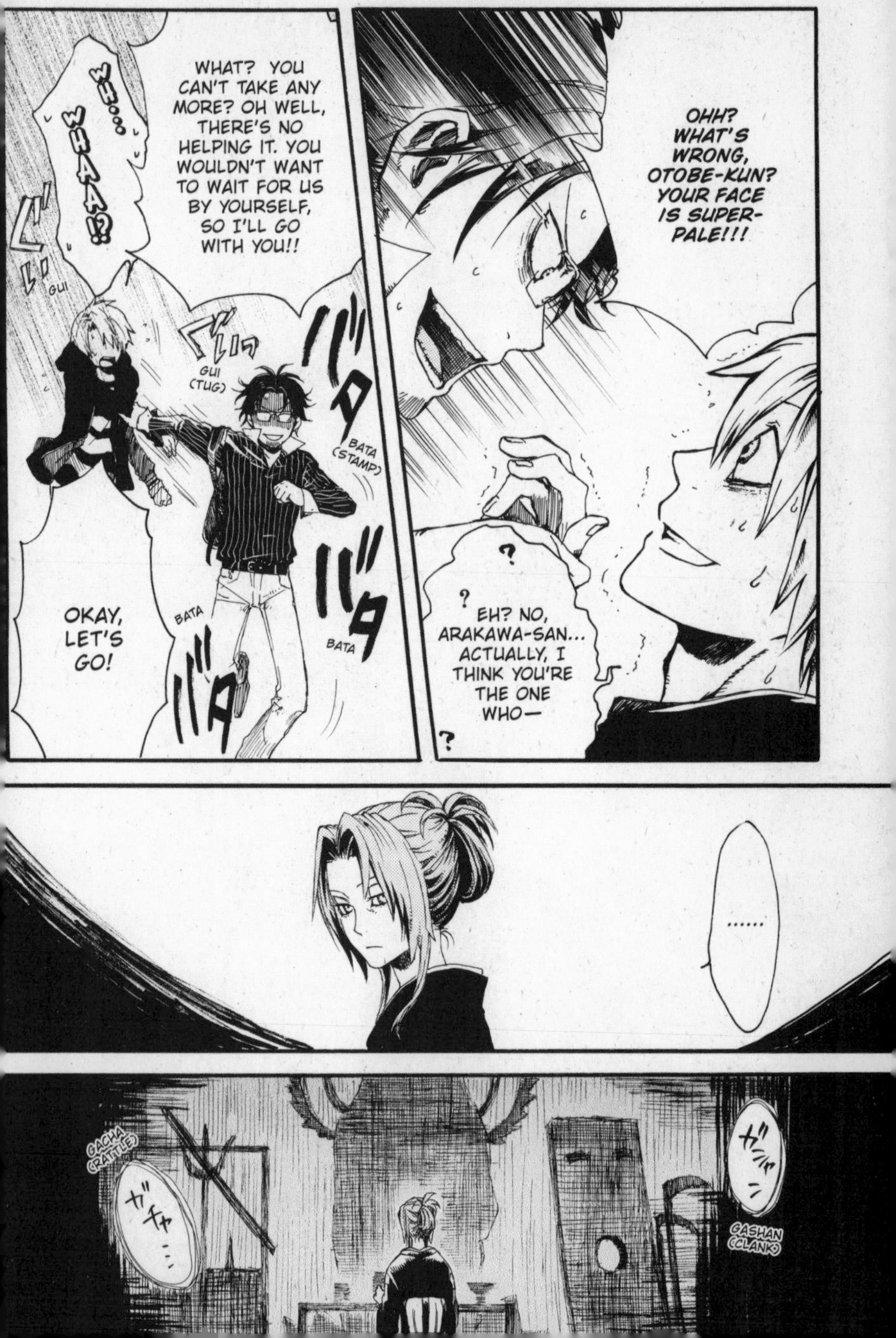
OHH? WHAT'S WRONG, OTOBE-KUN? YOUR FACE IS SUPER-PALE!!!
?
?
EH? NO, ARAKAWA-SAN... ACTUALLY, I THINK YOU'RE THE ONE WHO—
?
WHAT? YOU CAN'T TAKE ANY MORE? OH WELL, THERE'S NO HELPING IT. YOU WOULDN'T WANT TO WAIT FOR US BY YOURSELF, SO I'LL GO WITH YOU!!
WH... WHAA!?
GUI
GUI (TUG)
BATA (STAMP)
BATA
BATA
OKAY, LET'S GO!
......
GASHAN (CLANK)
GACHA (RATTLE)

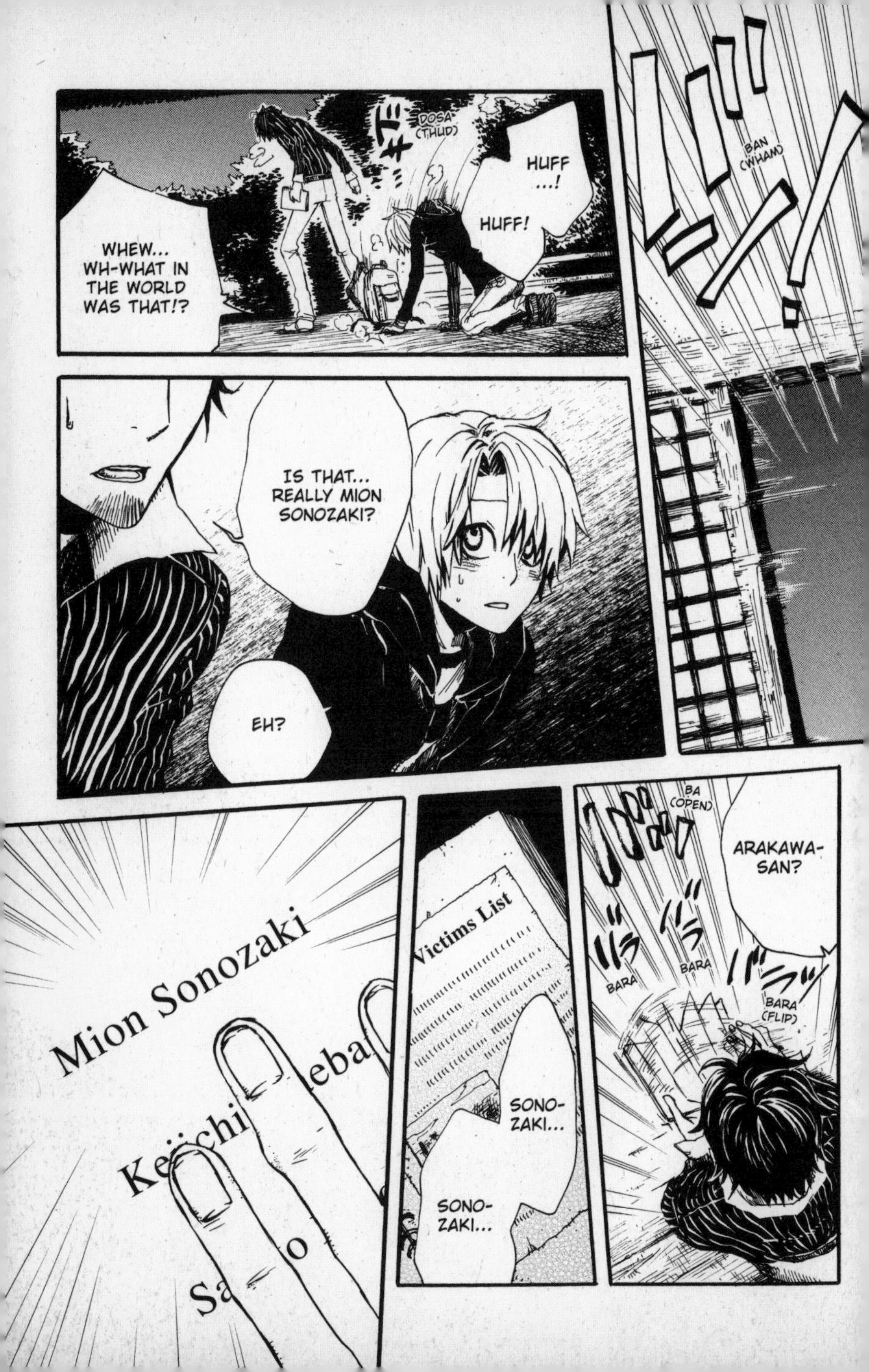
BAN (WHAM)
DOSA (THUD)
HUFF ...!
HUFF!
WHEW... WH-WHAT IN THE WORLD WAS THAT!?
IS THAT... REALLY MION SONOZAKI?
EH?
BA (OPEN)
ARAKAWA-SAN?
BARA
BARA
BARA (FLIP)
Victims List
SONO-ZAKI...
SONO-ZAKI...
Mion Sonozaki

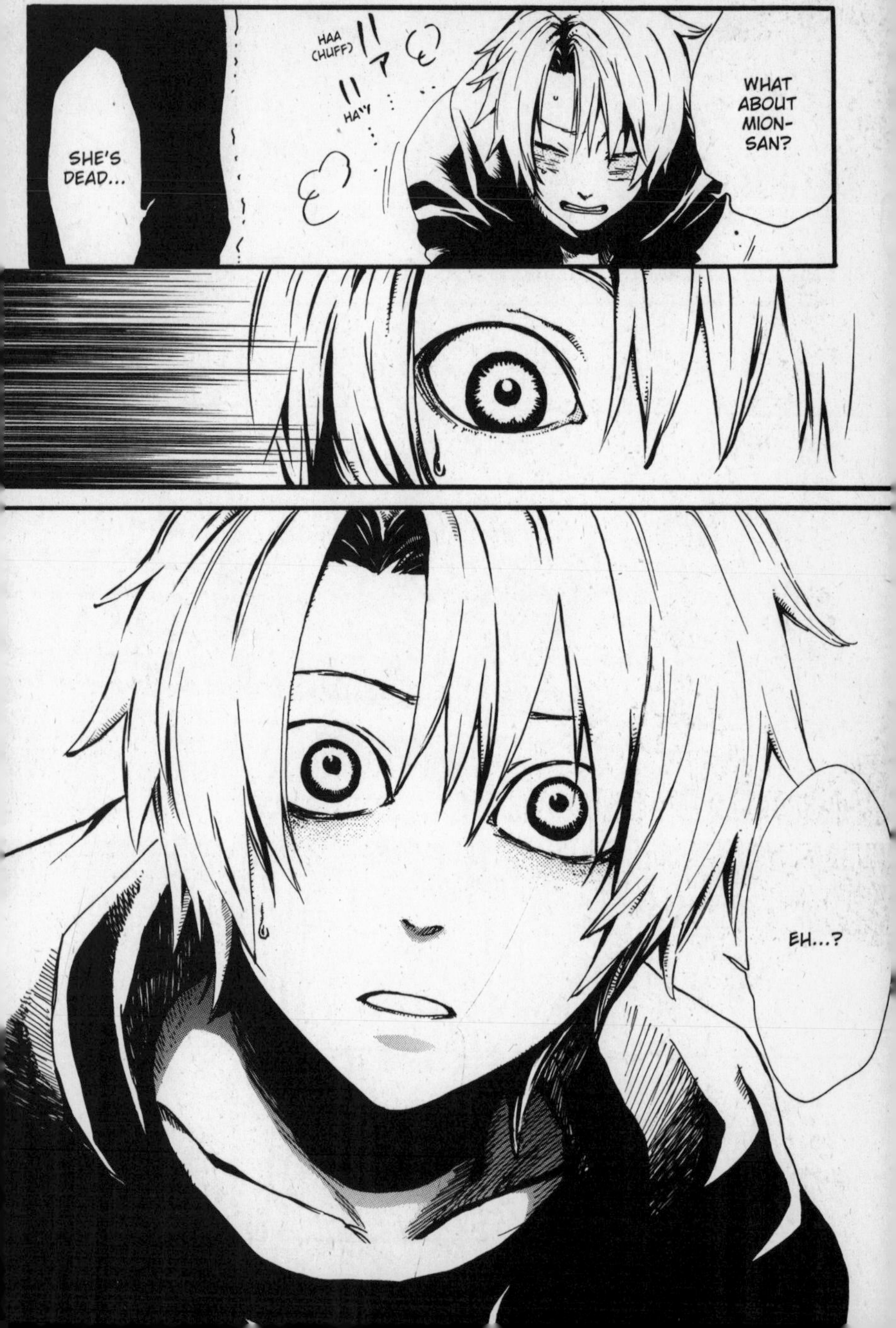
WHAT ABOUT MION-SAN?
ハァ
HAA (HUFF)
ハ
HAッ
SHE'S DEAD...
EH...?

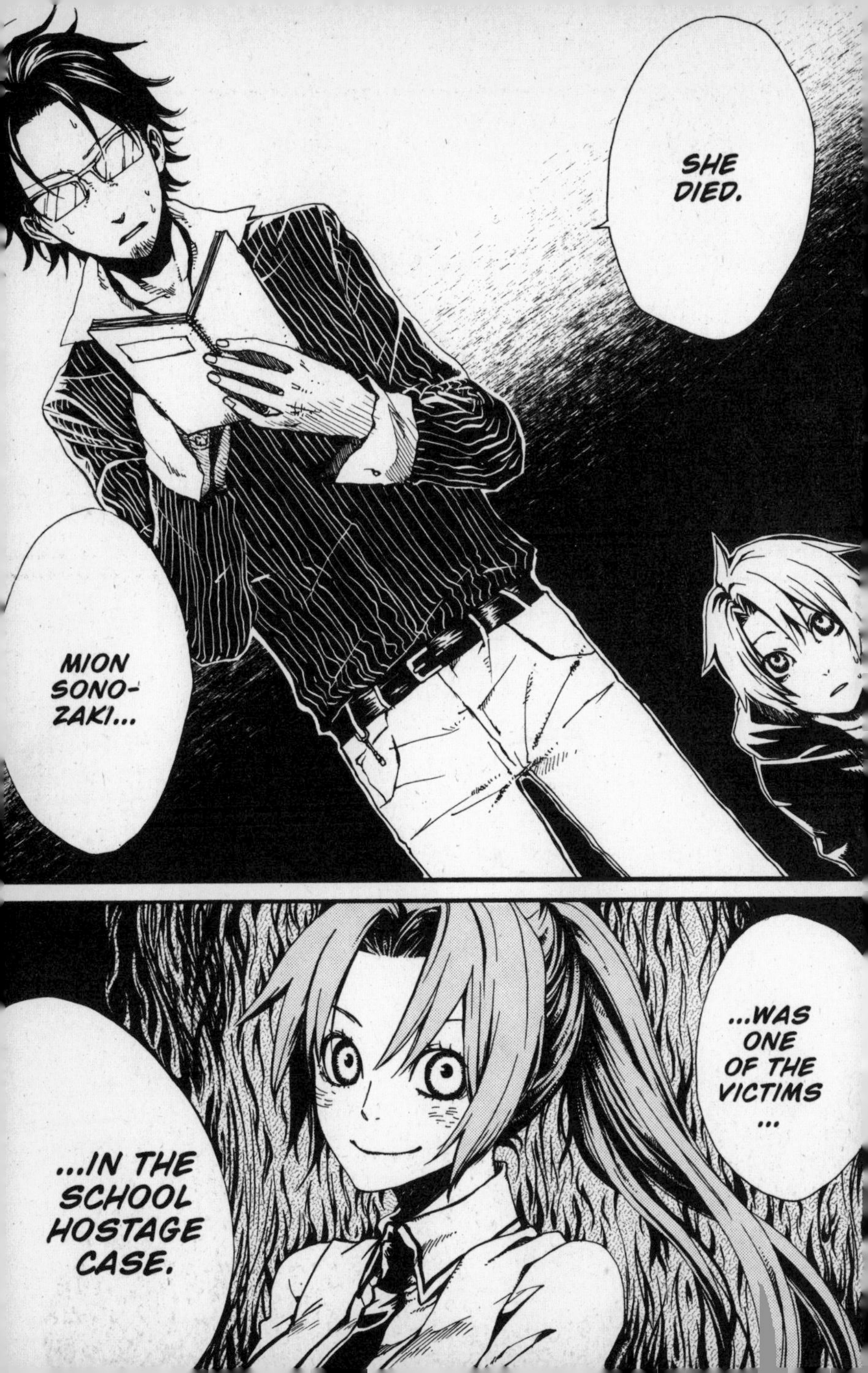
SHE DIED.
MION SONO-ZAKI...
...WAS ONE OF THE VICTIMS ...
...IN THE SCHOOL HOSTAGE CASE.

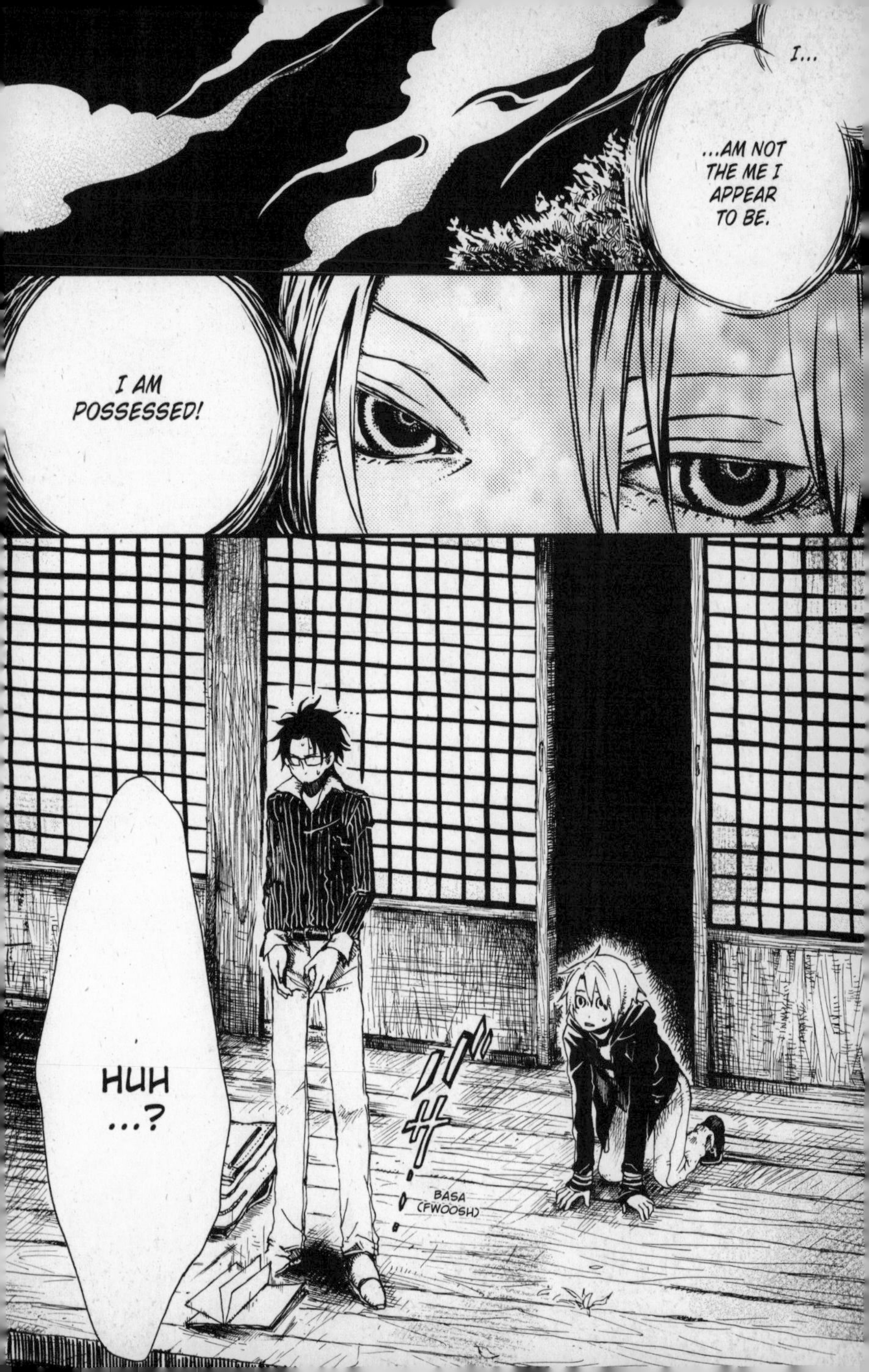
I...
...AM NOT THE ME I APPEAR TO BE.
I AM POSSESSED!
BASA (FWOOSH)
HUH ...?

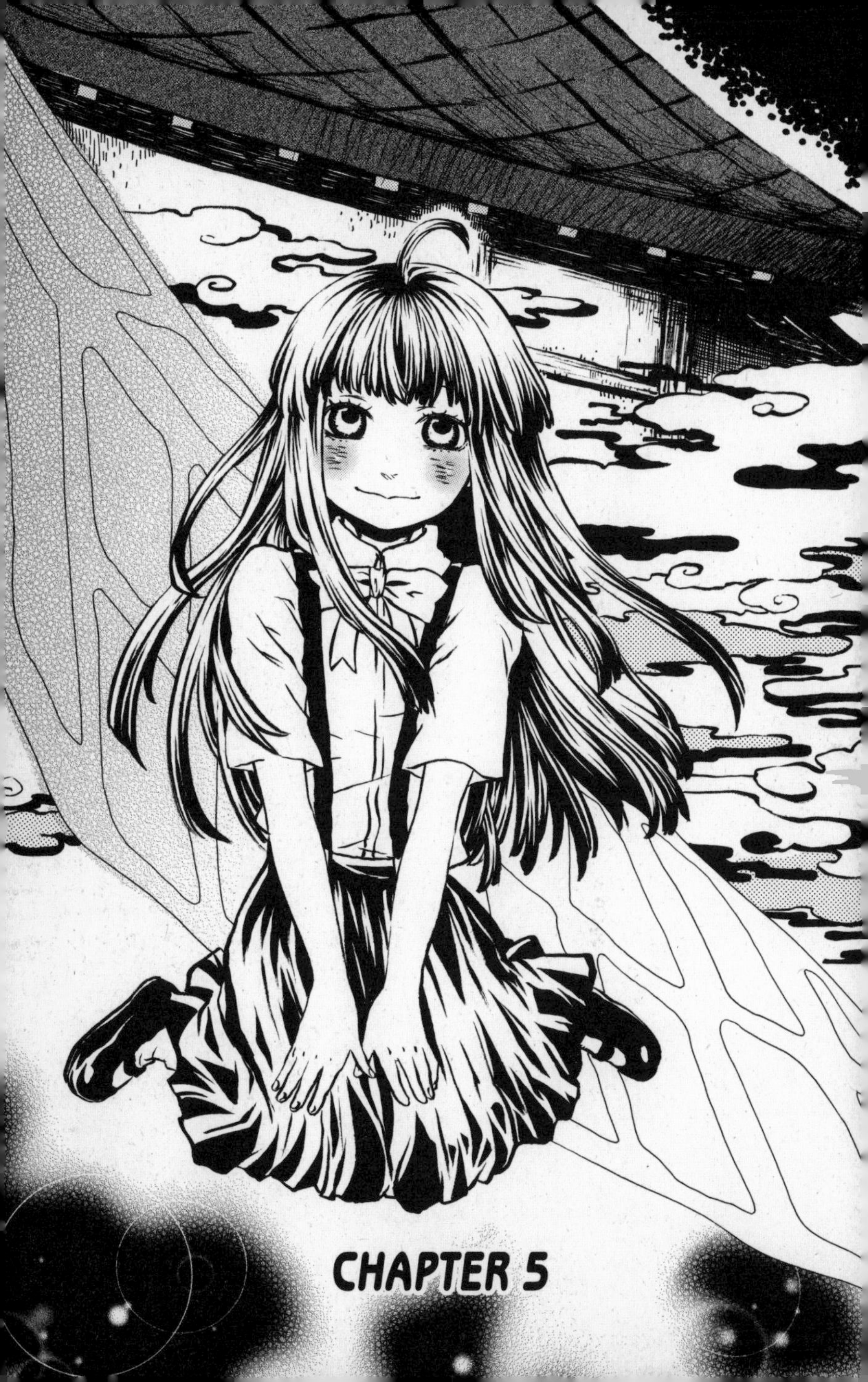
CHAPTER 5

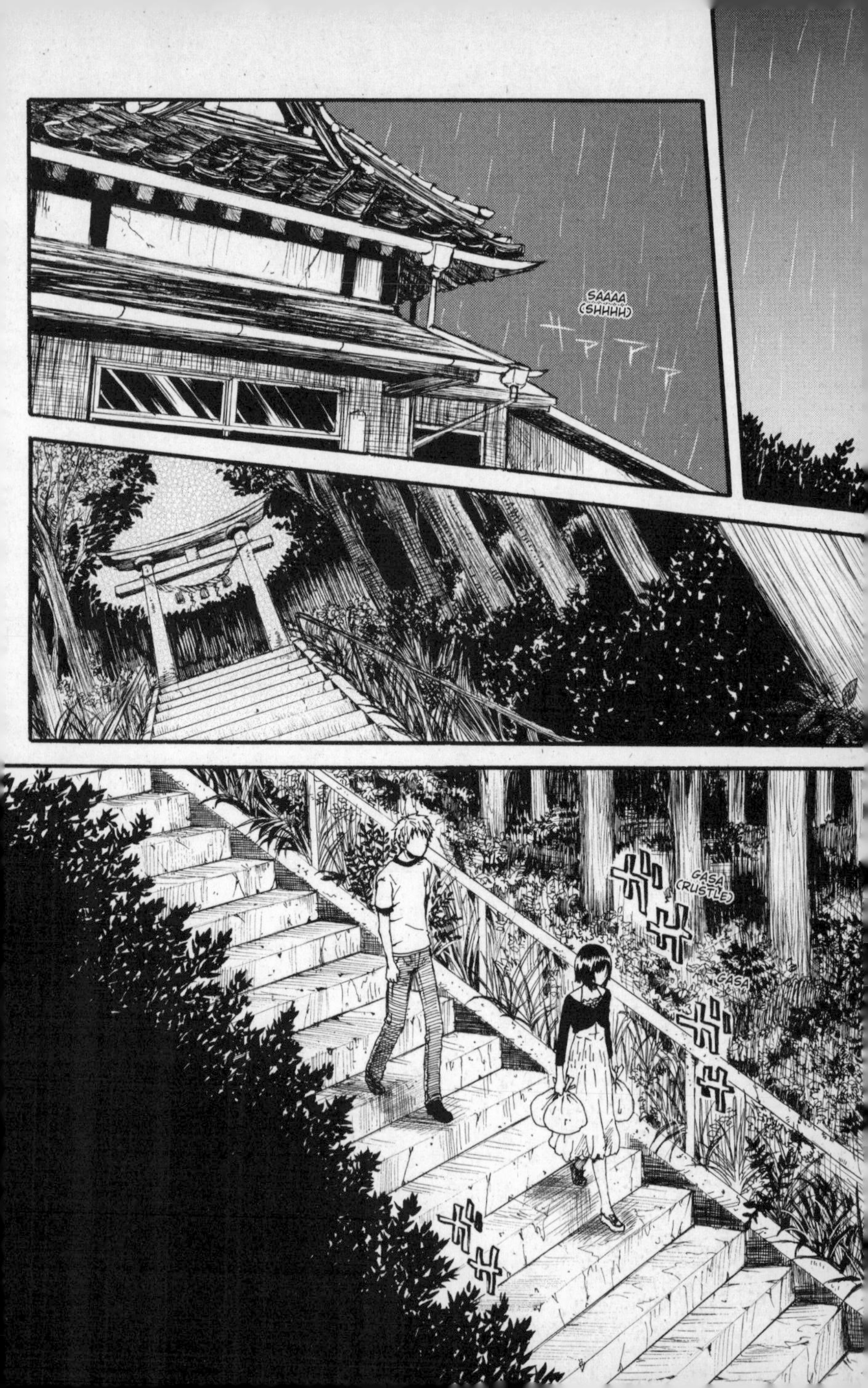
SAAAA
(SHHHH)
GASA
(RUSTLE)
GASA

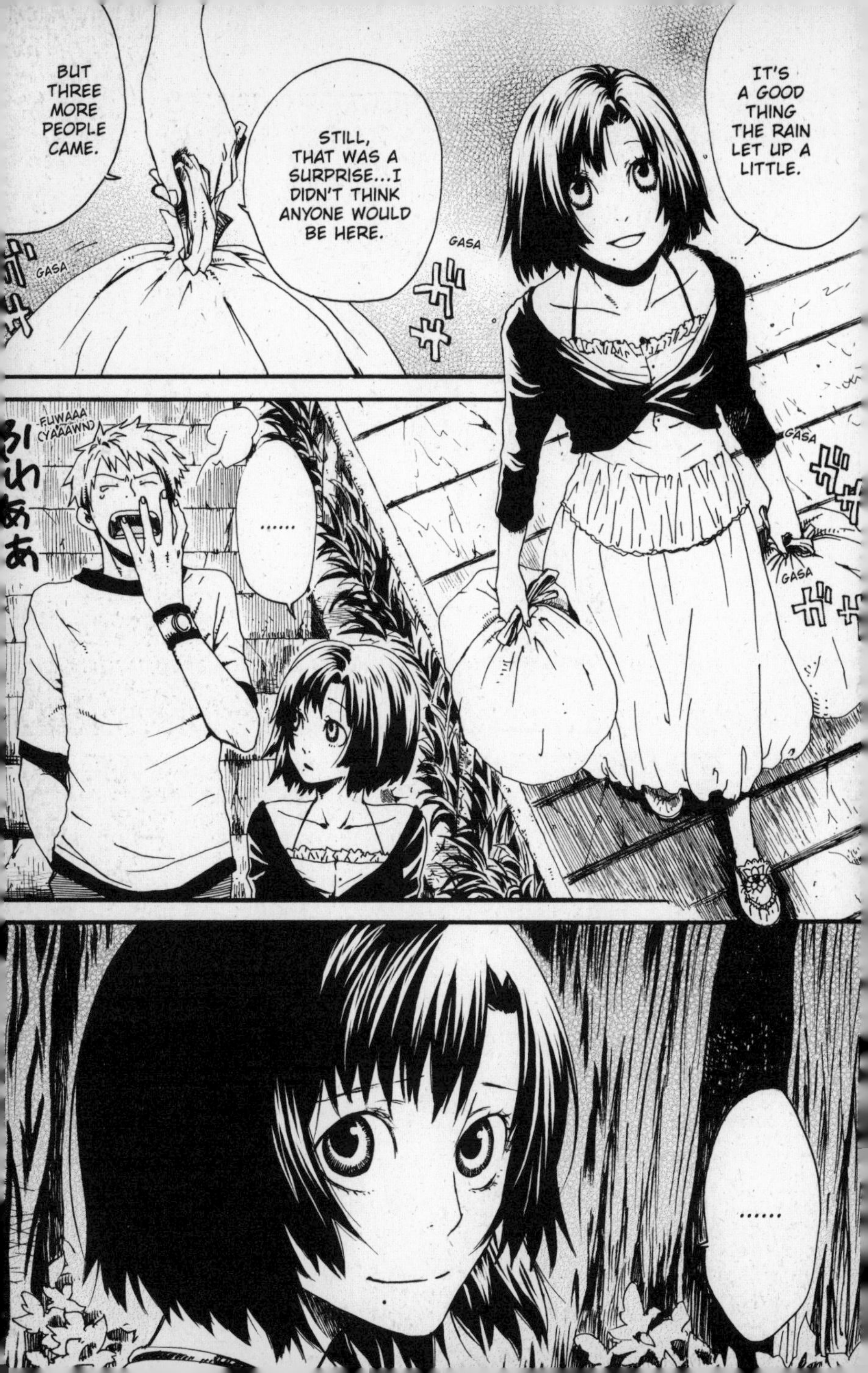

IT'S A GOOD THING THE RAIN LET UP A LITTLE.
GASA
GASA
GASA
STILL, THAT WAS A SURPRISE...I DIDN'T THINK ANYONE WOULD BE HERE.
GASA
BUT THREE MORE PEOPLE CAME.
GASA
......
FUWAAA (YAAAWN)
......

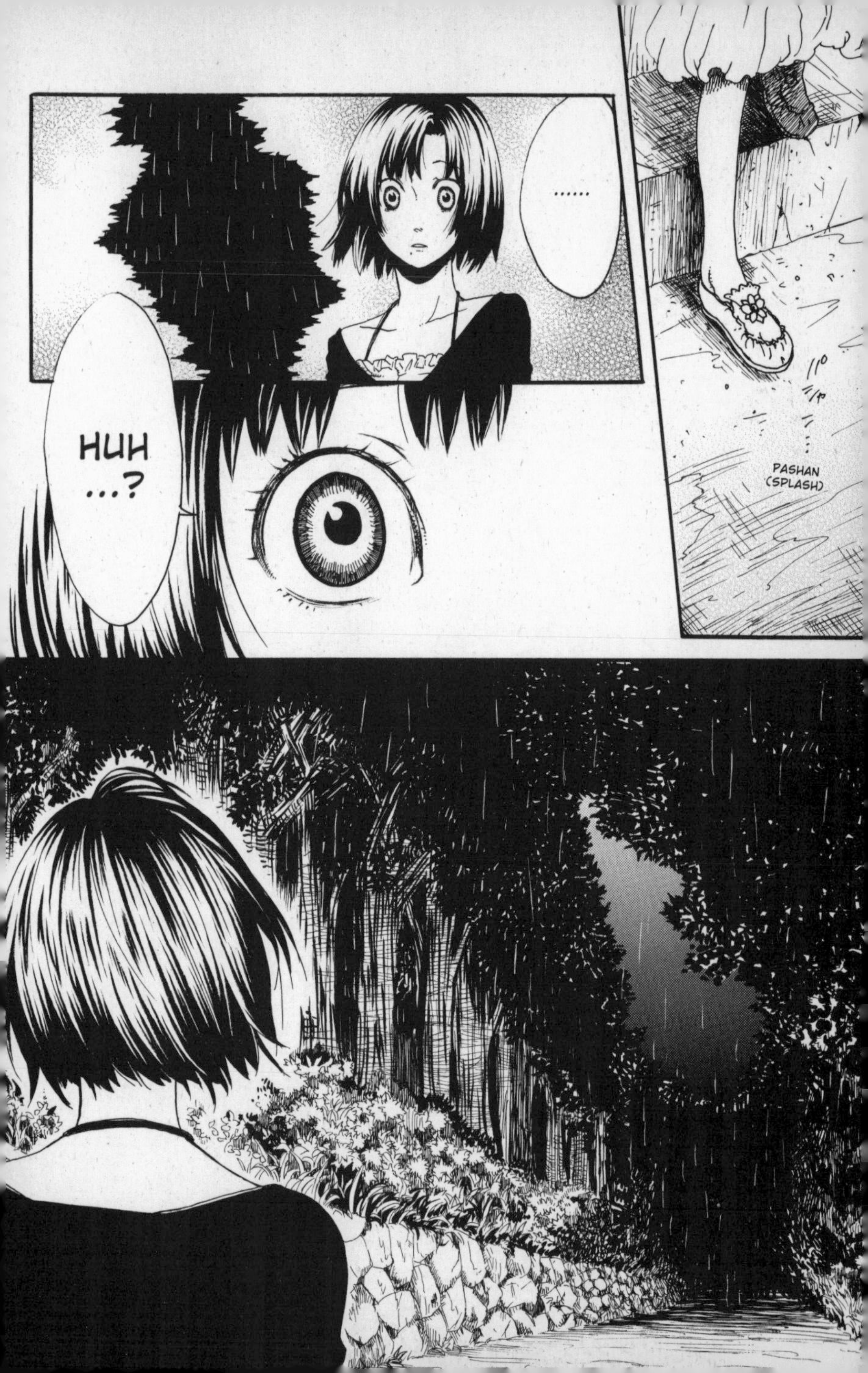
PASHAN (SPLASH)
......
HUH ...?

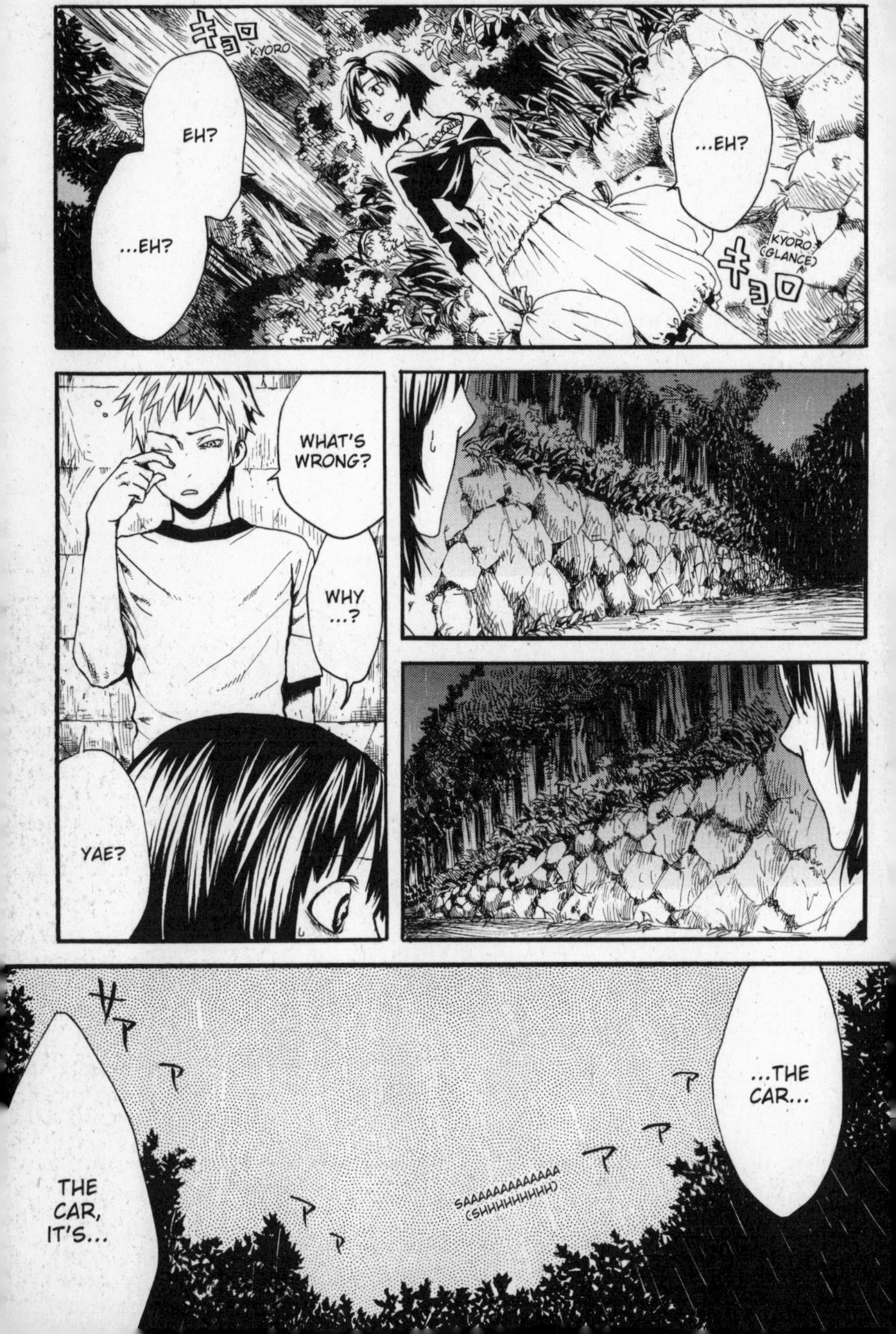
...EH?
キョロ
KYORO (GLANCE)
キョロ
KYORO
EH?
...EH?
WHAT'S WRONG?
WHY ...?
YAE?
...THE CAR...
SAAAAAAAAAAAAA (SHHHHHHHHHH)
THE CAR, IT'S...

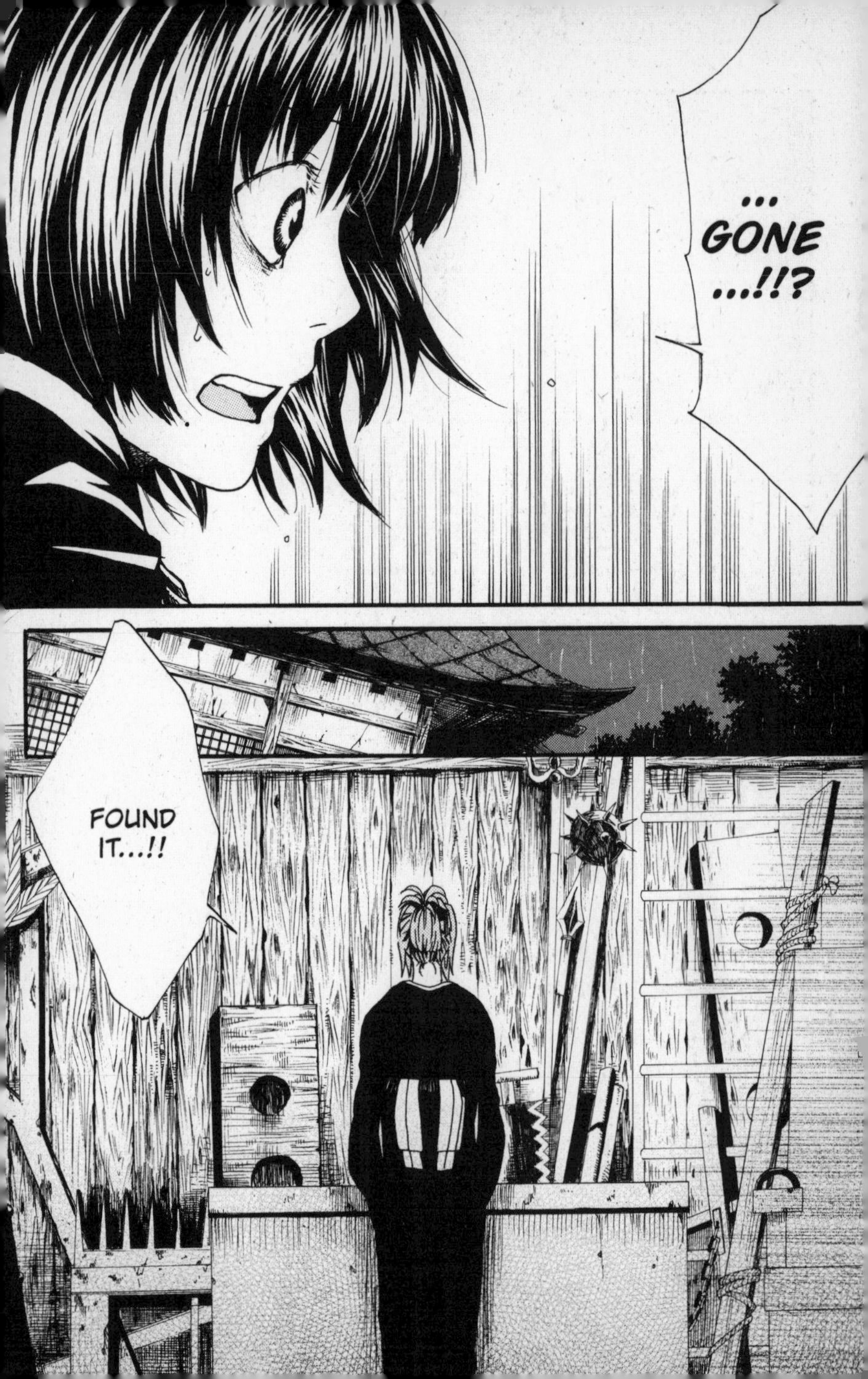

... GONE ...!!?
FOUND IT...!!

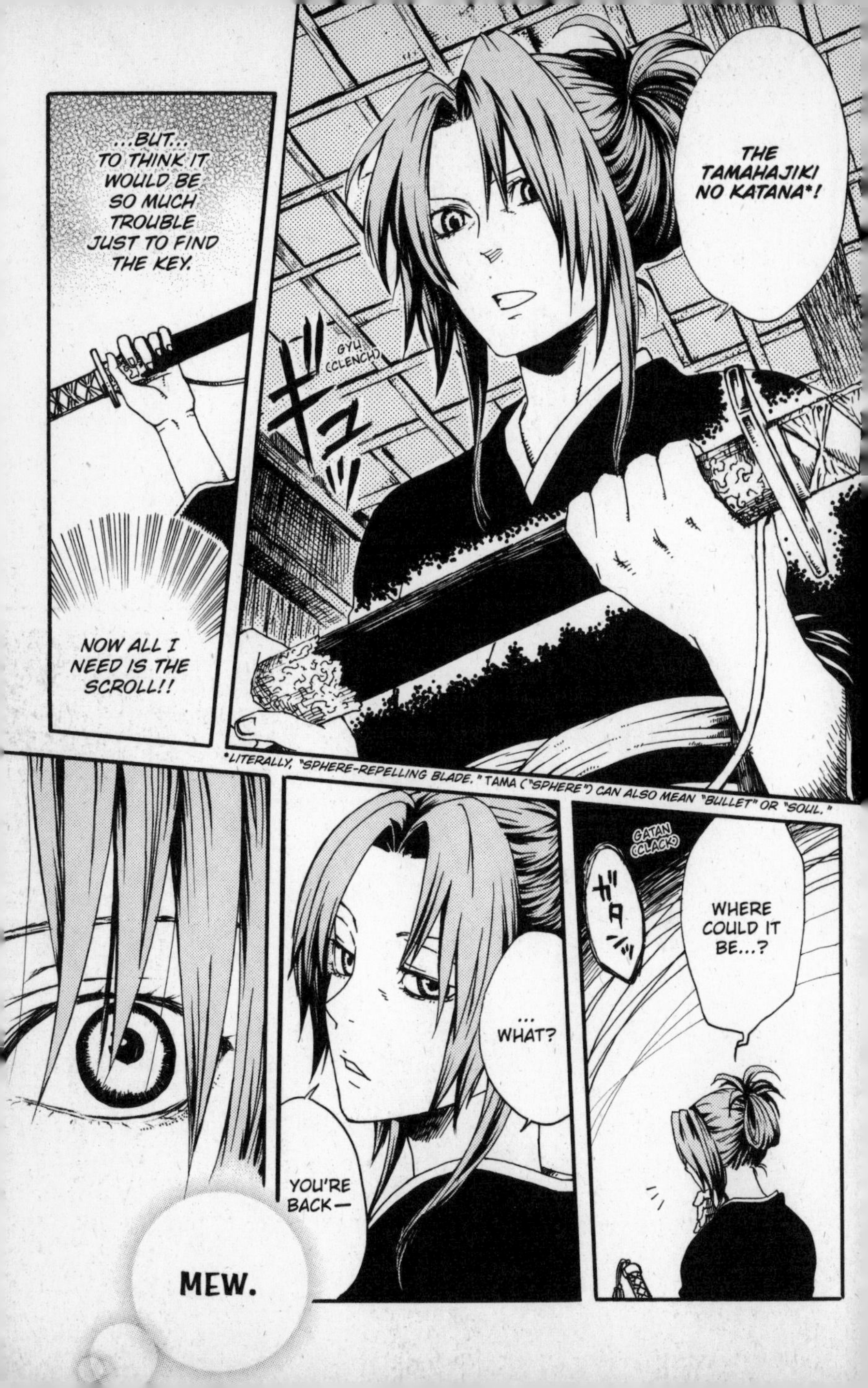
THE TAMAHAJIKI NO KATANA*!
GYU (CLENCH)
...BUT... TO THINK IT WOULD BE SO MUCH TROUBLE JUST TO FIND THE KEY.
NOW ALL I NEED IS THE SCROLL!!
GATAN (CLACK)
WHERE COULD IT BE...?
... WHAT?
YOU'RE BACK—
MEW.

*LITERALLY, "SPHERE-REPELLING BLADE." TAMA ("SPHERE") CAN ALSO MEAN "BULLET" OR "SOUL."

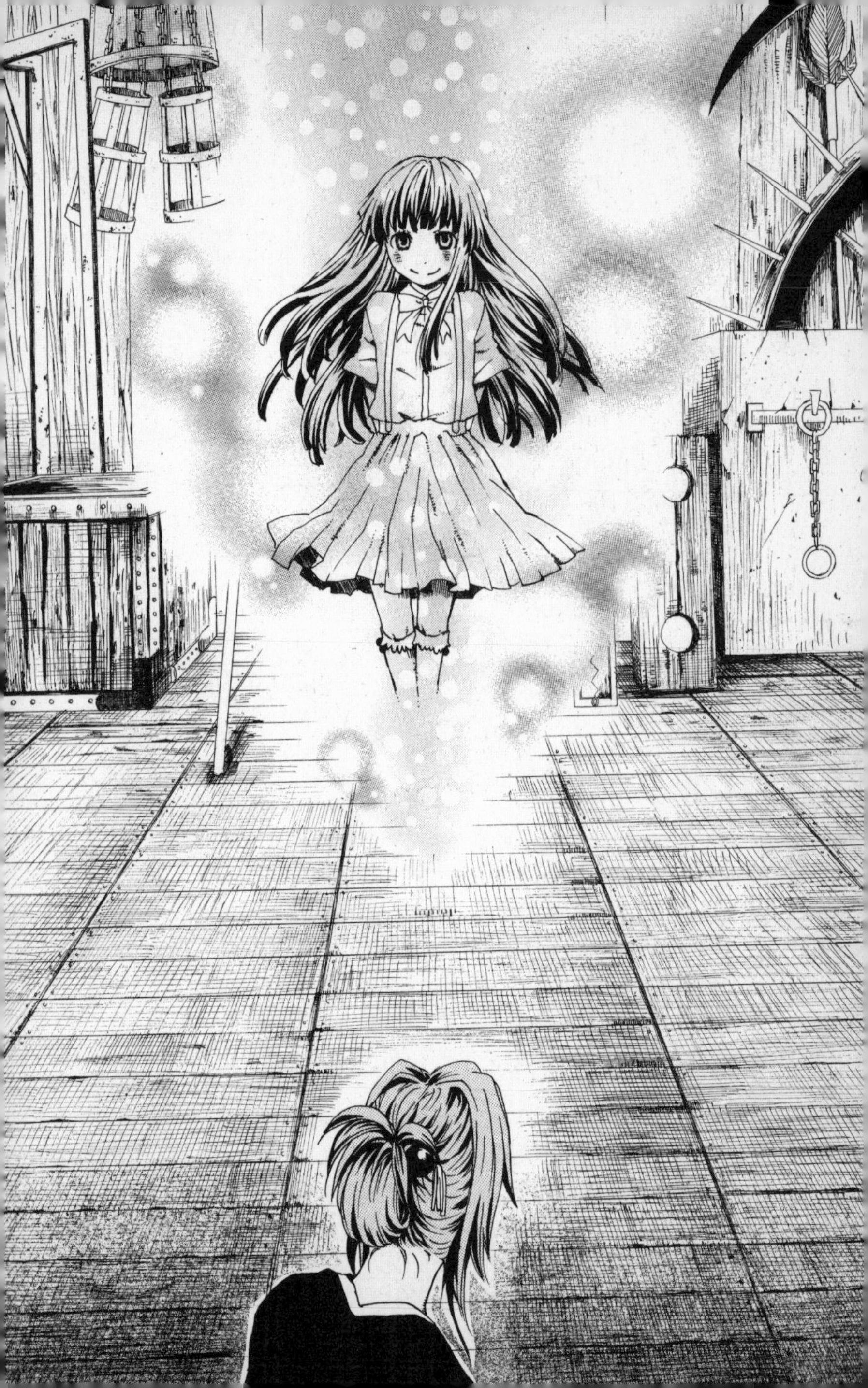

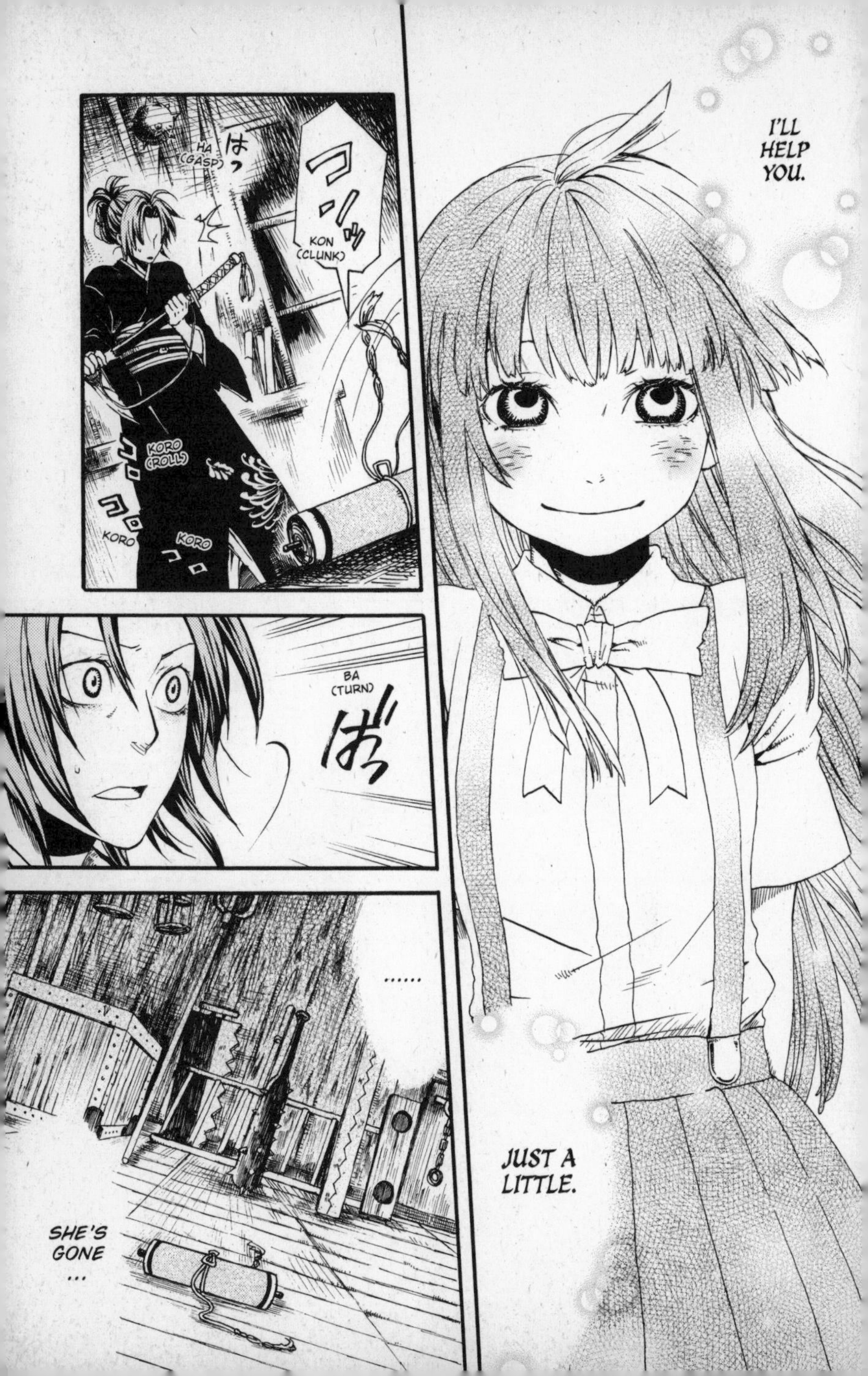
I'LL HELP YOU.
JUST A LITTLE.
KON (CLUNK)
コンッ
HA (GASP)
はっ
KORO (ROLL)
コロ
KORO
コロ
KORO
コロ
BA (TURN)
ばっ
......
SHE'S GONE ...

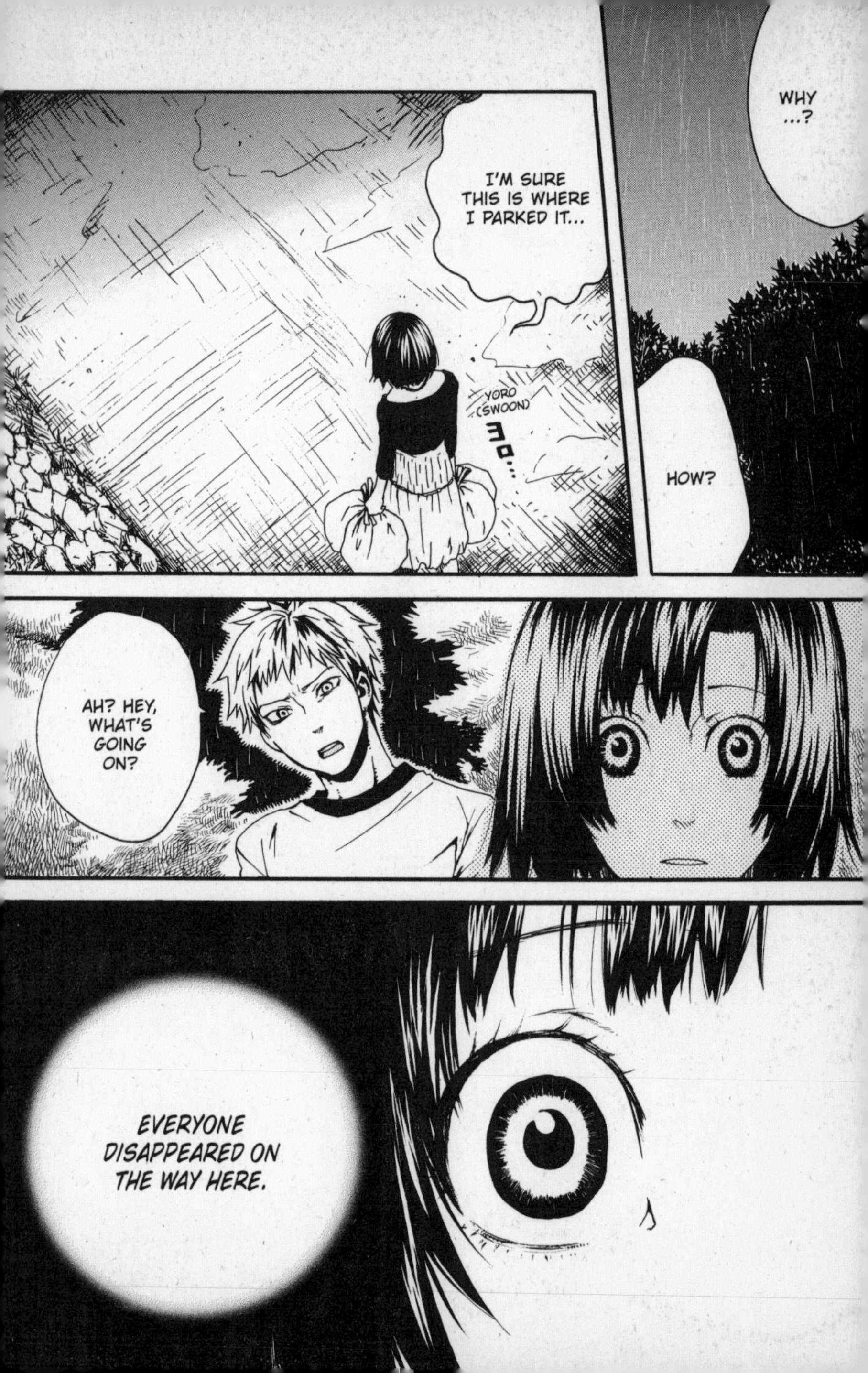
WHY ...?
HOW?
I'M SURE THIS IS WHERE I PARKED IT...
YORO (SWOON)
ヨロ...
AH? HEY, WHAT'S GOING ON?
EVERYONE DISAPPEARED ON THE WAY HERE.

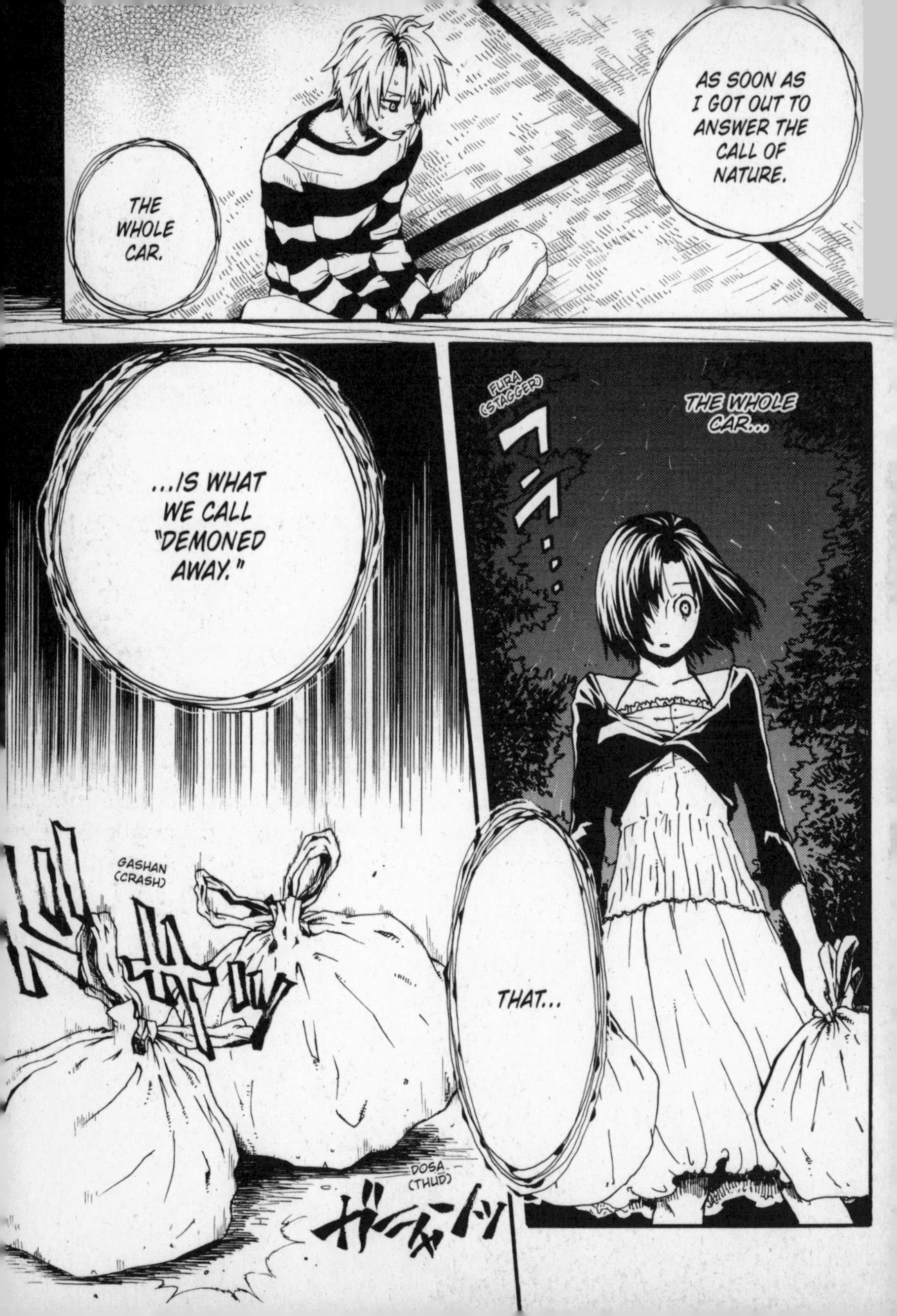
AS SOON AS I GOT OUT TO ANSWER THE CALL OF NATURE.
THE WHOLE CAR.
FURA (STAGGER)
THE WHOLE CAR...
THAT...
...IS WHAT WE CALL "DEMONED AWAY."
GASHAN (CRASH)
DOSA (THUD)

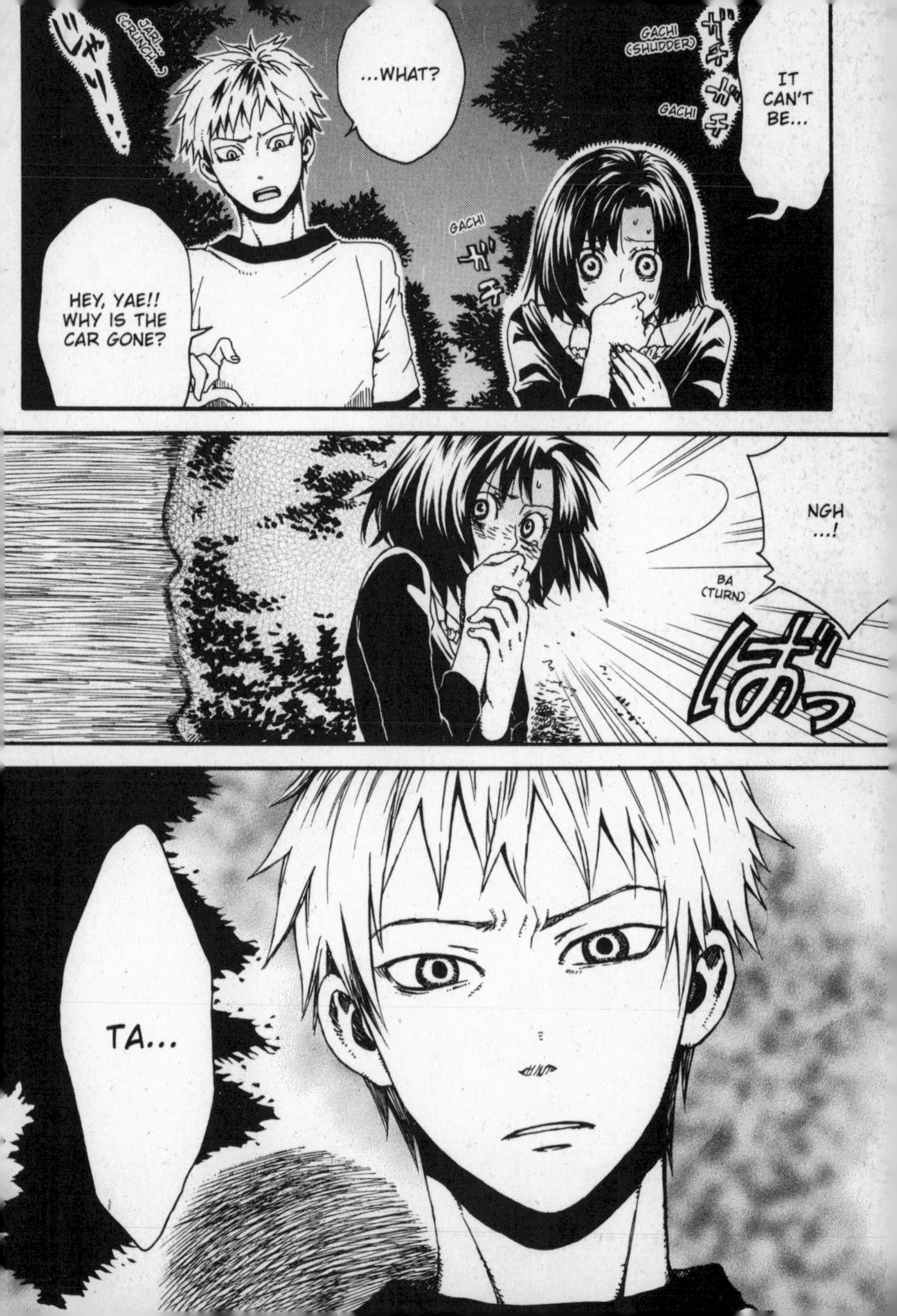
GACHI (SHUDDER)
ガチ
GACHI
ガチ
IT CAN'T BE...
...WHAT?
JARI... (CRUNCH...)
ジャリ...
GACHI
ガチ
HEY, YAE!! WHY IS THE CAR GONE?
NGH ...!
BA (TURN)
ばっ
TA...

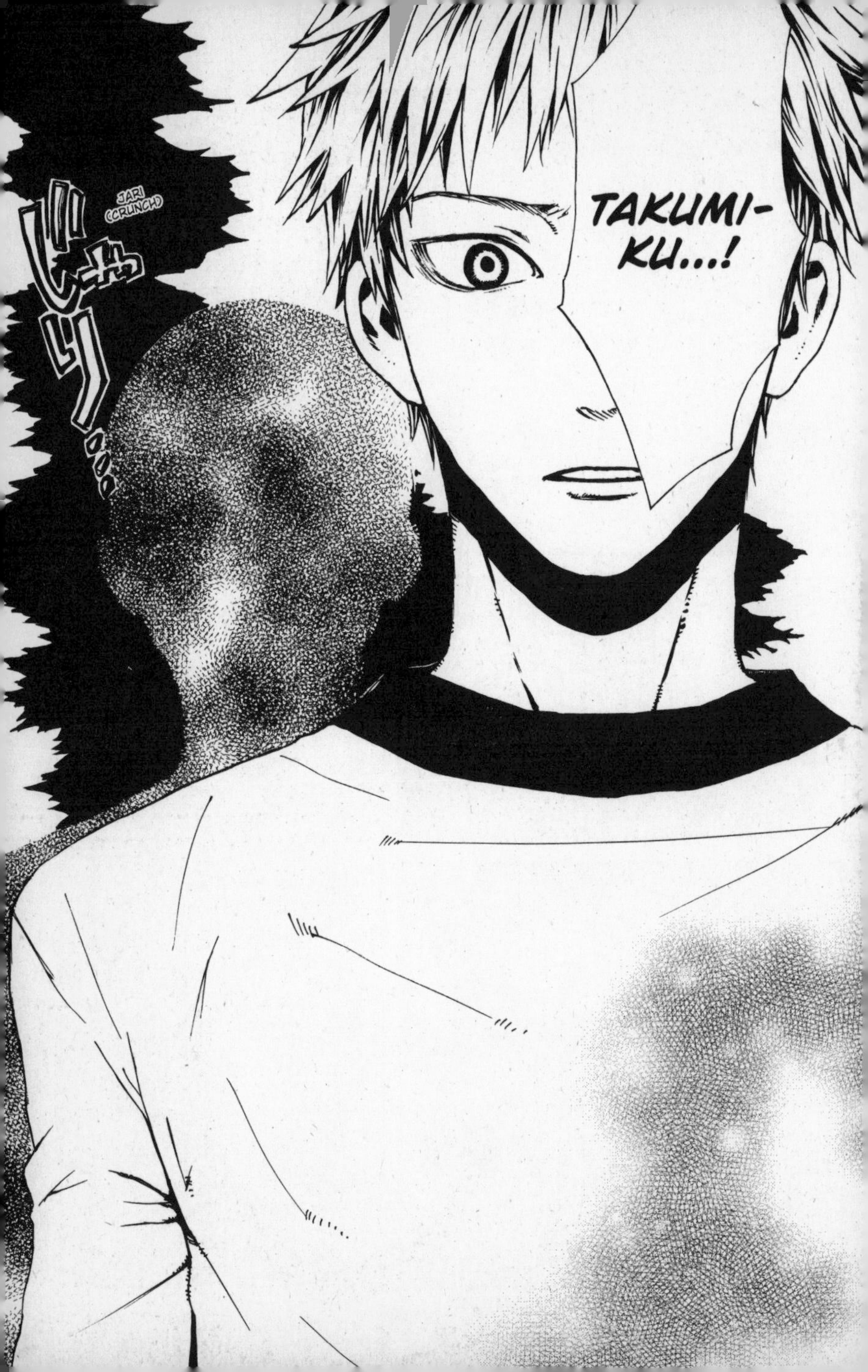
TAKUMI-KU...!
JARI (CRUNCH)

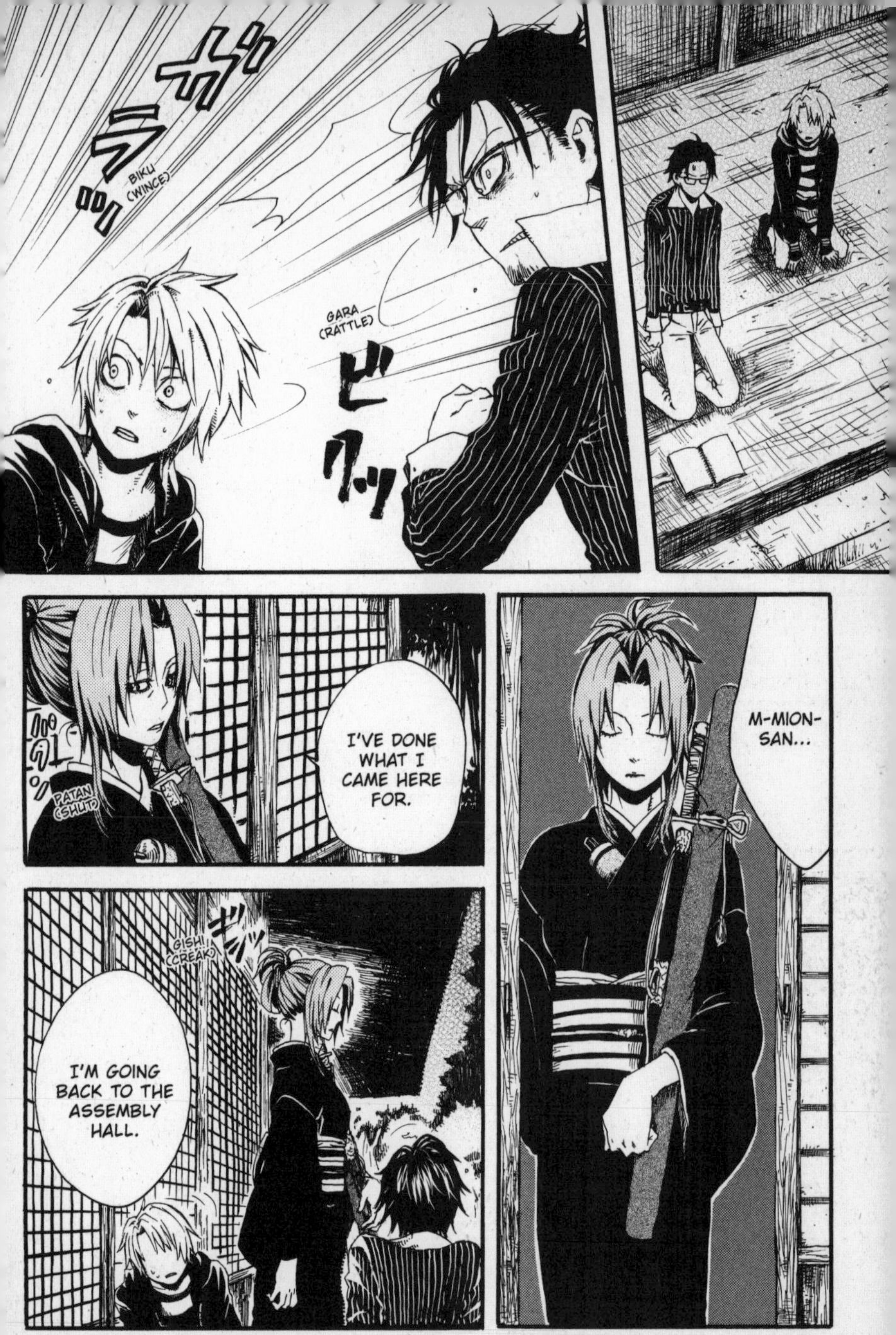
ガラッ
BIKU (WINCE)
GARA (RATTLE)
ビクッ
M-MION-SAN...
I'VE DONE WHAT I CAME HERE FOR.
パタン
PATAN (SHUT)
GISHI (CREAK)
ギシ
I'M GOING BACK TO THE ASSEMBLY HALL.

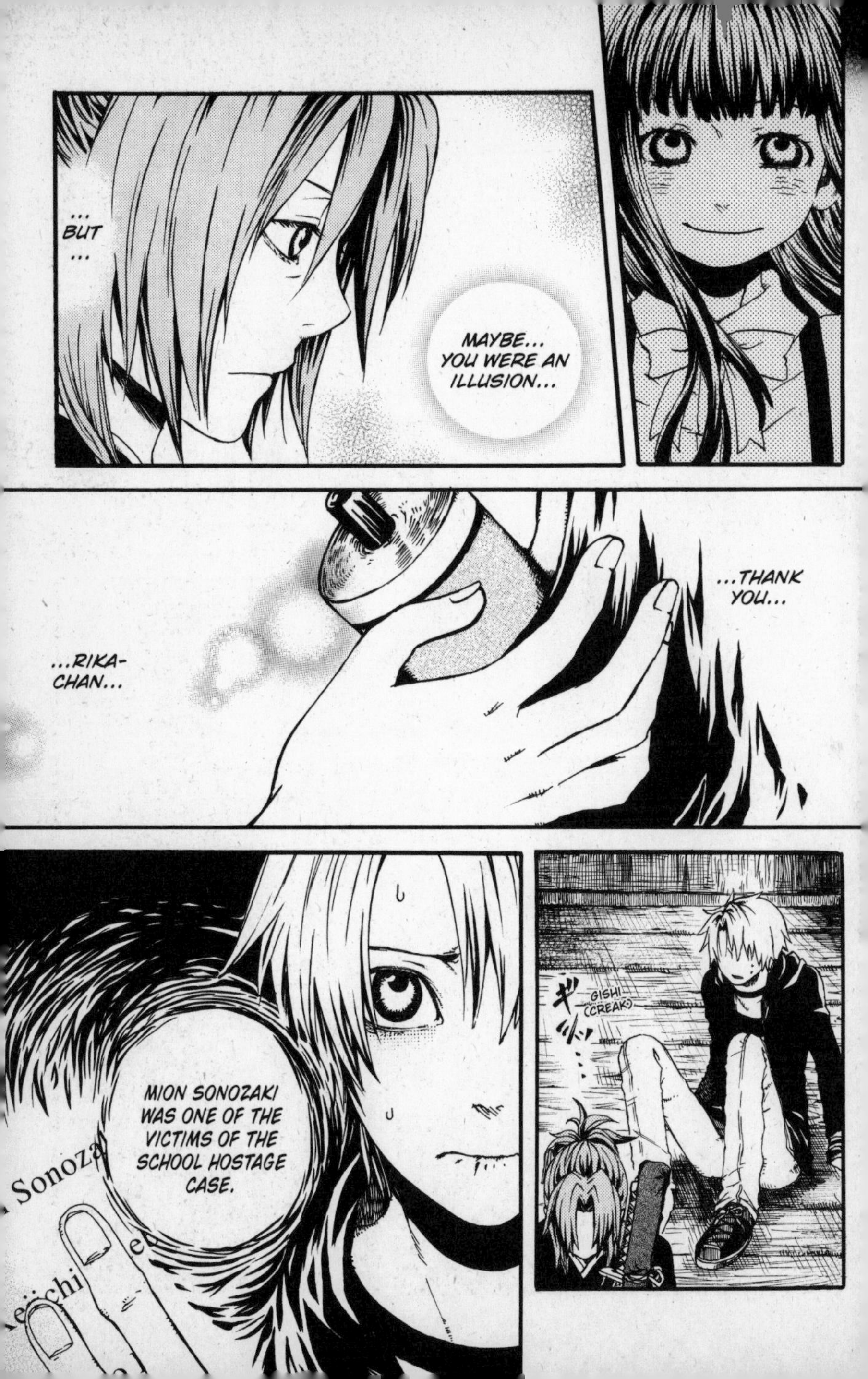
MAYBE... YOU WERE AN ILLUSION...
...BUT...
...THANK YOU...
...RIKA-CHAN...
GISHI (CREAK)
MION SONOZAKI WAS ONE OF THE VICTIMS OF THE SCHOOL HOSTAGE CASE.
Sonoza

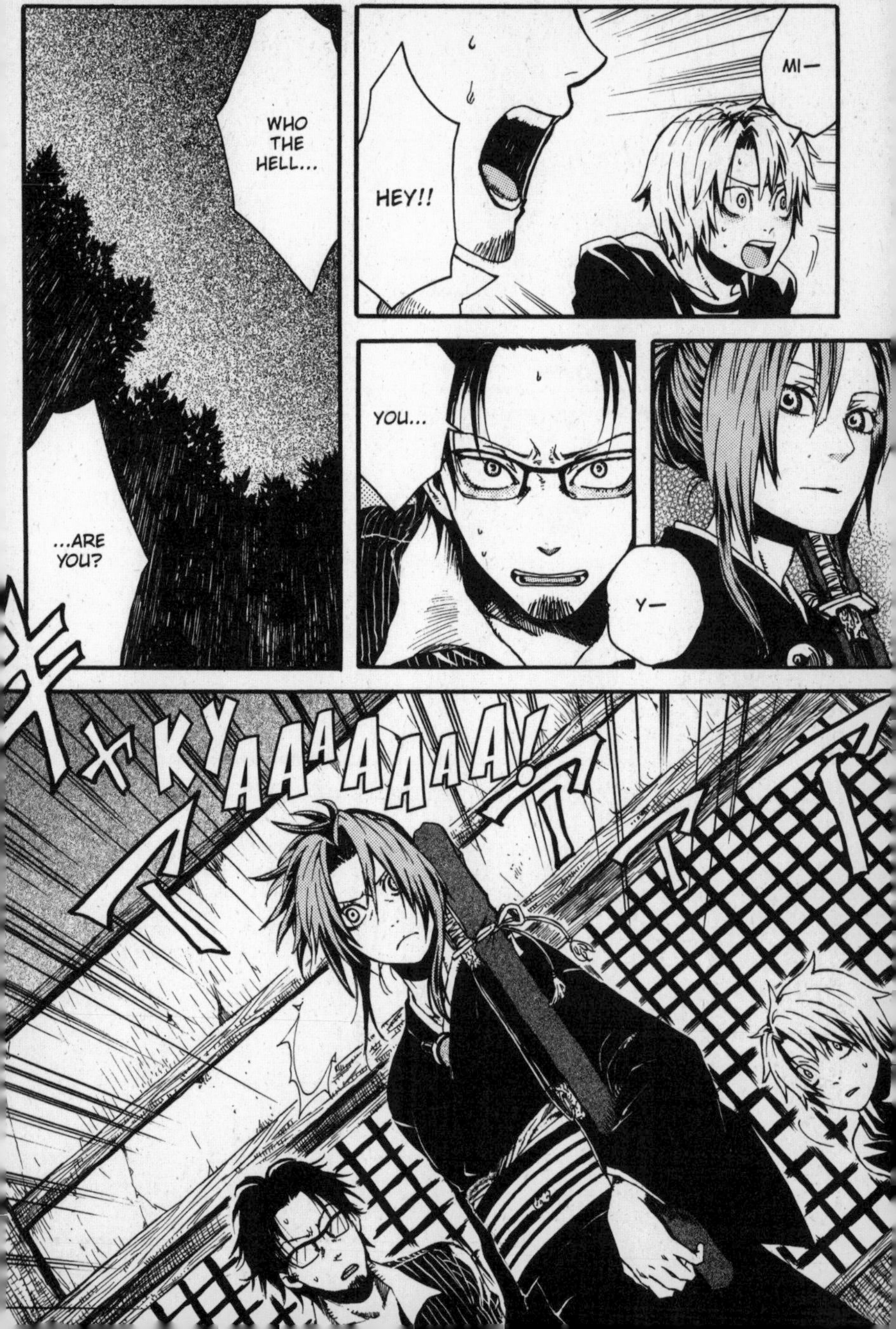
MI—
HEY!!
Y—
YOU...
WHO THE HELL...
...ARE YOU?
KYAAAAAAA!

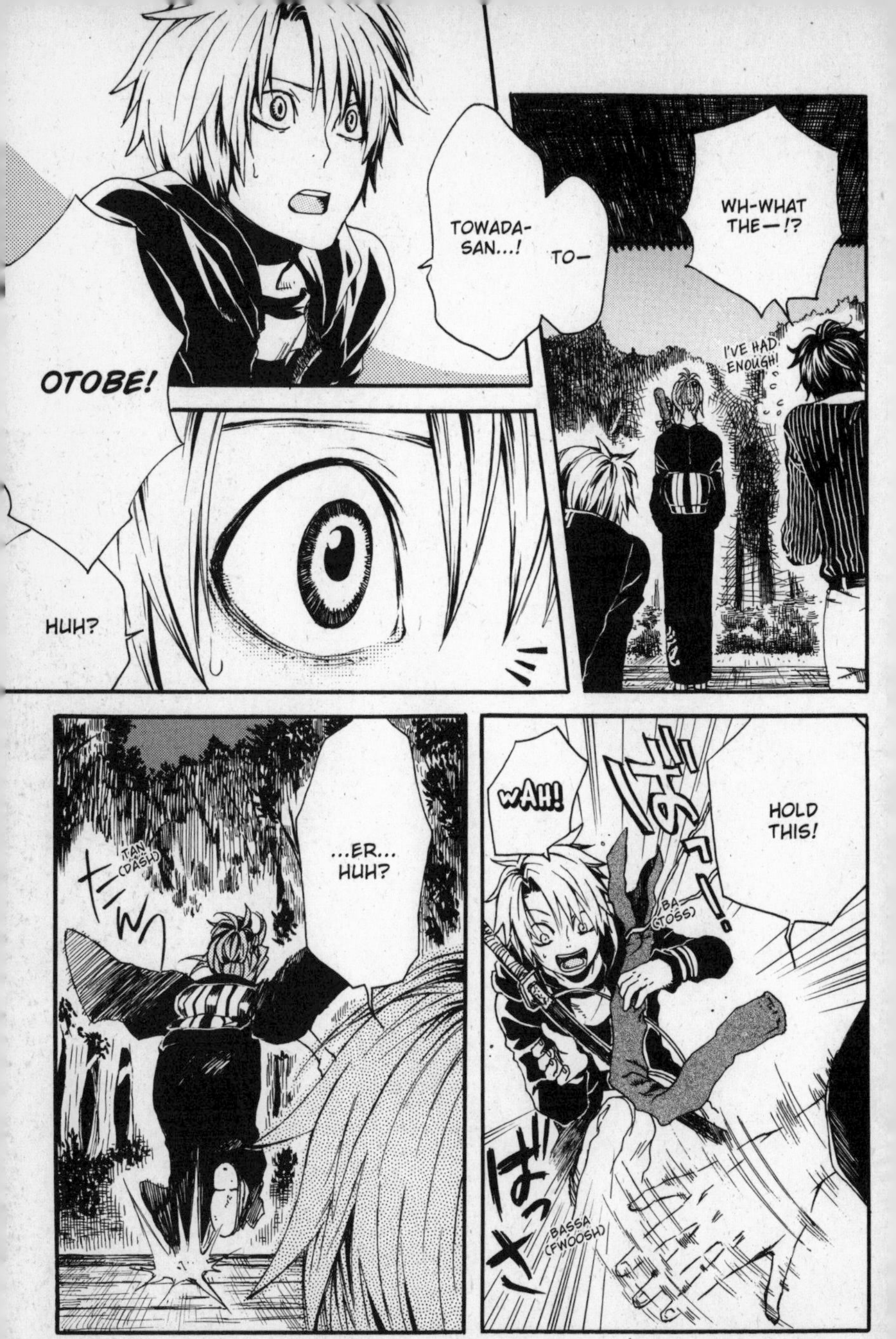
WH-WHAT THE—!?
TO—
I'VE HAD ENOUGH!
TOWADA-SAN...!
OTOBE!
HUH?
HOLD THIS!
WAH!
BA (TOSS)
BASSA (FWOOSH)
...ER... HUH?
TAN (DASH)

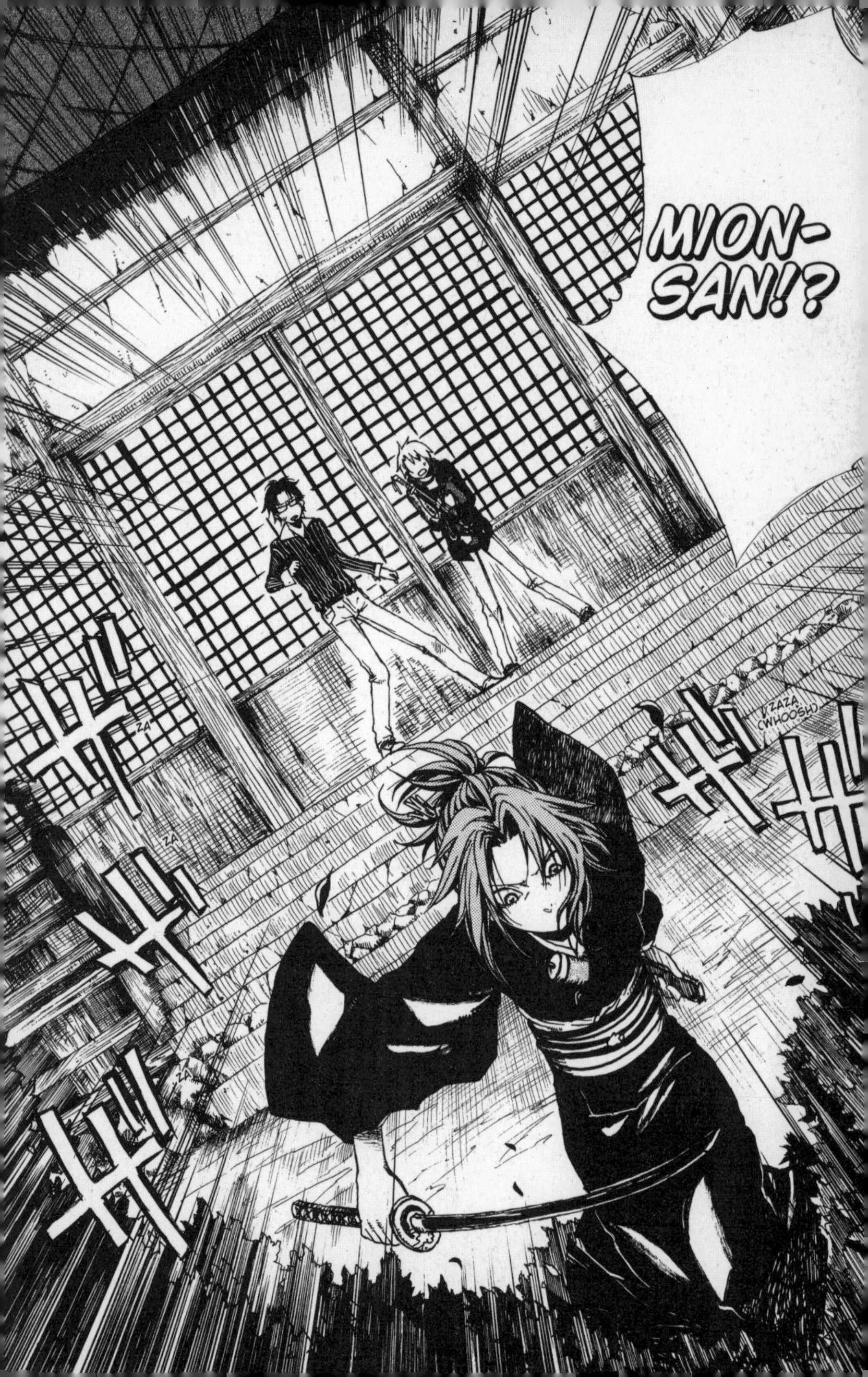
MION-SAN!?
ZAZA (WHOOSH)
ZA
ZA
ZA

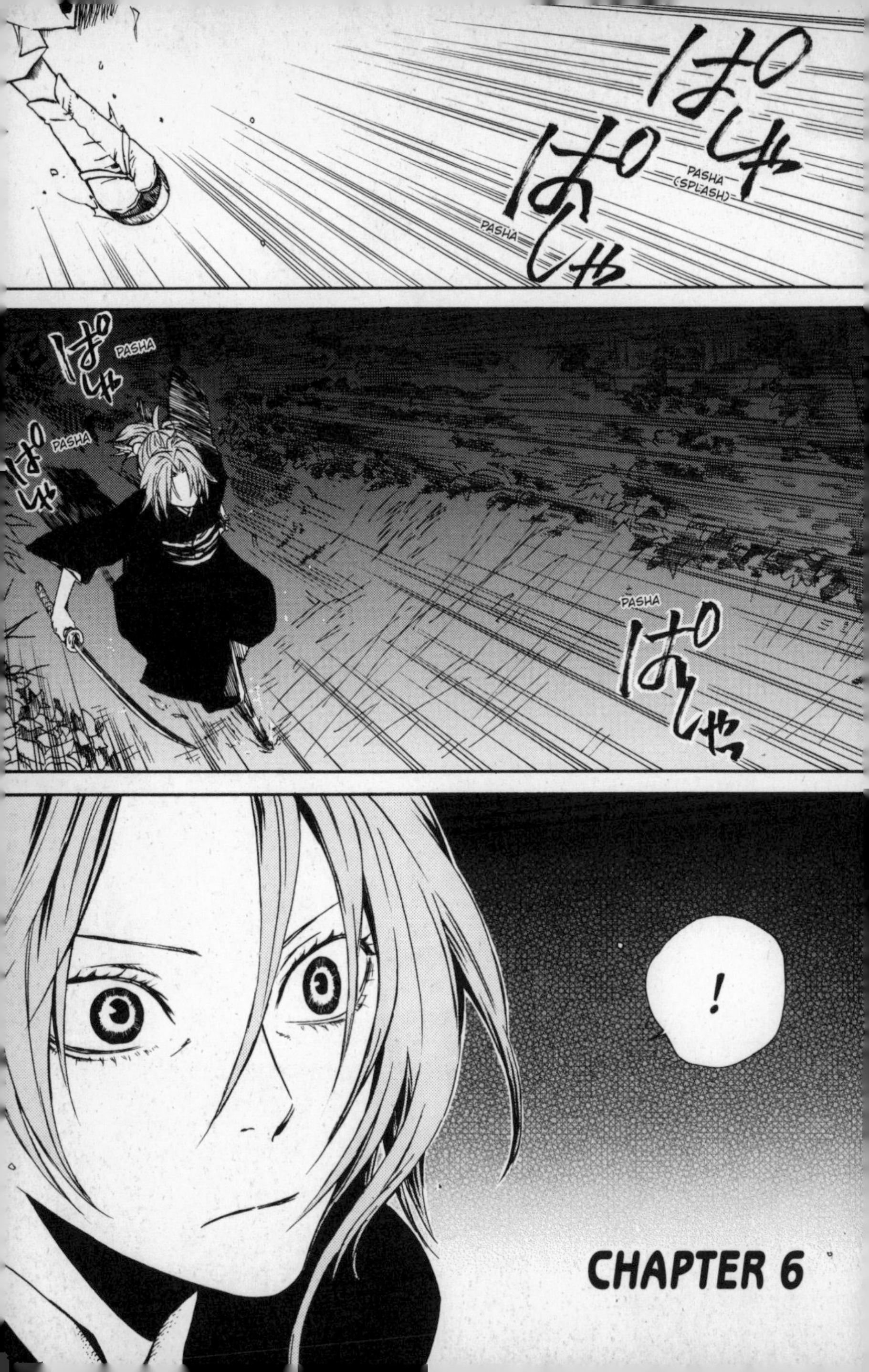
ぱしゃ
PASHA (SPLASH)
ぱしゃ
PASHA
PASHA
ぱしゃ
ぱしゃ
PASHA
ぱしゃ
PASHA
!
CHAPTER 6

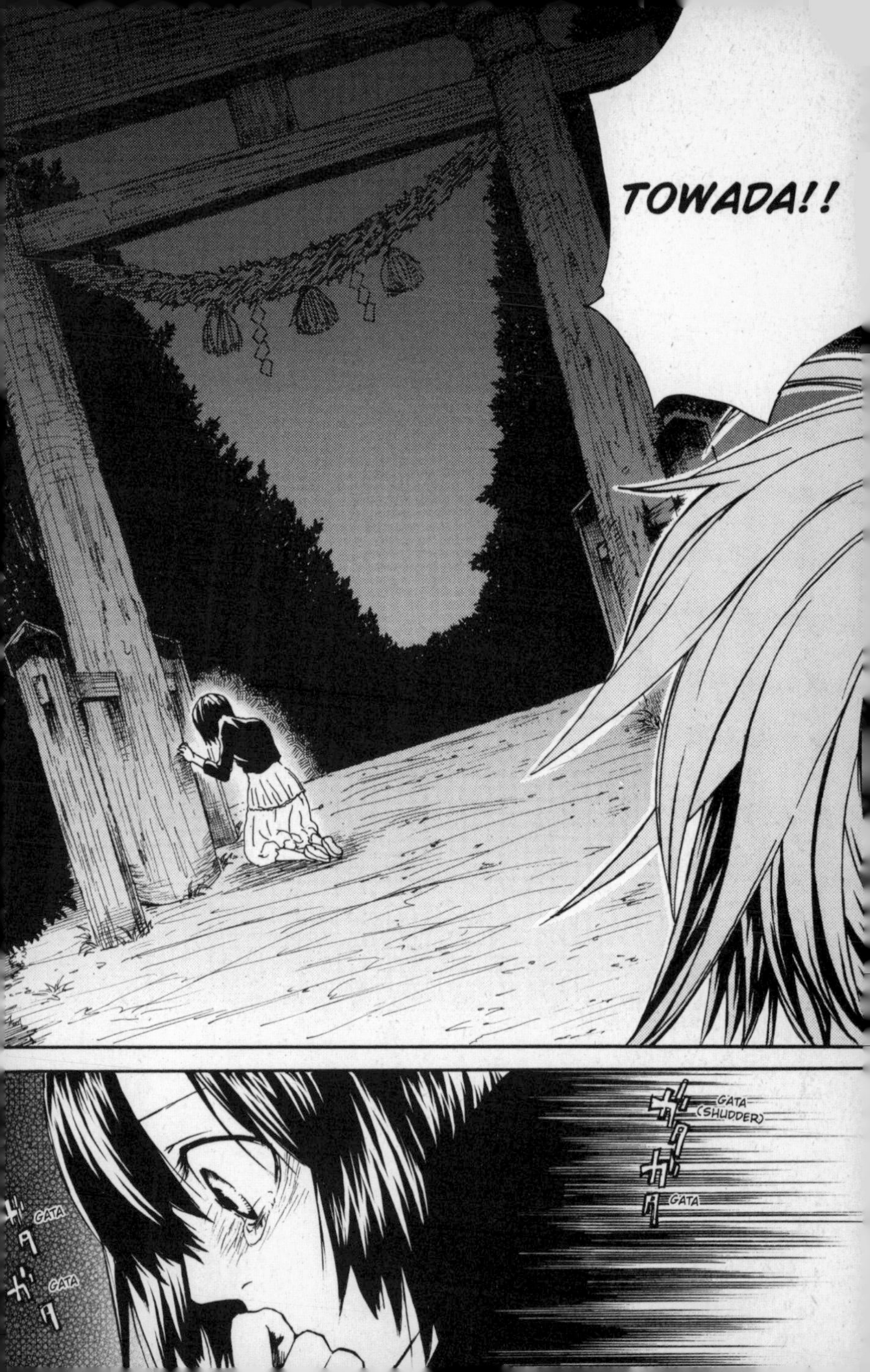
TOWADA!!
GATA (SHUDDER)
GATA
GATA
GATA

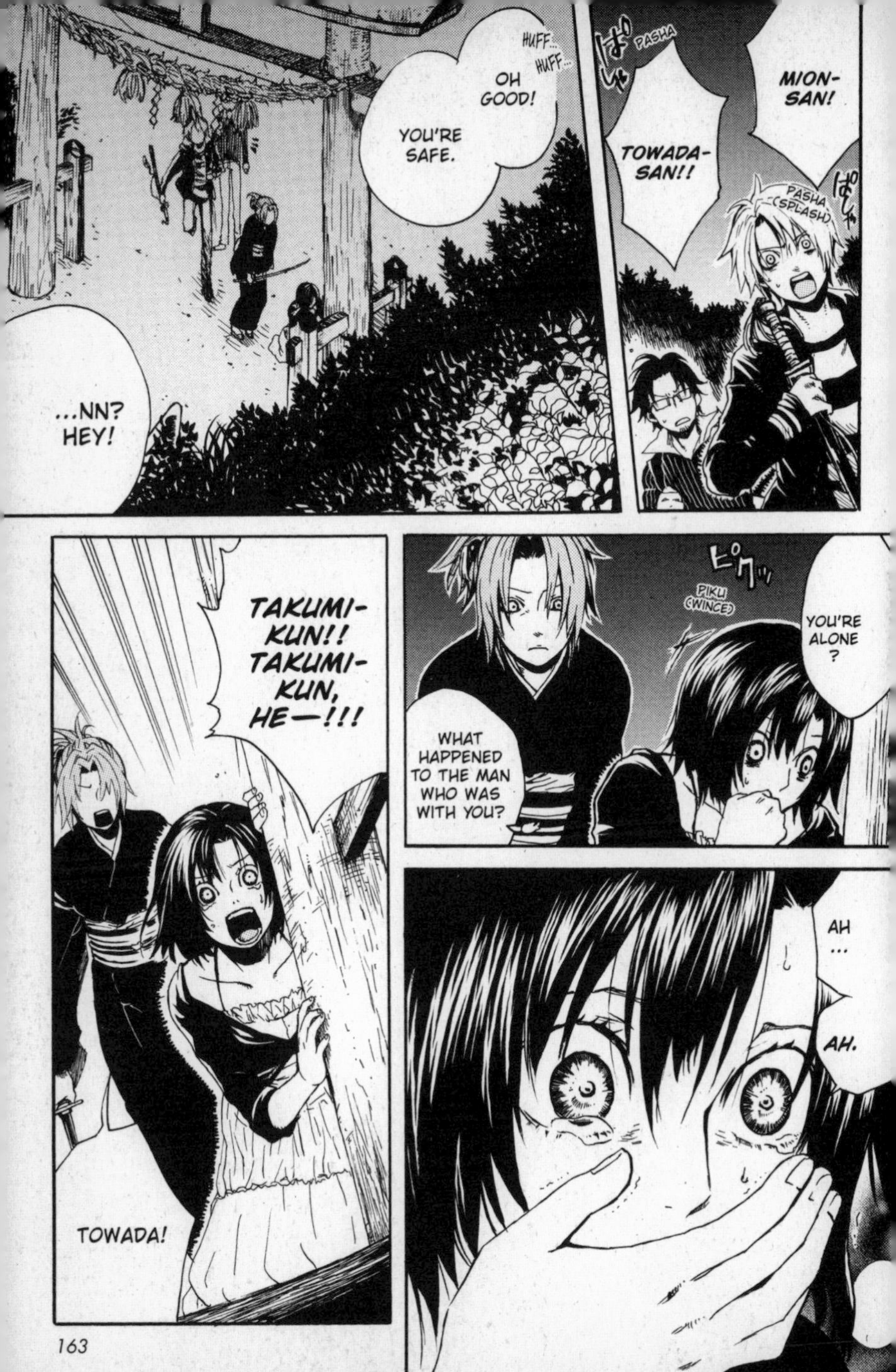

ぱしゃ
PASHA
MION-SAN!
TOWADA-SAN!!
ぱしゃ
PASHA (SPLASH)
HUFF... HUFF...
OH GOOD!
YOU'RE SAFE.
...NN? HEY!
ピクッ
PIKU (WINCE)
YOU'RE ALONE?
WHAT HAPPENED TO THE MAN WHO WAS WITH YOU?
AH...
AH.
TAKUMI-KUN!! TAKUMI-KUN, HE—!!!
TOWADA!

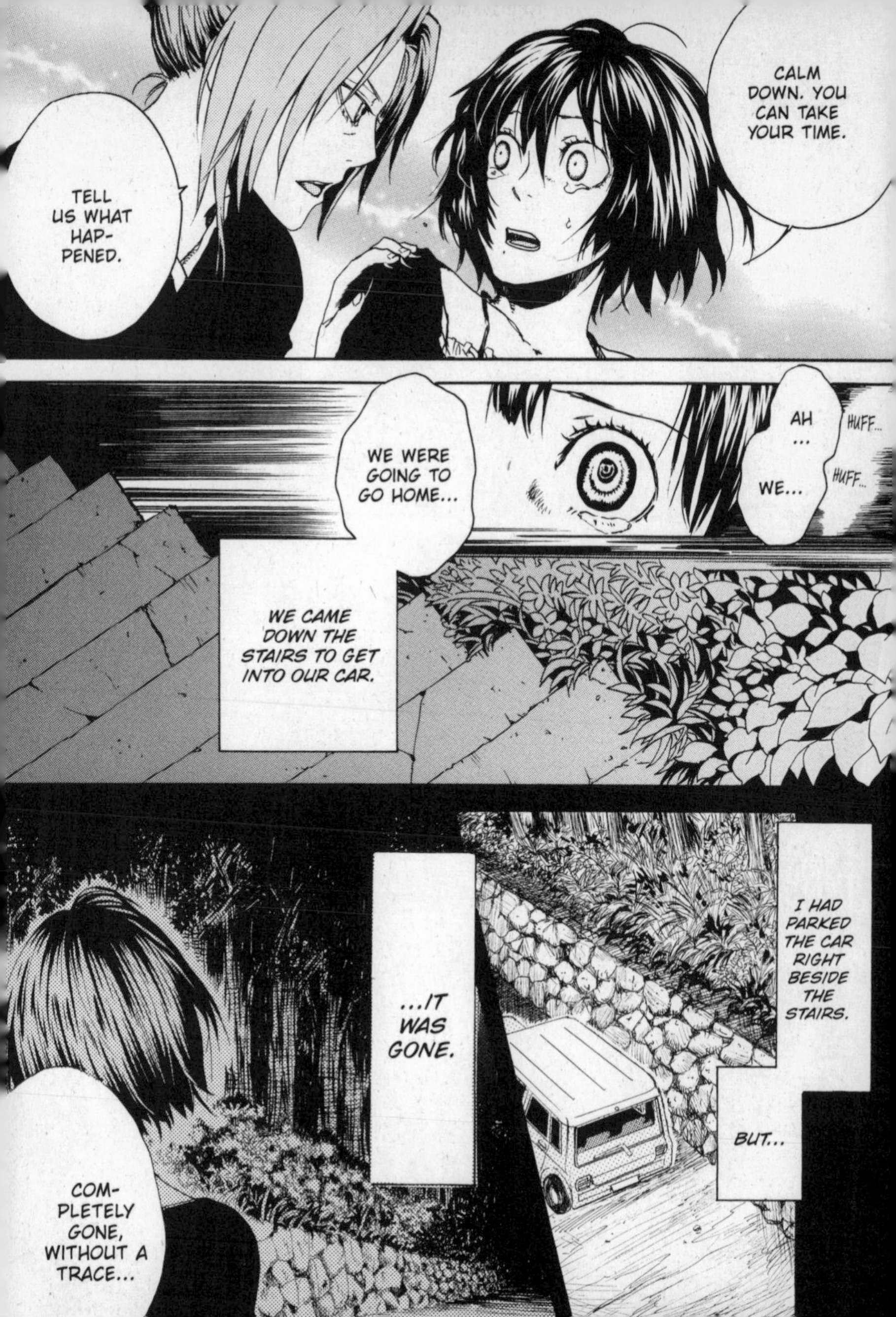
CALM DOWN. YOU CAN TAKE YOUR TIME.
TELL US WHAT HAP-PENED.
AH... WE...
HUFF...
HUFF...
WE WERE GOING TO GO HOME...
WE CAME DOWN THE STAIRS TO GET INTO OUR CAR.
I HAD PARKED THE CAR RIGHT BESIDE THE STAIRS.
BUT...
...IT WAS GONE.
COM-PLETELY GONE, WITHOUT A TRACE...

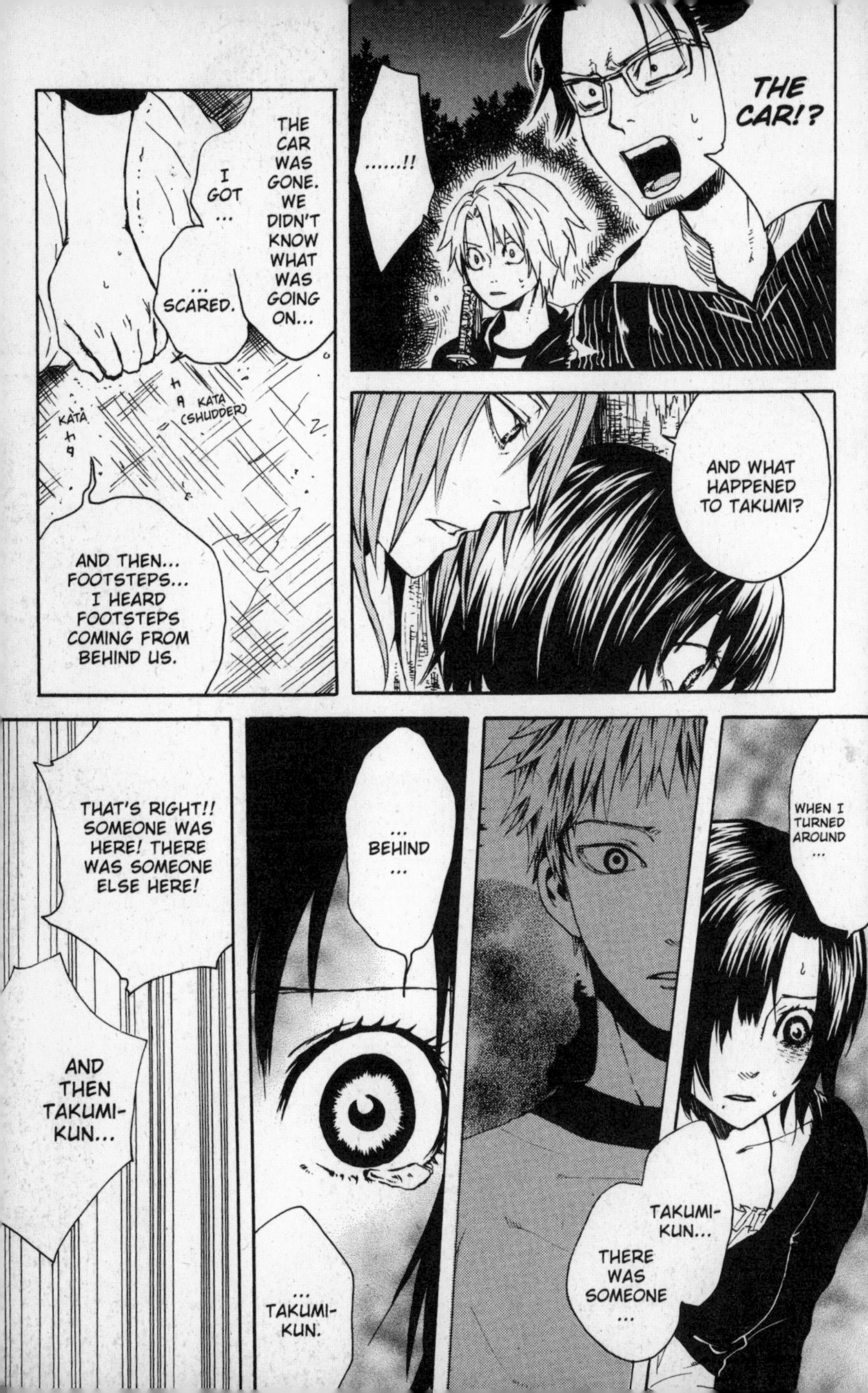
THE CAR!?
......!!
AND WHAT HAPPENED TO TAKUMI?
THE CAR WAS GONE. WE DIDN'T KNOW WHAT WAS GOING ON...
I GOT ...
... SCARED.
カタ KATA (SHUDDER)
KATA カタ
AND THEN... FOOTSTEPS... I HEARD FOOTSTEPS COMING FROM BEHIND US.
WHEN I TURNED AROUND ...
TAKUMI-KUN... THERE WAS SOMEONE ...
... BEHIND ...
... TAKUMI-KUN.
THAT'S RIGHT!! SOMEONE WAS HERE! THERE WAS SOMEONE ELSE HERE!
AND THEN TAKUMI-KUN...

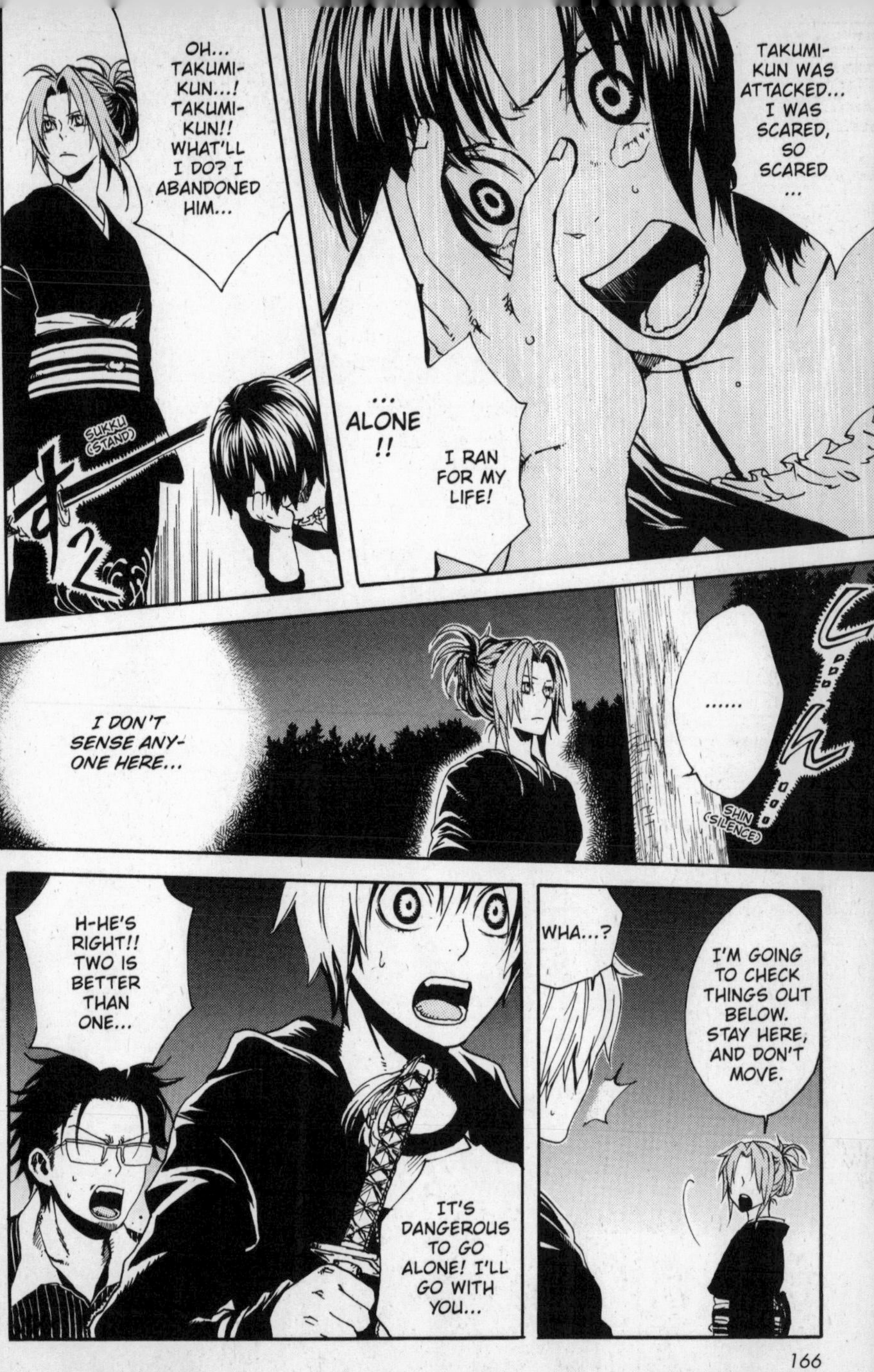
TAKUMI-KUN WAS ATTACKED... I WAS SCARED, SO SCARED ...
I RAN FOR MY LIFE!
... ALONE !!
OH... TAKUMI-KUN...! TAKUMI-KUN!! WHAT'LL I DO? I ABANDONED HIM...
SUKKU (STAND)
......
SHIN (SILENCE)
I DON'T SENSE ANY-ONE HERE...
I'M GOING TO CHECK THINGS OUT BELOW. STAY HERE, AND DON'T MOVE.
WHA...?
IT'S DANGEROUS TO GO ALONE! I'LL GO WITH YOU...
H-HE'S RIGHT!! TWO IS BETTER THAN ONE...

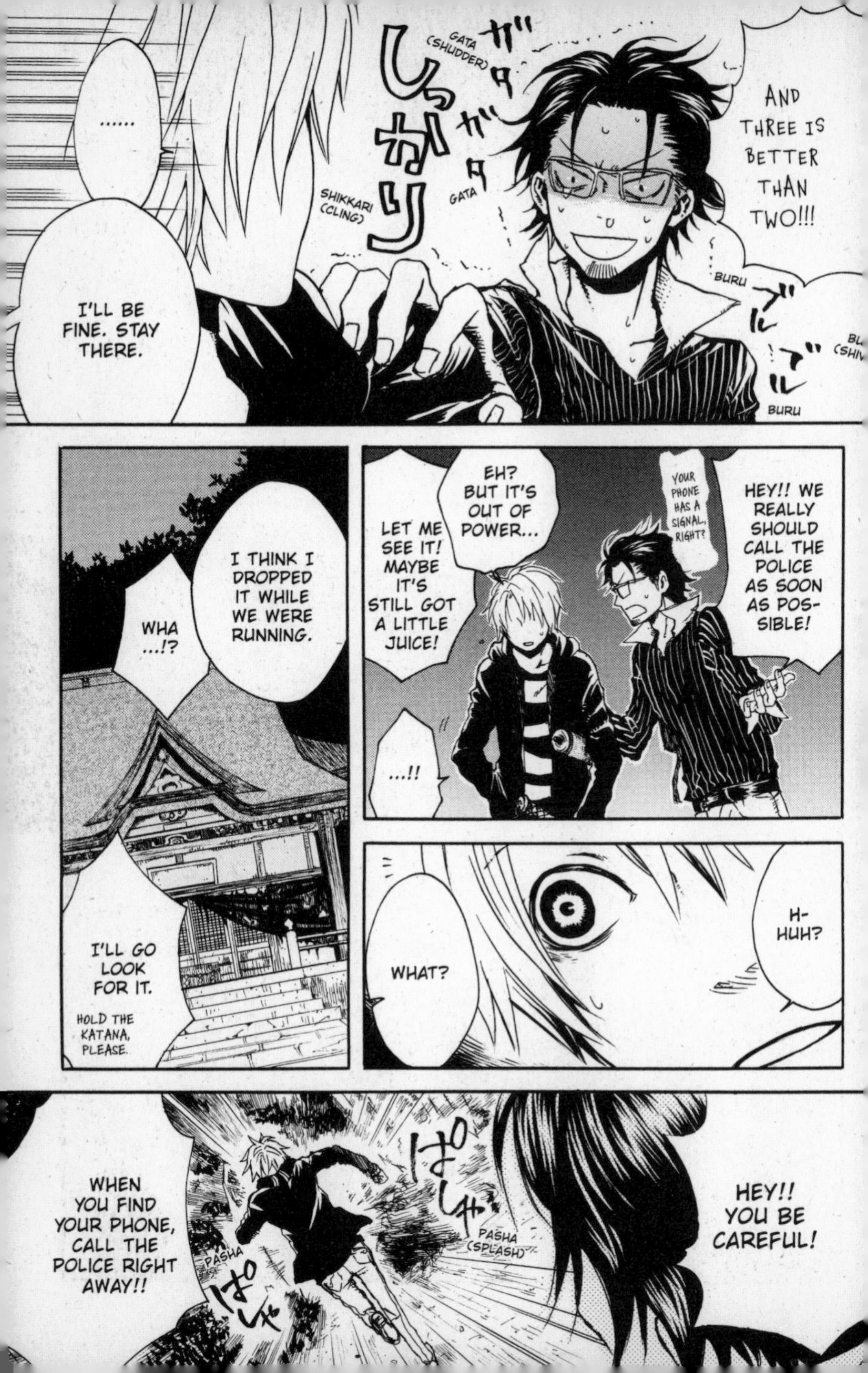
AND THREE IS BETTER THAN TWO!!!
BURU
ブル
ブル
BURU
GATA (SHUDDER)
ガタ
ガタ
GATA
しっかり
SHIKKARI (CLING)
......
I'LL BE FINE. STAY THERE.
HEY!! WE REALLY SHOULD CALL THE POLICE AS SOON AS POS-SIBLE!
YOUR PHONE HAS A SIGNAL, RIGHT?
EH? BUT IT'S OUT OF POWER...
LET ME SEE IT! MAYBE IT'S STILL GOT A LITTLE JUICE!
...!!
H-HUH?
WHAT?
I THINK I DROPPED IT WHILE WE WERE RUNNING.
WHA ...!?
I'LL GO LOOK FOR IT.
HOLD THE KATANA, PLEASE.
HEY!! YOU BE CAREFUL!
ぱしゃ
PASHA (SPLASH)
PASHA
ぱしゃ
WHEN YOU FIND YOUR PHONE, CALL THE POLICE RIGHT AWAY!!

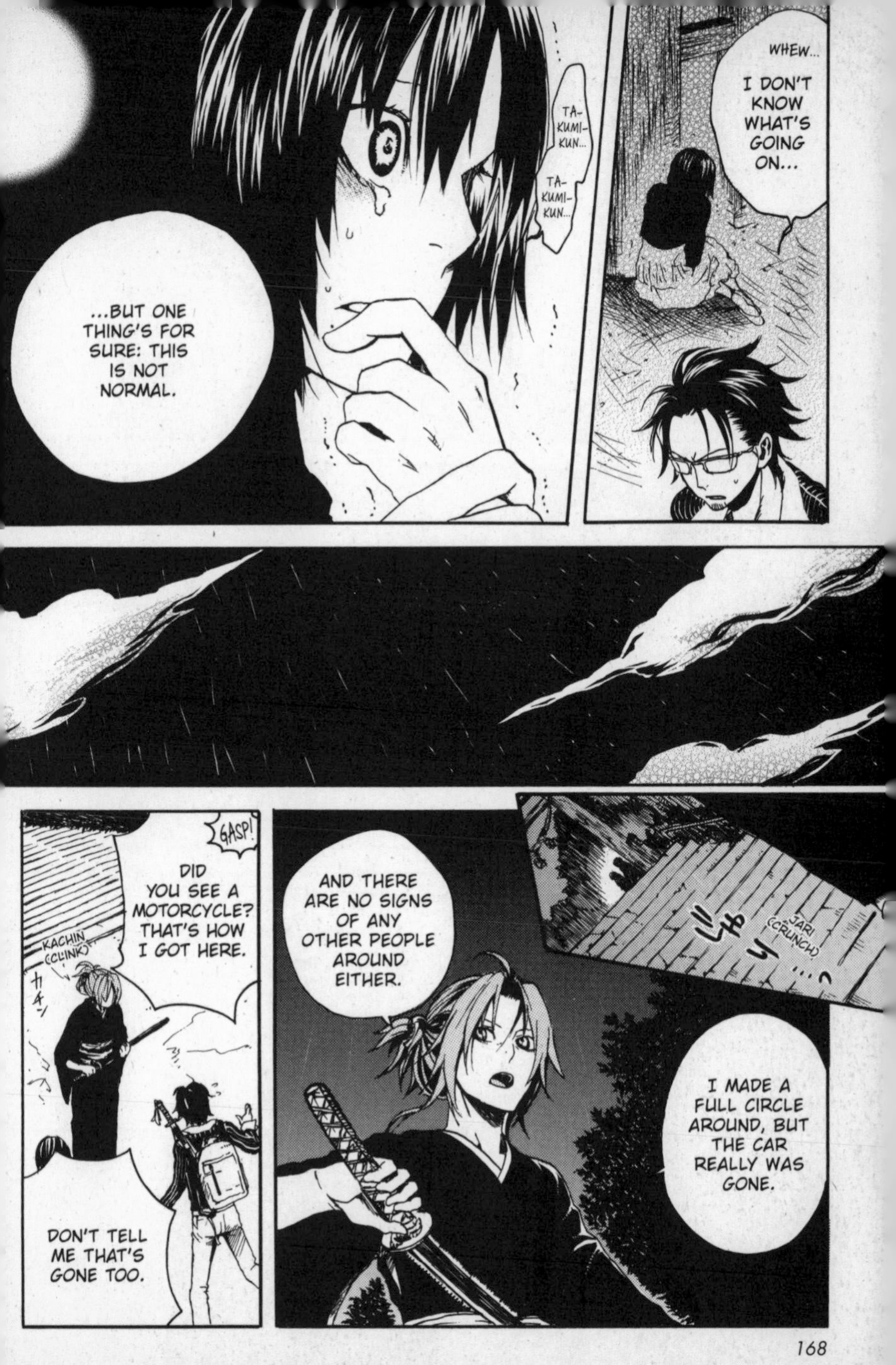
WHEW...
I DON'T KNOW WHAT'S GOING ON...
TA-KUMI-KUN...
TA-KUMI-KUN...
...BUT ONE THING'S FOR SURE: THIS IS NOT NORMAL.
JARI (CRUNCH)
I MADE A FULL CIRCLE AROUND, BUT THE CAR REALLY WAS GONE.
AND THERE ARE NO SIGNS OF ANY OTHER PEOPLE AROUND EITHER.
GASP!
DID YOU SEE A MOTORCYCLE? THAT'S HOW I GOT HERE.
KACHIN (CLINK)
DON'T TELL ME THAT'S GONE TOO.

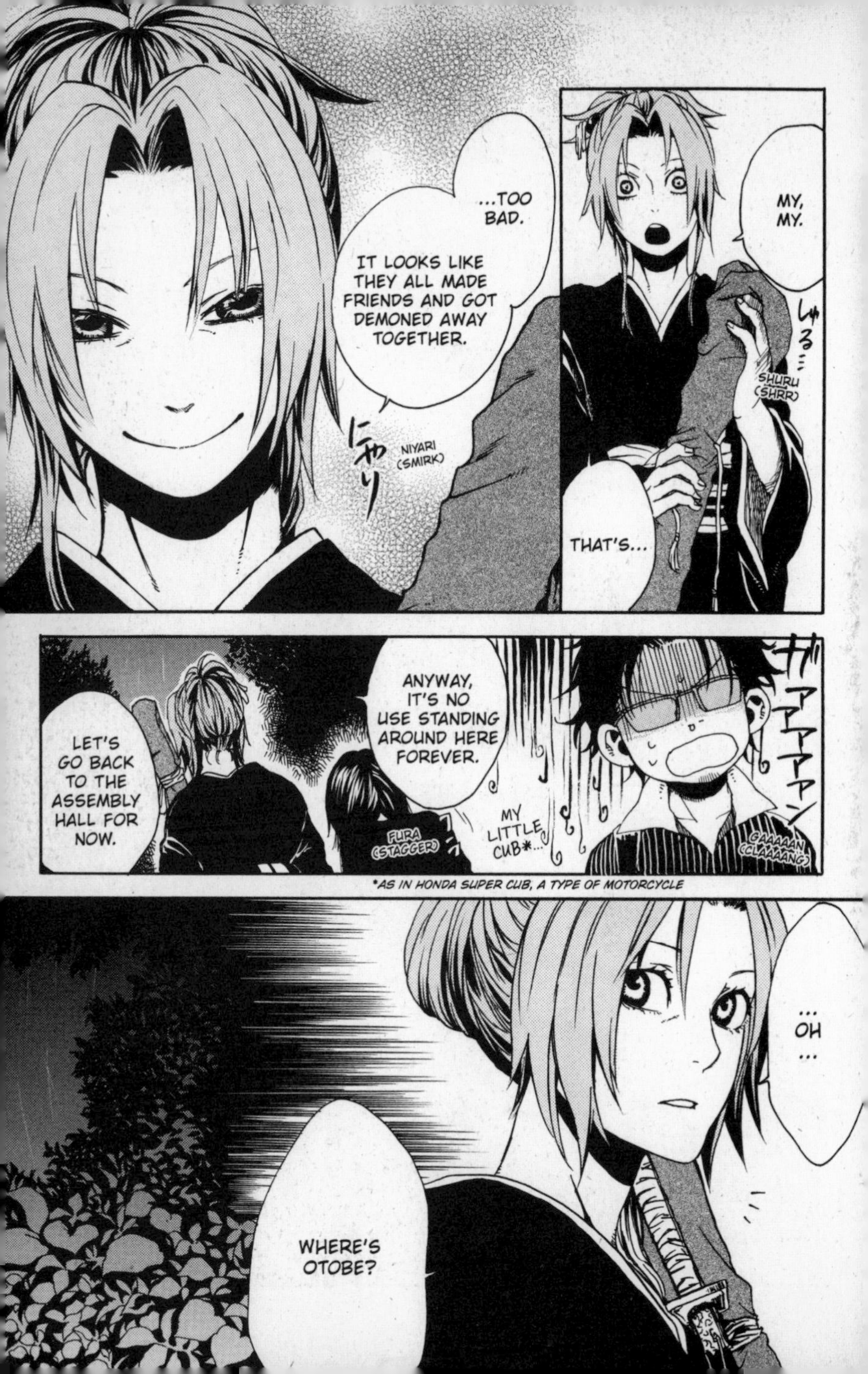
MY, MY.
しゅる
SHURU (SHRR)
THAT'S...
...TOO BAD.
IT LOOKS LIKE THEY ALL MADE FRIENDS AND GOT DEMONED AWAY TOGETHER.
にやり
NIYARI (SMIRK)
ガアアアアン
GAAAAAN (CLAAAANG)
MY LITTLE CUB*...
FURA (STAGGER)
ANYWAY, IT'S NO USE STANDING AROUND HERE FOREVER.
LET'S GO BACK TO THE ASSEMBLY HALL FOR NOW.
*AS IN HONDA SUPER CUB, A TYPE OF MOTORCYCLE
...OH...
WHERE'S OTOBE?

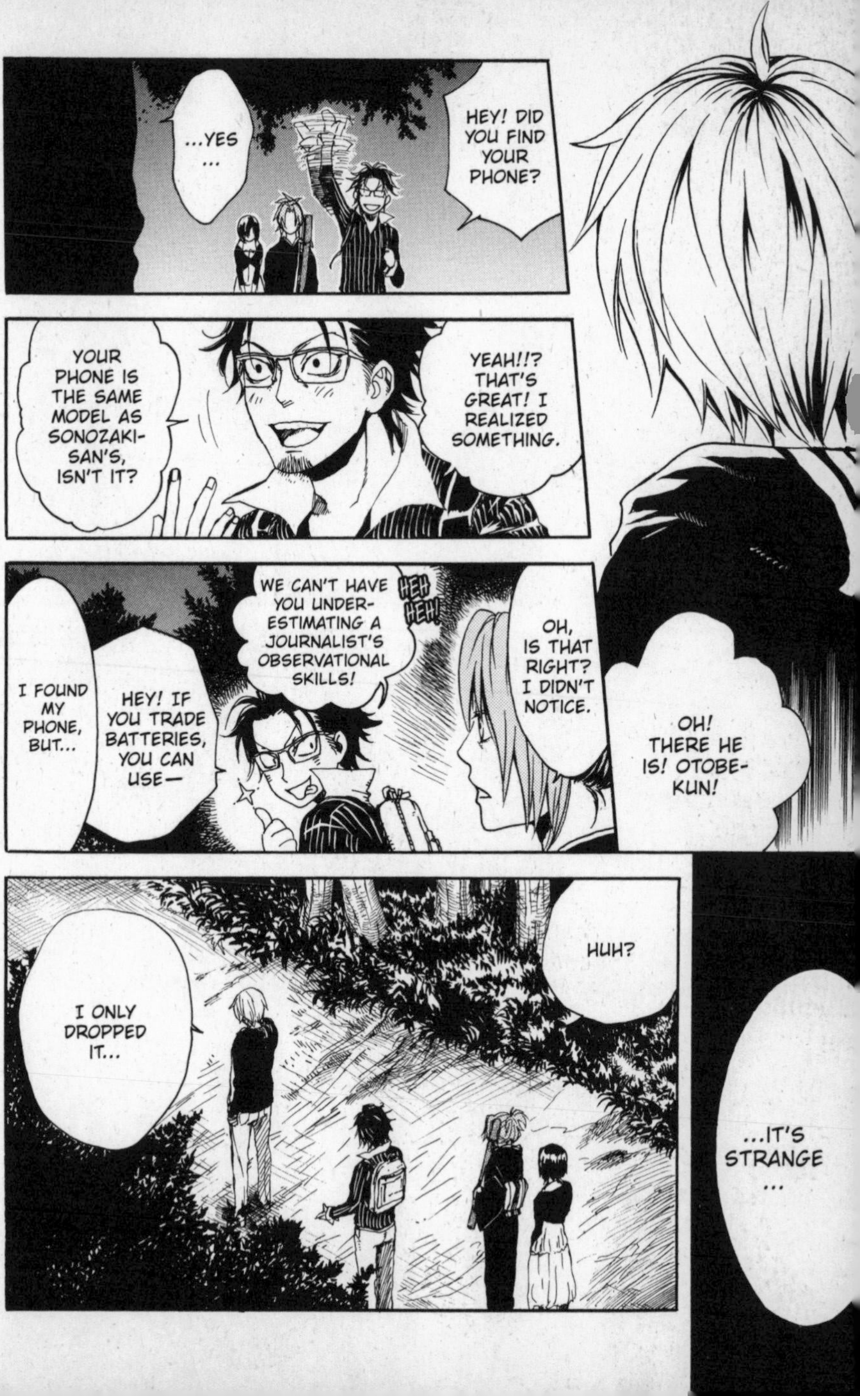
OH! THERE HE IS! OTOBE-KUN!
...IT'S STRANGE ...
HEY! DID YOU FIND YOUR PHONE?
...YES ...
YEAH!!? THAT'S GREAT! I REALIZED SOMETHING.
YOUR PHONE IS THE SAME MODEL AS SONOZAKI-SAN'S, ISN'T IT?
OH, IS THAT RIGHT? I DIDN'T NOTICE.
HEH HEH!
WE CAN'T HAVE YOU UNDER-ESTIMATING A JOURNALIST'S OBSERVATIONAL SKILLS!
HEY! IF YOU TRADE BATTERIES, YOU CAN USE—
I FOUND MY PHONE, BUT...
HUH?
I ONLY DROPPED IT...

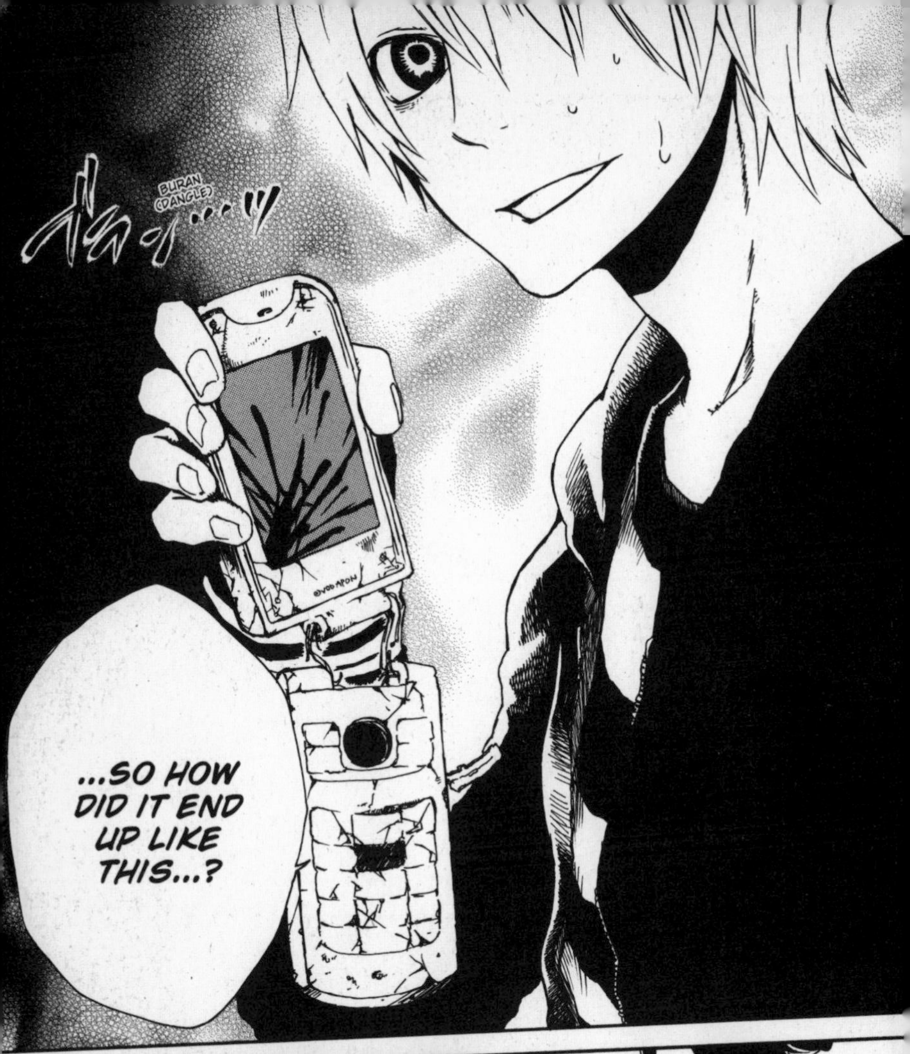
BURAN (DANGLE)
...SO HOW DID IT END UP LIKE THIS...?
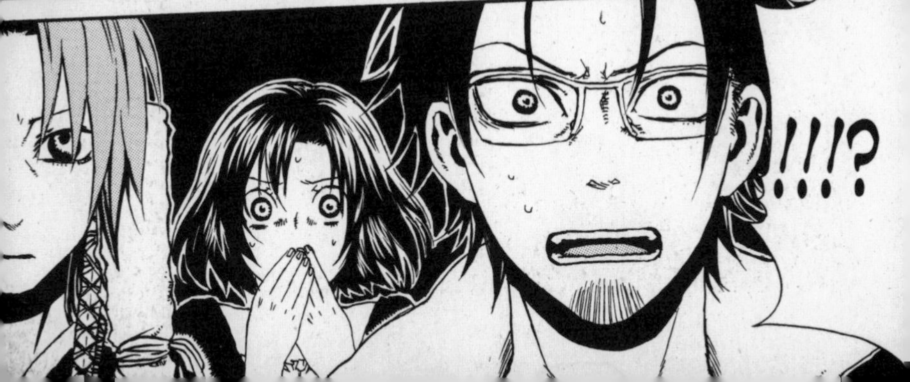
!!!?

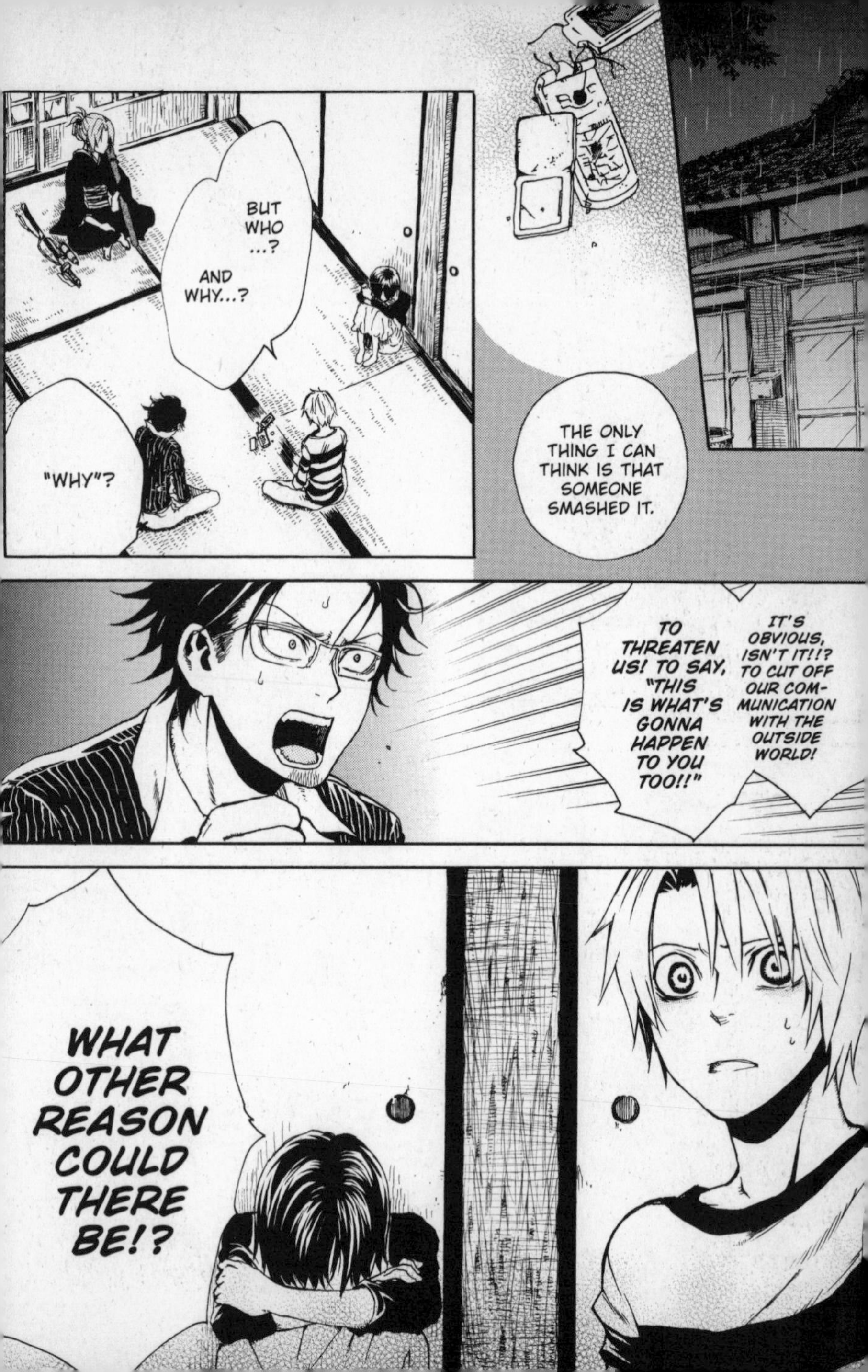
THE ONLY THING I CAN THINK IS THAT SOMEONE SMASHED IT.
BUT WHO ...?
AND WHY...?
"WHY"?
IT'S OBVIOUS, ISN'T IT!!? TO CUT OFF OUR COMMUNICATION WITH THE OUTSIDE WORLD!
TO THREATEN US! TO SAY, "THIS IS WHAT'S GONNA HAPPEN TO YOU TOO!!"
WHAT OTHER REASON COULD THERE BE!?

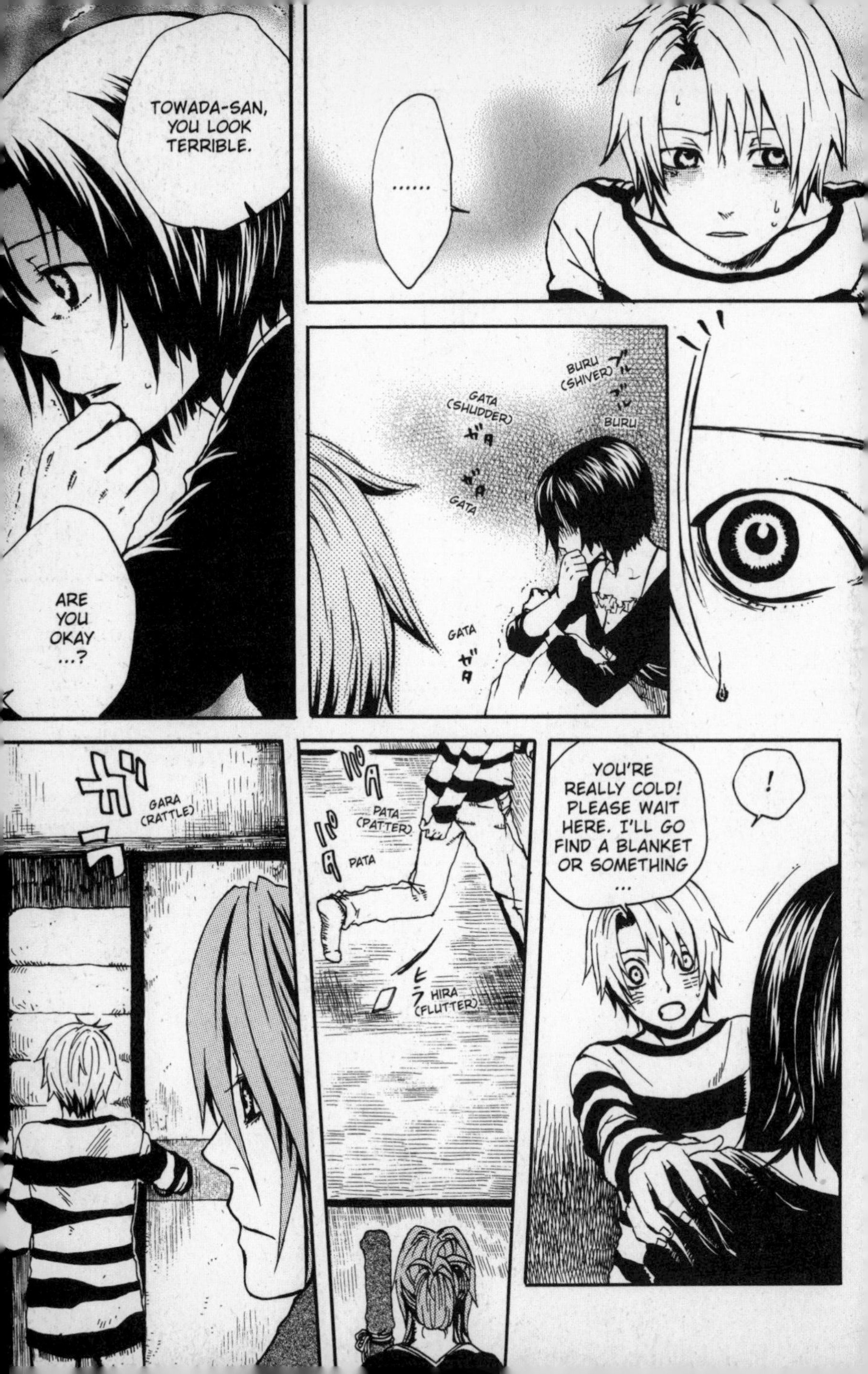
……
ブル
BURU (SHIVER)
ブル
BURU
GATA (SHUDDER)
ガタ
ガタ
GATA
GATA
ガタ
TOWADA-SAN, YOU LOOK TERRIBLE.
ARE YOU OKAY ...?
!
YOU'RE REALLY COLD! PLEASE WAIT HERE. I'LL GO FIND A BLANKET OR SOMETHING ...
パタ
PATA (PATTER)
パタ
PATA
ヒラ
HIRA (FLUTTER)
ガラ
GARA (RATTLE)

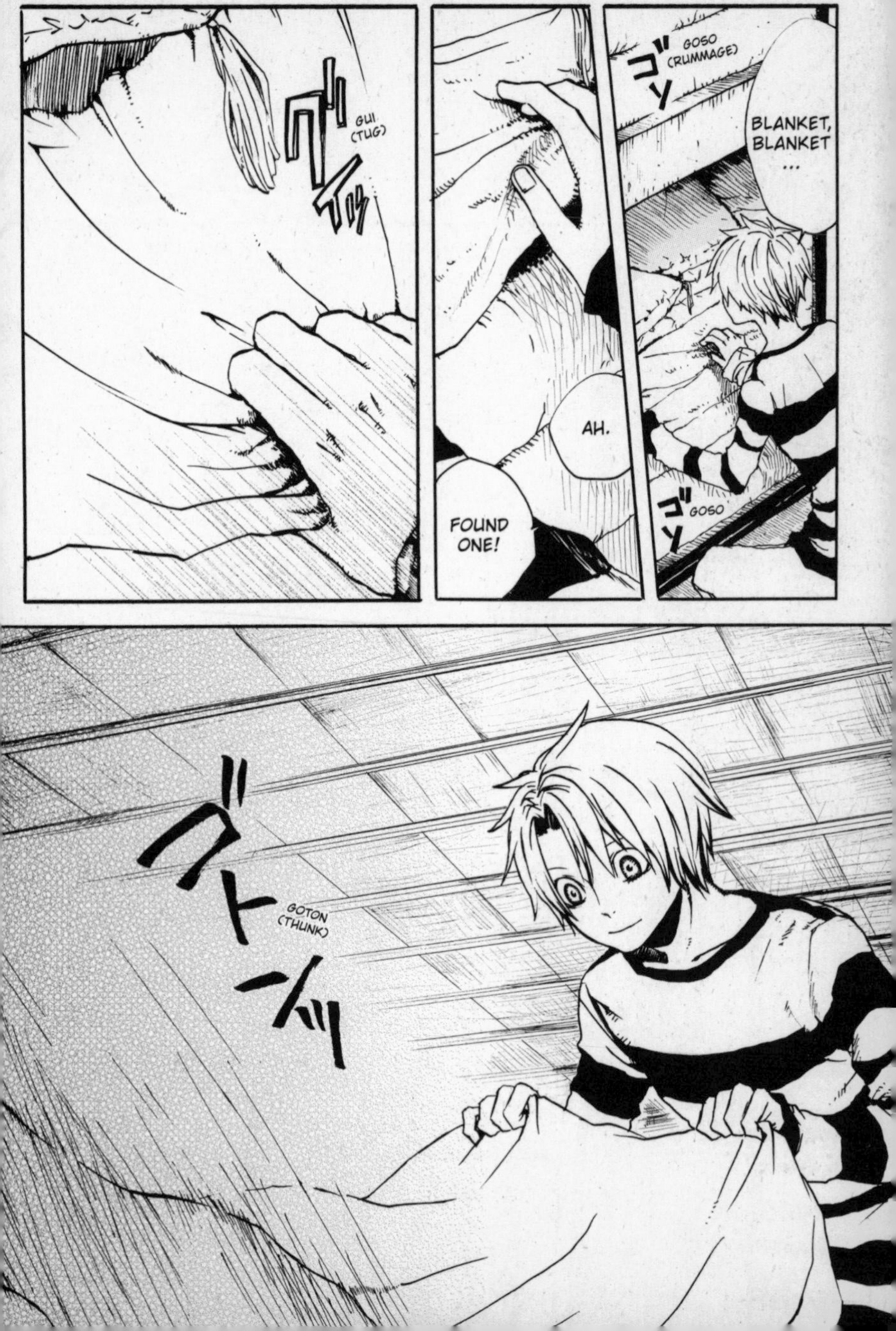
GOSO (RUMMAGE)
BLANKET, BLANKET ...
GOSO
AH.
FOUND ONE!
GUI (TUG)
GOTON (THUNK)

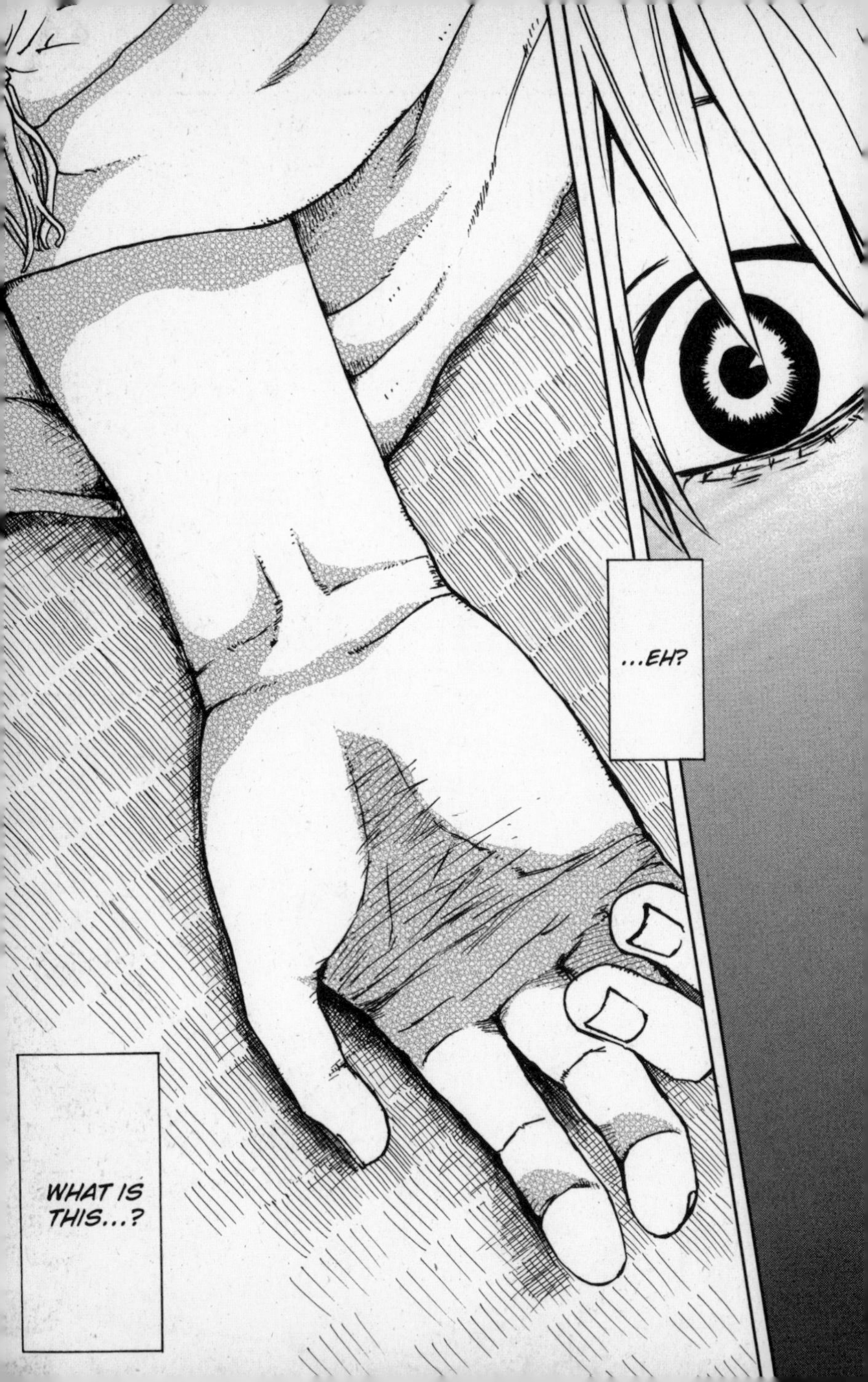
...EH?
WHAT IS THIS...?

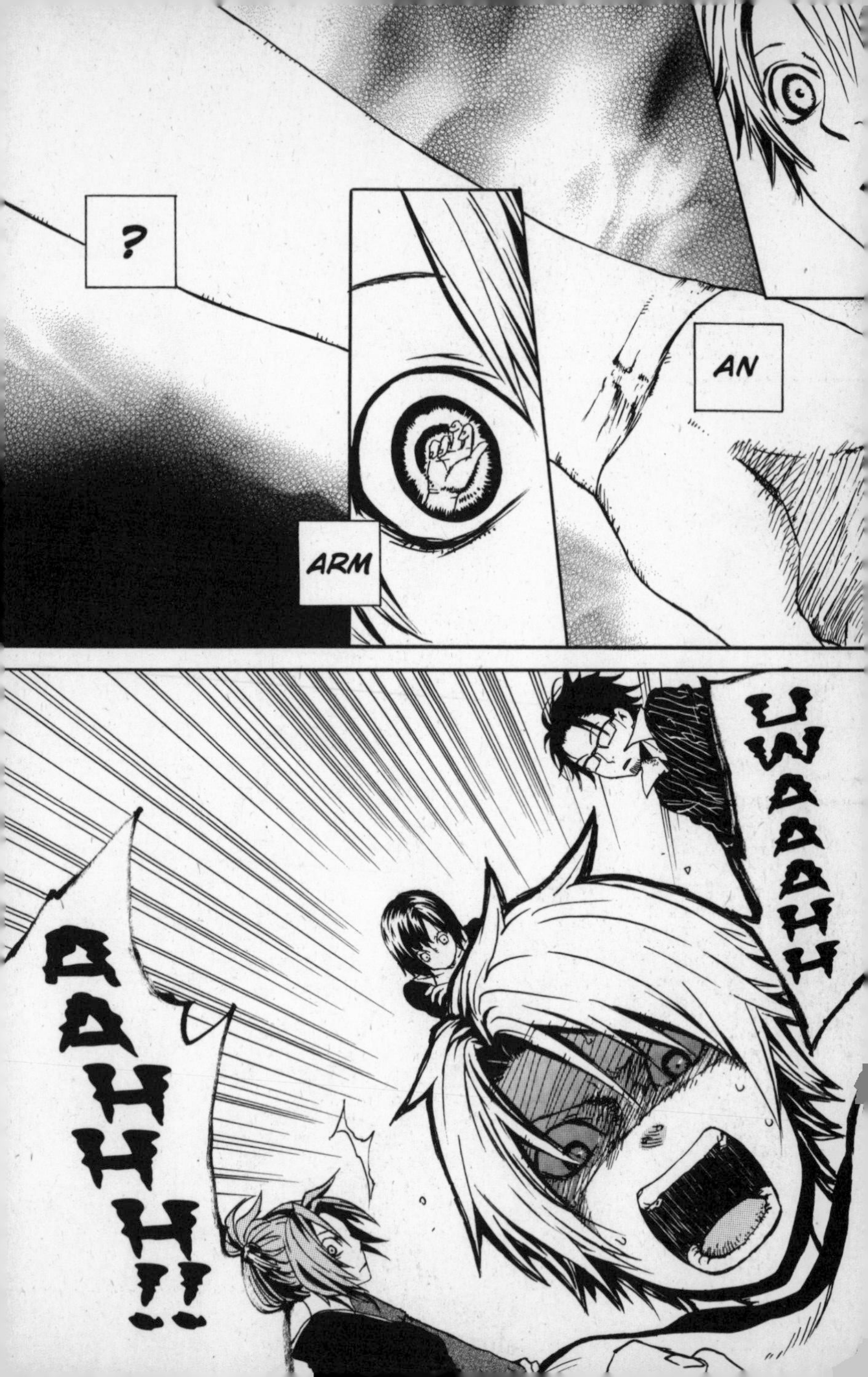
?
AN
ARM
UWAAAHH
AAHHH!!

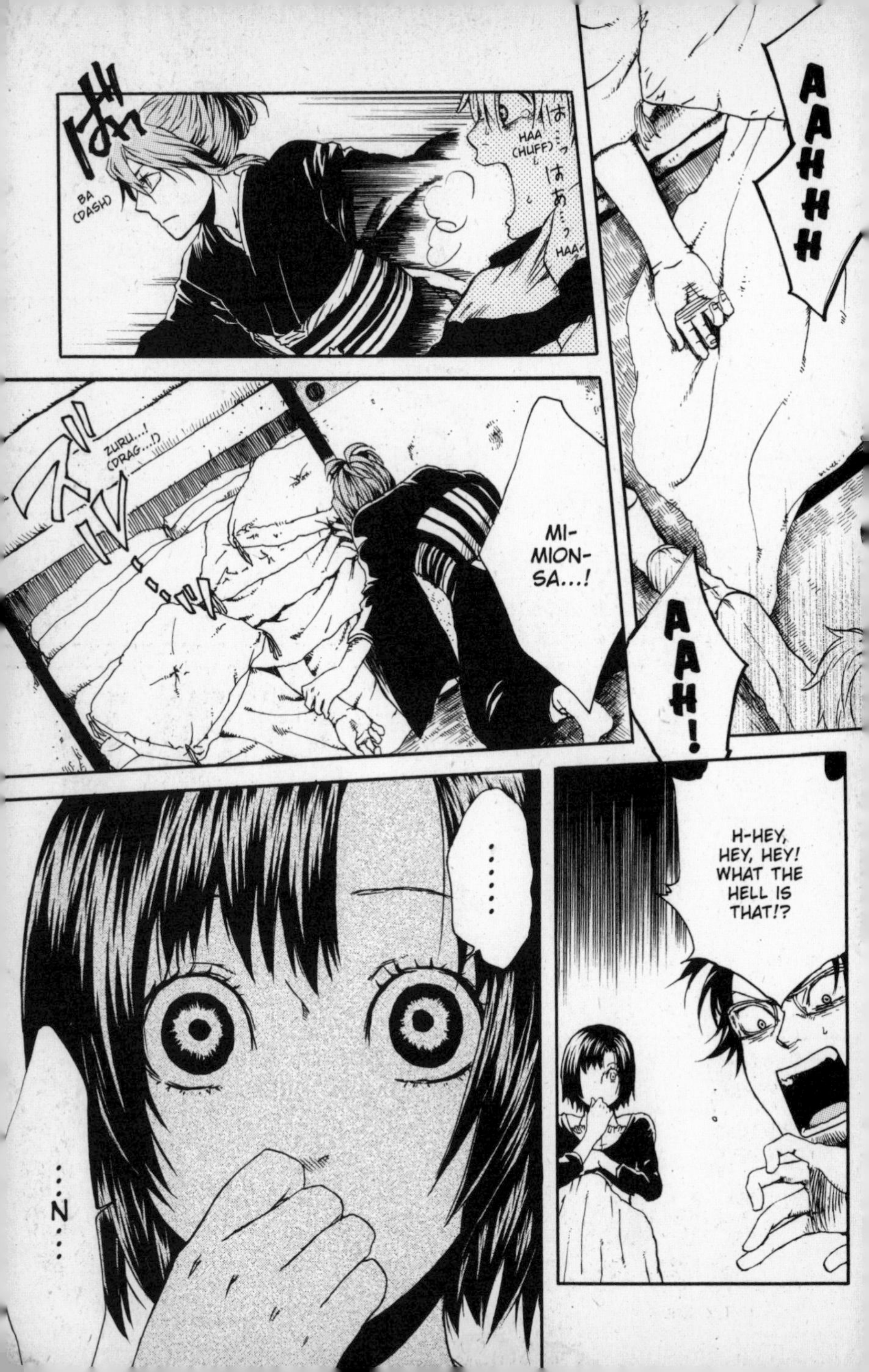
AAHHHH
AAH!
BA (DASH)
HAA (HUFF)
HAA
ZURU...! (DRAG...!)
MI-MION-SA...!
H-HEY, HEY, HEY! WHAT THE HELL IS THAT!?
......
...N...

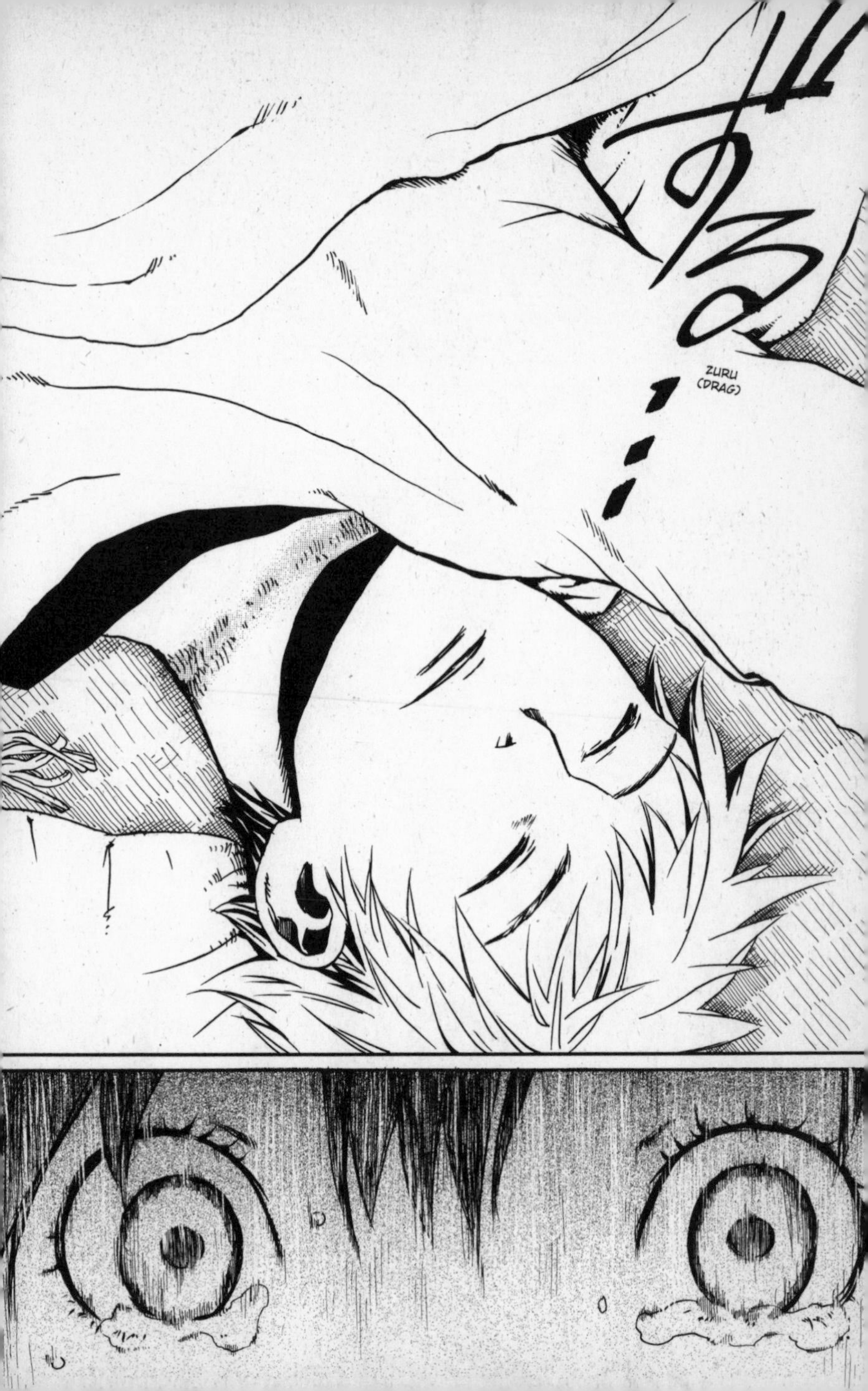
ずる…
ZURU
(DRAG)

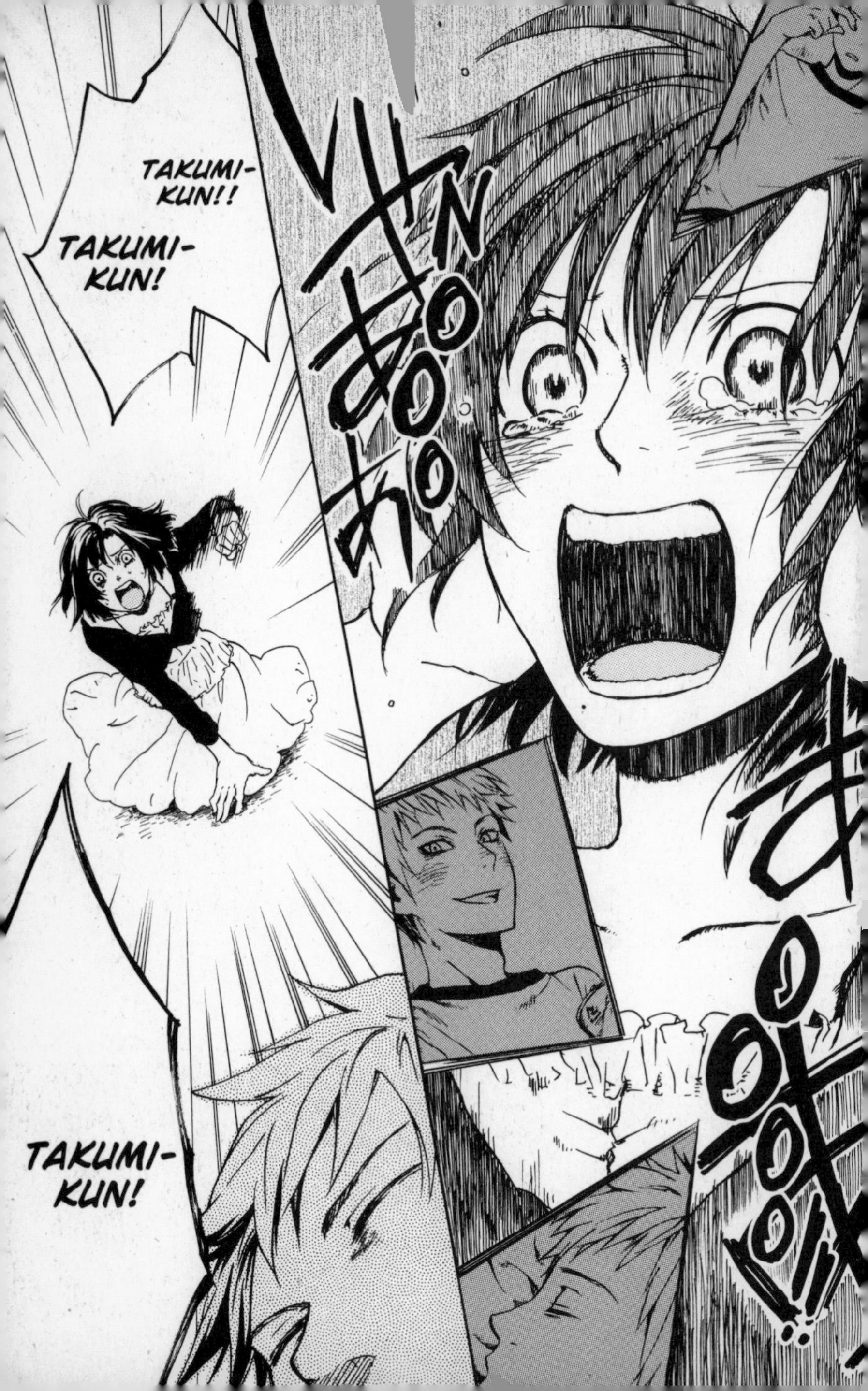
TAKUMI-KUN!!
TAKUMI-KUN!
TAKUMI-KUN!

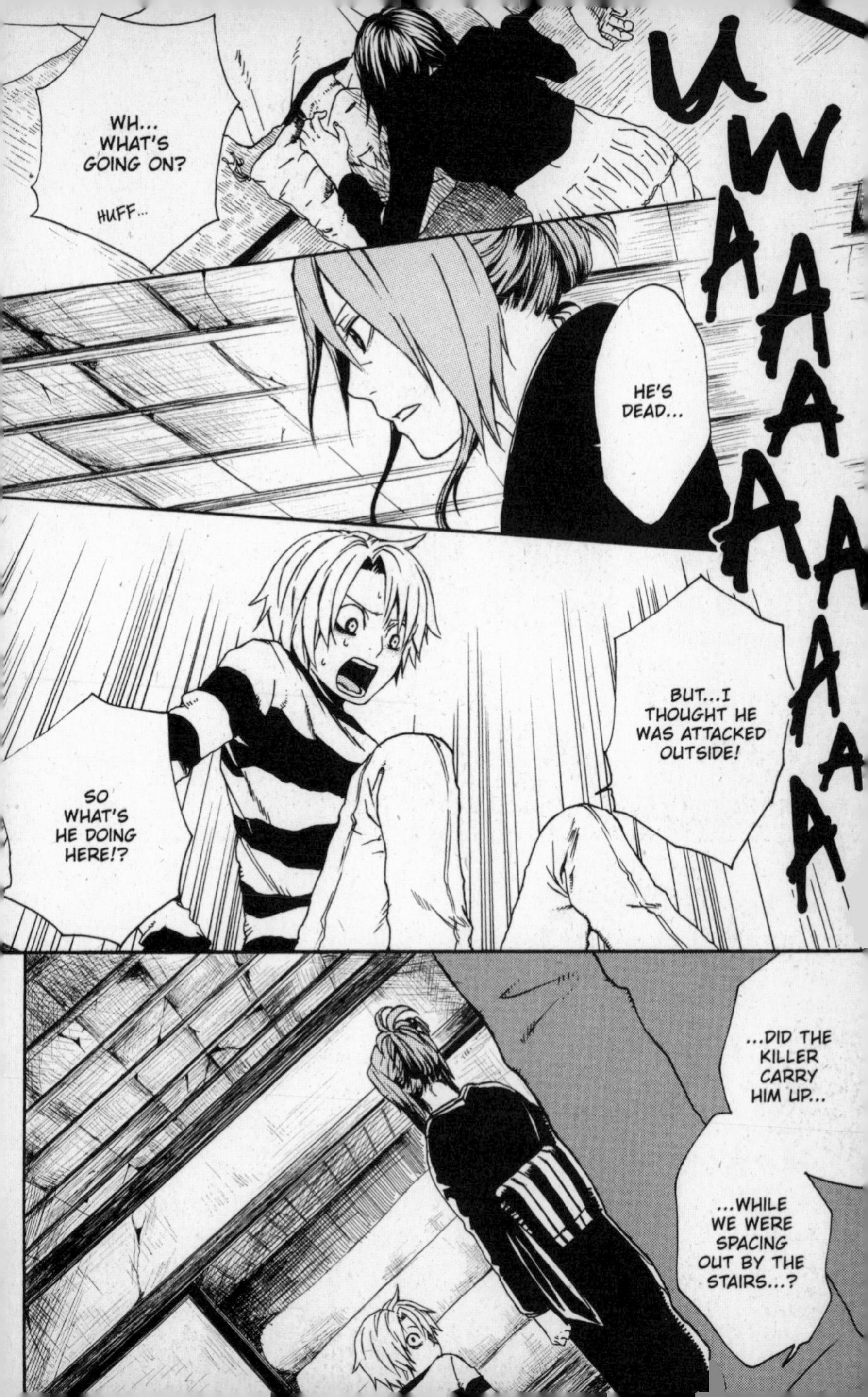
UWAAAAAAAA
WH... WHAT'S GOING ON?
HUFF...
HE'S DEAD...
BUT...I THOUGHT HE WAS ATTACKED OUTSIDE!
SO WHAT'S HE DOING HERE!?
...DID THE KILLER CARRY HIM UP...
...WHILE WE WERE SPACING OUT BY THE STAIRS...?

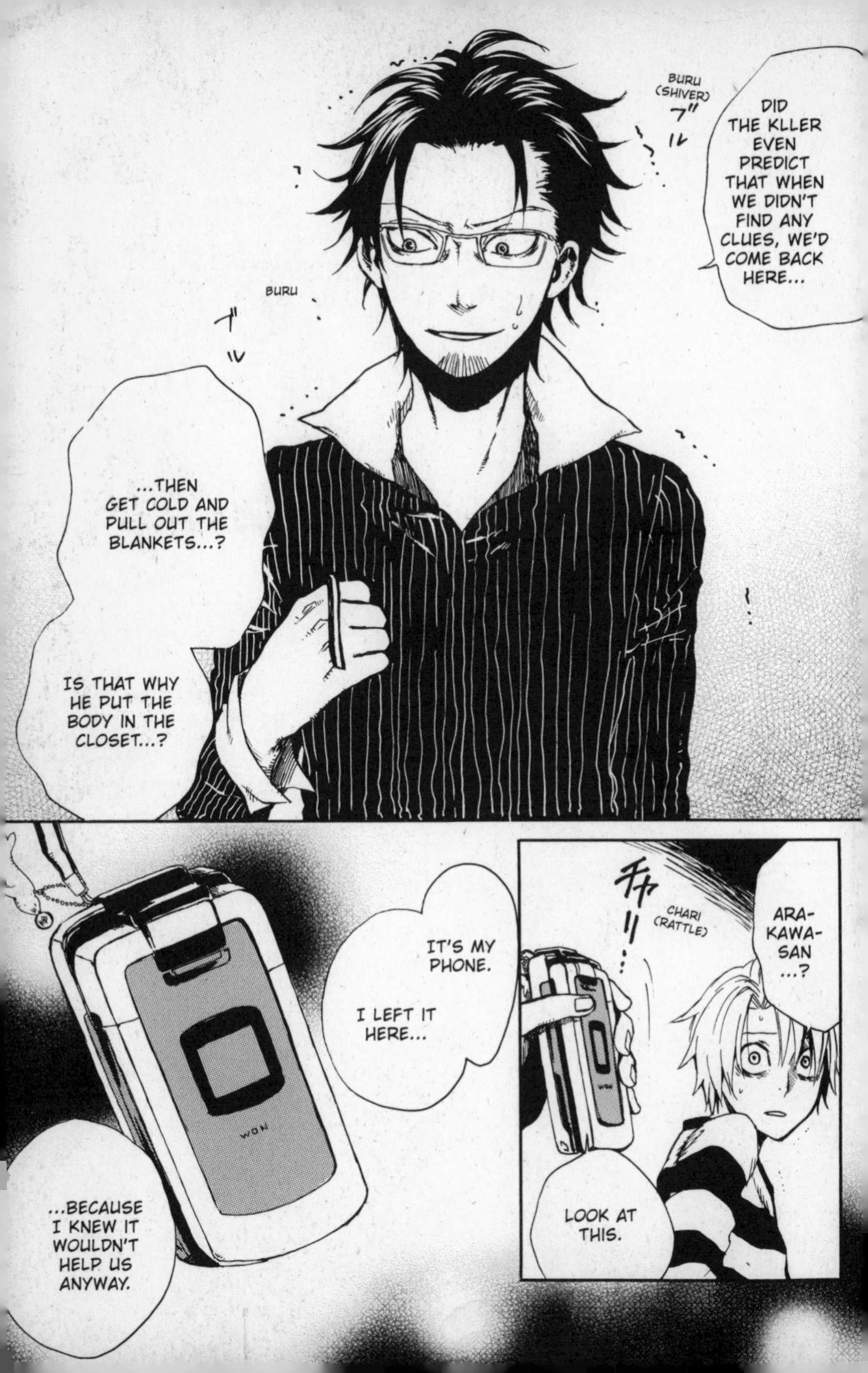
BURU (SHIVER)
DID THE KLLER EVEN PREDICT THAT WHEN WE DIDN'T FIND ANY CLUES, WE'D COME BACK HERE...
BURU
...THEN GET COLD AND PULL OUT THE BLANKETS...?
IS THAT WHY HE PUT THE BODY IN THE CLOSET...?
ARA-KAWA-SAN ...?
CHARI (RATTLE)
LOOK AT THIS.
IT'S MY PHONE.
I LEFT IT HERE...
...BECAUSE I KNEW IT WOULDN'T HELP US ANYWAY.

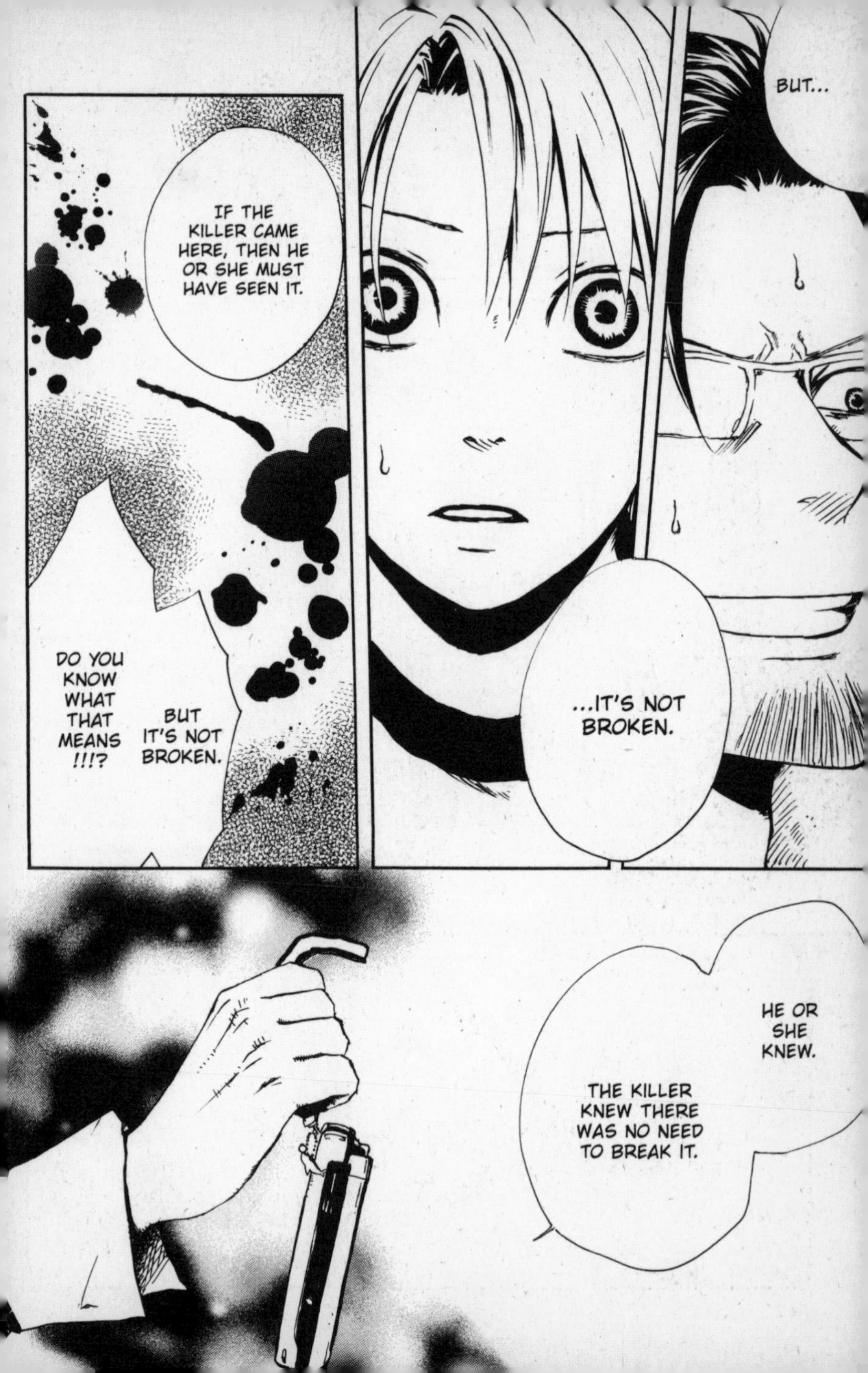
BUT...
...IT'S NOT BROKEN.
IF THE KILLER CAME HERE, THEN HE OR SHE MUST HAVE SEEN IT.
BUT IT'S NOT BROKEN.
DO YOU KNOW WHAT THAT MEANS !!!?
HE OR SHE KNEW.
THE KILLER KNEW THERE WAS NO NEED TO BREAK IT.

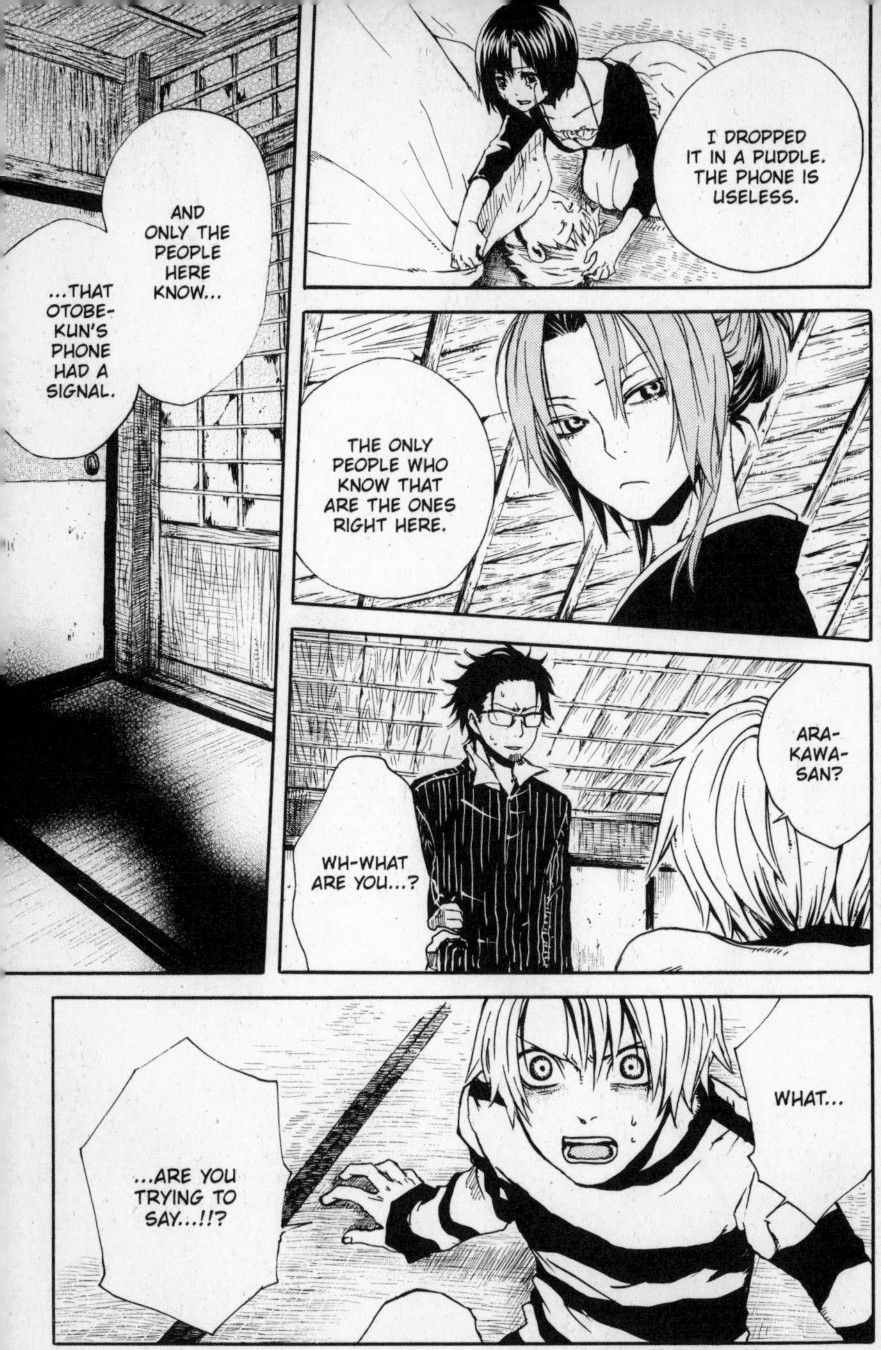
I DROPPED IT IN A PUDDLE. THE PHONE IS USELESS.
THE ONLY PEOPLE WHO KNOW THAT ARE THE ONES RIGHT HERE.
ARA-KAWA-SAN?
WH-WHAT ARE YOU...?
AND ONLY THE PEOPLE HERE KNOW...
...THAT OTOBE-KUN'S PHONE HAD A SIGNAL.
WHAT...
...ARE YOU TRYING TO SAY...!!?

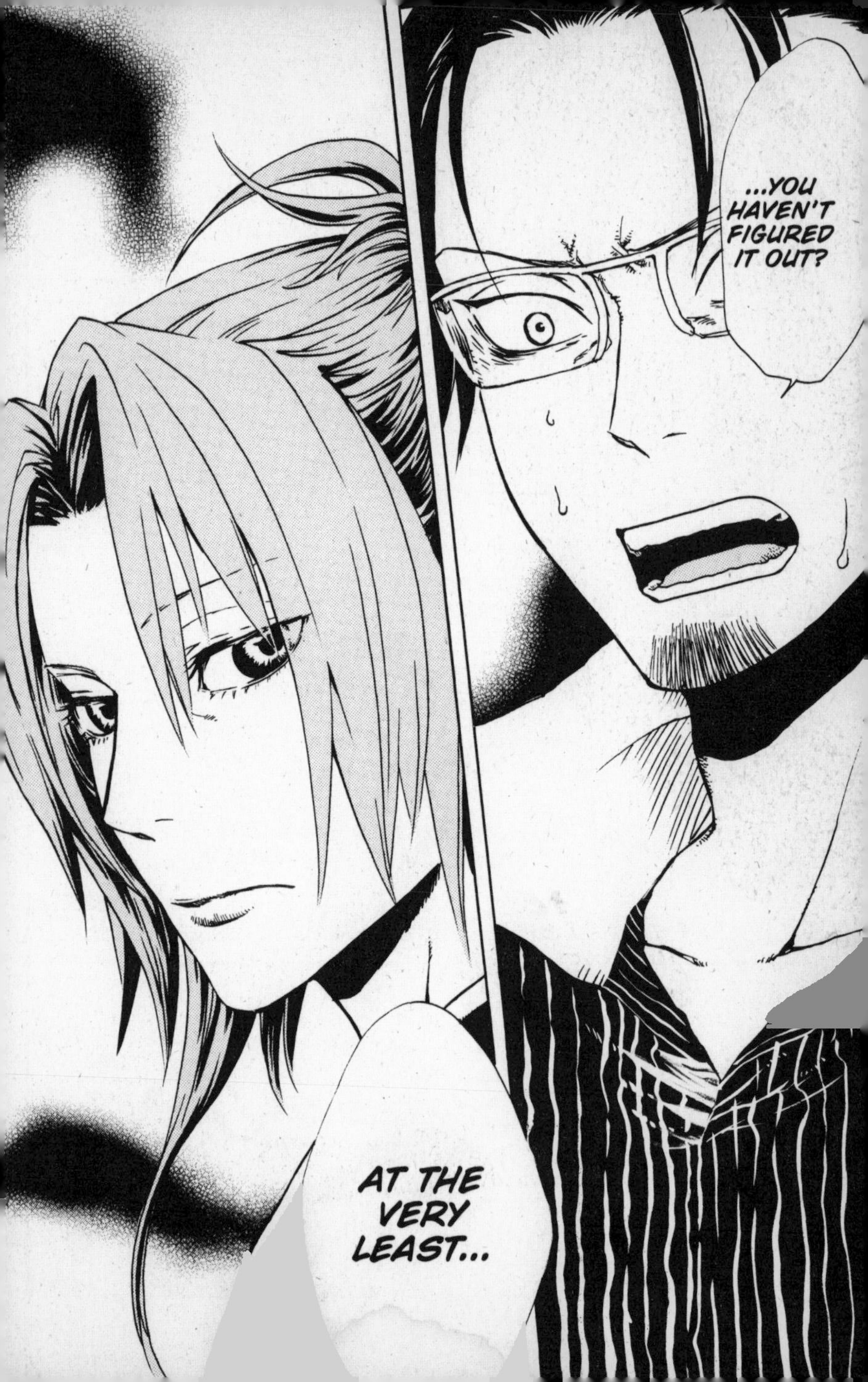
...YOU HAVEN'T FIGURED IT OUT?
AT THE VERY LEAST...

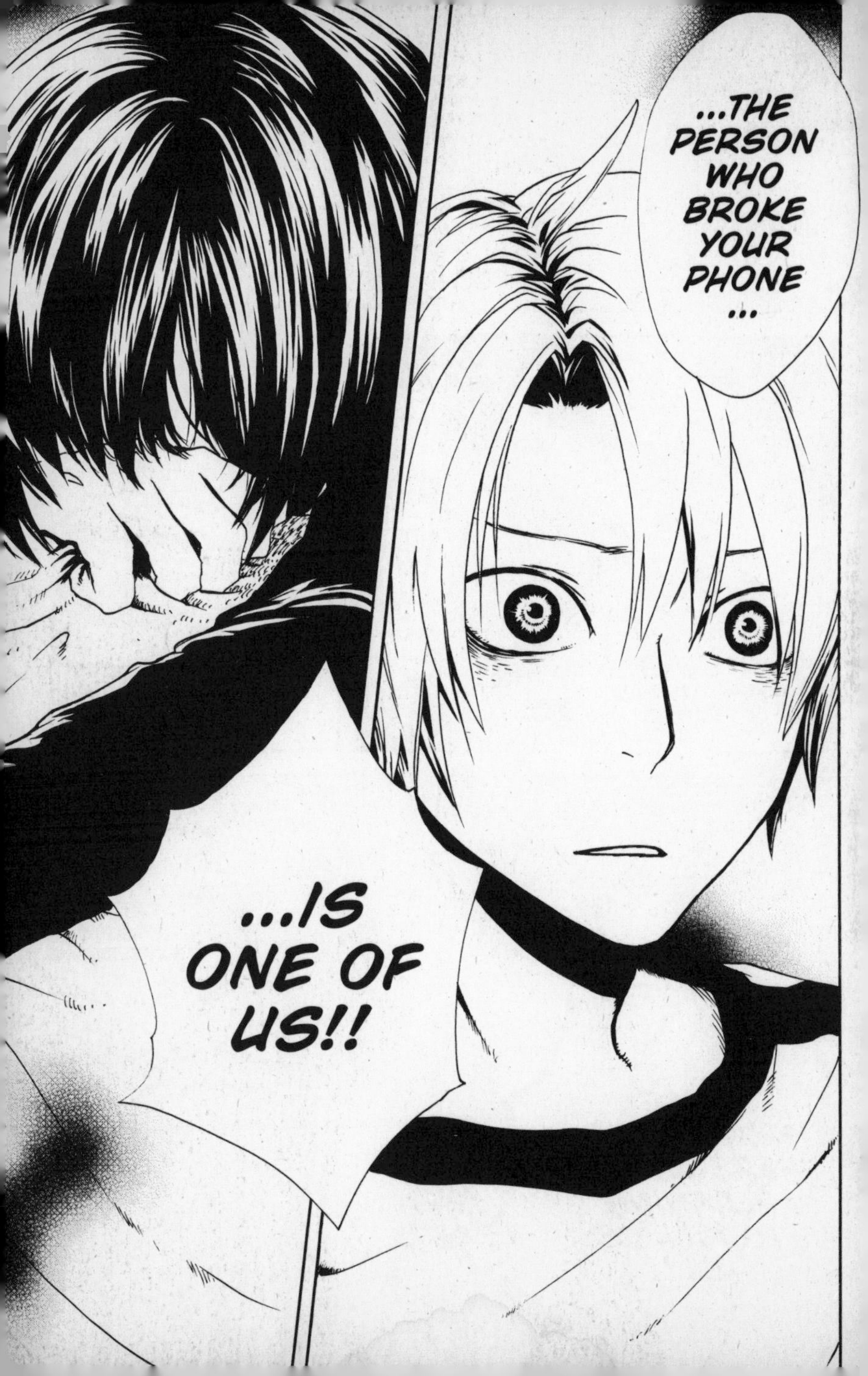
...THE PERSON WHO BROKE YOUR PHONE ...
...IS ONE OF US!!

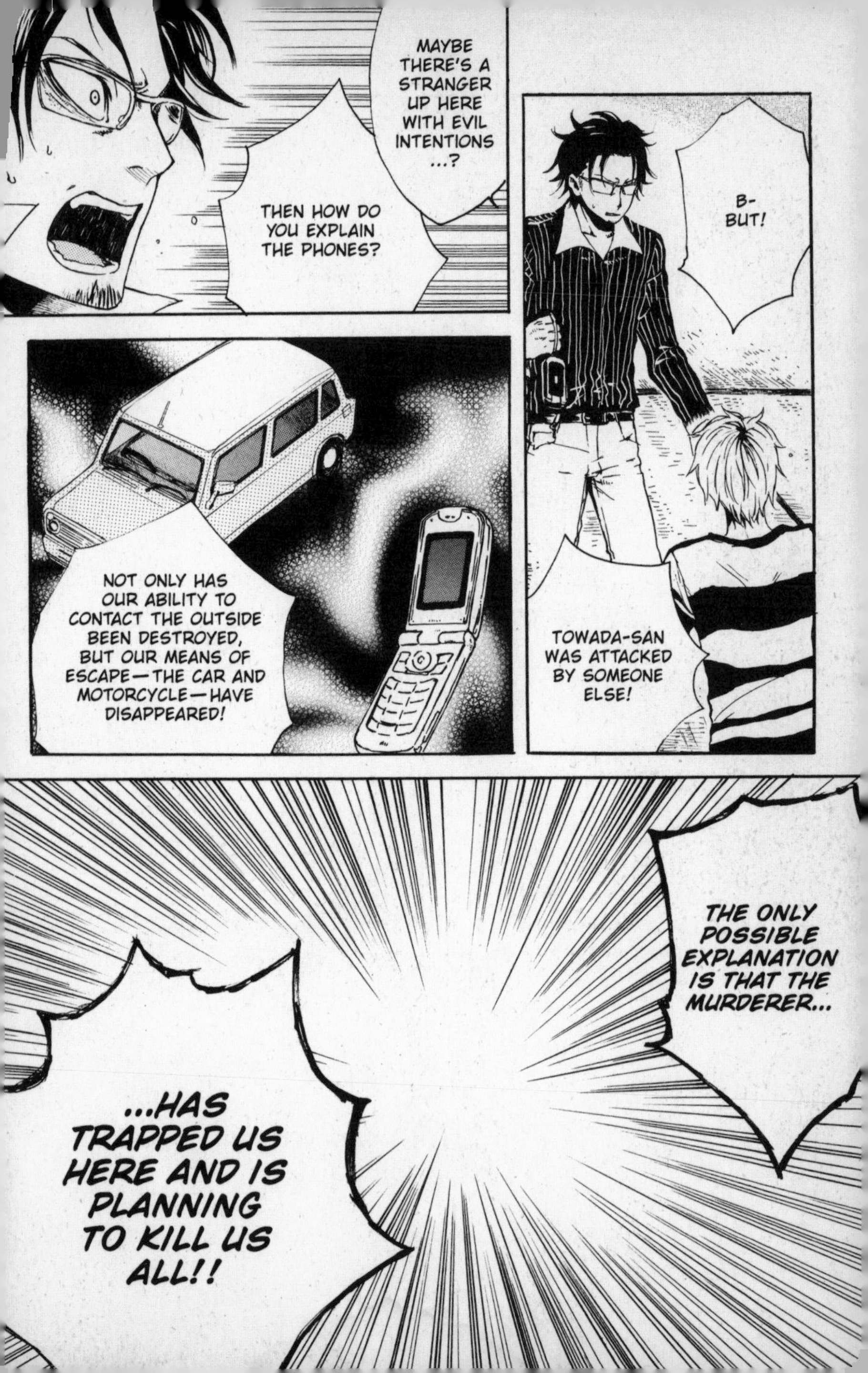
B-BUT!
TOWADA-SAN WAS ATTACKED BY SOMEONE ELSE!
MAYBE THERE'S A STRANGER UP HERE WITH EVIL INTENTIONS ...?
THEN HOW DO YOU EXPLAIN THE PHONES?
NOT ONLY HAS OUR ABILITY TO CONTACT THE OUTSIDE BEEN DESTROYED, BUT OUR MEANS OF ESCAPE—THE CAR AND MOTORCYCLE—HAVE DISAPPEARED!
THE ONLY POSSIBLE EXPLANATION IS THAT THE MURDERER...
...HAS TRAPPED US HERE AND IS PLANNING TO KILL US ALL!!

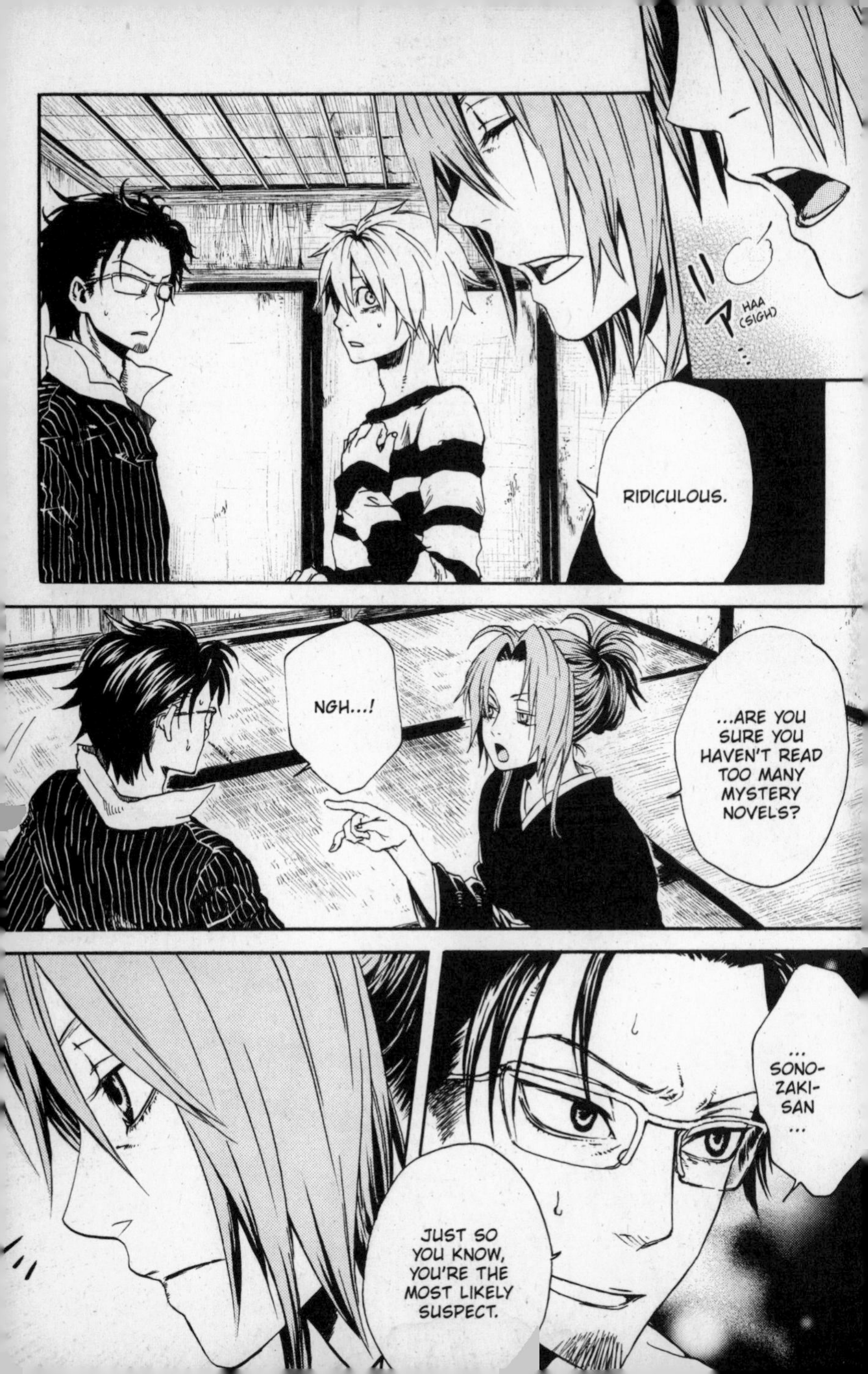
HAA (SIGH)
RIDICULOUS.
...ARE YOU SURE YOU HAVEN'T READ TOO MANY MYSTERY NOVELS?
NGH...!
... SONOZAKI-SAN ...
JUST SO YOU KNOW, YOU'RE THE MOST LIKELY SUSPECT.

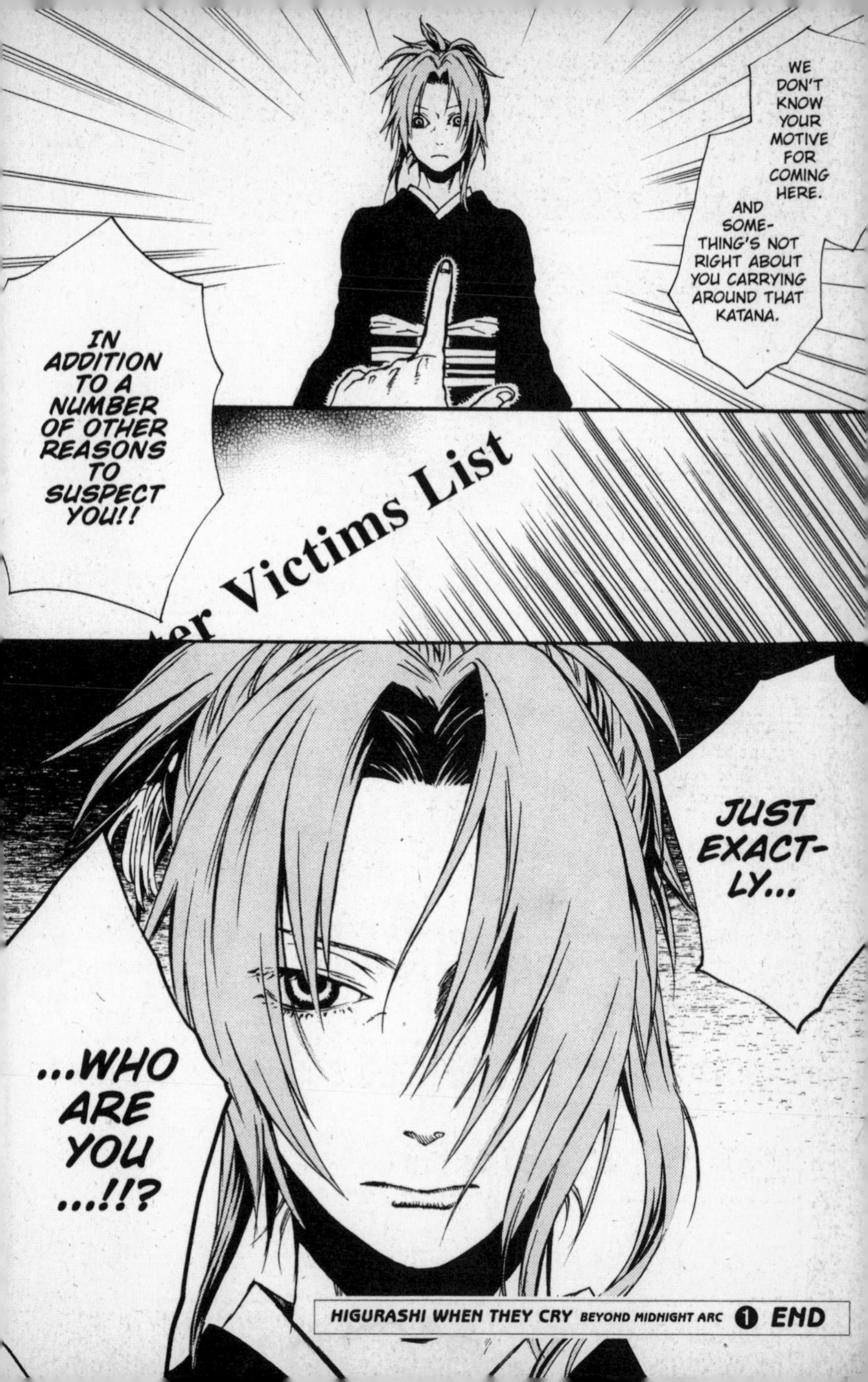
WE DON'T KNOW YOUR MOTIVE FOR COMING HERE. AND SOMETHING'S NOT RIGHT ABOUT YOU CARRYING AROUND THAT KATANA.
IN ADDITION TO A NUMBER OF OTHER REASONS TO SUSPECT YOU!!
er Victims List
JUST EXACTLY...
...WHO ARE YOU ...!!?
HIGURASHI WHEN THEY CRY BEYOND MIDNIGHT ARC 1 END

HIGURASHI LOVE DOODLES

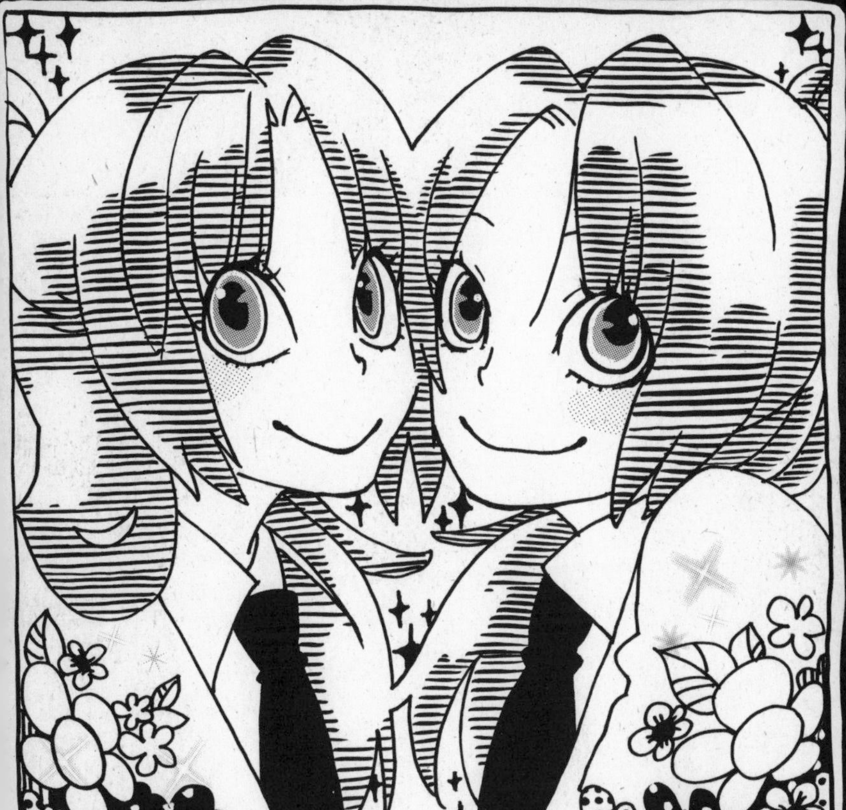

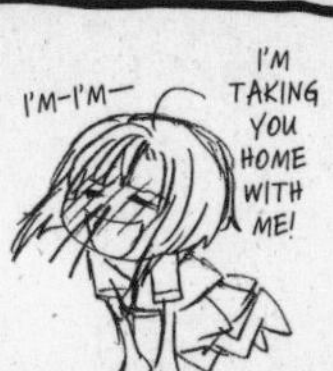
I'M TAKING YOU HOME WITH ME!
I'M-I'M—

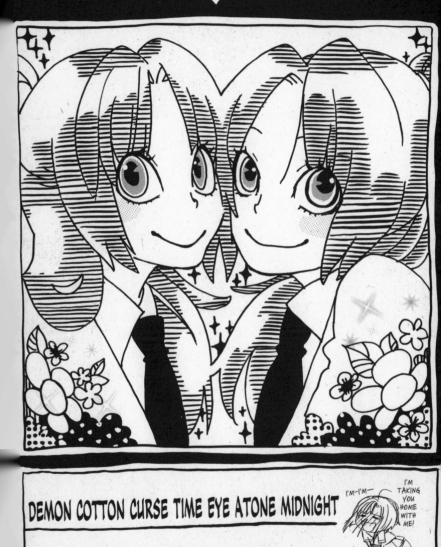

DEMON COTTON CURSE TIME EYE ATONE MIDNIGHT

First Grade Class K

Name: Mimori

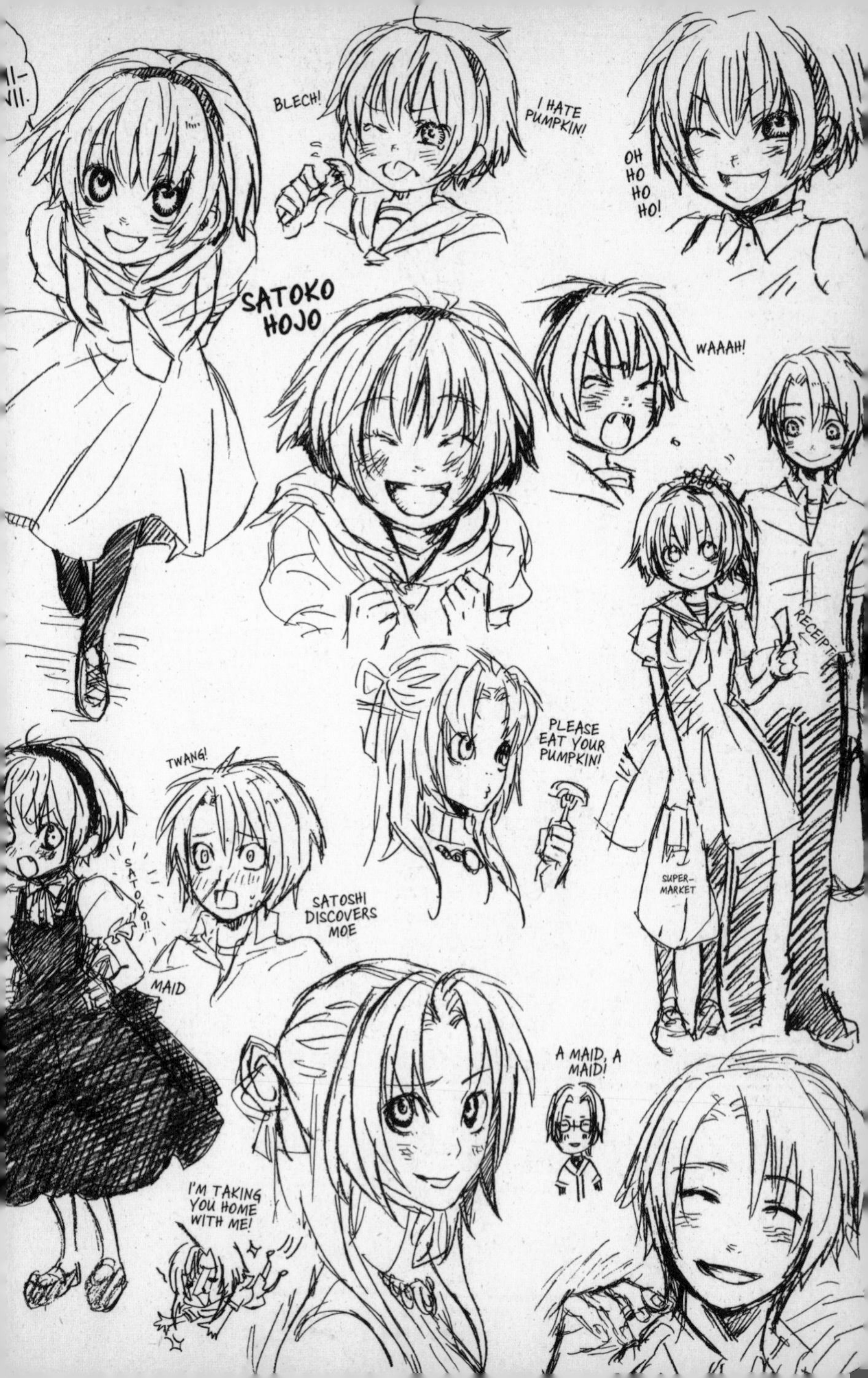
OH HO HO HO!
I HATE PUMPKIN!
BLECH!
WAAAH!
SATOKO HOJO
RECEIPT
SUPER-MARKET
PLEASE EAT YOUR PUMPKIN!
SATOSHI DISCOVERS MOE
TWANG!
SATOKO!!
MAID
A MAID, A MAID!
I'M TAKING YOU HOME WITH ME!

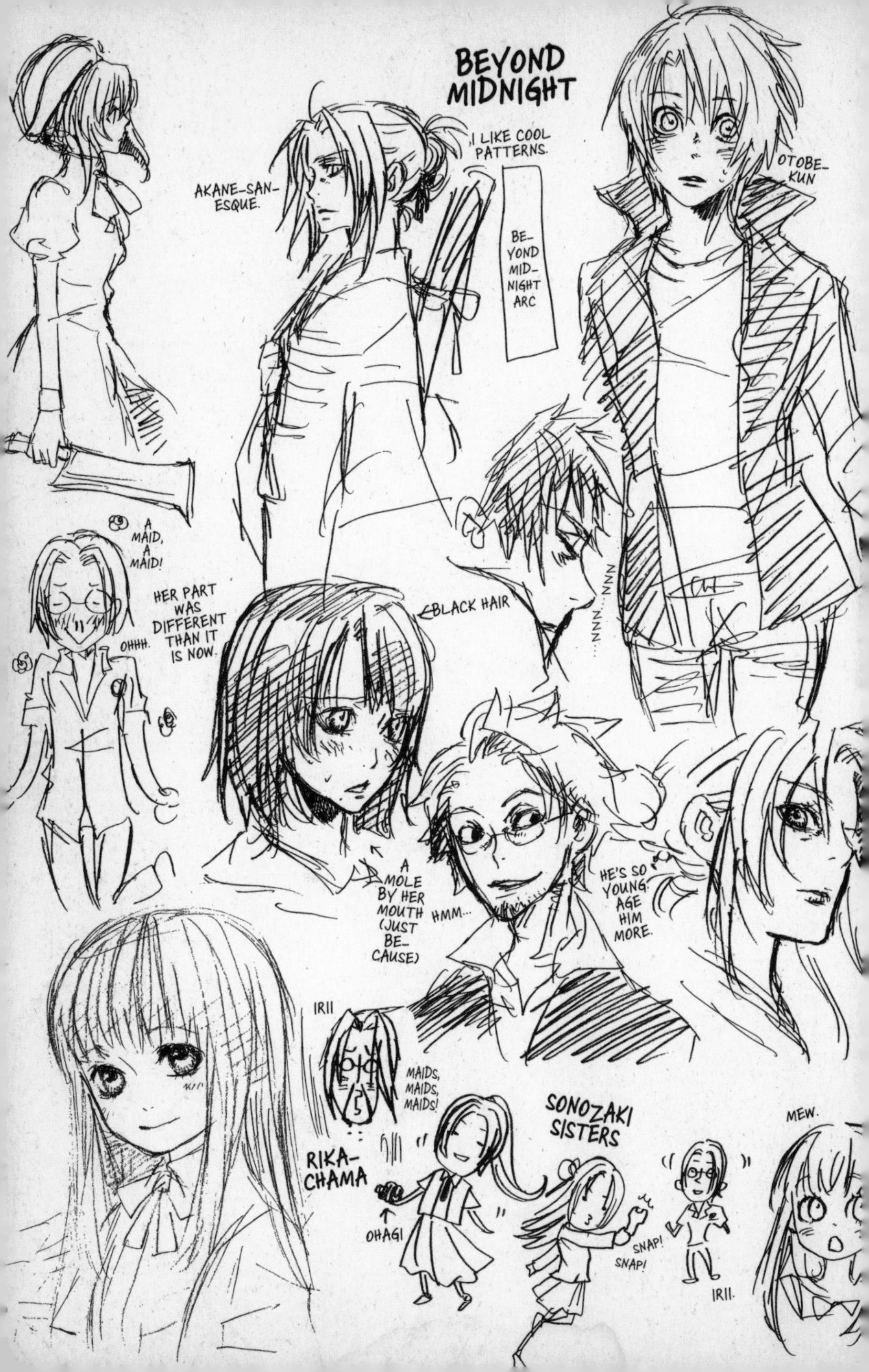
BEYOND MIDNIGHT
OTOBE-KUN
I LIKE COOL PATTERNS.
BE-YOND MID-NIGHT ARC
AKANE-SAN-ESQUE.
ZZZ... ZZZ...
BLACK HAIR
A MAID, A MAID!
HER PART WAS DIFFERENT THAN IT IS NOW.
OHHH.
HE'S SO YOUNG. AGE HIM MORE.
HMM...
A MOLE BY HER MOUTH (JUST BE-CAUSE)
IRII
MAIDS, MAIDS, MAIDS!
MEW.
SONOZAKI SISTERS
SNAP! SNAP!
IRII.
RIKA-CHAMA
OHAGI

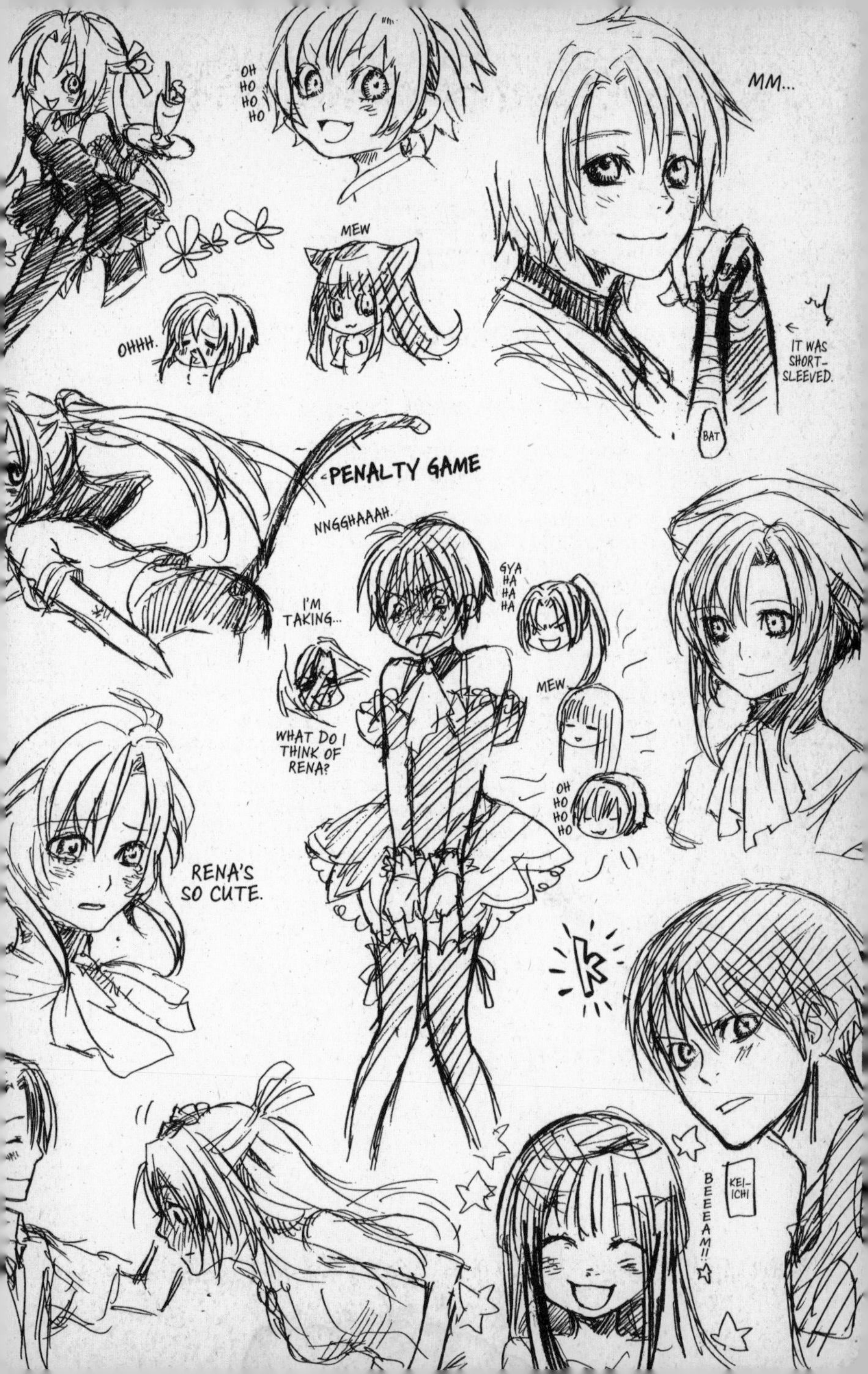
MM...
IT WAS SHORT-SLEEVED.
BAT
OH HO HO HO
MEW
OHHH.
PENALTY GAME
NNGGHAAAH.
GYA HA HA HA
I'M TAKING...
MEW.
WHAT DO I THINK OF RENA?
OH HO HO HO
RENA'S SO CUTE.
K
KEI-ICHI
BEEEAM!!

HIGURASHI WHEN THEY CRY

07th Expansion presents. Welcome to Hinamizawa.
"WHEN THEY CRY."

ABOUT THE "BEYOND MIDNIGHT ARC"

ORIGINAL STORY, SUPERVISOR: RYUKISHI 07

THE "BEYOND MIDNIGHT ARC" IS A NEW SIDE STORY THAT WASN'T IN THE ORIGINAL GAME SERIES.

THE SETTING IN THE SIDE STORY HAS LEFT THE YEAR 1983 AND TAKES PLACE IN THE PRESENT DAY, BUT THE WORLD AND LAWS THAT MAKE UP THE FOUNDATION OF THE "HIGURASHI" SERIES STILL CARRY OVER. IN THAT SENSE, I MAY CALL IT A SIDE STORY, BUT IT IS STILL A LEGITIMATE "HIGURASHI WHEN THEY CRY" ARC THAT IS IN NO WAY INFERIOR TO THE OTHERS.

THE OTHER EPISODES ARE FILLED WITH THE CRY OF THE HIGURASHI CICADAS, WHICH BRINGS A SAD FEELING IN THE MIDST OF TRANQUILLITY, BUT THOSE VOICES GO UNHEARD IN THE WORLD OF THIS "BEYOND MIDNIGHT ARC." INSTEAD, ALL WE HEAR IS THE GENTLE, MELANCHOLY SOUND OF THE RAIN LATE AT NIGHT. FOUR MEN AND WOMEN GATHER IN A QUIET, EERIE, ABANDONED VILLAGE, NOT KNOWING WHO THE OTHERS ARE. BY A STRANGE COINCIDENCE, THEY TAKE SHELTER FROM THE RAIN TOGETHER...IN THE DESERTED VILLAGE THAT WAS WIPED OUT IN A SINGLE NIGHT BY THE GREAT HINAMIZAWA DISASTER LONG AGO.

MIMORI-SENSEI HAS WONDERFULLY DEPICTED THAT MYSTERIOUS AND EERIE WORLD WITH THE TIP OF A PEN PREGNANT WITH DELICACY AND BEWITCHING CHARM. I HOPE YOU WILL ENJOY THE CONTINUATION OF THIS STORY OF A BIZARRE NIGHT IN THE RAIN....

HI
WH

RYUKISHI07
MIMORI

Translation: Alethea Nibley and Athena Nibley

Lettering: AndWorld Design

Higurashi WHEN THEY CRY Beyond Midnight Arc, Vol. 1 © RYUKISHI07
/ 07th Expansion © 2007 Mimori / SQUARE ENIX CO., LTD. All rights re-
served. First published in Japan in 2007 by SQUARE ENIX CO., LTD. Eng-
lish translation rights arranged with SQUARE ENIX CO., LTD. and Hachette Book Group through Tuttle-Mori Agency, Inc. Translation © 2010 by
SQUARE ENIX CO., LTD.

Yen Press
Hachette Book Group
237 Park Avenue, New York, NY 10017

www.HachetteBookGroup.com
www.YenPress.com

Yen Press is an imprint of Hachette Book Group, Inc. The Yen Press name
and logo are trademarks of Hachette Book Group, Inc.

First Yen Press Edition: October 2010

ISBN: 978-0-316-10240-7

10 9 8 7 6 5 4 3 2 1

BVG

Printed in the United States of America